Recreations in the Theory of Numbers

The Queen of Mathematics Entertains

by

ALBERT H. BEILER

*Engineering Department, American Electric Power
Service Corporation, New York, New York
Mathematics Department, Polytechnic Institute
of Brooklyn, Brooklyn, New York*

DOVER PUBLICATIONS, INC.

New York   New York

Recreations in the Theory of Numbers: The Queen of Mathematics Entertains is a new work published for the first time in 1964.

Library of Congress Catalog Card Number: 64–13458

Manufactured in the United States of America

Dover Publications, Inc.
180 Varick Street
New York 14, N.Y.

To Kliss

*Mathematics is the queen of the sciences
and arithmetic the queen of mathematics.*
— Karl Friedrich Gauss

PREFACE

WHILE the author was a student, an enthusiastic mathematics professor recommended to the class a book entitled *Mathematical Recreations and Essays*, by W. W. R. Ball. The students dutifully made a note of the title and most of them no doubt promptly forgot about it. Many years later when the book was mentioned to several of the author's own classes, an unexpected hilarity invariably greeted the announcement of the title, and inquiry elicited the fact that "recreations" and "mathematics" were considered practically contradictory terms. If this was the response from a group of engineering students whose proficiency in mathematics was probably above average, what must be the attitude toward mathematics of the vast horde who take this subject by compulsion?

It was found, however, that mention of just a few "puzzle" problems immediately awakened the class from the proverbial student lethargy and that a problem connected with the theory of numbers aroused such enthusiastic response that the students were loath to return to their regular work. The stimulus of such problems permeated the class for a long time, and the prescribed work in algebra, trigonometry, analytic geometry, and calculus took on an added zest because of it. It was like a catalyst, which, although not itself taking part in a chemical reaction, excites other substances to do so.

A little cautious experimenting with a few non-mathematically inclined friends—who, however, had been exposed to high-school algebra—aroused a similar gratifying response. And so the idea to write this book took form.

A number of mathematicians such as W. W. R. Ball and E. Lucas have written first-rate books on recreational aspects of mathematics in general; and others, such as Tobias Dantzig, E. T. Bell, and Edward Kasner, have given excellent interpretations of mathematical ideas and accounts of the men who are responsible for them. There is no book in English, however, which deals exclusively with the recreational aspects of this inherently recreational subject—the theory of numbers. This book attempts to present a few of these recreational jewels.

More can be found, encrusted by much dry technical matter, in books and periodicals on the shelves of almost any public library large enough to boast a section on mathematics.

One reason for the well-nigh irresistible appeal of number theory is the easily comprehended, yet puzzling nature of its problems. Another is that no long preliminary training is necessary; equipped with a knowledge of only high-school mathematics, a beginner can easily master some of the more important fundamentals of the subject. Like the man who, after reading a few detective stories, feels quite competent to go out and help the sleuth solve the murder mystery, so the beginner in number theory soon sprouts Icarian wings and boldly flies among primitive roots and quadratic residues.

The mathematician Karl Friedrich Gauss said: "The most beautiful theorems of higher arithmetic have this peculiarity, that they are easily discovered by induction, while on the other hand their demonstrations lie in exceeding obscurity and can be ferreted out only by very searching investigations. It is precisely this which gives to higher arithmetic the magic charm which has made it the favorite science of leading mathematicians, not to mention its inexhaustible richness, wherein it so far excels all other parts of mathematics."

The author was frequently faced with the dilemma of including or omitting the theory behind the subject matter. On the one hand, with too much theory the book would cease to be recreational; on the other, explanations are often as interesting as the results themselves—occasionally even more so. Considerable theory is included and the reader can follow his own inclination as to what to omit.

In general, the subject matter discussed in the latter part of the book is a little more difficult than the earlier chapters and it is advisable therefore to read them in sequence. Here and there problems have been interspersed for the entertainment of the reader, and where the solution is not immediately given, it will often be found in Chapter XXVI. One section, Chapter XXV, devoted entirely to problems and their solution has also been included.

Additional factors of Mersenne, repunit, and Fermat numbers, discussed respectively in Chapters III, XI, and XVII, have been discovered recently but too late for inclusion here. For these, see *Mathematics of Computation*, Vol. 17 (1963), pp. 447, 458.

ALBERT H. BEILER

New York, 1963

CONTENTS

FIGURES

TABLES

Recreations in
the Theory of Numbers

The Queen of Mathematics Entertains

The mathematical text book to which this is intended as an introduction . . . will be different from any other treatise on arithmetic in the world. It would have no very large numbers in it, for very large numbers . . . exert a malign influence upon the imagination; something unsocial and sinister and detached from reality and demoniac steals out of them like a vapor to corrode and corrupt the pink and innocent convolutions of the brain.

There will be a good many 7's in it and a good many 3's . . . sevens and threes are attractive numbers . . . 7 satisfies us . . . . There were Seven Pleiades, Seven Hills, Seven Sutherland sisters . . . [and 7 Brides for 7 Brothers].

—Don Marquis: *Prefaces*,
"Preface to a Moral Book of Arithmetic"

CHAPTER I

PRESENTATION AT COURT

ANYONE interested in puzzles will find the theory of numbers a delightful and inexhaustible source of puzzle problems. It has justly been called the "Queen of Mathematics" (itself the "Queen of the Sciences"), and fairly scintillates with intellectual gems contributed by the world's foremost mathematicians. There is an irresistible fascination in finding numbers having specified properties, and one soon falls under their spell and begins to understand why many men were willing to devote so much time to this subject. *Vita brevis, ars longa* is never felt more acutely than while pursuing some engrossing problem in number theory.

How would you go about solving these problems?

1. Find the divisors, if any, of 16000001.†

2. One side of a right-angled triangle is 48. Find ten pairs of whole numbers which may represent the other two sides.†

3. How many positive integers are there less than and having no divisor in common with 5929?†

4. Find the least number consisting solely of threes and sevens such that this number and also the sum of its digits is divisible by both 3 and 7.†

5. Find three square numbers in arithmetic progression. Can there be four such?†

6. Find the least number with exactly 100 divisors.†

7. Show that $1 \cdot 2 \cdot 3 \cdot 4 \ldots (n-1) + 1$ is always divisible by n if n is a prime, but never when n is composite.†

8. Prove that every prime number of the form $4x + 1$ is expressible as the sum of two integer squares in one and only one way.†

9. Find numbers each of which is equal to the sum of all its different divisors. (Exclude the number itself, but include unity among the divisors.)†

---

† Problems indicated by a dagger are solved in Chapter XXVI.

10. Find a general formula for the values of x for which $2^x - 1$ is a prime.

11. Prove that every even number can be expressed as the sum of two primes.

12. Prove that $x^n + y^n = z^n$ is impossible in integers if n is greater than 2.

The requirements of every one of these problems can be understood by the average high-school student, yet the actual solutions of some of them have withstood the intellectual assaults of centuries and are still unsolved. Such are Problems 10, 11, and 12. An entire book could easily be devoted to the history alone of Problem 10, and many volumes would be required to contain all the work which has been expended on it. An enormous amount has been written about Problem 12. Problem 8 requires keen analysis. Problems 2 and 5 involve a branch of number theory known as Diophantine analysis, after Diophantus, a mathematician of the early Christian era. A history of Diophantine analysis alone has been the subject of a volume of over 700 pages by L. E. Dickson.

The theory of numbers differs from many other branches of mathematics in that it is an almost purely theoretical science. Occasionally some brilliant engineer or scientist will apply a few of the elementary theorems, as has been done in the splicing of telephone cables, X-ray spectroscopy of cubic crystals, and radio technology; but in the main this study has remained aloof from mundane affairs. One of its greatest followers, E. E. Kummer, is said to have remarked on one occasion that of all his discoveries he appreciated his "ideal numbers" most because they had not soiled themselves as yet with any practical applications.

No other branch of mathematics has such ardent devotees. David Hilbert in the introduction to L. W. Reid's *Elements of the Theory of Algebraic Numbers* says, "In the theory of numbers, we value the simplicity of its foundations, the exactness of its conceptions and the purity of its truths; we extol it as the pattern for the other sciences, as the deepest, the inexhaustible source of all mathematical knowledge, prodigal of incitements to investigation in other departments of mathematics.... Moreover, the theory of numbers is independent of the change of fashion and in it we do not see, as is often the case in other departments of knowledge, a conception or method at one time given undue prominence, at another suffering undeserved neglect; in the theory of numbers the oldest problem is often today modern, like a genuine work of art from the past."

L. E. Dickson in his epochal *History of the Theory of Numbers* says, "The theory of numbers is especially entitled to a separate history on account of the great interest which has been taken in it continuously through the centuries from the time of Pythagoras, an interest shared on the one extreme by nearly every noted mathematician and on the other extreme by numerous amateurs attracted by no other part of mathematics."

An eminent mathematician and number-theory specialist, G. H. Hardy, said, "The elementary theory of numbers should be one of the very best subjects for early mathematical instruction. It demands very little previous knowledge; its subject matter is tangible and familiar; the processes of reasoning which it employs are simple, general and few; and it is unique among the mathematical sciences in its appeal to natural human curiosity. A month's intelligent instruction in the theory of numbers ought to be twice as instructive, twice as useful, and at least ten times more entertaining as the same amount of 'calculus for engineers.'"*

One enters this land of numbers and wanders timidly amongst integers, divisors, and primes, vaguely familiar names recalling arithmetic in elementary grades. We soon meet perfect and amicable numbers, then number of divisors of a number and their sum. The path beckons onward into the new and hitherto unsuspected land of congruences; then through the difficult thickets of Fermat's and Wilson's theorems. Primitive roots, quadratic residues, Diophantine analysis, Haupt-exponents, and quadratic reciprocity are revealed to us. It is so absorbing that we do not wish to leave this place. Ahead are craggy domains where the going will be slow and difficult: quadratic forms and partitions, ideals and idoneals, Pell equations, continued fractions, automorphs, theory of primes, analytic theory of numbers. Only the stoutest of hearts will want to continue to clearer, purer, more sublime heights. We shall confine ourselves to less lofty ones in this book to stay within purely recreational bounds.

Do you wish to take the journey? Not much equipment is necessary—one needs mostly a genuine willingness. It will be fun; to some, if the world's ills clamor too exigently at our doors, it may be

---

* *Bulletin of the American Mathematical Society*, **35** (1929), 818.

nepenthe—like that journey to far-off Shangri-La which James Hilton wrote about in *Lost Horizon*.

*   *   *

If we plan to go on a pleasure jaunt we need some sort of equipment to make the trip a pleasant one. We may have to buy a number of new things and overhaul some we own. A trip through the domain of numbers demands some essential equipment, if a rather modest amount of it. Elementary algebra is very useful. No more geometry is required than knowing what is meant by a square, various kinds of triangles, something about a circle. A general overhauling of our perhaps rusty arithmetical equipment may be necessary. We may find it advisable to consult the dictionary about integer, digit, prime number, composite number, factor, and divisor.

A *digit* is one of the 10 *numerals*—0, 1, 2, 3, 4, 5, 6, 7, 8, 9—so named from counting upon the fingers or digits. A *whole number* like 15 is an *integer*, distinguished from another number like 7/3 which is a fraction. The *integer* 15 is written with the *digits* 1 and 5. The number 15 is *composite* because it is composed of the two *factors* or *divisors* 3 and 5. Numbers like 13 or 97 or 67280421310721 are *primes* because they have no factors except unity and the number itself. No general method has yet been discovered for determining whether or not a number is a prime. For a 14-digit number like the one above, unless it has some special form, years of continuous effort may be required to resolve it.

When we were children we had to leap a considerable mental hurdle to advance from integers to fractions. Perhaps some of us remember the homely illustrations of our instructors: "Divide a pie into five parts and take three of them; that would represent the fraction 3/5." Later we had to leap more hurdles; you could not only chop up the interval between two integers and get fractions, but there were gaps between fractions, yielding numbers which were neither one nor the other. We called these *irrational numbers*, and the length of the diagonal of a unit square was cited as an illustration of such a number. Gradually, the idea of a continuous number stream took form in our minds.

In number theory we return to our elementary ideas. We abandon "continuity" and consider "discrete magnitudes," meaning not that the magnitude can be trusted to comport itself in a seemly fashion, but rather that it is disconnected from its neighbors. Thus there are no integers between 14 and 15, and only four of them between 15 and 20.

Because number theory deals with discrete magnitudes like integers, it requires a special viewpoint and special tools with which to attack its problems. Often the paths leading to a solution run parallel to, or even coincide with, those of algebraic problems—a perilous proximity, because if one does not watch the point of departure of the paths, it is easy to be led astray. This will be seen when we compare congruences and equations, and integers in different number realms.

Consider the problem: Solve for *positive* values of x and y in $5x + 3y = 17$. From the algebraic viewpoint there are an infinite number of sets of values of x and y which satisfy the equation, fractional and integral, corresponding to the infinite number of points on the straight line which is its graph. In number theory we consider only the *integral* values $x = 1, y = 4$ as solutions of such an equation.

We shall conclude this introduction to the court of the Queen of Mathematics by quoting from Uspensky and Heaslet's *Elementary Number Theory.*[*]

> What, then, compels men to spend a lot of time and effort on arithmetical investigations?... The answer is that the whole beauty of this science becomes apparent only to those who penetrate deep into it....
>
> It is natural that much preliminary study of things which are not so very interesting in themselves is required before one can appreciate some of the arithmetical treasures contained in...[number theory]. But this is inescapable: before learning to walk one first learns to crawl.

Unavoidably, therefore, we too shall have to crawl a little before learning to walk upright and turning our faces to the light.

BIBLIOGRAPHY[‡]

Ball, W. W. R. *Mathematical Recreations and Essays.* New York: Macmillan Co., 1939.

Dickson, L. E. *History of the Theory of Numbers.* 3 vols. New York: Chelsea Publishing Co., 1950.

[*] J. V. Uspensky and M. A. Heaslet, *Elementary Number Theory* (New York: McGraw-Hill Book Company, Inc., 1939).

[‡] In this and subsequent references at the end of each chapter, the publisher given is frequently that of the reprint rather than the original edition. This has been done in order that the reader might consult the most readily available reference.

Hardy, G. H. "An Introduction to the Theory of Numbers," *Bulletin of the American Mathematical Society*, **35** (1929), 778.

Lawther, H. P., Jr. "An Application of Number Theory to the Splicing of Telephone Cables," *American Mathematical Monthly*, **42** (1935), 81.

Reid, L. W. *Elements of the Theory of Algebraic Numbers.* Baltimore: Johns Hopkins Press, 1946.

Uspensky, J. V., and Heaslet, M. A. *Elementary Number Theory.* New York: McGraw-Hill Book Company, 1939.

Van Der Pol, B. "Radio Technology and Theory of Numbers," *Journal of the Franklin Institute*, **255** (1953), 475.

CHAPTER II

DIVISORS FOR DIVERSION

OF COURSE you know all about divisors. If you were asked to enumerate the divisors of, say, 24, you would write 1, 2, 3, 4, 6, 8, 12, and 24—a total of 8. Could you tell without listing them that 24 has 8 divisors and that 60 has 12? To determine this the given number must first be resolved into its "elementary" or prime factors and their powers, which can be done in one and only one way. Thus $24 = 2^3 \cdot 3$ and $60 = 2^2 \cdot 3 \cdot 5$. Then add unity to the exponent of each prime and multiply the results. Thus the exponents of the primes 2 and 3 in 24 are 3 and 1 respectively. So we have $(3+1)(1+1) = 8$. For 60, similarly, we have $(2+1)(1+1)(1+1) = 12$.

In the compact generalized symbolism of the mathematician, you would say that for a given number, $N = p_1{}^{a_1}p_2{}^{a_2}\ldots p_n{}^{a_n}$, where the p's are different primes greater than unity, the number of divisors is:

$$(a_1+1)(a_2+1)\ldots(a_n+1).$$

Don't be afraid of the subscripts. The p's are the Smith family; the a's the Joneses. Bill Smith, Fanny Smith, and John Smith are p_1, p_2, and p_3 respectively; whereas Mary Jones, Tom Jones, and Jane Jones are a_1, a_2, and a_3. We might have called the different primes p, q, r, etc., but then nothing would show that they are all members of the prime class. The subscripts differentiate the members of the class; like subscripts indicate that the respective members of the two classes are married to each other.

Then there is the converse problem. Find a number having 14 divisors. Here $14 = 2 \cdot 7$, and *subtracting* unity from each factor we have 1 and 6 as exponents to be applied to any primes we please. In general, to get the smallest answer apply the exponents to the smallest primes, namely 2 and 3 in this case. Thus $2^6 \cdot 3^1 = 192$, but any number of the form $p^6 q$ where p and q are primes greater than unity also has exactly 14 divisors. We could also have factored 14 into $1 \cdot 14$, resulting in the solution p^{13} such as $2^{13} = 8192$.

The determination of the *least* number having a given number of divisors is not always simple.　For instance if 12 is the given number of divisors and we write $12 = 2 \cdot 6$, the exponents are 1 and 5 and the number is $2^5 \cdot 3 = 96$.　But 12 also equals $3 \cdot 4$; the exponents are 2 and 3 and the number is $2^3 \cdot 3^2 = 72$.　Both of these results are larger than 60, which also has 12 divisors as found above.　How can that particular solution be found?　The number 12 should be factored into $2 \cdot 2 \cdot 3$, giving exponents 1, 1, and 2 and the number is then $2^2 \cdot 3 \cdot 5 = 60$.

The reader might wish to solve Problem 6 of Chapter I: Find the *least* number with 100 divisors; and then for comparison the *least* with 96.†

The *sum* of the divisors of a number gives rise to numerous interesting problems.　The number itself and unity are generally included among the divisors in such questions; if the number is not to be included, reference is made to "aliquot" divisors, meaning only those, including unity, which are less than the number.

One such problem is to find a number the sum of whose divisors is a perfect square.　The least number the sum of whose divisors is a square is 3, since 1 and 3 add to 4.　Then there is 22, since

$$1 + 2 + 11 + 22 = 36 = 6^2.$$

It is a pretty problem and, incidentally, one requiring essentially empirical methods to find such numbers even if one knows the formula for the sum of the divisors of a number.　A few other numbers possessing this property are the following:

TABLE 1

NUMBERS THE SUM OF WHOSE DIVISORS IS A SQUARE

Number	Divisors	Sum of Divisors = a Square
66	1; 2; 3; 6; 11; 22; 33; 66	$144 = 12^2$
70	1; 2; 5; 7; 10; 14; 35; 70	$144 = 12^2$
81	1; 3; 9; 27; 81	$121 = 11^2$
1501	1; 19; 79; 1501	$1600 = 40^2$
4479865	1; 5; 13; 41; 65; 205; 533; 1681; 2665; 8405; 21853; 68921; 109265; 344605; 895973; 4479865	$5934096 = 2436^2$

† Problems indicated by a dagger are solved in Chapter XXVI.

The great mathematician Fermat proposed in 1657 the problem: To find a cube which, when increased by the sum of its aliquot divisors, becomes a square. For example: $7^3 + (1 + 7 + 7^2) = 20^2$. Also: To find a square which when increased by the sum of its aliquot divisors becomes a cube. A few other solutions of the first problem are the following:

TABLE 2

CUBES WHICH, INCREASED BY THE SUM OF THEIR ALIQUOT DIVISORS, ARE SQUARES

Cube	Square = Cube + Its Aliquot Divisors
$(3^3 \cdot 5 \cdot 11 \cdot 13 \cdot 41 \cdot 47)^3$	$(2^8 \cdot 3^2 \cdot 5 \cdot 7 \cdot 11 \cdot 13 \cdot 17 \cdot 29 \cdot 61)^2$
$(2 \cdot 3 \cdot 5 \cdot 13 \cdot 41 \cdot 47)^3$	$(2^7 \cdot 3^2 \cdot 5^2 \cdot 7 \cdot 13 \cdot 17 \cdot 29)^2$
$(17 \cdot 31 \cdot 47 \cdot 191)^3$	$(2^{10} \cdot 3^2 \cdot 5 \cdot 13 \cdot 17 \cdot 29 \cdot 37)^2$
$(2^5 \cdot 5 \cdot 7 \cdot 31 \cdot 73 \cdot 241 \cdot 243 \cdot 467)^3$	$(2^{12} \cdot 3^2 \cdot 5^3 \cdot 11 \cdot 13^2 \cdot 17 \cdot 37 \cdot 41 \cdot 113 \cdot 193 \cdot 257)^2$
$(3 \cdot 11 \cdot 31 \cdot 443 \cdot 499)^3$	$(2^9 \cdot 3 \cdot 5^4 \cdot 13 \cdot 37 \cdot 61 \cdot 157)^2$

Some solutions of the second problem are:

TABLE 3

SQUARES WHICH, INCREASED BY THE SUM OF THEIR ALIQUOT DIVISORS, ARE CUBES

Square	Cube = Square + Its Aliquot Divisors
$(43098)^2 = (2 \cdot 3 \cdot 11 \cdot 653)^2$	$(1729)^3 = (7 \cdot 13 \cdot 19)^3$
$(2^2 \cdot 5 \cdot 7 \cdot 11 \cdot 37 \cdot 67 \cdot 163 \cdot 191 \cdot 263 \cdot 439 \cdot 499)^2$	$(3^2 \cdot 7^3 \cdot 13 \cdot 19 \cdot 31^2 \cdot 67 \cdot 109)^3$
$(7 \cdot 11 \cdot 29 \cdot 163 \cdot 191 \cdot 439)^2$	$(3 \cdot 7 \cdot 13 \cdot 19 \cdot 31 \cdot 67)^3$

Problems of this sort were often given as challenges by one mathematical coterie to another. The spirit of rivalry among mathematicians in different countries used to be, and often frequently still is, very keen, and nothing would delight one clique more than to propose to another a set of problems to which the proponents had the general solution. Many problems owed their existence to such a cause, and some of the most fruitful mathematical discoveries came about because of such rivalry.

Similar problems are to find squares such that the sum of their divisors is a square, or squares whose *aliquot* divisors only add up to a square.

A few examples are:

TABLE 4

SQUARES THE SUM OF WHOSE DIVISORS IS A SQUARE

Square	Sum of All Divisors = a Square
$81 = 9^2$	$1+3+9+27+81 = 121 = 11^2$
$400 = 20^2$	$1+2+4+5+8+10+16+20+25+40+50$
	$+80+100+200+400 = 961 = 31^2$
$(3 \cdot 7 \cdot 11 \cdot 29 \cdot 37)^2$	$(3 \cdot 7 \cdot 13 \cdot 19 \cdot 67)^2$

TABLE 5

SQUARES THE SUM OF WHOSE ALIQUOT DIVISORS IS A SQUARE

Square	Sum of Aliquot Divisors Only = a Square
$9 = 3^2$	$1+3 = 2^2$
$2401 = 49^2$	$1+7+49+343 = 400 = 20^2$

There are many other interesting relations involving divisors of numbers. A rather unusual one states that if a number N has p divisors, then the product of all these divisors is $\sqrt{N^p}$.

BIBLIOGRAPHY

Barlow, P. *Theory of Numbers.* London: J. Johnson & Co., 1811.
Carmichael, R. D. *Theory of Numbers and Diophantine Analysis.* New York: Dover Publications, Inc., 1959.
Dickson, L. E. *History of the Theory of Numbers.* 3 vols. New York: Chelsea Publishing Co., 1950.
Escott, E. B. "Solution of Problem: Find a Number, *x*, Such That the Sum of the Divisors of *x* Is a Perfect Square," *American Mathematical Monthly*, **23** (1916), 394.

CHAPTER III

PERFECTION

MAN EVER seeks perfection but inevitably it eludes him. He has sought "perfect numbers" throughout the ages and has found only a very few—twenty-two up to May, 1963. A perfect number is one which is equal to the sum of its aliquot divisors, that is, all the divisors including unity but excluding the number itself. Most numbers are either "abundant" or "deficient," the sum of their aliquot divisors either exceeding or being exceeded by the number, such as 24, whose aliquot divisors add to 36, or 15, whose aliquot divisors add to only 9. Six is the smallest perfect number, its aliquot divisors $1+2+3$ adding up to exactly 6.

Perfect numbers are few and far between; after 6 come 28; 496; 8128; and 33550336 in order. No odd perfect numbers are known. Six and 28 were regarded by some commentators on the Bible as the basic numbers of the Supreme Architect, the creation in six days and the 28-day lunar cycle being pointed out to substantiate this.

Euclid studied perfect numbers as did many another early Greek and also the early Hebrews. He knew the formula for even perfect numbers. Euclid lived about 2300 years ago. Since his time an enormous amount of labor has been expended on perfect numbers and the fields which were opened by investigating them. St. Augustine said, "Six is a number perfect in itself, and not because God created all things in six days; rather the inverse is true; God created all things in six days because this number is perfect. And it would remain perfect even if the work of the six days did not exist."

Nichomachus, a mathematician who flourished in about 100 A.D. and to whom the discovery of the perfect numbers 28 and 496 is sometimes attributed, wrote: "But it happens, that, just as the beautiful and the excellent are rare and easily counted, but the ugly and the bad are prolific, so also excessive and defective numbers are found to be very many and in disorder, their discovery being unsystematic. But the perfect are both easily counted and drawn up in a fitting order."

The followers of Pythagoras—the man who is responsible for "the sum of the squares on the legs of a right triangle is equal to the square on the hypotenuse"—called the perfect number 6 "marriage and health and beauty on account of the integrity of its parts and the agreement existing in it" (see Chapter XVIII).

Rabbi Josef ben Jehuda Ankin, in the twelfth century, recommended the study of perfect numbers in his book *Healing of Souls*.

In an Italian work the perfect number 6 was attributed to Venus, "for it is made by the union of the two sexes, that is, from triad, which is male since it is odd, and from diad, which is feminine since it is even."

Euclid's formula for *even* perfect numbers, N, is:

$$N = (2^{n-1})(2^n - 1) \qquad \text{(Formula 1)}$$

where n may be any positive integer exceeding unity which makes the second factor $(2^n - 1)$ a prime number. This is true when $n = 2, 3, 5, 7, 13$, etc., these values of n unfortunately following no regular sequence. The corresponding perfect numbers for these five values are: 6; 28; 496; 8128; and 33550336, as given previously.

It is a remarkable fact that Euclid knew the formula for even perfect numbers, and not till two thousand years later did the mathematician Euler prove that Euclid's formula is the only one for even perfect numbers. No one has yet been able to demonstrate whether or not an odd number can be perfect.

If an odd perfect number, N, is ever found, it will have to have met more stringent qualifications than exist in a legal contract and some almost as confusing. Here are just a *few*:

1. N must leave a remainder of 1 when divided by 12 and a remainder of 9 when divided by 36.

2. It must have at least six different prime divisors.

3. It must have the form $p^{4x+1} q_1^{2a_1} q_2^{2a_2} q_3^{2a_3} \ldots q_n^{2a_n}$, where p is a prime of only the form $4k+1$ while the q's may be *any* odd primes.

4. This can be further qualified by stating that if all the a's except the first equal 1, then a_1 cannot equal 2; also if all except the first two equal 1, then the first two, a_1 and a_2, cannot both equal 2.

5. Also N cannot be perfect if *all* the a's equal 2.

6. If all the exponents of the q's are increased by 1, the resulting exponents cannot have as a common divisor, 9, 15, 21, or 33.

7. If the exponent $4x+1$ of p is 5, then none of the a's may equal 1 or 2.

8. If N is not divisible by 3, it must have at least 9 different prime divisors, and if not divisible by 21 it must have at least 11 such divisors. If not divisible by 15, it must have at least 14 different prime divisors, and if not divisible by 105 it must have at least 27 such divisors. This requires N to be greater than 10^{44}.

9. If N has exactly r different prime divisors, the smallest of them will be smaller than $r+1$. Thus, should N (if it exists) have 28 different prime divisors, the smallest would not exceed 23.

For *even* perfect numbers, $(2^{n-1})(2^n-1)$, the problem therefore exists to find those values of n which make the second factor in $(2^{n-1})(2^n-1)$ a prime. W. W. R. Ball gave the name "Mersenne's numbers" to integers of the form (2^n-1) where n is a prime, because the French mathematician Mersenne made a statement in his *Cogitata* in 1644 regarding numbers of this type. The conjectures as to Mersenne's source of information and the ensuing discussions have given this investigation such a stimulus that Herculean labors of calculation have been performed to verify or contradict his statements and many important properties of numbers have incidentally been discovered. In modern times, digital computers have performed these difficult tasks.

Peter Bungus, who lived in the seventeenth century, was one of a host of mathematicians who combined numbers and general nonsense somewhat as the alchemists combined chemistry and alchemy. In a book entitled *Numerorum Mysteria*, he listed 24 numbers said to be perfect, of which Mersenne stated that only 8 were correct, namely those listed in Table 6. Mersenne then added on his own account the three values $n = 67; 127; 257$, and stated that these gave the next

TABLE 6

PERFECT NUMBERS

n	Perfect Number $= (2^{n-1})(2^n-1)$	Corresponding Mersenne Number, $M_n = 2^n - 1$
2	6	3
3	28	7
5	496	31
7	8128	127
13	33550336	8191
17	8589869056	131071
19	137438691328	524287
31	2305843008139952128	2147483647

three perfect numbers in order. Subsequent investigations showed that he was wrong in admitting the values 67 and 257 and that he omitted the perfect numbers corresponding to 89 and 107 for which the Mersenne numbers are primes. But it took 303 years, from 1644 to 1947, completely to check and correct Mersenne's statement.

There have been many conjectures as to how Mersenne arrived at his results, and after a lapse of over 300 years no answer has been found. He must have discovered or had available some theorem not yet rediscovered, since empirical methods could hardly have been used—the Mersenne number for $n = 257$ has 78 digits. Some have supposed that the talented mathematician Fermat communicated these results to him.

It is inevitable that with a problem having such universal appeal many false claims should have been made about discovering a new perfect number. That such claims were made in past centuries without any foundation in fact was more or less to be expected, as when Peter Bungus unblushingly gave 24 perfect numbers and achieved a batting average of only .333. But the twentieth century too brought forth some interesting claimants. As explorers were attracted to the North Pole, mathematicians have been lured by the Mersenne numbers having high exponents, particularly the one for $n = 257$.

On March 27, 1936, the Associated Press released an exciting report on a "new perfect number." Dr. S. I. Krieger of Chicago claimed he had found a 155-digit perfect number, meaning $2^{256}(2^{257} - 1)$; he thought, that is, he had proved $2^{257} - 1$ is a prime. Said the *New York Herald Tribune*:

PERFECTION IS CLAIMED FOR 155-DIGIT NUMBER

MAN LABORS 5 YEARS TO PROVE PROBLEM DATING FROM EUCLID

Chicago, March 26 (AP).—Dr. Samuel I. Krieger laid down his pencil and paper today and asserted he had solved a problem that had baffled mathematicians since Euclid's day—finding a perfect number of more than nineteen digits.

A perfect number was one that was equal to the sum of its divisors, he explained. For example, 28 is the sum of 1, 2, 4, 7, and 14, all of which may be divided into it. Dr. Krieger's perfect number contains 155 digits. Here it is: 26,815,615,859,885,194, 199,148,049,996,411,692,254,958,731,641,184,786,755,447,122,887, 443,528,060,146,978,161,514,511,280,138,383,284,395,055,028,465, 118,831,722,842,125,059,853,682,308,859,384,882,528,256.

Its formula is 2 to the 513th power minus 2 to the 256th power. The doctor said it took him seventeen hours to work it out and five years to prove it correct.

Two experts in the theory of numbers, M. Kraitchik and D. H. Lehmer, men of deservedly high reputation, had found the number composite, the former in 1922, the latter in 1931. Their method, however, while revealing the character of the number, did not disclose its factors. Who was correct, Dr. Krieger or Messrs. Kraitchik and Lehmer?

The mathematical journals subsequently chided the newspapers and deservedly so, for sacrificing accuracy to sensationalism. Four perfect numbers with more than the 19 digits mentioned in the article were known prior to its publication. These have 37, 54, 65, and 77 digits respectively; the 37-digit one, $2^{60}(2^{61}-1)$, was discovered as long ago as 1883. Dr. Krieger laid down his pencil prematurely, but the ghost was not properly laid until 1952 when the National Bureau of Standards' Western Automatic Computer "SWAC" confirmed that $2^{257}-1$ is indeed composite. More about this later.

The expression 2^n-1 is always composite when n is composite. For, if n is an even composite number, say $2y$, the expression becomes the difference of two squares, which is always factorable so that $2^{2y}-1 = (2^y+1)(2^y-1)$. For example:

$$(2^{14}-1) = (2^7+1)(2^7-1) = 129\cdot127 = 3\cdot43\cdot127.$$

If n is odd but composite as in $2^{pq}-1$, we can write:

$$\begin{aligned}2^{pq}-1 &= (2^p)^q-1\\ &= (2^p-1)[(2^p)^{q-1}+(2^p)^{q-2}+(2^p)^{q-3}+\ldots+(2^p)+1],\end{aligned}$$

as explained in any algebra textbook. For example:

$$\begin{aligned}2^{35}-1 &= (2^7)^5-1 = (2^7-1)[(2^7)^4+(2^7)^3+(2^7)^2+(2^7)+1]\\ &= 127\cdot270549121.\end{aligned}$$

Thus $2^{35}-1$ is composite since it has been resolved into at least two factors. It so happens that the last factor is also composite, finally resulting in the prime factors $127\cdot31\cdot71\cdot122921$.

Although 2^n-1 is *always* composite when n is composite, it is also frequently composite when n is a prime. Certain theorems can be applied in some cases which may either directly factor the number or place a reasonable limit on the number of divisors to be tried in factoring it. Fermat's theorem and its corollaries are most useful here.

This celebrated theorem, which we shall refer to again in Chapter VI, states that the number $a^{p-1}-1$ is always divisible by p if p is a prime and if the number a is not a multiple of p. For example, 2^6-1 is exactly divisible by 7. It may be that some lower exponent than $p-1$, say, n, would make a^n-1 divisible by p (for example, 2^3-1 is also divisible by 7); but if such is the case, the exponent n is always a divisor of $p-1$, that is, $p-1$ must be equal to, say, mn. Then $p = mn+1$.

In Mersenne's numbers, that is, numbers of the form 2^n-1, the exponent n is always a prime and therefore odd (except for $n = 2$, a trivial case). Hence, since in Fermat's theorem p is also a prime and odd, it follows that mn must be even, and therefore m must be even, equal to, say, $2r$, and then $p = 2rn+1$. This tells us, therefore, that if, for example, $2^{11}-1$ has a prime divisor, p (if it has any divisor, it has a prime divisor, of course), it must be of the form $2r\cdot11+1 = 22r+1$, and in fact when $r = 1$, the prime 23 divides $2^{11}-1$. Similarly, if $2^{17}-1$ has a prime divisor, it must be of the form $2r\cdot17+1 = 34r+1$, but in this case the only such prime divisor is the number itself because $2^{17}-1$ happens to be a prime. When n becomes large, the number of possible divisors to test, even though limited to the above form, becomes so large that other aids must be enlisted.

A modification of Fermat's theorem, however, gives divisors of certain Mersenne numbers directly. From this theorem we know that $2^{p-1}-1$ is always divisible by p when p is a prime. Since p is an odd number, $p-1$ is even and therefore composite, because it is divisible by 2. But Mersenne's numbers all have *prime* exponents, so that it would appear that Fermat's theorem cannot aid us in finding factors of these numbers. But it can be shown* that for the base 2, the exponent $p-1$ may be divided by 2 without affecting divisibility by p if p is a prime leaving 1 or 7 as a remainder when divided by 8, or, as we say, is of the form $8r+1$ or $8r+7$. Thus,

$$2^{[(8r+1)-1]/2}-1 \quad \text{and} \quad 2^{[(8r+7)-1]/2}-1$$

are respectively divisible by primes of the given forms. In the first case we have $2^{4r}-1$ divisible by a prime, $8r+1$, but since the exponent $4r$ is not a prime, the number is not of the Mersenne type. In the latter instance, however, we have $2^{4r+3}-1$, divisible by the prime $8r+7$, so that if both $4r+3$ and $8r+7$ are primes, then $8r+7$ will always divide the corresponding Mersenne number.

* See, for example, Uspensky and Heaslet's *Elementary Number Theory*.

Mersenne confined his remarks to numbers, $2^n - 1$, where n does not exceed 257; and up to this limit, the values of r and n fulfilling both conditions are shown in Table 7.

TABLE 7

DIVISORS OF MERSENNE'S NUMBERS

r	$n = 4r+3$, a Prime	$8r+7$, a Prime and Therefore a Divisor of $2^n - 1$
2	11	23
5	23	47
20	83	167
32	131	263
44	179	359
47	191	383
59	239	479
62	251	503

Very ingenious methods have been developed for limiting the trials of divisors of Mersenne's numbers, including a photoelectric factoring machine, of which mention is made in Chapter XXI. Modern digital computers have been extremely effective in finding large perfect numbers, sometimes accomplishing in seconds what it has taken a human computer years to calculate.

E. V. Lucas, a French mathematician, invented a test for the primality of a Mersenne number. D. H. Lehmer improved upon this test, making it so effective and practical that he and other investigators were soon able to demonstrate the composite character of many of the Mersenne numbers previously unknown. Lucas's test, as modified by Lehmer, employs the series: 4; 14; 194; 37634; ... $u_n = u_{n-1}^2 - 2$, where each term is obtained by squaring the previous term and then subtracting 2. Then if, and only if, the $(n-1)$th term of this series is exactly divisible by $N = 2^n - 1$, N is a prime; otherwise it is composite. Thus 37634 is the fourth term of the series, and if $2^5 - 1 = 31$ divides into it exactly, 31 is a prime. This proves to be the case. Unfortunately the terms of this series increase so rapidly that the test becomes almost impractical for large values of n unless this "immovable object" is met by an "irresistible force" such as a modern digital computer. The National Bureau of Standards' Western Automatic Computer "SWAC" was given this job in 1953. Lucas's rule had to be adapted to the computer's ability, requiring 184 separate commands. The five perfect numbers corresponding to $n = 521$; 607; 1279; 2203; and 2281 were found by SWAC. Dr. D. H. Lehmer, who had spent very many hours on Mersenne's numbers, saw the machine do in 48 seconds what it had taken him over 700 hours of arduous labor with a desk calculator to demonstrate 20 years before: that $2^{257} - 1$ is composite. Mersenne had stated that all eternity would not suffice to tell if a 15- or 20-digit number is prime. Within a few hours, SWAC tested 42 numbers, the *smallest* of which had 80 digits. It took $13\frac{1}{2}$ minutes to determine that $2^{1279} - 1$ is a prime. A human instead of a digital computer might have taken 125 years for this. It is fatuous to prophesy. Also the ability of a mere human is not to be discounted. H. S. Uhler, using only a desk calculator, found the six perfect numbers corresponding to $n = 157$; 167; 193; 199; 227; and 229.

Dr. Lehmer states that it takes approximately $(p/100)^3$ seconds to test a prime, p, to see if a Mersenne number, M_p, is a prime. In general, each minute of the SWAC is equivalent to one year of work by a person with a desk calculator.

The values of the twelve perfect numbers corresponding to Mersenne's limit of 257 are given in Table 8, as well as the value of the next ten perfect numbers, for n between 257 and 9941.

The most recent information known to the author regarding the factors of the Mersenne numbers, $M_n = 2^n - 1$, up to the limit 257 is as follows: prime for the twelve values $n = 2, 3, 5, 7, 13, 17, 19, 31, 61$ 89, 107, and 127; composite and completely factored for $n = 11, 23$ 29, 37, 41, 43, 47, 53, 59, 67, 71, 73, 79, 83, 97, 113, and 151; composite with two or more factors known for $n = 163, 173, 179, 181$ 223, 229, 233, 239, 251; composite with only one factor known for $n = 109, 131, 157, 167, 191, 193, 197, 211, 229,$ and 241; composite but no factor known for $n = 101, 103, 137, 139, 149, 199, 227,$ and 257 However, it is known that for $n = 101$ there are only two prime factors Table 9 gives the factors of those composite Mersenne numbers which have at least one known factor. The seven numbers known to be composite but none of whose factors are known are not listed; 101 however, is included.

Table 8 shows the exasperating irregularity of functions involving primes. The 12 prime Mersenne numbers occur within the range of the first 31 prime values of n, namely between 2 and 127 inclusive but not a single prime Mersenne number, M_n, occurs in the range of

TABLE 8

PERFECT AND MERSENNE'S NUMBERS

$n =$ a Prime	Mersenne's Number $M_n = (2^n - 1)$, a Prime	No. of Digits	Perfect Number $(2^{n-1})(2^n - 1)$	No. of Digits
2	3	1	$2^1(2^2 - 1) = 6$	1
3	7	1	$2^2(2^3 - 1) = 28$	2
5	31	2	$2^4(2^5 - 1) = 496$	3
7	127	3	$2^6(2^7 - 1) = 8128$	4
13	8191	4	$2^{12}(2^{13} - 1) = 33550336$	8
17	131071	6	$2^{16}(2^{17} - 1) = 8589869056$	10
19	524287	6	$2^{18}(2^{19} - 1) = 137438691328$	12
31	2147483647	10	$2^{30}(2^{31} - 1) = 2305843008139952128$	19
61	2305843009213693951	19	$2^{60}(2^{61} - 1)$	37
89	618970019642690137449562111	27	$2^{88}(2^{89} - 1)$	54
107	$2^{107} - 1$	33	$2^{106}(2^{107} - 1)$	65
127	$2^{127} - 1$	39	$2^{126}(2^{127} - 1)$	77
521	$2^{521} - 1$	157	$2^{520}(2^{521} - 1)$	314
607	$2^{607} - 1$	183	$2^{606}(2^{607} - 1)$	366
1279	$2^{1279} - 1$	386	$2^{1278}(2^{1279} - 1)$	770
2203	$2^{2203} - 1$	664	$2^{2202}(2^{2203} - 1)$	1327
2281	$2^{2281} - 1$	687	$2^{2280}(2^{2281} - 1)$	1373
3217	$2^{3217} - 1$	969	$2^{3216}(2^{3217} - 1)$	1937
4253	$2^{4253} - 1$	1281	$2^{4252}(2^{4253} - 1)$	2561
4423	$2^{4423} - 1$	1332	$2^{4422}(2^{4423} - 1)$	2663
9689	$2^{9689} - 1$	2917	$2^{9688}(2^{9689} - 1)$	5834
9941	$2^{9941} - 1$	2993	$2^{9940}(2^{9941} - 1)$	5985

the next 66 primes between 131 and 521. All the 24 Mersenne numbers between $2^{127}-1$ and $2^{257}-1$ are composite plus the 42 additional ones between $2^{257}-1$ and $2^{521}-1$. Between 521 and 607 there are only 12 primes which make M_n composite, but after that there are 95 primes between 607 and 1279, then a long run of 120 primes before $2^{2203}-1$ is a prime, and yet there are only 10 primes between 2203 and 2281, the next exponent which makes M_n a prime. Then there is another long run of 116 primes before the eighteenth perfect number is reached for which $n = 3217$. The intervals between the last four Mersenne primes listed in Table 8 are 128; 19; 594; and 30 primes respectively.

Some readers may wish to know how the formula for even perfect numbers is derived. In Chapter II the formula was given for the *number* of divisors of a number:

$$N = p_1{}^{a_1} p_2{}^{a_2} \ldots p_n{}^{a_n}.$$

The formula for the *sum* of the divisors of N is:

$$\frac{p_1{}^{a_1+1}-1}{p_1-1} \cdot \frac{p_2{}^{a_2+1}-1}{p_2-1} \cdots \frac{p_n{}^{a_n+1}-1}{p_n-1} \qquad \text{(Formula 2)}$$

For example, if $N = 240$, we express it as the product of powers of primes in the form $2^4 \cdot 3 \cdot 5$. Then the sum of the divisors of N, frequently symbolized as $S(N)$, is:

$$\frac{2^{4+1}-1}{2-1} \cdot \frac{3^{1+1}-1}{3-1} \cdot \frac{5^{1+1}-1}{5-1} = 31 \cdot 4 \cdot 6 = 744.$$

The number itself is included as a divisor in this sum.

Now we are ready to derive the perfect number formula. Suppose there is an even perfect number $N = 2^a q$ where q represents the product of all the odd prime powers. We shall show that q is in fact only a single prime and of a particular form. For convenience, to save writing out a complicated expression like Formula 2, let s be the sum of all the divisors of q (including q itself) and let d be the sum of its aliquot divisors only, so that $s = q+d$.

By Formula 2, the sum of the divisors of 2^a is $(2^{a+1}-1)/(2-1) = 2^{a+1}-1$. Therefore the sum of all the divisors of N is equal to $(2^{a+1}-1) \cdot s$, and this sum, in a perfect number, is equal to *twice* the number, because Formula 2 includes the number itself among its divisors. So we have $2N$ or $2(2^a q)$ or $2^{a+1}q = (2^{a+1}-1) \cdot s$ or $(2^{a+1}-1)(q+d)$.

TABLE 9

FACTORS OF MERSENNE'S NUMBERS

n, a Prime	Mersenne's Number $2^n - 1$
11	$2047 = 23 \cdot 89$ C*
23	$8388607 = 47 \cdot 178481$ C
29	$536870911 = 233 \cdot 1103 \cdot 2089$ C
37	$137438953471 = 223 \cdot 616318177$ C
41	$2199023255551 = 13367 \cdot 164511353$ C
43	$8796093022207 = 431 \cdot 9719 \cdot 2099863$ C
47	$2351 \cdot 4513 \cdot 13264529$ C
53	$6361 \cdot 69431 \cdot 20394401$ C
59	$179951 \cdot 3203431780337$ C
67	$193707721 \cdot 761838257287$ C
71	$228479 \cdot 48544121 \cdot 212885833$ C
73	$439 \cdot 2298041 \cdot 9361973132609$ C
79	$2687 \cdot 202029703 \cdot 1113491139767$ C
83	$167 \cdot 57912614113275649087721$ C
97	$11447 \cdot 13842607235828485645766393$ C
101	Prime $\cdot$ Prime C
109	$745988807 \cdot$?
113	$3391 \cdot 23279 \cdot 65993 \cdot 1868569 \cdot 1066818132868207$ C
131	$263 \cdot$?
151	$18121 \cdot 55871 \cdot 165799 \cdot 2332951$ $\cdot 7289088383388253664437433$ C
157	$852133201 \cdot$?
163	$150287 \cdot 704161 \cdot 110211473 \cdot$?
167	$2349023 \cdot$?
173	$730753 \cdot 1505447 \cdot$?
179	$359 \cdot 1433 \cdot$?
181	$43441 \cdot 1164193 \cdot 7648337 \cdot$?
191	$383 \cdot$?
193	$13821503 \cdot$?
197	$7487 \cdot$?
211	$15193 \cdot$?
223	$18287 \cdot 196687 \cdot 1466449 \cdot 2916841 \cdot$?
229	$1504073 \cdot 20492753 \cdot$?
233	$1399 \cdot 135607 \cdot 622577 \cdot$?
239	$479 \cdot 1913 \cdot 5737 \cdot 176383 \cdot 134000609 \cdot$?
241	$22000409 \cdot$?
251	$503 \cdot 54217 \cdot$?

* C indicates that the number has been *completely* factored; *all* its prime factors are given. For $n = 101$, the two factors are unknown.

Simplifying, we get

$$2^{a+1} - 1 = q/d.$$

This means that d is an aliquot divisor of q and, as defined previously, it is also equal to the sum of the aliquot divisors of q. Hence d must be the *only* aliquot divisor of q. Then the only possible value of d is 1, and if the sum of the aliquot divisors of a number is 1, obviously the number is a prime.

Therefore $q = 2^{a+1} - 1$ is a prime; and N, which equals $2^a q$, becomes $2^a(2^{a+1} - 1)$, which corresponds to Formula 1 if we let $a + 1 = n$. This completes the proof.

*   *   *

Except for the perfect number 6, where $a = 1$, every even perfect number, $2^a(2^{a+1} - 1)$, is the sum of the cubes of the first $2^{a/2}$ odd numbers. Thus for $a = 2$, the perfect number $28 = 1^3 + 3^3$; for $a = 4$, the perfect number $496 = 1^3 + 3^3 + 5^3 + 7^3$; for $a = 6$, the perfect number $8128 = 1^3 + 3^3 + 5^3 + 7^3 + 9^3 + 11^3 + 13^3 + 15^3$, etc. This is a rather unexpected relation between cubes and perfect numbers.

*   *   *

Not content with ordinary perfect numbers, mathematicians discovered multiply perfect ones—numbers the sum of *all* of whose divisors is an exact multiple of the number. Ordinary perfect numbers are called P_2's since their divisors add up to twice the number. A P_3 is one whose divisors add to three times the number, etc. An example of a P_3 is 120, whose divisors $1 + 2 + 3 + 4 + 5 + 6 + 8 + 10 + 12 + 15 + 20 + 24 + 30 + 40 + 60 + 120$ add to $360 = 3 \cdot 120$. Here are a few of many other multiply perfect numbers:

TABLE 10

MULTIPLY PERFECT NUMBERS

Multiplicity	Perfect Number
3	672
4	30240
4	$2^{41} \cdot 3^{12} \cdot 7^4 \cdot 11^2 \cdot 13^4 \cdot 17^2 \cdot 19^2 \cdot 43 \cdot 103 \cdot 127 \cdot 151 \cdot 191 \cdot 271 \cdot 307 \cdot 337 \cdot 467 \cdot 617 \cdot 911 \cdot 2801 \cdot 5419 \cdot 30941 \cdot 398581 \cdot 797161$
5	14182439040
6	$2^{23} \cdot 3^7 \cdot 5^3 \cdot 7^4 \cdot 11^3 \cdot 13^3 \cdot 17^2 \cdot 31 \cdot 41 \cdot 61 \cdot 241 \cdot 307 \cdot 467 \cdot 2801$
7	$2^{46} \cdot 3^{15} \cdot 5^3 \cdot 7^5 \cdot 11 \cdot 13 \cdot 17 \cdot 19^4 \cdot 23 \cdot 31 \cdot 37 \cdot 41 \cdot 43 \cdot 61 \cdot 89 \cdot 97 \cdot 151 \cdot 193 \cdot 911 \cdot 2351 \cdot 4513 \cdot 442151 \cdot 13264529$

The *product* instead of the sum of the aliquot divisors of a number may equal a power of the number, as shown in Table 11.

TABLE 11

NUMBERS THE PRODUCT OF WHOSE DIVISORS IS A POWER OF
THE NUMBER

N = number	$\pi(d)$ = Product of Aliquot Divisors of N	
12	$1 \cdot 2 \cdot 3 \cdot 4 \cdot 6 =$	$144 = 12^2$
20	$1 \cdot 2 \cdot 4 \cdot 5 \cdot 10 =$	$400 = 20^2$
45	$1 \cdot 3 \cdot 5 \cdot 9 \cdot 15 =$	$1225 = 45^2$
24	$1 \cdot 2 \cdot 3 \cdot 4 \cdot 6 \cdot 8 \cdot 12 =$	$13824 = 24^3$
40	$1 \cdot 2 \cdot 4 \cdot 5 \cdot 8 \cdot 10 \cdot 20 =$	$64000 = 40^3$
48	$1 \cdot 2 \cdot 3 \cdot 4 \cdot 6 \cdot 8 \cdot 12 \cdot 16 \cdot 24 =$	$5308416 = 48^4$
80	$1 \cdot 2 \cdot 4 \cdot 5 \cdot 8 \cdot 10 \cdot 16 \cdot 20 \cdot 40 =$	$40960000 = 80^4$
405	$1 \cdot 3 \cdot 5 \cdot 9 \cdot 15 \cdot 27 \cdot 45 \cdot 81 \cdot 135 =$	$26904200625 = 405^4$

Aside from perfect numbers, the numbers $2^n \pm 1$ have been investigated for their own sake. Such numbers have been either partially or completely factored for many high values of n. The Army Ordinance Electronic Numerical Integrator and Computer ENIAC has been used to calculate such factors and also composite numbers n and their prime factors, p, for which $2^n \equiv 2 \bmod n$. Examples are $n = 100463443$, $p = 75771$; and $n = 199674721$, $p = 4261$.

There are very few *even* numbers, m, satisfying the congruence $2^m - 2 \equiv 0 \bmod m$. One is $161038 = 2 \cdot 73 \cdot 1103$, and three others are 215326, 2568226, and 143742226.

BIBLIOGRAPHY

Archibald, R. C. "Mersenne's Numbers," *Scripta Mathematica*, **3** (1935), 112.

Associated Press. "Perfection Is Claimed for 155-Digit Number," *New York Herald Tribune*, **95** (March 27, 1936), 21.

Ball, W. W. R. *A Short Account of the History of Mathematics.* New York: Dover Publications, Inc., 1960.

———. *Mathematical Recreations and Essays.* New York: Macmillan Co., 1939.

Barker, C. B. "Proof That the Mersenne Number M_{167} Is Composite," *Bulletin of the American Mathematical Society*, **51** (1945), 388.

Barlow, P. *Theory of Numbers.* London: J. Johnson & Co., 1811.

Beeger, N. G. W. H. "On Even Numbers m Dividing $2^m - 2$," *American Mathematical Monthly*, **58** (1951), 553.

Bell, E. T.   *The Last Problem.*   New York: Simon and Schuster, 1961.

Bickmore, C. E.   "On the Numerical Factors of $a^n - 1$," *Messenger of Mathematics*, **25** (1895), 1.

Brauer, A.   "On the Non-Existence of Odd Perfect Numbers of the Form $p^a q_1^2 q_2^2 \ldots q_{t-1}^2 q_t^4$," *Bulletin of the American Mathematical Society*, **49** (1943), 712.

Brillhardt, J., and Johnson, G. D.   "On the Factors of Certain Mersenne Numbers," *Mathematics of Computation*, **14** (1960), 365.

Carmichael, R. D.   *Theory of Numbers and Diophantine Analysis.*   New York: Dover Publications, Inc., 1959.

———.   "A Table of Multiply-Perfect Numbers," *Bulletin of the American Mathematical Society*, **13** (1907), 383.

Carmichael, R. D., and Mason, T. E.   "Note on Multiply-Perfect Numbers...," *Proceedings of the Indiana Academy of Science* (1911), 257.

Dantzig, T.   *Number: The Language of Science.*   New York: Macmillan Co., 1954.

Dickson, L. E.   *History of the Theory of Numbers.*   3 vols.   New York: Chelsea Publishing Co., 1950.

Franque, B., and Garcia, M.   "Some New Multiply-Perfect Numbers," *American Mathematical Monthly*, **60** (1953), 459.

Gillies, D. B.   "Computer Discovers New Prime Number," *Science News Letter*, **83** (May 11, 1963), 291.

Hurwitz, A.   "New Mersenne Primes," *Mathematics of Computation*, **16** (1962), 249.

Kraitchik, M.   "On the Factorization of $2^n \pm 1$," *Scripta Mathematica*, **18** (1952), 39.

Lehmer, D. H.   "On the Converse of Fermat's Theorem," *American Mathematical Monthly*, **43** (1936), 347.

———.   "Factor Tables for the First Ten Million," *American Mathematical Monthly*, **56** (1949), 103.

———.   "Test for Primality by the Converse of Fermat's Theorem," *Bulletin of the American Mathematical Society*, **33** (1927), 327.

———.   "A Further Note on the Converse of Fermat's Theorem," *Bulletin of the American Mathematical Society*, **34** (1928), 54.

———.   "Note on Mersenne Numbers," *Bulletin of the American Mathematical Society*, **38** (1932), 383.

———.   "Some New Factorizations of $2^n \pm 1$," *Bulletin of the American Mathematical Society*, **39** (1933), 105.

———.   "On the Factors of $2^n \pm 1$," *Bulletin of the American Mathematical Society*, **53** (1947), 164.

———.   "On Lucas's Test for the Primality of Mersenne's Numbers," *Journal of the London Mathematical Society*, **10** (1935), 162.

Licks, H. E.   *Recreations in Mathematics.*   New York: D. Van Nostrand Co., 1921.

National Bureau of Standards.   "National Bureau of Standards' Western Automatic Computer," *Technical News Bulletin*, **37** (Oct., 1953), 145.

Powers, R. E. "The Tenth Perfect Number," *American Mathematical Monthly*, **18** (1911), 195.

———. "Note on a Mersenne Number," *Bulletin of the American Mathematical Society*, **40** (1934), 883.

Reid, C. "Perfect Numbers," *Scientific American*, **188** (March, 1953), 84.

Riessel, H. "Mersenne Numbers," *Mathematical Tables and Other Aids to Computation*, **12** (1958), 207.

———. "All Factors $q < 10^8$ in All Mersenne Numbers, $2^p - 1$, p a Prime $< 10^4$," *Mathematics of Computation*, **16** (1962), 478.

Touchard, J. "On Prime Numbers and Perfect Numbers," *Scripta Mathematica*, **19** (1953), 35.

Uhler, H. S. "Note on the Mersenne Numbers M_{157} and M_{167}," *Bulletin of the American Mathematical Society*, **52** (1946), 178.

———. "On Mersenne's Number M_{199} and Lucas's Sequences," *Bulletin of the American Mathematical Society*, **53** (1947), 162.

———. "On Mersenne's Number M_{227} and Cognate Data," *Bulletin of the American Mathematical Society*, **54** (1948), 378.

———. "A Brief History of the Investigation of Mersenne Numbers and the Latest Immense Pairs," *Scripta Mathematica*, **18** (1952), 122.

———. "Full Values of the First Seventeen Perfect Numbers," *Scripta Mathematica*, **20** (1954), 240.

Uspensky, J. V., and Heaslet, M. A. *Elementary Number Theory*. New York: McGraw-Hill Book Co., 1939.

Van Der Pol, B. "Radio Technology and Theory of Numbers," *Journal of the Franklin Institute*, **255** (1953), 476.

———. "Addendum and Correction to 'Radio Technology and Theory of Numbers,'" *Journal of the Franklin Institute*, **256** (1953), 265.

Woodall, H. J. "Mersenne's Numbers," *Manchester Literary and Philosophical Society, Memoirs and Proceedings*, **56** (1911–1912), 1.

CHAPTER IV

JUST BETWEEN FRIENDS

IF YOU WISH to convey an original valentine greeting to someone, expressing sincere friendship, make use of number theory. Send a card on which is printed something like this:

John—1184
Mary—1210

or you might substitute a question mark for the name of the sender. Subsequently you can explain that 1184 and 1210 are "amicable numbers," and if you do a convincing job perhaps you may be able to adopt 6 or some other perfect number as the token of your mutual happiness, since it symbolizes the union of the two sexes. The numbers 1184 and 1210 are amicable because they have the remarkable property that the sum of the aliquot divisors of either number equals the other number. Thus

$$1+2+4+8+16+32+37+74+148+296+592 = 1210,$$

and

$$1+2+5+10+11+22+55+110+121+242+605 = 1184.$$

As might be expected, such a sentimental attachment had many interpretations by some of our mystically inclined ancestors. Thus in Genesis 32: 14, Jacob's present of 200 she-goats and 20 he-goats was, according to one Bible commentator, a "hidden secret arrangement," because 220 is one of the pair of amicable numbers 220–284 and Jacob tried this means of securing the friendship of Esau. Pythagoras said that a friend is "one who is the other I such as are 220 and 284."

El Madschriti, an Arab of the eleventh century, tested the erotic effects of these numbers by giving someone the smaller number 220 to eat, and himself eating the larger. This may prove a valuable suggestion to a modern lover, who might perhaps offer one of these numbers made of cake or candy to his inamorata, the while he avidly consumed the other. It might lend added effect to wait until both delicacies had been eaten before explaining the significance of this ceremonial.

In spite of interest in amicable numbers dating from biblical times, there is much about their law of formation still to be cleared up. The master mathematician Euler listed 60 correct pairs of amicable numbers in 1750; yet he omitted the second smallest pair, 1184 and 1210, which were discovered by a 16-year-old boy, B. N. I. Paganini, as late as 1866. All the experts living within that mathematically fruitful intervening century failed to find that pair.

There are many rules for finding amicable number sets in contrast with the single formula for perfect numbers. One fairly simple one taken from the Arabian mathematician Thabit ben Korrah is: Take any power of 2, such as 2^x where x is greater than 1, and form the numbers:

$$a = 3 \cdot 2^x - 1$$
$$b = 3 \cdot 2^{x-1} - 1$$
$$c = 9 \cdot 2^{2x-1} - 1.$$

If these are all primes, then $2^x ab$ and $2^x c$ are amicable. When x is 2, this gives the numbers 220 and 284. A few other pairs are shown in Table 12.

TABLE 12

AMICABLE NUMBER PAIRS

2620	5020	6232	10744	17296
2924	5564	6368	10856	18416
	9363584		111448537712	
	9437056		118853793424	

It was inevitable that someone should investigate what happens if you add the aliquot divisors of the number which itself represents the sum of the aliquot divisors of a number, and so on. The sum of the aliquot divisors of 20 is $1+2+4+5+10 = 22$; the sum of the aliquot divisors of 22 is $1+2+11 = 14$; the aliquot divisors of 14 add to $+2+7 = 10$, whose aliquot divisors $1+2+5$ add to 8. The aliquot divisors of 8 add to 7, and finally we find that the aliquot divisors of 7 add only to 1. Most numbers eventually end up in this manner, but on the other hand some divisor sums increase indefinitely.

In passing through such a cycle, one of the sums may turn out to equal the original number and then we have an "amicable number of a higher order" or, recently, a "sociable number." Obviously, if the original number is reached after one addition, we have a perfect number; if after two additions we have a set of common amicable numbers, since the first addition of the aliquot divisors of a number n gives a number m, the sum of whose aliquot divisors is n. Mathematicians use the symbol $s(n)$ for the sum of the aliquot divisors of n, and for compactness, instead of $s[s(n)]$ representing the second cycle, they write $s^2(n)$. This does not mean the square of s multiplied by n but a two-times cycle of divisor additions. Thus $s(n) = n$ in perfect numbers and $s^2(n) = n$ in common amicable numbers. Proceeding further, $s^k(n) = n$ represents an amicable number of order k with a k-cycle addition starting and ending with n; the k respective sums are all amicable numbers of order k.

An example is 12496, whose $s(n) = 14288$; $s^2(n) = 15472$; $s^3(n) = 14536$; $s^4(n) = 14264$; and $s^5(n) = 12496 = n$, the original number. But a really marvelous number is 14316 which has a 28-link chain, that is, $s^{28}(14316) = 14316$. Perhaps the reader would like to verify this before looking at Table 14 and Figure 1 which give the values of each link.

Like the Three Musketeers, there are amicable triplets, that is, three numbers such that the sum of the aliquot divisors of any one of them is equal to the sum of the remaining two numbers. Two such triplets are shown in Table 13.

FIG. 1. A WONDERFUL 28-LINK AMICABLE NUMBER CHAIN

TABLE 13

Amicable Number Triplets

$2^{14} \cdot 3 \cdot 5 \cdot 19 \cdot 31 \cdot 89 \cdot 151$	$2^5 \cdot 3 \cdot 13 \cdot 293 \cdot 337$
$2^{14} \cdot 5 \cdot 11 \cdot 19 \cdot 29 \cdot 31 \cdot 151$	$2^5 \cdot 3 \cdot 5 \cdot 13 \cdot 16561$
$2^{14} \cdot 5 \cdot 19 \cdot 31 \cdot 151 \cdot 359$	$2^5 \cdot 3 \cdot 13 \cdot 99371$

TABLE 14

Amicable Number Chain of 28 Links
(The Sum of the Aliquot Divisors of Any Link = the Succeeding Link)

Link No.	Link Value As Integer	Link Value As Product of Powers of Primes	Number of Aliquot Divisors
1	14316	$2^2 \cdot 3 \cdot 1193$	11
2	19116	$2^2 \cdot 3^4 \cdot 59$	29
3	31704	$2^3 \cdot 3 \cdot 1321$	15
4	47616	$2^9 \cdot 3 \cdot 31$	39
5	83328	$2^7 \cdot 3 \cdot 7 \cdot 31$	63
6	177792	$2^7 \cdot 3 \cdot 463$	31
7	295488	$2^6 \cdot 3^5 \cdot 19$	83
8	629072	$2^4 \cdot 39317$	9
9	589786	$2 \cdot 294893$	3
10	294896	$2^4 \cdot 7 \cdot 2633$	19
11	358336	$2^6 \cdot 11 \cdot 509$	27
12	418904	$2^3 \cdot 52363$	7
13	366556	$2^2 \cdot 91639$	5
14	274924	$2^2 \cdot 13 \cdot 17 \cdot 311$	23
15	275444	$2^2 \cdot 13 \cdot 5297$	11
16	243760	$2^4 \cdot 5 \cdot 11 \cdot 277$	39
17	376736	$2^5 \cdot 61 \cdot 193$	23
18	381028	$2^2 \cdot 95257$	5
19	285778	$2 \cdot 43 \cdot 3323$	7
20	152990	$2 \cdot 5 \cdot 15299$	7
21	122410	$2 \cdot 5 \cdot 12241$	7
22	97946	$2 \cdot 48973$	3
23	48976	$2^4 \cdot 3061$	9
24	45946	$2 \cdot 22973$	3
25	22976	$2^6 \cdot 359$	13
26	22744	$2^3 \cdot 2843$	7
27	19916	$2^2 \cdot 13 \cdot 383$	11
28	17716	$2^2 \cdot 43 \cdot 103$	11
29	14316	$2^2 \cdot 3 \cdot 1193$	11

BIBLIOGRAPHY

Barlow, P.   *Theory of Numbers*.   London: J. Johnson & Co., 1811.

Dickson, L. E.   *History of the Theory of Numbers*.   3 vols.   New York: Chelsea Publishing Co., 1950.

Ozanam, J.   *Recreations in Science and Natural Philosophy*.   London: T. Tegg, 1884.

CHAPTER V

INVENTION OF THE MASTER

HERE IS an effective trick that will bear considerable repetition. Ask anyone to select a number less than 1000, and to divide it respectively by 7, 11, and 13, giving you the three remainders. You will then be able to tell him what number he originally selected. This is done by multiplying the three remainders respectively by the "magic numbers" 715, 364, and 924, adding the resulting products, and subtracting from the sum the greatest multiple of 1001 that will still leave a positive remainder. This remainder is the selected number. Thus if the remainders were 5, 6, and 3 you would write

$$715 \cdot 5 = 3575$$
$$364 \cdot 6 = 2184$$
$$924 \cdot 3 = \underline{2772}$$
$$8531$$

Multiples of 1001 start and end with the same digits, such as 2002, 16016, 35035, etc. In this case subtract 8008, the largest multiple of 1001 contained in 8531, leaving 523, which was the number originally selected.

Before explaining, it will be desirable to learn something about congruences, the elegant invention of that "Prince of Mathematicians," Karl Friedrich Gauss. In number theory we often wish to test whether a number, n, is exactly divisible by another, m. The quotient isn't so important; we are interested in the remainder and the condition under which it is zero. Gauss invented a compact and highly efficient symbolism for this. By disregarding irrelevancies, we obtain entirely new and illuminating conceptions of integers and divisibility. In ordinary arithmetic if we want to find the remainder when 31 is divided by 13, we write

$$\frac{31}{13} = 2 + \frac{5}{13}.$$

Compare this with $31 \equiv 5 \bmod 13$, which is read, "Thirty-one is congruent to 5, modulo 13," and means, 31 leaves the remainder 5 when divided by the divisor (or modulus) 13. By thus arranging the congruence so that it resembles an equation, we can perform many operations permissible on the latter. For example, adding 3 to both sides, we obtain

$31 \equiv 5 \mod 13$

$$34 \equiv 8 \mod 13.$$

Again, by subtracting 5 from both sides,

$$26 \equiv 0 \mod 13.$$

Also, by multiplying both sides by 2,

$$62 \equiv 10 \mod 13.$$

Had we multiplied by 4 instead we would have had

$$124 \equiv 20 \mod 13.$$

But since

$$20 \equiv 7 \mod 13,$$

we may write

$$124 \equiv 7 \mod 13.$$

Further, squaring the original congruence,

$$31^2 \equiv 5^2 \equiv 12 \mod 13,$$

and since 12 lacks one unit for divisibility by 13, we can write

$$31^2 \equiv 5^2 \equiv 12 \equiv -1,$$

a negative remainder.

Not all congruence laws are the same as those for equations, and discretion must be used when dividing both sides of a congruence by the same number. For instance, $16 \equiv 1 \mod 5$, but we do not usually have 8 congruent to 1/2 modulo 5. (Quite recently, however, the congruence notation has been extended to include this interpretation.) Again, although $40 \equiv 10 \mod 15$, we cannot have $4 \equiv 1 \mod 15$. We can divide both members of a congruence by an integer only if it is prime to the modulus; otherwise the modulus must be divided by the common factor. Thus $4 \equiv 1 \mod 3$.

This method really begins to show its power with exponents (no pun intended).

To verify that $97^{104} - 1$ is divisible by 105, that is,

$$97^{104} \equiv 1 \bmod 105 = 3 \cdot 5 \cdot 7,$$

we proceed as follows:

$$97 \equiv 1 \bmod 3 \quad \text{therefore} \quad 97^{104} \equiv 1^{104} \equiv 1 \bmod 3.$$

Again

$$97 \equiv 2 \bmod 5$$
$$97^2 \equiv 2^2 \equiv 4 \equiv -1 \bmod 5.$$

Negative remainders are also permissible.

$$97^4 \equiv (-1)^2 \equiv 1 \bmod 5,$$

therefore

$$(97^4)^{26} \equiv 97^{104} \equiv 1^{26} \equiv 1 \bmod 5.$$

Finally

$$97 \equiv -1 \bmod 7$$
$$97^{104} \equiv (-1)^{104} \equiv 1 \bmod 7.$$

Combining the three moduli, since the divisibility by one of them will not affect the divisibility by the others because they have no factor in common, we have:

$$97^{104} \equiv 1 \bmod 3 \cdot 5 \cdot 7 = 105,$$

which, when you get used to it, is quite easy.

Now verify that

$$2^{12} \equiv 1 \bmod 13.$$

It had once been incorrectly conjectured that numbers of the form $2^{2^x} + 1$ are primes. Actually 5 is the least value of x for which the resulting number is composite and divisible by 641. By congruences the verification for this value is readily made. We must show that

$$2^{32} + 1 \equiv 0 \bmod 641,$$

or

$$2^{32} \equiv -1 \bmod 641.$$

Start with a power of 2 as near to the value of the modulus as possible, or, if this is not very close, to a multiple of the modulus. In this case, $3 \times 641 = 1923$ is quite close to the eleventh power 2048 of 2, and moreover the difference, 125, is itself a power, making for additional convenience. Thus

$$2^{11} \equiv 125 \equiv 5^3 \bmod 641.$$

Then
$$2^{22} \equiv 5^6 = 5^4 \cdot 5^2 \equiv -2^4 \cdot 5^2.$$

Since it is permissible to divide both sides of a congruence by the same number provided the divisor is prime to the modulus, we can divide by 2:
$$2^{21} \equiv -2^3 \cdot 5^2,$$

and multiplying this result by $2^{11} \equiv 5^3$, we have
$$2^{32} \equiv -2^3 \cdot 5^5 = -2^3 \cdot 5 \cdot 5^4 \equiv -40(-16) = 640 \equiv -1.$$

Perhaps a more obvious and direct way of solving this problem is to make use of the fact that every number is the sum of powers of 2 (see Chapter IX). The exponent 32 is already a power of 2 so we proceed as follows, utilizing for convenience a table of squares, such as Barlow's:

$$
\begin{aligned}
2 &\equiv 2 \\
2^2 &\equiv 4 \\
2^4 &\equiv 16 \qquad\qquad \text{all modulo 641} \\
2^8 &\equiv 256 \\
2^{16} &\equiv 256^2 \equiv 65536 \equiv 154 \\
2^{32} &\equiv 154^2 \equiv 23716 \equiv 640 \equiv -1
\end{aligned}
$$

* * *

Now for the magic numbers: 715; 364; and 924. Let x be the selected unknown number, and a, b, c the respective remainders when divided by 7, 11, and 13. Then

$$
\begin{aligned}
x &\equiv a \quad \mod 7 &&\text{and} \quad 715x \equiv 715a \quad \mod 7 \\
x &\equiv b \quad \mod 11 &&\text{and} \quad 364x \equiv 364b \quad \mod 11 \\
x &\equiv c \quad \mod 13 &&\text{and} \quad 924x \equiv 924c \quad \mod 13.
\end{aligned}
$$

Transposing:

$$
\begin{aligned}
715(x-a) &\equiv 0 \quad \mod 7 &&(1) \\
364(x-b) &\equiv 0 \quad \mod 11 &&(2) \\
924(x-c) &\equiv 0 \quad \mod 13 &&(3)
\end{aligned}
$$

But congruence (1) is divisible by 11 and by 13 and therefore by 11, 13, and 7, or 1001; congruence (2) is divisible by 7 and by 13 and therefore by 7, 13, and 11, or 1001; and finally, congruence (3) is

divisible by 7 and by 11 and therefore by 7, 11, and 13, or 1001.
Adding, we have to the new modulus 1001:

$$2003x - (715a + 364b + 924c) \equiv 0 \quad \text{mod } 1001$$

or

$$x \equiv 715a + 364b + 924c \quad \text{mod } 1001.$$

We have thus found the value of x in terms of the three magic numbers
and the three remainders a, b, and c, and since it must not exceed
1000 we drop multiples of 1001 from the right-hand side of the
congruence so that a solution below this limit is obtained.

A slightly different method of performing this trick is to remember
the numbers 5, 4, -1 and the numbers $143 = 11 \cdot 13$; $91 = 7 \cdot 13$;
and $77 = 7 \cdot 11$. For the given remainders a, b, c, find the least
residues (remainders) of $5a$ mod 7; $4b$ mod 11; and $-c$ mod 13.
Multiply 143, 91, and 77 respectively by these residues, add the
products, and subtract multiples of 1001. Thus for the remainders
5, 6, 3, we have

$$5 \cdot 5 \equiv 4 \quad \text{mod } 7$$
$$4 \cdot 6 \equiv 2 \quad \text{mod } 11$$
$$(-1) \cdot 3 \equiv -3 \quad \text{mod } 13.$$

Multiplying 143, 91, and 77 by the respective residues 4, 2, -3, and
adding, we have $572 + 182 - 231 = 523$. Some may prefer this
method because of the smaller numbers involved; it may be easier to
keep in mind the two sets 5, 4, -1 and 143, 91, and 77 than the
larger numbers, 715, 364, and 924. The reader may now wish to
test his grasp of the congruence method by actually deriving the
magic numbers, instead of assuming them as above.†

If a congruence holds for several moduli, it holds for a modulus
equal to the lowest common multiple of these moduli. Thus if

$$x \equiv a \quad \text{mod } 2$$
$$x \equiv a \quad \text{mod } 6$$
$$x \equiv a \quad \text{mod } 8,$$

then

$$x \equiv a \quad \text{mod } 24.$$

† Problems indicated by a dagger are solved in Chapter XXVI.

By means of this property, problems like the following are easily solved:

The men in a certain army could not be divided into groups of 2, 3, 4, 5, 6, 7, 8, 9, 10, 11, or 12, as in each case one man was left over. However, it was possible to arrange them exactly into groups of 13. What was the least number of men in the army?

Here we have:

$$x \equiv 1 \quad \text{mod } 2, 3, 4, 5, 6, 7, 8, 9, 10, 11, 12$$

and

$$x \equiv 0 \quad \text{mod } 13.$$

The L.C.M. of 2, 3, 4, 5, 6, 7, 8, 9, 10, 11, and 12 is 27720, and therefore

$$x \equiv 1 \quad \text{mod } 27720,$$

so that for the first condition x may equal 1 or 1 added to any multiple of 27720, that is,

$$x = 27720m + 1.$$

But $27720 \equiv 4 \text{ mod } 13$. Therefore $27720m + 1 \equiv 4m + 1 \text{ mod } 13$ and if we select $m = 3$, then $4m + 1 \equiv 0 \text{ mod } 13$, as required. Hence the *least* number to fulfill the conditions is $27720 \cdot 3 + 1 = 83161$. However, m may be any number of the form $13n + 3$, and therefore x may be any number of the form $27720(13n + 3) + 1 = 360360n + 83161$. When $n = 0$ we get 83161 as before; when $n = 1$, we obtain the second solution $x = 443521$, etc., and it may readily be confirmed that all the integers from 1 to 12 leave a remainder of 1 when divided into either of these numbers, whereas 13 divides them exactly.

*   *   *

A similar example is the one about a pile of bricks in which one brick was left over when the pile was divided by 2; 2 over when divided by 3; 3 over when divided by 4, etc.; but the pile was exactly divisible by 13. What was the least number of bricks in the pile? This problem appears more difficult than the previous one if we start with:

$$x \equiv 1 \quad \text{mod } 2,$$
$$x \equiv 2 \quad \text{mod } 3,$$
$$x \equiv 3 \quad \text{mod } 4, \text{ etc.}$$

But we may also write:

$$x \equiv -1 \quad \mod 2$$
$$x \equiv -1 \quad \mod 3$$
$$x \equiv -1 \quad \mod 4, \text{ etc.,}$$

so that

$$x \equiv -1 \quad \mod 27720$$

and therefore

$$x = 27720m - 1.$$

Then

$$27720m - 1 \equiv 4m - 1 \equiv 0 \quad \mod 13.$$

But in this case we find by trial that $m \equiv 10$, that is, 39 is exactly divisible by 13. Hence $m = 13n + 10$ and

$$x = 27720(13n + 10) - 1 = 360360n + 277199.$$

For the least number of bricks in the pile, $n = 0$ and $x = 277199$. The next possible value, for $n = 1$, is 637559.

* * *

Many readers may have heard that famous problem about the five castaways and the monkey on the desert island. The men gathered a pile of coconuts one evening to be divided the next day. During the night one man arose and divided the pile into five equal parts, throwing the monkey one coconut which happened to be left over. Lacking faith in his comrades, he hid his share in a cave and returned to sleep. Each of the remaining four were similarly distrustful and repeated the process in turn, always hiding one-fifth of the pile which he found on awakening and each time throwing a leftover coconut to the monkey. The next day they divided the nuts into five exactly equal piles but this time none remained for the monkey. What was the minimum number of nuts in the original pile?

In this form, the problem is capable of solution by almost standard algebraic methods. However, the general case of "n" men and "r" monkeys is not so simple, but the solution is facilitated by enlisting the aid of congruences. The solution is given in the answers for Chapter XXV.

* * *

Any pair of relatively prime integers has the remarkable property that multiples of each can always be found such that their difference is unity. Stated another way, there always exists some multiple of an integer N, which leaves a remainder of unity when divided by another integer prime to it, and the multiplier of N is always a smaller number than the divisor of the product. Thus for 15 and 28, there exist two integers x and y, such that $15x - 28y = 1$. If this were written in congruence form we might have either:

$$15x \equiv 1 \quad \bmod 28$$

or

$$28y \equiv -1 \quad \bmod 15.$$

There are direct methods for solving such congruences, or in fact any equation like $ax + by = c$ where a, b, and c are given numbers. Often there is more than one set of solutions. Here are a few such equations to solve:

1. $71x + 37y = 3000.$†
2. $599x + 107y = 100000.$
3. Find the smallest positive integer b for which the equation $1001x + 770y = 1000000 + b$ is possible and show that it has then 100 solutions in positive integers.

See Chapter XXII for the method of solving equations of this type.

Congruences of higher degree form one of the most intriguing branches of number theory, quadratic congruences in particular leading to extremely elegant theorems. We shall devote more time to these in the chapter on quadratic residues.

BIBLIOGRAPHY

Ball, W. W. R. *Mathematical Recreations and Essays*. New York: Macmillan Co., 1939.

Dickson, L. E. *Introduction to the Theory of Numbers*. New York: Dover Publications, Inc., 1957.

Reid, L. W. *Elements of the Theory of Algebraic Numbers*. Baltimore: Johns Hopkins Press, 1946.

Uspensky, J. V., and Heaslet, M. A. *Elementary Number Theory*. New York: McGraw-Hill Book Co., 1939.

Vinogradov, I. M. *Elements of Number Theory*. New York: Dover Publications, Inc., 1954.

CHAPTER VI

OPEN SESAME

It is difficult if not impossible to state why some theorems in arithmetic are considered "important" while others, equally difficult to prove, are dubbed trivial. One criterion, although not necessarily conclusive, is that the theorem shall be of use in other fields of mathematics. Another is that it shall suggest researches in arithmetic or in mathematics generally, and a third that it shall be in some respects universal. Fermat's theorem...satisfies all of these somewhat arbitrary demands...it is universal in the sense that it states a property of all prime numbers—such general statements are extremely difficult to find and very few are known.

—E. T. Bell in *Men of Mathematics.*

In our everyday affairs we frequently apply the process of logic called inductive reasoning. From a number of observed facts we generalize and make a rule. Flowers have been blooming for many springs and it is safe to conclude that whenever there is spring, flowers will bloom. In mathematics, inductive reasoning isn't good enough. You find that under certain conditions something is true once, twice, even a hundred times. If you say incautiously, "It must always be true," it may turn out that the next time your statement will be contradicted. Mathematics demands more than the induction due to mere observation. *Mathematical* induction is the name of the method fulfilling the exacting requirements.

The theory of numbers is full of readily observed facts tempting to be generalized by common inductive reasoning, and great care must be exercised to steer clear of the pitfalls. Suppose you multiplied 2 by itself 7 times and subtracted 2, namely, $2^7 - 2 = 126$. This is divisible by the exponent 7. Again, $2^5 - 2$ is divisible by 5; $2^{11} - 2$ is divisible by 11. Then you try $2^4 - 2$, which is not divisible by 4; $2^6 - 2$, which is not divisible by 6; $2^8 - 2$, indivisible by 8.

You might stop here and, surveying your results, conclude: Whenever the exponent is odd, the expression seems to be exactly divisible; when the exponent is even, it isn't. Then, just to make sure, and having a little spare time on your hands, you try $2^9 - 2 = 510$

and find to your surprise that it is not divisible by 9, nor is $2^{15} - 2 = 32766$ divisible by 15. Apparently it is necessary to revise your hastily drawn conclusion. And then an idea dawns; the rule holds for 2, 3, 5, 7, 11 but not for 4, 6, 8, 9, 10, 12, 14, 15. The evidence seems to be clear.

Exact divisibility occurs when the exponent is a prime but not when it is a composite number. Your first assumption about odd and even is evidently untenable. If you were curious enough you might even try the exponents from 16 to, perhaps, 25 which include the odd composite numbers 21 and 25 and the primes 17, 19, 23. Sure enough $2^{17} - 2$, $2^{19} - 2$, $2^{23} - 2$ are respectively divisible by 17, 19, and 23, whereas none of the even-exponent combinations, nor $2^{21} - 2$ and $2^{25} - 2$, are divisible by their exponents.

Your conclusion would nevertheless require considerable amending. The Chinese as long ago as 500 B.C. thought that $2^p - 2$ is always divisible by p when p is a prime, but never so when p is composite. While it is true that $2^p - 2$ is always divisible by p if p is a prime, it is not true that $2^p - 2$ is never divisible by p if p is composite. The least *composite* exponent for which the rule holds is $341 = 31 \cdot 11$, and $2^{341} - 2$ is exactly divisible by 341. This was discovered as recently as the year 1819. You might easily spend several hours verifying this division by ordinary means, but it can easily be done in just a few steps by congruences.

Pierre de Fermat, the "Prince of Amateurs," rediscovered the relationship which had apparently sunk into oblivion since the days of Confucius and generalized the previous result to show that $x^p - x$ is always divisible by p if p is a prime. He was able to *prove* this relation, a simple yet elusive matter and something the Chinese had not succeeded in doing. In the general result, x may of course be any number, not just 2. Suppose we factor $x^p - x$; then $x(x^{p-1} - 1)$ must, by the theorem, be divisible by p. Now suppose x is not a multiple of p; then p cannot divide x, so that if p divides the entire expression it must divide $x^{p-1} - 1$. Hence we have Fermat's simple theorem in its usual form:

"If x is any integer not divisible by the prime p, then $x^{p-1} - 1$ is exactly divisible by p." In congruence notation (see Chapter V), $x^{p-1} \equiv 1 \bmod p$.

As it stands thus—a bald statement of an algebraic relationship—it does not appear very impressive. Yet it leads to so many intriguing avenues of thought and subtle mathematical logic that it is considered a cornerstone of the number-theory edifice. "Breathes there a man with soul so dead" who does not thrill when first becoming acquainted with this beautiful theorem and its proof? A number like

$$2^{134217826} - 1$$

has over 40 million digits and would require more than 40 volumes of 500 pages each at 2000 digits per page; yet by Fermat's theorem we know positively and immediately that it is divisible by the prime number 134217827. (We must of course be told that 134217827 is a prime.)

There are many proofs of this theorem; a proof by congruences is both short and elegant. Let us arbitrarily select the prime 13 for our proof although it would be almost as simple if we had selected *any* unspecified prime, p. Consider the series of integers 1, 2, 3,...12 from 1 to 12, each less than 13. If we multiply each of these by some arbitrary integer prime to 13, say 3, we get the series 3, 6, 9, 12, 15, 18,...36. To the modulus 13 this series is congruent to 3, 6, 9, 12, 2, 5, 8, 11, 1, 4, 7, 10 respectively. There are no repetitions. But this is the original series 1, 2, 3, 4,...12 except in a different order.

Now let us multiply together all the terms of the first series. The product is $1 \cdot 2 \cdot 3 \ldots 12$, written for convenience as 12! and called—it will be remembered from algebra—"factorial 12." If we similarly multiply together the terms 3, 6, 9,...36, we can first factor out a 3 from each and write the product as $3^{12} \cdot 12!$ These two products are congruent to each other, with respect to the modulus 13 since the terms of the 3, 6, 9,...36 series are congruent to those of the 1, 2, 3,...12 series although not respectively. Thus $3^{12} \cdot 12! \equiv 12!$ mod 13, and, dividing by 12!, $3^{12} \equiv 1$ mod 13. If we had used p instead of 13 and x instead of 3, we would have had $x^{p-1} \equiv 1$ mod p, the simple Fermat theorem. (A few minor details to make the proof "rigid" have been omitted for simplicity.)

If Fermat's theorem were true for primes only, one would have a practical criterion for recognizing a prime number, since if a number, p, divided $x^{p-1} - 1$ exactly, the divisor would be a prime, and, if not, it would be composite. Unfortunately we have no such practical criterion. Fermat's theorem is *always* true of prime numbers and *sometimes* true of composite numbers. The converse of the theorem is often misunderstood on this account.

Strangely enough, an infinite number of composite numbers can be found for which the relationship holds true. Besides the example

TABLE 15

Least Composite Divisor m, Greater Than x, For Which $x^{m-1} - 1$ Is Divisible by m

Base = x	Divisor = m	Base = x	Divisor = m
2	$341 = 11 \cdot 31$	52	$85 = 5 \cdot 17$
3	$91 = 7 \cdot 13$	53	$65 = 5 \cdot 13$
4	$15 = 3 \cdot 5$	54	$55 = 5 \cdot 11$
5	$124 = 2^2 \cdot 31$	55	$63 = 3^2 \cdot 7$
6	$35 = 5 \cdot 7$	56	$57 = 3 \cdot 19$
7	$25 = 5^2$	57	$65 = 5 \cdot 13$
8	$9 = 3^2$	58	$95 = 5 \cdot 19$
9	$28 = 2^2 \cdot 7$	59	$87 = 3 \cdot 29$
10	$33 = 3 \cdot 11$	60	$341 = 11 \cdot 31$
11	$15 = 3 \cdot 5$	61	$91 = 7 \cdot 13$
12	$65 = 5 \cdot 13$	62	$63 = 3^2 \cdot 7$
13	$21 = 3 \cdot 7$	63	$341 = 11 \cdot 31$
14	$15 = 3 \cdot 5$	64	$65 = 5 \cdot 13$
15	$341 = 11 \cdot 31$	65	$133 = 7 \cdot 19$
16	$51 = 3 \cdot 17$	66	$91 = 7 \cdot 13$
17	$45 = 3^2 \cdot 5$	67	$85 = 5 \cdot 17$
18	$25 = 5^2$	68	$69 = 3 \cdot 23$
19	$45 = 3^2 \cdot 5$	69	$85 = 5 \cdot 17$
20	$21 = 3 \cdot 7$	70	$169 = 13^2$
21	$55 = 5 \cdot 11$	71	$105 = 3 \cdot 5 \cdot 7$
22	$69 = 3 \cdot 23$	72	$85 = 5 \cdot 17$
23	$33 = 3 \cdot 11$	73	$111 = 3 \cdot 37$
24	$25 = 5^2$	74	$75 = 3 \cdot 5^2$
25	$28 = 2^2 \cdot 7$	75	$91 = 7 \cdot 13$
26	$27 = 3^3$	76	$77 = 7 \cdot 11$
27	$65 = 5 \cdot 13$	77	$95 = 5 \cdot 19$
28	$87 = 3 \cdot 29$	78	$341 = 11 \cdot 31$
29	$35 = 5 \cdot 7$	79	$91 = 7 \cdot 13$
30	$49 = 7^2$	80	$81 = 3^4$
31	$49 = 7^2$	81	$85 = 5 \cdot 17$
32	$33 = 3 \cdot 11$	82	$91 = 7 \cdot 13$
33	$85 = 5 \cdot 17$	83	$105 = 3 \cdot 5 \cdot 7$
34	$35 = 5 \cdot 7$	84	$85 = 5 \cdot 17$
35	$51 = 3 \cdot 17$	85	$129 = 3 \cdot 43$
36	$91 = 7 \cdot 13$	86	$87 = 3 \cdot 29$
37	$45 = 3^2 \cdot 5$	87	$91 = 7 \cdot 13$
38	$39 = 3 \cdot 13$	88	$91 = 7 \cdot 13$
39	$95 = 5 \cdot 19$	89	$99 = 3^2 \cdot 11$
40	$91 = 7 \cdot 13$	90	$91 = 7 \cdot 13$
41	$105 = 3 \cdot 5 \cdot 7$	91	$115 = 5 \cdot 23$
42	$205 = 5 \cdot 41$	92	$93 = 3 \cdot 31$
43	$77 = 7 \cdot 11$	93	$301 = 7 \cdot 43$
44	$45 = 3^2 \cdot 5$	94	$95 = 5 \cdot 19$
45	$76 = 2^2 \cdot 19$	95	$141 = 3 \cdot 47$
46	$133 = 7 \cdot 19$	96	$133 = 7 \cdot 19$
47	$65 = 5 \cdot 13$	97	$105 = 3 \cdot 5 \cdot 7$
48	$49 = 7^2$	98	$99 = 3^2 \cdot 11$
49	$66 = 2 \cdot 3 \cdot 11$	99	$145 = 5 \cdot 29$
50	$51 = 3 \cdot 17$	100	$259 = 7 \cdot 37$
51	$65 = 5 \cdot 13$		

previously given, we have $3^{90} - 1$, divisible by 91; $4^{14} - 1$, divisible by 15, etc. The least composite divisors of this kind, greater than the base, for all bases from 2 to 100 are given in Table 15.

Note that the smallest base 2 requires as high a divisor as 341, which is not exceeded by the divisor of any other base up to 100. It is scarcely to be wondered at, therefore, that the Chinese did not find the composite exception to their inductively discovered law. Chapter XIII explains how such composite divisors can be found.

Two interesting problems in composite divisors are:

1. The determination of such divisors for which Fermat's theorem holds when the base x is some given number.

2. The determination of such divisors for which Fermat's theorem holds for *every* base x prime to the composite divisor.

Table 15 furnishes examples of a single solution of the first problem for every base x up to 100. For any particular base, there are, of course, many solutions; a few for the bases 2 and 3 are given in Tables 16 and 17 respectively.

TABLE 16

COMPOSITE DIVISORS m, FOR WHICH $2^{m-1} - 1$ IS DIVISIBLE BY m

$$m =$$

$11 \cdot 31$
$23 \cdot 89$
$3 \cdot 5 \cdot 43$
$3 \cdot 5 \cdot 29 \cdot 43$
$3 \cdot 5 \cdot 29 \cdot 43 \cdot 113$
$3 \cdot 11 \cdot 29 \cdot 31 \cdot 43 \cdot 281$
$7 \cdot 11 \cdot 13 \cdot 31 \cdot 41 \cdot 61 \cdot 331$
$7 \cdot 11 \cdot 13 \cdot 31 \cdot 41 \cdot 61 \cdot 151 \cdot 1321$
$3 \cdot 11 \cdot 29 \cdot 31 \cdot 41 \cdot 43 \cdot 71 \cdot 113 \cdot 127 \cdot 281$
$5 \cdot 7 \cdot 17 \cdot 19 \cdot 37 \cdot 73 \cdot 97 \cdot 109 \cdot 241 \cdot 433 \cdot 673 \cdot 38737$

also any number $m = 2^p - 1$ where p is a prime that makes $2^p - 1$ composite.

TABLE 17

COMPOSITE DIVISORS m, FOR WHICH $3^{m-1} - 1$ IS DIVISIBLE BY m

$$m =$$
$23 \cdot 3851$
$17 \cdot 193$
$19 \cdot 37$
$31 \cdot 271$

*   *   *

The second problem is more difficult. For instance, $2^{340}-1$ is divisible by 341, but $3^{340}-1$ is not so divisible. The reader can again test his newly acquired knowledge of congruences to verify this fact. Similarly, although $3^{90}-1$ is divisible by 91, $2^{90}-1$ is not so divisible. The problem here is to find a composite number, n, such that $x^{n-1}-1$ is divisible by n for *all* numbers which are prime to x. The solution is not too easy. At least three prime factors must compose the divisor. The least solution is $x^{560}-1$ which is divisible by the composite number $561 = 3 \cdot 11 \cdot 17$. Here x can take on *any* values except 3, 11, 17, or their multiples. Thus $2^{560}-1$ is divisible by 561, but so are $4^{560}-1$, $5^{560}-1$, $7^{560}-1$, etc., a really remarkable relation. Such composite numbers are few and far between.

If the composite modulus, n, consists of just three prime factors and if one of them, say p, is assigned a value, then there are only a *finite* number of values for the other two primes; they cannot be increased indefinitely. Assigning such values to p from 3 to 43, there are only 52 composite moduli possible. Oddly enough, $p = 11$ yields no solution. These 52 values are listed in Table 18.

TABLE 18

COMPOSITE MODULI, n, FOR WHICH $a^{n-1} \equiv 1$ MOD n
FOR ALL BASES PRIME TO THE MODULUS

$3 \cdot 11 \cdot 17$	$19 \cdot 43 \cdot 409$	$41 \cdot 61 \cdot 101$
$5 \cdot 13 \cdot 17$	$19 \cdot 199 \cdot 271$	$41 \cdot 73 \cdot 137$
$5 \cdot 17 \cdot 29$	$23 \cdot 199 \cdot 353$	$41 \cdot 101 \cdot 461$
$5 \cdot 29 \cdot 73$	$29 \cdot 113 \cdot 1093$	$41 \cdot 241 \cdot 521$
$7 \cdot 13 \cdot 19$	$29 \cdot 197 \cdot 953$	$41 \cdot 241 \cdot 761$
$7 \cdot 13 \cdot 31$	$31 \cdot 61 \cdot 211$	$41 \cdot 881 \cdot 12041$
$7 \cdot 19 \cdot 67$	$31 \cdot 61 \cdot 271$	$41 \cdot 1721 \cdot 35281$
$7 \cdot 23 \cdot 41$	$31 \cdot 61 \cdot 631$	$43 \cdot 127 \cdot 211$
$7 \cdot 31 \cdot 73$	$31 \cdot 151 \cdot 1171$	$43 \cdot 127 \cdot 1093$
$7 \cdot 73 \cdot 103$	$31 \cdot 181 \cdot 331$	$43 \cdot 127 \cdot 2731$
11 None	$31 \cdot 271 \cdot 601$	$43 \cdot 211 \cdot 337$
$13 \cdot 37 \cdot 61$	$31 \cdot 991 \cdot 15361$	$43 \cdot 211 \cdot 757$
$13 \cdot 37 \cdot 97$	$37 \cdot 73 \cdot 109$	$43 \cdot 271 \cdot 5827$
$13 \cdot 37 \cdot 241$	$37 \cdot 73 \cdot 181$	$43 \cdot 433 \cdot 643$
$13 \cdot 61 \cdot 397$	$37 \cdot 73 \cdot 541$	$43 \cdot 547 \cdot 673$
$13 \cdot 97 \cdot 421$	$37 \cdot 109 \cdot 2017$	$43 \cdot 631 \cdot 1597$
$17 \cdot 41 \cdot 233$	$37 \cdot 613 \cdot 1621$	$43 \cdot 631 \cdot 13567$
$17 \cdot 353 \cdot 1201$		$43 \cdot 3361 \cdot 3907$

To top this off, we have a 4-prime value of

$$n = 13 \cdot 37 \cdot 73 \cdot 457 = 16046641$$

so that $a^{16046640} \equiv 1 \bmod 16046641$.

*　　*　　*

In logic, there is a term called an "implication": "If p, then q." The "converse" of this implication is, "If q, then p." Converses are *sometimes* but not necessarily *always* true. Then there is the "inverse" which states, "If not p, then not q." This again may only sometimes be true. Finally there is the "contrapositive": "If not q, then not p." This is *always* true. Applying this to Fermat's theorem, we let $p =$ "a prime" and $q =$ "$x^{p-1} \equiv 1 \bmod p$." The converse, "If $x^{p-1} \equiv 1 \bmod p$, then p is a prime," is only sometimes true because the relation also holds for some composite numbers, as Table 18 shows. The inverse, "If p is not a prime, then $x^{p-1} \not\equiv 1 \bmod p$" also is not always true, as Table 18 shows. But the contrapositive, "If x^{p-1} is not congruent to 1 mod p, then p is not a prime [is composite]," is *always* true.

The true converse of Fermat's theorem states that if an integer x is prime to m and $x^{m-1} \equiv 1 \bmod m$, but if there is no integer, e, smaller than $m-1$ for which $x^e \equiv 1 \bmod m$, then m is a prime. Thus $3^{16} \equiv 1 \bmod 17$, and no exponent smaller than 16 would make the congruence possible; hence 17 is a prime. This does not mean that if there *is* such an integer, e, then m is *not* a prime; for instance both $2^6 \equiv 1$ and $2^3 \equiv 1 \bmod 7$, yet 7 is a prime. Had the base 3 been selected, 6 would have been the smallest exponent.

At this point it will be desirable to define two new terms which will be met later. If $x^e \equiv 1 \bmod m$ and e is the *smallest* exponent for which this congruence is possible, then we say that "x belongs to the exponent e, modulo m." On the other hand, if this smallest exponent is $m-1$, then we say that "x is a primitive root of m." There is a more general definition of primitive roots but this one will serve our purpose here. In $2^3 \equiv 1 \bmod 7$, 2 belongs to the exponent 3, mod 7. In $3^6 \equiv 1 \bmod 7$, 3 is a primitive root of 7.

Fermat's "simple" theorem is just a corollary of a more general theorem applicable to both prime and composite moduli which states that if x and m have no common factor and m is any integer (prime or composite), then $x^{\phi(m)} - 1$ is exactly divisible by m. The expression

$\phi(m)$ does not mean ϕ times m. It means the number of integers less than m and prime to it. If m is a prime, every integer less than it is prime to it and, thus, $\phi(m) = m-1$. This results in Fermat's "simple" theorem. As an instance of the general case, the number of integers less than 15 and prime to it is 8; namely, the integers 1, 2, 4, 7, 8, 11, 13, 14. (The integer 1 is arbitrarily taken as prime to every other integer.) Thus $\phi(15) = 8$, and taking x as any number prime to 15, $x^8 - 1$ is divisible by 15. For example, $2^8 - 1 = 255$ is so divisible, also $7^8 - 1 = 5764800$, etc.

*   *   *

Sometimes $x^{p-1} - 1$ is divisible by p several times. For instance, $3^{10} - 1$ is divisible by $11^2 = 121$ and so is $9^{10} - 1$. Many investigators thought there was no solution of this kind for the bases 2 and 10, and only in comparatively recent times has it been found that $2^{1092} - 1$ is divisible by 1093^2, $2^{3510} - 1$ is divisible by 3511^2, and $10^{486} - 1$ is divisible by 487^2. More remarkable still is $68^{112} - 1$, which is divisible by 113^3. Besides 1093 and 3511 there is no other prime below 200183 for which this relation holds for the base 2. As a matter of fact, some base can always be found for which the relation holds for the square of *any* given prime. Table 19 lists some of the values for which $x^{p-1} - 1$ is divisible by p^2.

TABLE 19

$x^{p-1} \equiv 1 \text{ MOD } p^2$

x	p	x	p	x	p	x	p
2	1093	18	37	31	79	62	127
2	3511	18	331	38	17	65	163
3	11	19	7	38	127	68	113
7	5	19	13	43	103	69	631
8	3	19	43	51	41	71	331
9	11	19	137	53	29	78	151
10	487	22	673	53	47	78	181
11	71	26	71	53	59	84	163
14	29	28	19	53	97	96	109
18	7	28	23	58	131	99	83

As an illustration of the fact that solutions can be found for the square of *any* prime, Table 20 lists values for all primes smaller than 200 not previously given in Table 19.

TABLE 20

$$x^{p-1} \equiv 1 \text{ MOD } p^2$$

p	x	p	x	p	x
31	115	101	181	173	259
53	338	107	164	179	532
61	264	139	328	191	176
67	143	149	313	193	276
73	306	157	226	197	143
89	184	167	253	199	174

A few larger values, including many for higher powers of primes than squares, are given in Table 21.

TABLE 21

$$x^{p-1} \equiv 1 \text{ MOD } p^a$$

a	x	p	a	x	p	a	x	p
2	100	487	3	18	7	4	239	13
2	175	487	3	19	7	5	1353	7
2	196	353	3	158	17	5	1354	7
2	252	997	3	338	19	6	1068	5
2	307	487	4	2819	19	6	390112	17
2	324	331	4	2820	19	7	82681	7
2	484	673				7	82682	7

* * *

The "Fermat quotient" $(2^{p-1}-1)/p$ is a square for only two primes. Can the reader find them?†

One often feels that Fermat's theorem may some day be the "Open Sesame" that will unlock boundless mathematical treasures now hidden from mortal gaze. One may even imagine the ghost of that secretive man chuckling at the twentieth-century mortals, who, despite their profound and esoteric discoveries since his demise, are still vainly seeking the lost trails once trodden by the master.

BIBLIOGRAPHY

Barlow, P. *Theory of Numbers.* London: J. Johnson & Co., 1811.
Beeger, N. G. W. H. "Quelques Remarques sur les Congruences $r^{p-1} \equiv 1 \pmod{p^2}$ et $(p-1)! \equiv -1 \pmod{p^2}$," *Messenger of Mathematics,* **43** (1913), 73.

† Problems indicated by a dagger are solved in Chapter XXVI.

Beeger, N. G. W. H.   "On Composite Numbers, n, for Which $a^{n-1} \equiv 1$ mod n for Every a Prime to n," *Scripta Mathematica*, **16** (1950), 133.

Bell, E. T.   *Men of Mathematics.*   New York: Simon and Schuster, 1937.

Bickmore, C. E.   "On the Numerical Factors of $a^n - 1$," *Messenger of Mathematics*, **25** (1895), 1.

Carmichael, R. D.   *Theory of Numbers and Diophantine Analysis.*   New York: Dover Publications, Inc., 1959.

————.   "On Composite Numbers P Which Satisfy the Fermat Congruence $a^{p-1} \equiv 1$ mod P," *American Mathematical Monthly*, **19** (1912), 22.

Cunningham, A.   *Haupt-Exponents, Residue Indices, Primitive Roots.*   London: F. Hodgson, 1922.

————.   "Problem: Find Numbers N, Such that $1/N^2$, etc., Have the Same Number of Figures in the Scale of Radix r," *Mathematical Gazette*, **4** (1907–1908), 209.

————.   "Period Lengths of Circulates," *Messenger of Mathematics*, **29** (1898–1899), 145.

————.   "Haupt-Exponents of 2," *Quarterly Journal of Pure and Applied Mathematics*, **37** (1905), 122.

————.   "On Haupt-Exponents of 2," *Quarterly Journal of Pure and Applied Mathematics*, **42** (1911), 241.

————.   "On Haupt-Exponents of 2," *Quarterly Journal of Pure and Applied Mathematics*, **44** (1912–1913), 41.

————.   "On Haupt-Exponents of 2," *Quarterly Journal of Pure and Applied Mathematics*, **44** (1912–1913), 237.

————.   "On Haupt-Exponents of 2," *Quarterly Journal of Pure and Applied Mathematics*, **45** (1914), 114.

Dickson, L. E.   *History of the Theory of Numbers.*   3 vols.   New York: Chelsea Publishing Co., 1950.

————.   *Introduction to the Theory of Numbers.*   New York: Dover Publications, Inc., 1957.

Escott, E. B.   "The Converse of Fermat's Theorem," *Messenger of Mathematics*, **36** (1906), 175.

Herzer, H.   "Über die Zahlen der Form $a^{p-1} - 1$, wenn p eine Primzahl," *Archiv der Mathematik und Physik*, **13–14**, Series 3 (1908–1909), 107.

Kraitchik, A. M.   *Recherches sur la Théorie des Nombres.*   Paris: Gauthier-Villars et Cie., 1924.

Lehmer, D. H.   "On the Converse of Fermat's Theorem," *American Mathematical Monthly*, **43** (1936), 347.

Pearson, E. H.   "On the Congruences $(p-1)! \equiv -1$ and $2^{p-1} \equiv 1$ mod p^2," *Mathematics of Computation*, **17** (1963), 194.

Reid, L. W.   *Elements of the Theory of Algebraic Numbers.*   Baltimore: Johns Hopkins Press, 1946.

Rosser, B.   "On the First Case of Fermat's Last Theorem," *Bulletin of the American Mathematical Society*, **45** (1939), 636.

Vandiver, H. S.   "Divisibility Problems in Number Theory," *Scripta Mathematica*, **21** (1955), 16.

Vinogradov, I. M.   *Elements of Number Theory.*   New York: Dover Publications, Inc., 1954.

CHAPTER VII

THE CUP OF TANTALUS

AN UNOBTRUSIVE English judge has found a place in the Valhalla of mathematicians by being credited with discovering one of the very few relationships in number theory whose converse is also true. He thought so little of it that it might have been forgotten completely or perhaps rediscovered only after many years, as was the case with Fermat's theorem, were it not for his friend Edward Waring, professor of mathematics at Cambridge, who published the discovery.

But neither Sir John Wilson, nor his friend Waring, nor Leibnitz, co-inventor of the calculus and Wilson's predecessor in discovering the relation, proved its truth. Leibnitz knew the theorem long before the close of the seventeenth century; Waring reported Wilson's find in his algebra of 1770; and Lagrange proved it in 1771, more than 100 years after Leibnitz reported it. It would be more just, therefore, to call this Leibnitz's instead of "Wilson's" theorem, but, as has so often happened, once the archives register the credit to one man, not even a papal encyclical can change it.

Here is what Wilson rediscovered: Take all the integers from unity up to some prime number, say 11, and write their product: $1 \cdot 2 \cdot 3 \cdot 4 \cdot 5 \cdot 6 \cdot 7 \cdot 8 \cdot 9 \cdot 10 \cdot 11$. Symbolically this is condensed into 11! and called "factorial eleven." It is easy to see that 11! is exactly divisible by every integer from 1 up to and including 11. Now omit the 11, and it is clear that the product of the remaining 10 integers, namely, 10! is *not* divisible by 11, since 11 is a prime, and a product not containing 11 or one of its multiples can obviously never be divided by 11. But if we add unity to the product—presto! the result *is* divisible by 11. Similarly $6! + 1 = (1 \cdot 2 \cdot 3 \cdot 4 \cdot 5 \cdot 6) + 1 = 721$ is divisible by 7. This holds in the above two examples because 7 and 11 are prime numbers and it is *always* true for prime numbers and *never* true for composite numbers.

Generalizing the above, $(p-1)! + 1$ is divisible by p if, and only if, p is a prime. This is Wilson's theorem and it vies with Fermat's theorem in importance.

49

Table 22 indicates how Wilson's theorem may be applied in testing for a prime.

TABLE 22

WILSON'S CRITERION FOR PRIME NUMBERS

n		$(n-1)!$	$(n-1)!+1$	Remainder of $[(n-1)!+1] \div n$	Character
2	1! =	1	2	0	Prime
3	2! =	2	3	0	Prime
4	3! =	6	7	3	Composite
5	4! =	24	25	0	Prime
6	5! =	120	121	1	Composite
7	6! =	720	721	0	Prime
8	7! =	5040	5041	1	Composite
9	8! =	40320	40321	1	Composite
10	9! =	362880	362881	1	Composite
11	10! =	3628800	3628801	0	Prime
12	11! =	39916800	39916801	1	Composite
13	12! =	479001600	479001601	0	Prime
14	13! =	6227020800	6227020801	1	Composite
15	14! =	87178291200	87178291201	1	Composite

Theoretically, the theorem is a criterion for determining whether or not a number is a prime. For, to determine whether 421783 is a prime, it would be necessary only to multiply together all the numbers from 1 to 421782, add 1 and see whether 421783 divides this number exactly, in which case 421783 is a prime; if not, it is composite. Obviously the labor of applying this test would be prohibitive for even such a comparatively small number as this; nor is there any easy way to determine by congruences or other means what the remainder is when $(n-1)!+1$ is divided by n. Practical considerations thus snatch from us an insight into the nature of numbers even though a conclusive test for primes is at hand.

There are several elegant proofs of this theorem. To avoid being too technical we shall prove the theorem for a specific prime as was done for Fermat's theorem in Chapter VI. Here we shall take $p = 17$. Consider the sixteen integers less than 17—1, 2, 3, ... 16—and again take any integer, say 3, less than 17 and form the products 3, 6, 9, 12, ... 48. To the modulus 17, these are respectively congruent to 3, 6, 9, 12, 15, 1, 4, 7, 10, 13, 16, 2, 5, 8, 11, 14. There is no repetition (this can easily be proved in the general case); hence one of the numbers must be unity, in this case the sixth number in the series. If some other multiplier than 3 had been used, say 5, another series would have resulted where again one of the numbers would have been unity, namely $5 \times 7 \equiv 1$ mod 17. Thus each number in the series $2 \cdot 3 \cdot 4 \ldots 15$ could be used as a multiplier, finally resulting in seven pairs, the product of each pair congruent to unity mod 17:

$$\begin{aligned}
2 \cdot \ 9 &\equiv 1 \\
3 \cdot \ 6 &\equiv 1 \\
4 \cdot 13 &\equiv 1 \\
5 \cdot \ 7 &\equiv 1 \quad \text{all to mod 17} \\
8 \cdot 15 &\equiv 1 \\
10 \cdot 12 &\equiv 1 \\
11 \cdot 14 &\equiv 1
\end{aligned}$$

Thus all the numbers in the series $1, 2, 3, \ldots 16$ were used up in pairs except the first and last, and for these

$$1 \cdot 16 \equiv -1 \quad \text{mod 17,}$$

the exception needed to prove our rule.

Combining these eight congruences as a product, we have

$$16! \equiv -1 \quad \text{mod 17,}$$

that is to say, $(17-1)!+1$ is exactly divisible by 17, as was to be proved. Only slight changes would be required to prove the general theorem that if p is a prime,

$$(p-1)!+1 \equiv 0 \quad \text{mod } p.$$

It is a truly remarkable property that the numbers in the set are exhausted in pairs in this manner, without duplication.

Like Fermat's, Wilson's theorem has generalizations. For instance, it is not necessary to limit the modulus to prime numbers if we amend the rule to state that the product of all integers less than a given number and prime to it leaves a remainder of 1 when divided by that number, with these exceptions: If the number is 4, a power of a prime, or twice such a power, then the remainder is -1. Suppose the number is 12, which is neither a power of a prime nor twice such a number. The product of all the integers less than and prime to 12 is $1 \cdot 5 \cdot 7 \cdot 11 = 385$, which leaves a remainder of 1 when divided by 12. For 4 we have $1 \cdot 3$, which leaves a remainder of -1. For a power of a prime such as $3^2 = 9$, the product, $1 \cdot 2 \cdot 4 \cdot 5 \cdot 7 \cdot 8 = 2240$, leaving a remainder of -1 when divided by 9.   Finally, we can try twice a power of a prime such as $18 = 2 \cdot 3^2$ and $1 \cdot 5 \cdot 7 \cdot 11 \cdot 13 \cdot 17 = 85085$, which is congruent to -1 mod 18.

*   *   *

On rare occasions $(p-1)! + 1$ is divisible not only by p but also by p^2.   The only primes less than 200183 for which this is true are 5, 13, and 563.   Here

$$(5-1)! + 1 = 25 = 5^2 \cdot 1;$$
$$(13-1)! + 1 = 479001601 = 13^2 \cdot 2834329;$$
$$(563-1)! + 1 = 563^2 \cdot N.$$

N is a very large number.

*   *   *

A corollary of Wilson's theorem having far-reaching results states that if, and only if, the prime p is of the form $4x+1$, then

$$(1 \cdot 2 \cdot 3 \ldots 2x)^2 + 1$$

is a multiple of p, that is, $[(2x)!]^2 \equiv -1 \mod p$.   For example, when $x = 3$, the prime 13 exactly divides

$$(1 \cdot 2 \cdot 3 \cdot 4 \cdot 5 \cdot 6)^2 + 1 = 518401.$$

The proof is easy enough to be given here.   We start with $4x$, which is obviously congruent to -1 mod $(4x+1) = p$; for instance, 12 leaves a remainder of -1 when divided by 13.   Then we have:

$$4x \equiv -1 \mod p$$
$$4x-1 \equiv -2 \mod p$$
$$4x-2 \equiv -3 \mod p.$$

We continue for $2x$ congruences to the term, $4x - (2x-1) = 2x+1$, of the consecutive numbers descending from $4x$:

$$2x+1 \equiv -2x \mod p.$$

Multiplying the congruences together, but this time using the algebraic expressions for the consecutive integers *ascending* from $(2x+1)$ instead of *descending* from $4x$, we have

$$(2x+1)(2x+2) \ldots 4x \equiv (-1)^{2x}(1 \cdot 2 \cdot 3 \cdot 4 \ldots 2x) \equiv +1(2x)!$$

Multiplying both sides of the congruence by $(2x)!$, we have

$$(4x)! \equiv [(2x)!]^2,$$

and since by the original Wilson theorem, $(4x)! + 1 \equiv 0 \bmod p$, we have, by substitution, $[(2x)!]^2 + 1 \equiv 0 \bmod p$.

This theorem is the first link in a chain of beautiful logic which proves that every prime of the form $4x+1$ is expressible as the sum of two integer squares, and in only one way. Succeeding links show that every divisor of a composite number that is the sum of two relatively prime squares is itself the sum of two squares; in particular, this is true of the prime divisors. But $[(2x)!]^2 + 1$ is the sum of two such squares; hence, every divisor of it must be the sum of two squares, and since the prime p, of the form $4x+1$, is such a divisor, it follows that every prime p of the form $4x+1$ is expressible as the sum of two squares, necessarily co-prime. (Two integers are said to be co-prime when they have no common factor except unity. "Relatively prime" and "co-prime" mean the same thing.)

* * *

A prime $p = 4x - 1$ cannot be the sum of two squares. For since p is odd, one of the two squares would have to be even and the other odd. But every even square $(2A)^2$ is of the form $4A^2$ and every odd square $(2B+1)^2$ is of the form $4B^2 + 4B + 1$ and their sum

$$4A^2 + 4B^2 + 4B + 1$$

is of the form $4x+1$ instead of $4x-1$.

BIBLIOGRAPHY

Barlow, P. *Theory of Numbers*. London: J. Johnson & Co., 1811.

Carmichael, R. D. *Theory of Numbers and Diophantine Analysis*. New York: Dover Publications, Inc., 1959.

DeMorgan, A. *Budget of Paradoxes*. 2 vols. Chicago: Open Court Publishing Co., 1915.

Dickson, L. E. *Introduction to the Theory of Numbers*. New York: Dover Publications, Inc., 1957.

Pearson, E. H. "On the Congruences $(p-1)! \equiv -1$ and $2^{p-1} \equiv 1 \bmod p^2$," *Mathematics of Computation*, **17** (1963), 194.

Reid, L. W. *Elements of the Theory of Algebraic Numbers*. Baltimore: Johns Hopkins Press, 1946.

Uhler, H. S. "Nine Exact Factorials Between 449! and 751!," *Scripta Mathematica*, **21** (1955), 138.

Vandiver, H. S. "Divisibility Problems in Number Theory," *Scripta Mathematica*, **21** (1955), 16.

Vinogradov, I. M. *Elements of Number Theory*. New York: Dover Publications, Inc., 1954.

CHAPTER VIII

DIGITS—AND THE MAGIC OF 9

THE CURIOUS properties of the digit 9 are frequently the bases of many tricks by magicians and "numerologists." This number has aroused the interest of scholars and mathematicians since ancient times, and it offers many striking instances of number magic readily comprehensible to the layman. The reader may recall the rule taught in elementary school, that if the sum of the digits of a number is divisible by 9, the number itself is so divisible. A rather startling example of this principle is the following equation which appeared in a popular magazine some years ago: $2A99561 = [3(523+A)]^2$. You are required to find the digit A within sixty seconds, an apparently impossible feat. However, a quick thinker would see that the right-hand expression had $3^2 = 9$ as a factor and that therefore the left-hand expression must also be divisible by 9. Its digits, exclusive of A, adding to only 32, it is immediately evident that A must be 4, so that the sum, 36, shall be divisible by 9.

The method of "casting out 9's," or the "Hindu check," as it is sometimes called, was frequently used by bookkeepers in checking addition, but it can be employed in any of the four elementary arithmetical processes. It depends on the fact that the sum of the digits of a number leaves the same remainder when divided by 9 as does the number itself. When the remainder of the digit-sum division is zero, the number also leaves that remainder, that is, it is exactly divisible by 9—the rule given previously. Bearing this in mind, the following two examples in addition and multiplication, illustrating the casting out of 9's, should be evident:

Addition	*Remainder When Sum of Digits Is Divided by* 9
4671	0
2198	2
7422	6
5611	4
1105	7
Total 21007	19 = sum of remainders

The digits in the total add to 10, and so do the digits in the total of the remainders, thus verifying the process. The check is not absolutely reliable, but it is improbable that errors in addition would be made in just the right amount to compensate one another and thus obtain the correct remainders. It is advisable when the sums of the digits in the totals exceed 10 to add *their* sum until finally a number less than 9 results. Thus, in 21007, the sum of the digits is 10, the sum of whose digits is 1. Similarly for 19. This shows that the number 21007 leaves a remainder of 1 when divided by 9.

	Multiplication	*Remainder When Sum of Digits Is Divided by 9*
Multiplicand	5327	8
Multiplier	649	1
	47943	
	21308	
	31962	
Product	3457223	8

And here again, the sum of the digits in the product equals 26, and $2+6 = 8$, giving the same digit as the product of the remainders 8 and 1.

The method of congruences makes the reason for these tests almost self-evident. Thus, in the addition problem, to the modulus 9,

$$4671 \equiv 0$$
$$2198 \equiv 2$$
$$7422 \equiv 6$$
$$5611 \equiv 4$$
$$1105 \equiv 7$$

$$21007 \equiv 19 \equiv 1$$

*   *   *

Such "tricks" as "write a number as large as you please, erase one figure, and I will immediately fill in a figure so that the entire number becomes divisible by 9," then become childishly easy. For example, if you write:

53219645*2789,

it is necessary only to add the digits, whose sum is 61; the sum of 6 and 1 in turn is 7, and the missing place must obviously be filled with a 2. The trick can be varied by offering to fill the vacant place with a digit so as to leave a given remainder when the number is divided by 9.

This "magic," resident in the digit 9, is of course due to the fact that we count in the denary system or scale of 10 and each digit in a number really stands for the product of that digit by a power of 10. For instance, 7312 signifies

$$(7 \cdot 10^3) + (3 \cdot 10^2) + (1 \cdot 10^1) + 2,$$

and 907450 is actually

$$(9 \cdot 10^5) + (0 \cdot 10^4) + (7 \cdot 10^3) + (4 \cdot 10^2) + (5 \cdot 10^1) + 0.$$

Each digit has a local value depending on its place in the order of the digits, besides its own absolute value. This understood, the reason for the remainder test is easily shown. For, to modulus 9:

$$10 \equiv 1,$$

therefore

$$10^y \equiv 1,$$

where y is any positive integer. Then

$$a \cdot 10^y \equiv a,$$

where a also is any positive integer and, for our requirements, any one of the 10 digits. But any number, N, expressed as above in powers of 10, becomes:

$$N = (a \cdot 10^y) + (b \cdot 10^{y-1}) + (c \cdot 10^{y-2}) + \ldots + (q \cdot 10^1) + r,$$

and we have, all to the modulus 9:

$$a \cdot 10^y \equiv a$$
$$b \cdot 10^{y-1} \equiv b$$
$$c \cdot 10^{y-2} \equiv c$$
$$\ldots$$
$$q \cdot 10^1 \equiv q$$
$$r \equiv r.$$

Adding the congruences, we find that

$$N \equiv a + b + \ldots + q + r \quad \text{mod } 9.$$

That is, a number leaves the same remainder when divided by 9 as does the sum of its digits.

* * *

Here is a test for the reader's concept of the place value of digits. Can you guess which sum is the greater?†

1	2	3	4	5	6	7	8	9								1
1	2	3	4	5	6	7	8								2	1
1	2	3	4	5	6	7								3	2	1
1	2	3	4	5	6								4	3	2	1
1	2	3	4	5								5	4	3	2	1
1	2	3	4								6	5	4	3	2	1
1	2	3								7	6	5	4	3	2	1
1	2								8	7	6	5	4	3	2	1
1								9	8	7	6	5	4	3	2	1

* * *

E. Lucas, in his *Récréations Mathématiques*, gives the following curious tabulations:

TABLE 23

$$
\begin{aligned}
1\cdot 9 + 2 &= 11 \\
12\cdot 9 + 3 &= 111 \\
123\cdot 9 + 4 &= 1111 \\
1234\cdot 9 + 5 &= 11111 \\
12345\cdot 9 + 6 &= 111111 \\
123456\cdot 9 + 7 &= 1111111 \\
1234567\cdot 9 + 8 &= 11111111 \\
12345678\cdot 9 + 9 &= 111111111 \\
123456789\cdot 9 + 10 &= 1111111111
\end{aligned}
$$

The reason for this phenomenon is apparent if we write the general or nth expression on the left-hand side as:

$$(10^{n-1} + 2\cdot 10^{n-2} + 3\cdot 10^{n-3} + \ldots + r\cdot 10^{n-r} + \ldots + n)$$
$$\times (10-1) + (n+1)$$

† Problems indicated by a dagger are solved in Chapter XXVI.

which, when multiplied out and simplified, becomes:

$$10^n + 10^{n-1} + 10^{n-2} + 10^{n-3} + \ldots + 10 + 1 = (10^{n+1} - 1)/9.$$

In common notation this becomes unity repeated $(n+1)$ times.

* * *

TABLE 24

$$9 \cdot 9 + 7 = 88$$
$$98 \cdot 9 + 6 = 888$$
$$987 \cdot 9 + 5 = 8888$$
$$9876 \cdot 9 + 4 = 88888$$
$$98765 \cdot 9 + 3 = 888888$$
$$987654 \cdot 9 + 2 = 8888888$$
$$9876543 \cdot 9 + 1 = 88888888$$
$$98765432 \cdot 9 + 0 = 888888888$$

Here the general nth expression is:

$$[9 \cdot 10^{n-1} + 8 \cdot 10^{n-2} + 7 \cdot 10^{n-3} + \ldots + r \cdot 10^{n-10+r} + \ldots + (10-n)]$$
$$\times (10-1) + (8-n)$$

which, multiplied out and grouped, becomes:

$$9 \cdot 10^n - (10^{n-1} + 10^{n-2} + 10^{n-3} + \ldots + 10 + 1) - 1 = 8(10^{n+1} - 1)/9.$$

And since $(10^{n+1} - 1)/9$ in common notation is the digit 1 written $(n+1)$ times in succession, 8 times this result gives the required product. If $n = 5$, then

$$8(10^6 - 1)/9 = 8 \cdot 111111 = 888888.$$

* * *

TABLE 25

$$1 \cdot 8 + 1 = 9$$
$$12 \cdot 8 + 2 = 98$$
$$123 \cdot 8 + 3 = 987$$
$$1234 \cdot 8 + 4 = 9876$$
$$12345 \cdot 8 + 5 = 98765$$
$$123456 \cdot 8 + 6 = 987654$$
$$1234567 \cdot 8 + 7 = 9876543$$
$$12345678 \cdot 8 + 8 = 98765432$$
$$123456789 \cdot 8 + 9 = 987654321$$

TABLE 26

$$987654321 \cdot \ 9 = \qquad 888888888 \ 9$$
$$987654321 \cdot 18 = 1 \ 777777777 \ 8$$
$$987654321 \cdot 27 = 2 \ 666666666 \ 7$$
$$987654321 \cdot 36 = 3 \ 555555555 \ 6$$
$$987654321 \cdot 45 = 4 \ 444444444 \ 5$$
$$987654321 \cdot 54 = 5 \ 333333333 \ 4$$
$$987654321 \cdot 63 = 6 \ 222222222 \ 3$$
$$987654321 \cdot 72 = 7 \ 111111111 \ 2$$
$$987654321 \cdot 81 = 8 \ 000000000 \ 1$$

TABLE 27

$$12345679 \cdot \ 9 = 111111111$$
$$12345679 \cdot 18 = 222222222$$
$$12345679 \cdot 27 = 333333333$$
$$12345679 \cdot 36 = 444444444$$
$$12345679 \cdot 45 = 555555555$$
$$12345679 \cdot 54 = 666666666$$
$$12345679 \cdot 63 = 777777777$$
$$12345679 \cdot 72 = 888888888$$
$$12345679 \cdot 81 = 999999999$$

The number 12345679 can be expressed as $(10^9-1)/81$, which, when multiplied by a multiple of 9, say $9K$, becomes

$$9K(10^9-1)/81 = K(10^9-1)/9 = K(111111111);$$

and as K takes on the values 1, 2, 3, etc., we get the results of the table.

This relationship can be utilized as a trick by writing 12345679 and asking a person to select his favorite digit. Mentally multiply the digit he selected by 9, then write the result under the number above. Then say that inasmuch as he is fond of that digit he shall have plenty of it. Multiply the two numbers together and the digit he selected will result. Thus suppose 4 was selected; multiply 12345679 by 36, resulting in 444444444.

Another example is

$$1/891 = (1/81)(1/11) = .001122334455667789\ldots.$$

If we multiply by 99 we get

$$99/891 = 1/9 = .11111\ldots.$$

A person may be asked which digit he prefers. Suppose he says 7. Multiply 99 by 7 mentally, giving 693. Multiplying the large number above by 693 is equivalent to finding the value of

$$693/891 = 7/9 = .77777\ldots$$

The fraction 1/81 can jump through more hoops for us. (For simplicity, decimal points will be omitted.)

$$
\begin{aligned}
1/81 &= 1/81 = 12345679\ldots \\
3/81 &= 1/27 = 37037037\ldots \\
6/81 &= 2/27 = 74074074\ldots \\
12/81 &= 4/27 = 148148148\ldots \\
15/81 &= 5/27 = 185185185\ldots \\
66/81 &= 22/27 = 814814814\ldots
\end{aligned}
$$

By remembering the value of $3/81 = 1/27$, the others can be derived as simple multiples of it.

From $1/891 = 1/(81 \cdot 11) = 1122334455667789$, we have

$$33/891 = 1/27$$

and therefore,

$$
\begin{aligned}
1122334455667789 \cdot 33 &= 37037037037037037 \\
1122334455667789 \cdot 3 &= 3367003367003367
\end{aligned}
$$

The reader might like to find the fraction corresponding to

$$111222333444555666777889.\dagger$$

We then have

$$
\begin{aligned}
111222333444555666777889 \cdot 3 &= 333667000333667000333667 \\
111222333444555666777889 \cdot 333 &= 37037037037037037037037037
\end{aligned}
$$

* * *

Here is one for the children:

TABLE 28

$$
\begin{aligned}
3 \cdot 37 &= 111 && \text{and} && 1+1+1 = 3 \\
6 \cdot 37 &= 222 && \text{and} && 2+2+2 = 6 \\
9 \cdot 37 &= 333 && \text{and} && 3+3+3 = 9 \\
12 \cdot 37 &= 444 && \text{and} && 4+4+4 = 12 \\
15 \cdot 37 &= 555 && \text{and} && 5+5+5 = 15 \\
18 \cdot 37 &= 666 && \text{and} && 6+6+6 = 18 \\
21 \cdot 37 &= 777 && \text{and} && 7+7+7 = 21 \\
24 \cdot 37 &= 888 && \text{and} && 8+8+8 = 24 \\
27 \cdot 37 &= 999 && \text{and} && 9+9+9 = 27
\end{aligned}
$$

* * *

The following tables were taken from an article by F. B. Selkin in the *Teachers College Record*, Vol. 12, p. 68.

TABLE 29

$$
\begin{array}{rcl}
1 \cdot 1 & = & 1 \\
11 \cdot 11 & = & 121 \\
111 \cdot 111 & = & 12321 \\
1111 \cdot 1111 & = & 1234321 \\
11111 \cdot 11111 & = & 123454321 \\
111111 \cdot 111111 & = & 12345654321 \\
1111111 \cdot 1111111 & = & 1234567654321 \\
11111111 \cdot 11111111 & = & 123456787654321 \\
111111111 \cdot 111111111 & = & 12345678987654321
\end{array}
$$

TABLE 30

$$
\begin{array}{rcl}
7 \cdot 7 & = & 49 \\
67 \cdot 67 & = & 4489 \\
667 \cdot 667 & = & 444889 \\
6667 \cdot 6667 & = & 44448889 \\
66667 \cdot 66667 & = & 4444488889 \\
666667 \cdot 666667 & = & 444444888889 \\
6666667 \cdot 6666667 & = & 44444448888889 \\
& \text{etc.} &
\end{array}
$$

TABLE 31

$$
\begin{array}{rcl}
4 \cdot 4 & = & 16 \\
34 \cdot 34 & = & 1156 \\
334 \cdot 334 & = & 111556 \\
3334 \cdot 3334 & = & 11115556 \\
33334 \cdot 33334 & = & 1111155556 \\
& \text{etc.} &
\end{array}
$$

TABLE 32

$$
\begin{array}{rcl}
9 \cdot 9 & = & 81 \\
99 \cdot 99 & = & 9801 \\
999 \cdot 999 & = & 998001 \\
9999 \cdot 9999 & = & 99980001 \\
99999 \cdot 99999 & = & 9999800001 \\
999999 \cdot 999999 & = & 999998000001 \\
9999999 \cdot 9999999 & = & 99999980000001 \\
& \text{etc.} &
\end{array}
$$

TABLE 33

$$7 \cdot 9 = 63$$
$$77 \cdot 99 = 7623$$
$$777 \cdot 999 = 776223$$
$$7777 \cdot 9999 = 77762223$$
$$77777 \cdot 99999 = 7777622223$$
$$777777 \cdot 999999 = 777776222223$$

etc.

*   *   *

A German-American algebra dated 1837 tabulates the following:

TABLE 34

$$1 \cdot 7 + 3 = 10$$
$$14 \cdot 7 + 2 = 100$$
$$142 \cdot 7 + 6 = 1000$$
$$1428 \cdot 7 + 4 = 10000$$
$$14285 \cdot 7 + 5 = 100000$$
$$142857 \cdot 7 + 1 = 1000000$$
$$1428571 \cdot 7 + 3 = 10000000$$
$$14285714 \cdot 7 + 2 = 100000000$$
$$142857142 \cdot 7 + 6 = 1000000000$$
$$1428571428 \cdot 7 + 4 = 10000000000$$
$$14285714285 \cdot 7 + 5 = 100000000000$$
$$142857142857 \cdot 7 + 1 = 1000000000000$$

This obviously originates from the decimal period of $1/7$.

*   *   *

The following relations are of interest, and those given without proof will be good exercises for the reader.

$$7 \cdot 15873 = 111111$$
$$14 \cdot 15873 = 222222$$
$$21 \cdot 15873 = 333333$$
$$28 \cdot 15873 = 444444$$

etc.

Why is this so?†   Again:

$$91 \cdot 1221 = 111 \ 111$$

and

$$900991 \cdot 123321 = 111 \ 111 \ 111 \ 111†$$

*   *   *

If we multiply 1001 by a three-digit number, the product is the three-digit number and one repetend of its digits.   Thus

$$352 \cdot 1001 = 352352$$
$$621 \cdot 1001 = 621621$$

This relation can be used in an effective trick.   The number

$$1001 = 7 \cdot 11 \cdot 13 = 7 \cdot 143.$$

Ask someone to mention a three-digit number, say 352.   Mentally multiply it by 7 and write the answer 2464 as the multiplicand of an example in rapid multiplication.   Underneath place 143 as a multiplier and immediately write the product as 352352.

Similar curious results are derived from $10001 = 73 \cdot 137$ and $100001 = 11 \cdot 9091$.   Thus a four-digit number such as 7319 multiplied successively by 137 and by 73 gives as a product 73197319, and a five-digit one multiplied by 11 and 9091 gives a five-digit repetend.

*   *   *

A common trick with an almost infinite number of variations is to have someone write a three-digit number, then write the number with the digits in reverse order, subtract the smaller from the larger, reverse the digits again and *add* this time; you will then be able to give the answer without having received any information about the number.   The answer is 1089.   Suppose any number, say 173, were taken.   Subtract from 371, leaving 198, reverse, giving 891, and the sum of the last two numbers is 1089.

A slightly ribald tale about an old maid and her cat utilizes this principle in an amusing way.   Wishing to give the cat a name and being quite vague about the gender of the feline, she decided to visit a numerologist for further information, as she was too shy to ask her friends.   She broached the subject with considerable trepidation and circumlocution, and he informed her that number lore could easily determine the cat's sex.   It was necessary only for the lady to mention the alternate names she had decided to call her cat.   She coyly replied that it would be "Emma," in memory of a dear departed friend, in case it belonged to the gentle, and "Toy-Toy" if it belonged to the roving category.   With considerable flourish the necromancer wrote:

$$\text{E M M A}\quad\text{T O Y}\quad\text{T O Y}$$
$$9\ 8\ 7\ 6\quad\ 5\ 4\ 3\quad\ 2\ 1\ 0$$

and underneath, the 10 numerals.

"Now, Madam," he said, "the subconscious plays an indispensable part in these matters. The two essential elements in nature must be properly commingled. Will you therefore choose any digit you please from the 'Emma' group and two figures from the 'Toy-Toy' group?" Timidly she selected 7 from the first, 3 and 2 from the second. (Any other choices would have done equally well.) The numerologist wrote 732 and under it 237, subtracted, reversed digits again, added and got the result 1089. "Now, Madam," he continued, "all animals have sex numbers and the cat's is 20. Let us multiply our result by 20, giving 21780, and we are ready to receive the answer through the mysterious voice of the integers. The first digit, 2, corresponds to T in the names, 1 corresponds to O, 7 to M, 8 to M, and zero to Y. Your cat, Madam," he concluded dramatically, "is clearly a TOMMY."

The fact that the reversal operations mentioned result in 1089 is easily demonstrated. Any three-digit number can be written as $a \cdot 10^2 + b \cdot 10 + c$, and the number with the digits reversed then becomes $c \cdot 10^2 + b \cdot 10 + a$. It is assumed that the larger number is written first, hence "a" is greater than "c" and we must "borrow" in both the units and tens columns. Borrowing means that the coefficient of the power of 10 in the column to the left of the one which is borrowing is reduced by 1, whereas it is *increased* by 10 in the borrowing column. The numbers can then be written:

$$(a-1) \cdot 10^2 + (b+10-1) \cdot 10 + (c+10)$$
$$c \cdot 10^2 + \qquad b \cdot 10 + \qquad a$$

Difference =	$(a - 1 - c) \cdot 10^2 +$	$9 \cdot 10 + c + 10 - a$
Reversing the digits gives	$(c + 10 - a) \cdot 10^2 +$	$9 \cdot 10 + a - 1 - c$
Adding, this results in	$9 \cdot 10^2 +$	$180 + \quad 9 = 1089$

*   *   *

Some students and self-taught enthusiasts often discover a rule of numbers which they think may revolutionize mathematics but which depends only on some elementary property of the digit 9. In most cases such rules reduce to trivial results easily demonstrable by congruences or other means. However, it must always be remembered that the theory of numbers is probably the only branch of mathematics where an inexperienced but curious and energetic pioneer may hope to discover something really original.

*   *   *

The number 9 has the "magical" property that every prime except 2 and 5 divides an *infinite* number of integers all of whose digits are 9. Thus 999 contains 37 and so does 999999 or 999999999, etc. Again 41 divides 99999 and any other group of $5K$ nines; 73 divides 99999999. It takes only 4 nines to be divisible by 101, but no less than 96 to contain 97. The prime 271 divides 99999, but the previous prime, 269, requires 268 nines. The prime 4649 divides 9999999, but the next prime 4651 requires 4650 nines in succession. Only 10 nines are required for 9091, but 9102 of them for the prime 9103. And of course, 20, 30, 40, 50, etc., nines also contain 9091; but after the group of 9102 nines, divisible by 9103, it takes twice that many, or 18204 nines in succession, before the resulting integer is again divisible by 9103.

The proof is much simpler than one would expect. The discerning reader will discover that this property is true not only of the digit 9 but of any of the 9 digits repeated.†

*   *   *

The following curious table shows how to arrange the 9 digits so that the product of 2 groups is equal to a number represented by the remaining digits.

TABLE 35

PRODUCTS OF NUMBERS, UTILIZING ALL NINE DIGITS

$12 \cdot 483 = 5796$	$27 \cdot 198 = 5346$
$42 \cdot 138 = 5796$	$39 \cdot 186 = 7254$
$18 \cdot 297 = 5346$	$48 \cdot 159 = 7632$

$$28 \cdot 157 = 4396$$
$$4 \cdot 1738 = 6952$$
$$4 \cdot 1963 = 7852$$

The product of 51249876 and 3 (all the digits used once only) is 153749628, which again contains all 9 digits used once. Again:

$$16583742 \cdot 9 = 149253678$$
$$32547891 \cdot 6 = 195287346$$

*   *   *

The number 142857 can be multiplied by 3 simply by transferring the 7 from the right to the left. The number

3529411764705882

may be multiplied by 3 and divided by 2 by similarly transferring the digit 2.

*   *   *

For a number of interesting digit problems see Chapter XXV.

BIBLIOGRAPHY

Abbott, H. E.   *Mathematical Excursions.*   New York: Dover Publications, Inc. (in prep.).

Brooks, E.   *Philosophy of Arithmetic.*   Lancaster, Pa.: Normal Publishing Co., 1880.

Jones, S. I.   *Mathematical Nuts.*   Nashville, Tenn.: S. I. Jones, 1932.

Lucas, E.   *Récréations Mathématiques.*   Paris: Gauthier-Villars et Cie., 1882.

Selkin, F. B.   "Number Games Bordering on Arithmetic and Algebra," *Teachers College Record,* **13** (1912), 68.

Simons, L. G.   "A German-American Algebra of 1837," *Scripta Mathematica,* **1** (1932), 29.

Smith, D. E.   *Wonderful Wonders of 1, 2, 3.*   New York: McFarlane, Ward, McFarlane, 1937.

White, W. F.   *Scrap Book of Elementary Mathematics.*   Chicago: Open Court Publishing Co., 1910.

CHAPTER IX

SCALES AND DISCORDS

"ONE TIMES six is six. Two times six is fifteen. Three times six is twenty-four; four times six makes thirty-three; five times six makes forty-two; six times six makes fifty-one; and 'ten' times six is sixty."

A strange multiplication table! But that is the way to recite the six-times table if the "radix" of our number system is 7 instead of 10. In such a system, the digits 7, 8, and 9 would be unknown; after 6 we would jump to the two-digit combination 10, representing 7 of our units. Hence "ten" above means 7 units.

It is fairly difficult for children to memorize their multiplication tables, and it takes much practice to develop the skill to multiply in our "denary" system or scale of 10. No intuition guided us into $2 \times 4 = 8$. We just had to learn that that was so, and if as children we had learned instead that $2 \times 4 = 11$, which it does in the 7 system, it would have been no queerer than $2 \times 4 = 8$.

In this system we count consecutively 1, 2, 3, 4, 5, 6, 10, 11, 12, 13, 14, 15, 16, 20, 21, 22, 23, 24, 25, 26, 30, etc., then consecutively 61, 62, 63, 64, 65, 66, 100, etc. The first two-digit number can be arbitrarily called anything; to avoid confusion, we will call it "ten," but it could be called "seven" or "wiget." A number in the 7 system is *not* seven-tenths of a number in the denary system. *Powers* of 7 correspond to powers of 10. In the denary system, the number 329 means $3 \cdot 10^2 + 2 \cdot 10 + 9$. To convert this to the *scale* where 7 is the *radix*, we divide by successive sevens and note the remainders. Thus $329 \div 7 = 47$, and no remainder; $47 \div 7 = 6$, and 5 remainder; $6 \div 7 = $ zero, and 6 remainder. The remainders in *reverse* order correspond to the coefficients of powers of 7 and the number 329 in the 7 scale is 650. Similarly 5218 of "our" scale gives:

Dividend				Remainder
7|5	2	1	8	
7|	7	4	5	3
	7|	1	0 6	3
		7|	1 5	1
			7| 2	1
			0	2

and this number in the scale whose radix is 7 is 21133. To convert a number, as 21133, from the 7 scale back to the denary scale, we give each digit its *place* value as a coefficient of a power of 7 and evaluate. Thus we have:

$$2 \cdot 7^4 + 1 \cdot 7^3 + 1 \cdot 7^2 + 3 \cdot 7^1 + 3 = 4802 + 343 + 49 + 21 + 3 = 5218.$$

The above method of successive divisions by 7 is merely a convenient way of determining the highest power of 7 in the number, then the next higher power, etc., together with their coefficients. Thus, we might have said: "$7^5 = 16807$ is too large; $7^4 = 2401$ is contained twice in 5218; $7^3 = 343$ is contained once in the remainder $416 = 5218 - 2 \cdot 2401$; $7^2 = 49$ is contained once in the new remainder 73; 7^1 is contained 3 times in the remainder 24; and finally the last remainder corresponding to the units place is 3."

Here are the multiplication tables we would have to learn in the world of seven.

TABLE 36

Multiplication Tables—Radix 7

One-Times Table	Two-Times Table	Three-Times Table
$1 \times 1 = 1$	$1 \times 2 = 2$	$1 \times 3 = 3$
$2 \times 1 = 2$	$2 \times 2 = 4$	$2 \times 3 = 6$
$3 \times 1 = 3$	$3 \times 2 = 6$	$3 \times 3 = 12$
$4 \times 1 = 4$	$4 \times 2 = 11$	$4 \times 3 = 15$
$5 \times 1 = 5$	$5 \times 2 = 13$	$5 \times 3 = 21$
$6 \times 1 = 6$	$6 \times 2 = 15$	$6 \times 3 = 24$

Four-Times Table	Five-Times Table	Six-Times Table
$1 \times 4 = 4$	$1 \times 5 = 5$	$1 \times 6 = 6$
$2 \times 4 = 11$	$2 \times 5 = 13$	$2 \times 6 = 15$
$3 \times 4 = 15$	$3 \times 5 = 21$	$3 \times 6 = 24$
$4 \times 4 = 22$	$4 \times 5 = 26$	$4 \times 6 = 33$
$5 \times 4 = 26$	$5 \times 5 = 34$	$5 \times 6 = 42$
$6 \times 4 = 33$	$6 \times 5 = 42$	$6 \times 6 = 51$

Now let us try an addition and a multiplication problem, remembering, in adding, that after 6 comes 10; after 16, 20; after 26, 30, etc., and after 66 comes 100. The addition of the following sum should then be evident. The numbers are already in the scale of 7; their place value is now a power of 7, not a power of ten.

```
      2514
      5603
      2051
      6643
      ─────
     23444
```

Here we add as usual, but for each multiple of 7 we say "ten" and carry one digit, writing down the remainder in the sum.   Note that the digits 7, 8, and 9 are of necessity absent.

A multiplication problem can also be performed readily by referring to the multiplication table (we would have to develop skill and speed by memorizing, if we wished to do without the table), just as we did with our common tables when we were children.

```
       6542
       3105
      ─────
      46003
      65420
     26256
     ─────────
     30322203
```

Here the first line of the products is sufficiently special to merit some explanation.   We say (referring to the multiplication tables), "Five times 2 is 13, put down 3 and carry 1; five times 4 is 26 and one carried makes 30, put down zero and carry 3; five times 5 is 34 and 3 carried makes 40, put down zero and carry 4; five times 6 is 42 and 4 carried makes 46."   (Had it been 5 carried it would have been 42 plus 5 makes 50.)

*   *   *

Needless to state, there can be scales of notation with other *radices*— many people have advocated the duodecimal scale which uses the radix 12.   Here two new symbols would have to be invented for 10 and 11 since we would not get to the two-digit combination until two units beyond 10.

The binary scale with radix 2 has become well known in recent years because it is used in digital computers.   In this scale, every integer must be expressed in terms of zeros and ones only.   To find the expression for the number 54 in the binary scale, we divide by 2 successively until no quotient remains and the remainders then give the number.   Thus:

	Dividend		Remainder
2	5 4		
	2	2 7	0
		2	1 3	1
			2	6	1
				2	3	0
					2	1	1
						0	1

and 54 is 110110 in the scale of 2.

Since only the two symbols 0 and 1 are used in the binary scale, a one-to-one correspondence can be established between them and (1) relay contacts which are open or closed and (2) power-supply terminals "plus" and "minus."   This is why the system is so useful in digital computers.

If what has gone before is somewhat confusing, imagine the conversion of fractions to a scale of notation other than 10, and then the conversion of these in turn to the "decimal" system in that scale. The reader is referred to a text such as Chrystal's *Algebra** for an extended discussion of this subject.

The fact that when a number is written in the binary scale, the coefficients of the powers of 2 are only zero or unity means that any number can be expressed as the sum of powers of 2, each power with coefficient unity; thus, $54 = 2^5 + 2^4 + 2^2 + 2$.

In the scale of 3, the coefficients are either zero, 1, or 2, and if we substitute $(3-1)$ for 2, this means that any number can be expressed as the *sum* or *difference* of powers of 3.   Thus 65 in the scale of 3 is

$$2 \cdot 3^3 + 1 \cdot 3^2 + 2 \cdot 3^0 = (3-1)3^3 + 1 \cdot 3^2 + (3-1)3^0$$
$$= 3^4 - 3^3 + 3^2 + 3^1 - 3^0.$$

A well-known weight problem depends on this last principle. Since sums of powers of 2 can represent any integer, we may select weights of 1, 2, 4, 8, 16, etc., pounds to weigh any exact number of

* G. Chrystal, *Textbook of Algebra* (2 vols.; New York: Dover Publications, Inc., 1961).

pounds on a balance scale. But powers of 3 work equally well—in fact better—if it is permitted to place weights in either scale pan. This corresponds to adding or subtracting powers of 3. By using only four weights of 1, 3, 9, and 27 pounds, it is possible to weigh any integral number of pounds to 40, and by just one additional weight of 81 pounds, any integral number to 121 pounds, and so on.

* * *

A story is told of the peasant who knew addition but could divide or multiply only by 2, yet, equipped with this limited knowledge, managed to multiply "any two numbers." For example, taking 89 and 107 he would place these at the head of two columns, then repeatedly divide the first number by 2, placing the results under one another. Remainders would be rejected. The number heading the second column would correspondingly be successively multiplied by 2, placing the results in the second column. Finally, he added only those numbers in the second column corresponding to odd numbers in the first column (indicated by an asterisk) and so obtained the correct product. The example below makes the method clear.

89*	107
44	214
22	428
11*	856
5*	1712
2	3424
1*	6848

Product $89 \cdot 107 = 107 + 856 + 1712 + 6848 = 9523.$

The reason for this process is not difficult to understand. Dividing 89 successively by 2 is the method for expressing it in the binary scale (as was done for the number 54). Only the odd numbers in the first column leave the remainder unity which determines the inclusion of a power of 2. Thus, the remainders are: 1, 0, 0, 1, 1, 0, 1, and applying these remainders in reverse order as coefficients of powers of 2, we have

$$89 = 1 \cdot 2^6 + 0 \cdot 2^5 + 1 \cdot 2^4 + 1 \cdot 2^3 + 0 \cdot 2^2 + 0 \cdot 2^1 + 1 \cdot 2^0.$$

Then,

$$107 \cdot 89 = 107 \cdot 2^6 + 107 \cdot 2^4 + 107 \cdot 2^3 + 107 \cdot 2^0$$
$$= 6848 + 1712 + 856 + 107 = 9523.$$

BIBLIOGRAPHY

Barlow, P. *Theory of Numbers.* London: J. Johnson & Co., 1811.

Chrystal, G. *Textbook of Algebra.* 2 vols. New York: Dover Publications, Inc., 1961.

CHAPTER X

CYCLING TOWARDS INFINITY

DECIMAL FRACTIONS were rather a bore at school, but there are some interesting relations and principles governing them which were little dreamt of in our juvenile philosophy. Let us review some of the elementary ones.

$$1/3 = .333\ldots \qquad 1/7 = .142857142857\ldots$$
$$1/4 = .25 \qquad 1/9 = .111\ldots$$
$$1/5 = .2 \qquad 1/11 = .0909\ldots$$
$$1/6 = .1666\ldots \qquad 1/13 = .076923076923\ldots$$

Why do some of the decimals terminate without a remainder, others repeat the first digit indefinitely, some repeat after dissimilar digits preceding them, and still others (as 1/7, 1/11, and 1/13) have digits repeating in cycles? Most readers are probably aware of the fact that in order for the reciprocal of an integer to terminate when expressed as a decimal—to "come out exactly"—it is necessary that the integer consist *only* of powers of 2, 5, or both. Numbers such as 2, 4, 5, 8, 10, 16, 20, 25, 32, 40, 50, 64, 80, 100—to mention *all* those not exceeding 100—consist only of powers of 2 and 5, and therefore their reciprocals are *terminate* decimals. No other integers less than 100 can be so expressed. As an example, 1/64 = .015625 exactly.

It is the behavior of these other integers which furnishes recreational aspects of decimals. To understand about the cycle of repetition it is convenient to think of a power of 10 divided by the given integer. Thus for the reciprocal of the integer 7, we think of $10^x/7$. Now by Fermat's theorem $10^{p-1} \equiv 1 \bmod p$, that is to say, we need raise 10 to an exponent no higher than $(p-1)$ before the remainder becomes 1 when divided by a prime p. Sometimes the exponent may be a smaller number; if so this exponent is always a factor of $p-1$. If $10^e \equiv 1 \bmod p$, where e is the *smallest* exponent that gives 1 as a remainder, the number e represents the number of decimal places that the reciprocal of p must be carried to before it repeats.

By Fermat's theorem, $10^2 \equiv 1 \bmod 3$, but the lower exponent 1 also applies, so that $10^1 \equiv 1 \bmod 3$. Hence 1/3 should repeat after only one digit, and in fact $1/3 = .333\ldots$. Similarly $10^6 \equiv 1 \bmod 7$, but in this case the congruence would hold for no lower exponent than 6; therefore there must be six places in the period of 1/7 and indeed $1/7 = .142857\ 142857\ldots$. Repetition of the cycle takes place when the remainder 1 is reached because the division by 7 started with unity as the first digit in the dividend. And it is the eth remainder which is 1. Again, $10^{10} \equiv 1 \bmod 11$, but also $10^2 \equiv 1 \bmod 11$, so that 1/11 repeats after two digits and in fact $1/11 = .0909\ldots$.

Continuing for higher primes, although $10^{12} \equiv 1 \bmod 13$, the lowest exponent for which the congruence holds is 6, and 1/13 repeats after six places, that is, $1/13 = .076923\ 076923\ldots$. For the prime 17, it is necessary to raise 10 to the sixteenth power before the remainder 1 is reached. Ten is called a *primitive* root of 17 and $1/17 = .0588235294117647\ldots$. Then the cycle repeats starting with zero. Ten is a primitive root of 19 also, and 1/19, therefore, has 18 places of decimals in one period. Table 37 shows the least exponent e for which 10^e leaves a remainder of 1 when divided by the prime p and, therefore, indicates the number of decimal places in one cycle of $1/p$. Ten is said to "belong to e, mod p." It is interesting to note that of the 23 odd primes between 1 and 100, 10 is a primitive root of only nine of them, indicated by a double asterisk. The greatest prime less than 100 is 97, and it so happens that 10 is a primitive root of 97; consequently, 1/97 must be carried to 96 places of decimals before the cycle repeats! If this seems like a large amount of work, consider the labors of one W. H. H. Hudson, who calculated the 1860 digits in the period of 1/1861, and of William Shanks, who calculated the period of 17388 digits in 1/17389.

Messrs. Suffield and Lunn in 1863 found the 7698 digits in the period of 1/7699 in illustration of a "new" method of synthetic division which Suffield thought he had discovered. But the French mathematician Fourier had discovered the method in the early part of the nineteenth century and it has been "rediscovered" many times since. The writer of *Ecclesiastes* said, "There is no new thing under the sun." It should now be clear why the decimal equivalents of 1/2, 1/4, and 1/5 terminate, why 1/3 repeats after one digit, 1/7 after six digits, and why in general $1/p$ repeats after e decimal places where e is the *smallest* integer that will make $10^e \equiv 1 \bmod p$.

TABLE 37

Exponents to Which 10 Belongs, for Primes 3 to 97*

Prime = p	Least Exponent = e	Prime = p	Least Exponent = e
3	1	47†	46
7†	6	53	13
11	2	59†	58
13	6	61†	60
17†	16	67	33
19†	18	71	35
23†	22	73	8
29†	28	79	13
31	15	83	41
37	3	89	44
41	5	97†	96
43	21		

* Least exponent "e" to which 10 must be raised so that $10^e - 1$ is divisible by the prime, p.

† 10 is a primitive root of this prime.

Table 37 is the merest beginning of a much more extensive one, illustrating the extent to which calculators are willing to devote large parts of their lives on work that can be only its own reward. William Shanks, a perfect demon of energy—he calculated π to 707 places but was correct only to the 528th place—extended the table to all primes not exceeding 120000. To obtain some idea of what this means, consider the prime 97. We know that $10^{96} \equiv 1 \bmod 97$, and also that if there is a smaller exponent for which this congruence holds, that exponent must divide 96 exactly. Therefore, it is necessary to examine the remainders of 10^2, 10^3, 10^4, 10^6, 10^8, 10^{12}, 10^{16}, 10^{24}, 10^{32}, and 10^{48} when divided by 97 to find the lowest power leaving a remainder of 1. And this is for only *one* prime! Imagine performing these calculations for all the primes up to 120000. Of course, there are numerous short cuts and Shanks referred to previous smaller tables, but even with these, the labor is still great. And subsequent investigators like Allan Cunningham have checked Shanks's computations!

One wonders at these patient souls in all corners of the globe, working ceaselessly under some inexplicable urge to contribute their share to the world's small store of knowledge. One delves through dusty tomes in the sanctuary of a library and comes upon pages and pages of such tables compiled by Germans, Frenchmen, Italians, Americans, Englishmen, a scientific brotherhood transcending all boundaries and prejudices. It is a revelation just to thumb through the *Proceedings of the Royal Society of London*, Volume 22, 1873, for example, and see some of these computations by Shanks.*

* * *

TABLE 38

DECIMAL PERIODS OF *a*/7 AND *a*/17

1/7 = .142 857...	1/17 = .05882352 94117647...
2/7 = .285 714...	2/17 = .11764705 88235294...
3/7 = .428 571...	3/17 = .17647058 82352941...
4/7 = .571 428...	14/17 = .82352941 17647058...
5/7 = .714 285...	15/17 = .88235294 11764705...
6/7 = .857 142...	16/17 = .94117647 05882352...

The fractions in Table 38 exhibit a curious property. It will be noted that each multiple of 1/7 is a cyclic rearrangement of the same six digits and a similar property holds for the 16 multiples of 1/17. This property is exhibited by the reciprocals of all primes of which 10 is a primitive root and would consequently hold true also of 1/19, 1/23, 1/29, and so on.

Since p is a prime and odd, $p-1$ is even, and the $p-1$ decimal places in one period, when 10 is a primitive root, can therefore be divided into two equal parts. It will be noticed that the corresponding digits in the two parts always add to 9; consequently, if we have half the period we can write the digits of the second half merely by subtracting from 9 those already found.

This property holds not only for primes of which 10 is a primitive root but for *any* prime having an even number of digits in its period as, for example, 13 which has a six-digit period. Table 37 shows that 31, 37, 41, 43, 53, 67, 71, 79, and 83 have an odd number of digits in their respective periods; therefore, for these primes there are no half periods. But for all the remaining primes less than 100, there are an even number of digits in the period and the corresponding digits in the half periods add to 9.

The reciprocal of a composite number may or may not have the digits in the half periods complementary even though there are an

---

* Should the reader have occasion to refer to these, he will find that the printed tables in the *Proceedings* go only to the prime 29989, but the Archives of the Society contain in manuscript form the balance to 120000.

even number of digits in the period. For example, the reciprocal of the composite number 403 has an even number of digits, 30, in its period, which is 002481389578163 771712158808933, but the two halves are not complementary. This is due to the fact that $403 = 31 \cdot 13$, and 1/31 has an odd number of digits in its period, thus affecting the result. Other examples are 1/21, 1/33, 1/39, and 1/51, which fail to follow the rule because 3, a factor of each denominator, has an odd number of places in its period.

There are many methods of determining the digits of a period. For a conveniently small remainder occurring in the division, as many more digits as have already been found can be written down immediately by multiplying what has already been found by that remainder. For example, since 10 is a primitive root of 97, the period of 1/97 has 96 places. Starting to calculate these by ordinary division, we have

$$1/97 = .01030927835 \frac{5}{97}.$$

The remainder, 5/97, expressed decimally, is five times as large as 1/97, and the number represented by the next 11 digits is five times as large as the number represented by the first 11, or 05154639175, and $5(5/97) = 25/97$ is the new remainder. The numerator is again a convenient multiplier because to multiply by 25 we merely multiply by 100 (or move the decimal point two places to the right) and divide by 4. Doing this to the 22-digit number already found, we have 1.03092783505154639175, which, after dividing by 4, gives the next 22 places: 2577319587628865979375, with a remainder of $25 \cdot 25 = 625$. But

$$625/97 = 6 \frac{43}{97},$$

so we add 6 to the previous result, writing 81 instead of 75 in the last two places and proceeding with the remainder, 43. The next four digits by actual division of 43 by 97 are 4432, and since, after 48 places or a half period, corresponding digits add to 9, we easily obtain the whole period of 96 digits, having actually divided for only 15 of them. The whole period is:

1/97 = .0103092783505154639175257731958762886859793814432
98969072164948453608247422680412371134020618556 7...

and then it starts all over again with 0103....

If 10 is *not* a primitive root of p, the result is somewhat different.

TABLE 39

DECIMAL PERIODS OF $a/13$

Group 1	Group 2
1/13 = .076 923...	2/13 = .153 846...
3/13 = .230 769...	5/13 = .384 615...
4/13 = .307 692...	6/13 = .461 538...
9/13 = .692 307...	7/13 = .538 461...
10/13 = .769 230...	8/13 = .615 384...
12/13 = .923 076...	11/13 = .846 153...

Here there are two sets of cyclic arrangements. Each decimal in one group consists of the same six digits in the same cyclic order, but each decimal starts with a different digit. If 10 "belongs" to a still lower exponent than half of $p-1$, we get more groups. The 36 fractions with 37 as denominator have 12 groups of *different* cycles, each group containing three fractions because $10^3 \equiv 1$ mod 37. But $10^5 \equiv 1$ mod 41, and there are eight groups with five members per group for multiples of 1/41.

TABLE 40

DECIMAL PERIODS OF $a/41$

Group			Fractions		
1	1/41 = .02439	10/41 = .24390	16/41 = .39024	18/41 = .43902	37/41 = .90243
2	2/41 = .04878	20/41 = .48780	32/41 = .78048	33/41 = .80487	36/41 = .87804
3	3/41 = .07317	7/41 = .17073	13/41 = .31707	29/41 = .70731	30/41 = .73170
4	4/41 = .09756	23/41 = .56097	25/41 = .60975	31/41 = .75609	40/41 = .97560
5	5/41 = .12195	8/41 = .19512	9/41 = .21951	21/41 = .51219	39/41 = .95121
6	6/41 = .14634	14/41 = .34146	17/41 = .41463	19/41 = .46341	26/41 = .63414
7	11/41 = .26829	12/41 = .29268	28/41 = .68292	34/41 = .82926	38/41 = .92682
8	15/41 = .36585	22/41 = .53658	24/41 = .58536	27/41 = .65853	35/41 = .85365

*   *   *

The integer 49 is unique among composite integers less than 100 used as denominators of proper fractions. If k is prime to 49, all fractions $k/49$ have the same cyclic arrangement of their digits. There are 42 such fractions and each has 42 digits in its period. Thus

$1/49 = .020408163265306122448\ 97959183673469387755 1...$

and

$3/49 = .061224489795918367346\ 938775510204081632653...$

etc., the second number in this case starting with the fourteenth digit of the first.   The only composite numbers which possess this property are powers of a single prime exceeding 3, and 10 must be a primitive root of that prime.

*   *   *

In most instances the number of the digits, n, in the decimal equivalent of the reciprocal of a *power* of a prime, p^a, is $r \cdot p^{a-1}$, where r is the number of digits in the reciprocal of the prime's first power. For instance, since $1/11$ has the two-digit period, 09, $1/11^2$ has 22 digits, and since $1/13$ has 6 digits, $1/13^3$ has $6 \cdot 13^2 = 1014$ digits.

Two noteworthy exceptions are $1/9 = 1/3^2$ whose period of one digit is the same as that of $1/3$ and $1/487^2$ whose period of 486 digits is the same as that of $1/487$.   No other prime up to 1000 possesses this very rare property.

*   *   *

A cycle of quotients and remainders can be shown in an interesting manner by means of a diagram like Figure 2.   The inner ring gives the quotients, the outer one the remainders, of $1/29$, starting with the digits below the asterisk and proceeding clockwise.

1. It will be noted that diametrically opposite digits in the quotient circle add to 9.

2. The sum of diametrically opposite remainders is 29.

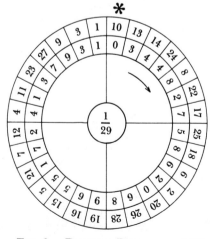

Fig. 2.   Decimal Periods of $1/29$

3. The period for any fraction, say 13/29, can be obtained by first finding 13 in the remainder circle and the corresponding quotient 3 on the inner circle.   Then start with the next quotient clockwise from 3, namely, 4, and the period for 13/29 is .44827586.... Other properties of periodic fractions can easily be discovered by constructing a few of these circles.

*   *   *

It is interesting to note that decimals can be written following an altogether different pattern from the finite or recurring ones just described.   Only a brief mention of them can be made here because they would lead us far afield and along unexplored paths.   The decimal 0.101001000100001 follows the law that the number of zeros after each unit progressively increases and this number may be expressed by:

$$10^{-1} + 10^{-3} + 10^{-6} + 10^{-10} + 10^{-15} + \ldots + 10^{-n(n+1)/2},$$

the exponents being triangular numbers (see Chapter XVIII), that is, sums of an arithmetic progression.   We also have

$$0.1101000100000001,$$

where the unit occupies the first, second, fourth, eighth, sixteenth, $\ldots 2^n$ place, to which corresponds

$$10^{-1} + 10^{-2} + 10^{-4} + 10^{-8} + \ldots + 10^{-2^n}.$$

The exponents are terms of a geometric progression.   More complicated is 0.11101010001010 where the units occupy the first, second, third, fifth, seventh, eleventh, and thirteenth places—that is, the places of prime rank.   Then there is 0.123571113171923, obtained from writing down the primes in their *natural order*.

*   *   *

In 1823 Henry Goodwyn published in London a table 107 pages long, giving the decimal periods of every fraction having a prime or composite denominator that is relatively prime to 10 and not exceeding 1024.   For example, all the digits in the decimal periods of 1/127, 2/127, 3/127, etc., are given in full.   Goodwyn would have published additional tables if this work had been well received, but apparently it was not greeted with particular warmth.   An enormous mount of his unpublished matter on fractions was purchased by the Royal Society in 1842. We blush to state that thirty years later no record of this manuscript was found in the files of the Society, and one may permit himself a vision of some stolid street-cleaner phlegmatically depositing in his cart the wasted efforts of one Henry Goodwyn. *Sic transit gloria mundi.*

*   *   *

Every repeating decimal, no matter how long its period—so long as the period has a finite ending—is a rational number, which means that it can be expressed as the quotient of two integers. To find this fraction—the inverse process of obtaining the decimal from the fraction—we proceed as follows: Suppose $N = .076923076923\ldots$ is given, having six places in its period. Then $10^6 N = 76923.076923\ldots.$ Subtracting the original number, we have $999999N = 76923$ exactly. Then $N = 76923/999999 = 1/13$. Once again, $N = .0731707317\ldots$ with five places in the period. Then $10^5 N = 7317.07317\ldots$, and $10^5 N - N = 99999N = 7317$ exactly. Then

$$N = 7317/99999 = 3/41.$$

BIBLIOGRAPHY

Bickmore, C. E. "On the Numerical Factors of $a^n - 1$," *Messenger of Mathematics*, **25** (1895), 1.

Brooks, E. *Philosophy of Arithmetic*. Lancaster, Pa.: Normal Publishing Co., 1880.

Carmichael, R. D. *Theory of Numbers and Diophantine Analysis*. New York: Dover Publications, Inc., 1959.

Cunningham, A. *Haupt-Exponents, Residue Indices, Primitive Roots*. London: F. Hodgson, 1922.

———. "Note on Factors of $(10^n - 1)$ [Corrections]," *Messenger of Mathematics*, **33** (1903), 95.

Dickson, L. E. *History of the Theory of Numbers*. 3 vols. New York: Chelsea Publishing Co., 1950.

Escott, E. B. "Note Concerning the Numerical Factors of $a^n - 1$," *Messenger of Mathematics*, **33** (1903), 49.

Glaisher, J. W. L. "On Circulating Decimals...," *Proceedings of the Cambridge Philosophical Society*, **3** (1876–1880), 185.

Guttman, S. "On Cyclic Numbers," *American Mathematical Monthly*, **41** (1934), 159.

Hardy, G. H. "An Introduction to the Theory of Numbers," *Bulletin of the American Mathematical Society*, **35** (1929), 778.

Lehmer, D. H. "Test for Primality by the Converse of Fermat
    Theorem," *Bulletin of the American Mathematical Society*, **33** (1927), 32

Shanks, W.   "On the Number of Figures in the Period of the Reciproc:
    of Every Prime Number Below 20000," *Proceedings of the Royal Socie*
    of London, **22** (1873), 200.

———.   "Given the Number of Figures (Not Exceeding 100) in th
    Reciprocal of a Prime Number, to Determine the Prime Itself,
    Proceedings of the Royal Society of London, **22** (1873), 381.

———.   "On the Number of Figures in the Reciprocal of Every Prim
    Between 20000 and 30000," *Proceedings of the Royal Society of London*, ?
    (1873), 384.

White, W. F.   *Scrap Book of Elementary Mathematics*.   Chicago: Op(
    Court Publishing Co., 1910.

CHAPTER XI

11111...111

NUMBERS consisting of the digit 1 repeated a finite number of times have aroused a great deal of curiosity, and much time has been expended trying to find their factors. Has 11 111 111 111 111 111 any exact divisors, and if so, what are they? A number of this type may be written:

$$10^x + 10^{x-1} + 10^{x-2} + \ldots + 10^2 + 10 + 1,$$

and summing up this geometric progression by the usual algebraic formula, we get $(10^{x+1} - 1)/9$. The 17-digit number above is represented by $(10^{17} - 1)/9$, and the problem reduces to the discovery of the factors of a number of the form $10^y - 1$.

A number which consists of a repetend of a single digit is sometimes called a monodigit number, and for convenience the author has used the term "repunit number" (repeated unit) to represent monodigit numbers consisting solely of the digit 1.

As far as the author knows, the "latest" information available of the factors of repunit numbers consisting of a prime number of digits each, is given in Table 41. As will be recalled from the discussion of Mersenne's numbers in Chapter III, a binomial of this type is factorable immediately if y is composite, so that only when y is a prime is there any difficulty in determining the character of the expression. Methods similar to those used for Mersenne's numbers assist in factoring numbers of the form $a^x - 1$ where the base is 10 instead of 2.

By Fermat's theorem $a^{p-1} \equiv 1 \bmod p$. Since $p - 1$ is even when p is a prime, the theorem cannot apply directly to numbers of the form $a^x - 1$ when x is a prime and therefore odd. With Mersenne's numbers, where the base is 2, it was found in Chapter III that the exponent could be halved without affecting divisibility provided p is of the form $8r + 7$. That is, $2^{4r+3} \equiv 1 \bmod 8r + 7$. Table 7 lists the prime numbers, $4r + 3$, not exceeding 257, and the corresponding primes, $8r+7$ dividing $2^{4r+3}-1$. A similar relation holds for the base 10. We have that

$$10^{(p-1)/2} \equiv 1 \mod p,$$

provided that p is a prime having one of the forms $40r \pm 1$, $40r \pm 3$, $40r \pm 9$, or $40r \pm 13$.

If $x = (p-1)/2$ is composite, the relation is of no particular interest since we already know how to factor $a^x - 1$ for composite exponents, using common algebra. But if x is a prime, no algebraic method applies, and then the above relation, where applicable, can be used to factor $a^x - 1$. The only prime values of x less than 100 for which p is also a prime of one of the eight required forms are 41 and 53, the corresponding values of p being 83 and 107.

TABLE 41

FACTORS OF "REPUNIT" NUMBERS,
$R_y = 111\ldots111$ (y UNITS) $= (10^y - 1)/9$

y, a Prime	Factors of $(10^y - 1)/9 = R_y$	Character
1	1	Prime
2	11	Prime
3	$3 \cdot 37$	Composite
5	$41 \cdot 271$	Composite
7	$239 \cdot 4649$	Composite
11	$21649 \cdot 513239$	Composite
13	$53 \cdot 79 \cdot 265371653$	Composite
17	$2071723 \cdot 5363222357$	Composite
19	1111111111111111111	Prime
23	11111111111111111111111	Prime
29	$3191 \cdot 16763 \cdot 43037 \cdot 62003 \cdot 77843839397$	Composite
31	$2791 \cdot ?$	Composite
37	?	Composite
41	$83 \cdot 1231 \cdot ?$	Composite
43	$173 \cdot ?$	Composite
47	?	?
53	$107 \cdot ?$	Composite
59	?	?
61	$733 \cdot 4637 \cdot ?$	Composite
67	?	?
71	?	?
73	?	?
79	$317 \cdot 6163 \cdot 10271 \cdot ?$	Composite
83	?	?
89	?	?
97	?	?

Thus $10^{41} - 1$ is divisible by 83, and $10^{53} - 1$ is divisible by 107. A few other theorems are available for finding divisors of repunit numbers, but on the whole there are wide gaps in our knowledge of them, as Table 41 shows.

Although only prime exponents were considered in Table 41, the resolution of $10^y - 1$ into all its prime factors, even when the exponent is a composite number, is by no means easy nor has it been accomplished for all composite values of y even to so low a limit as 100. Suppose y is an even multiple of 3, for instance 48. Let us factor the corresponding number. Then $10^{48} - 1$ is the difference of two squares and is factorable into $(10^{24} + 1)(10^{24} - 1)$. The first factor is the sum of two cubes and is factorable into $(10^8 + 1)(10^{16} - 10^8 + 1)$; the second is again the difference of two squares and can be further resolved. Expressions like $10^{16} - 10^8 + 1$ are frequently almost intractable to factorization. "Algebraically" this factor is prime, that is, no general factoring method enables $a^{16} - a^8 + 1$ to be resolved into real factors of lower degree. In particular instances the expression may have factors but it so happens that $10^{16} - 10^8 + 1 = 9\ 999\ 999\ 900\ 000\ 001$ is prime. The determination of this last was by no means easy, and its character remained unknown until relatively recently. The curious table below indicates that expressions of this type seem to follow a rule for a short interval and then act irregularly, an all too frequent occurrence in number theory and an indication of the danger of hasty generalization.

TABLE 42

NUMERICAL FACTORS OF $(a^{2x} - a^x + 1)$,
THE ALGEBRAIC PRIME FACTOR OF $(a^{3x} + 1)/(a^x + 1)$

x	$(a^{2x} - a^x + 1)$	Numerical Value	Nature
1	$10^2 - 10 + 1$	91	Composite
2	$10^4 - 10^2 + 1$	9901	Prime
3	$10^6 - 10^3 + 1$	999001	Composite
4	$10^8 - 10^4 + 1$	99990001	Prime
5	$10^{10} - 10^5 + 1$	9999900001	Composite
6	$10^{12} - 10^6 + 1$	999999000001	Prime
7	$10^{14} - 10^7 + 1$	99999990000001	Composite
8	$10^{16} - 10^8 + 1$	9999999900000001	Prime
9	$10^{18} - 10^9 + 1$	999999999000000001	Composite
10	$10^{20} - 10^{10} + 1$	99999999990000000001	Composite (unfortunately)

If we follow to completion the factors of $10^{48}-1$, we continue $10^{24}-1$ to

$$(10^{12}+1)(10^6+1)(10^3+1)(10^3-1) = (10^4+1)(10^8-10^4+1)$$
$$\times (10^2+1)(10^4-10^2+1)$$
$$\times (10+1)(10^2-10+1)$$
$$\times (10-1)(10^2+10+1).$$

The table shows us that the second and fourth factors are numerically prime. The first factor $10^4+1 = 10001$ is small enough to be looked up in a factor table, where we find it equal to $73 \cdot 137$. The factor $10^2+1 = 101$ is prime; $10+1 = 11$ is prime;

$$10^2-10+1 = 91 = 7 \cdot 13; \qquad 10-1 = 9 = 3^2;$$

and

$$10^2+10+1 = 111 = 3 \cdot 37.$$

The factor 10^8+1 is divisible by 17, and the quotient 5882353 is a prime. The final resolution of $10^{48}-1$ into prime factors is

$$17 \cdot 5882353 \cdot 9999999900000001 \cdot 73 \cdot 137 \cdot 99990001 \cdot 101$$
$$\cdot 9901 \cdot 11 \cdot 7 \cdot 13 \cdot 3^3 \cdot 37.$$

Therefore, the digit 1 repeated 48 times, or $(10^{48}-1)/9$, has the above factors except that 3 must be substituted for 3^3 to take account of the denominator 9.

The terse description "Prime" or "Composite" in Table 41 gives a very inadequate conception of what it means to determine the nature of a repunit number such as $(10^{23}-1)/9$. M. Kraitchik in his *Recherches sur la Théorie des Nombres*, Volume II, devotes a chapter to the description of his labors to prove the number a prime. It was an immense piece of work and not altogether devoid of humor on account of the apparent discrepancies between his conclusions and those of Dr. D. H. Lehmer (see Chapter III). Let the ambitious reader refer to Kraitchik's efforts before rashly embarking on the exploration of $(10^{47}-1)/9$.

High powers of 10 have more than a purely recreational interest. Although not entirely germane to our discussion here, it may be noted that the amplification of a telephone conversation over a long transmission line is of the order of 10^{4000}. There is also the whimsey of Professor Edward Kasner of Columbia University, who referred to 10^{100} as a "googol" and $10^{10^{100}}$ as a "googolplex." Thus the

40000 decibel (4000 bel) attenuation of the telephone conversation is subjected to more than a (googol)^{40} of amplification. For comparison with this superastronomical figure, the ratio of 15 billion light years (which is as far as the radio telescope at Big Pine, California, can reach) to the radius of a small atomic nucleus is only 10^{39}.

BIBLIOGRAPHY

Bickmore, C. E. "On the Numerical Factors of $a^n - 1$," *Messenger of Mathematics*, **25** (1895), 1.

Dickson, L. E. *History of the Theory of Numbers*. 3 vols. New York: Chelsea Publishing Co., 1950.

Green, E. I. "The Evolving Technology of Communication," *Electrical Engineering*, **78** (1959), 473.

Kasner, E., and Newman, J. *Mathematics and the Imagination*. New York: Simon and Schuster, 1940.

Kraitchik, M. *Recherches sur la Théorie des Nombres, Vols. I, II*. Paris: Gauthier-Villars et Cie., 1924, 1929.

Lehmer, D. H. "Test for Primality by the Converse of Fermat's Theorem," *Bulletin of the American Mathematical Society*, **33** (1927), 327.

――――. "A Further Note on the Converse of Fermat's Theorem," *Bulletin of the American Mathematical Society*, **34** (1928), 54.

――――. "On the Number $(10^{23} - 1)/9$," *Bulletin of the American Mathematical Society*, **35** (1929), 349.

Reid, L. W. *Elements of the Theory of Algebraic Numbers*. Baltimore: Johns Hopkins Press, 1946.

Shanks, W. "On the Number of Figures in the Period of the Reciprocal of Every Prime Number Below 20000," *Proceedings of the Royal Society of London*, **22** (1873), 200.

――――. "Given the Number of Figures (Not Exceeding 100) in the Reciprocal of a Prime Number, to Determine the Prime Itself," *Proceedings of the Royal Society of London*, **22** (1873), 381.

――――. "On the Number of Figures in the Reciprocal of Every Prime Between 20000 and 30000," *Proceedings of the Royal Society of London*, **22** (1873), 384.

CHAPTER XII

Φ, FIE—FO—FUM

Some apparently guileless problems bristling with snares for the unwary arise in connection with Euler's ϕ function—the number of integers less than and prime to a given integer. If one were asked to express some relatively simple number, say 72, as a "product of powers of primes," no particular difficulty would be experienced. We decompose the number as a chemical compound might be decomposed into its essential elements. Prime numbers are the elements of arithmetic. Dividing 72 by 2 and 3 as many times as is possible, we finally get $72 = 2^3 \cdot 3^2$. In a similar way $120 = 2^3 \cdot 3 \cdot 5$; and 60840, which obviously contains twos, threes, and fives, resolves into $2^3 \cdot 3^2 \cdot 5 \cdot 13^2$. We have already noted that the general expression for any positive integer, N, as the product of powers of primes is

$$N = p_1{}^{a_1} p_2{}^{a_2} p_3{}^{a_3} \ldots p_n{}^{a_n}. \qquad \text{(Formula A)}$$

It is shown in textbooks that the number of integers less than N and prime to it, that is, having no factor, except unity, in common with it is given by the expression:

$$\phi(N) = p_1{}^{a_1 - 1}(p_1 - 1)p_2{}^{a_2 - 1}(p_2 - 1)p_3{}^{a_3 - 1}(p_3 - 1) \ldots p_n{}^{a_n - 1}(p_n - 1).$$
$$\text{(Formula B)}$$

It is written $\phi(N)$ and read "fee of N." Thus:

$$\phi(72) = \phi(2^3 \cdot 3^2) = 2^2(2-1) \cdot 3^1(3-1) = 4 \cdot 1 \cdot 3 \cdot 2 = 24$$
$$\phi(120) = \phi(2^3 \cdot 3 \cdot 5) = 2^2(2-1) \cdot 3^0(3-1) \cdot 5^0(5-1)$$
$$= 4 \cdot 1 \cdot 1 \cdot 2 \cdot 1 \cdot 4 = 32$$
$$\phi(60840) = \phi(2^3 \cdot 3^2 \cdot 5 \cdot 13^2)$$
$$= 2^2(2-1) \cdot 3^1(3-1) \cdot 5^0(5-1) \cdot 13^1(13-1)$$
$$= 4 \cdot 1 \cdot 3 \cdot 2 \cdot 1 \cdot 4 \cdot 13 \cdot 12 = 14976. \quad \cdot$$

It is to be noted that whenever a prime appears to only the first power in Formula A, it does not appear in Formula B since $p^0 = 1$. Because of this absence and also for many other reasons, many interesting problems are presented by the ϕ function:

I. To find *all* the ways, if any, of expressing a given number $b = \phi(N)$ in the form of Formula B, and to formulate a practical procedure for doing so.

II. To obtain all numbers, N, from these values of $\phi(N)$.

III. To find numbers, b, which cannot be put into this form.

It is not even necessary to know that $\phi(N)$ means the number of integers less than N and prime to it in order to solve these problems. Formula A defines a number N, and Formula B is a function involving N. Solely from these two relations, the problems can be solved, but considerable ingenuity must be exercised to obtain all the solutions N for a given number b, and to make a set of practical rules for doing so.

In I, if $b = 6$, then $3^1(3-1)$ is one way of expressing it in the form of Formula B. For $b = 8$, one solution is $2^3(2-1)$. But try as we may, $b = 14$ cannot be expressed in this manner. At first glance there also does not seem to be a solution for the number 10, but $11^0(11-1)$ satisfies the requirements. Now find a second solution.† Then find three ways of expressing the number 2 in this form.†

If $N = 1$, then by Formula B,

$$\phi(1) = 1^{1-1}(1-1) = 1^0 \cdot 0 = 1 \cdot 0 = 0;$$

but arbitrarily, unity is considered prime to every integer *including itself*, so that $\phi(1) = 1$ despite Formula B.

Expressing an integer, b, in the form of Formula B implies a corresponding value of N as given by Formula A; hence there will be as many numbers, N, satisfying $\phi(N) = b$ as there are ways of writing b in the form of Formula B. (The exception unity has already been noted; both $\phi(2)$ and $\phi(1)$ equal 1, but for $b = 1$ only the *single* form, $2^0(2-1)$, can be written, since $\phi(1) = 1$ by definition, not by formula.) This raises a fascinating question: Is there an integer, N, whose $\phi(N) = b$ is unique, that is, can there be only a single solution, N, for some $b = \phi(N)$? It has been proved that there is no such integer N smaller than 10^{400}, and it seems highly improbable that such integers exist. (The number of drops of water on this earth is less than 10^{30}.) Below this limit, it is always possible to find at least two solutions, N, for a given $b = \phi(N)$. Thus if an odd number, N, is a solution, $2N$ is also a solution; if an even number, $N = 2(2x+1)$, is

† Problems indicated by a dagger are solved in Chapter XXVI.

a solution, then the odd number, $2x+1$, is also a solution.   Thus if number, N, exists whose $\phi(N)$ is unique, N must be a multiple of 4.

It is easily shown that the number b cannot be odd, except fo $b = 1$ which has the solution $2^0(2-1)$: Formula B shows that ther is at least one factor (p_1-1) of b and this factor must be even if th prime is greater than 2.   If $p_1 = 2$, then $p_1^{a_1-1}$ is even.   If $a_1 = 1$ we have the one odd-number exception mentioned above.

The solution $3^1(3-1)$ is only one of four ways of writing the numbe 6 in the form of Formula B.   The other three are:

$$7^0(7-1) \qquad\qquad = 6$$
$$2^0(2-1) \cdot 7^0(7-1) = 6$$
$$2^0(2-1) \cdot 3^1(3-1) = 6$$

To show that these are all distinct, we can write the respectiv values of N, for these values of $\phi(N)$, with the aid of Formulas A an B.   These are listed in Table 43.

One could work backwards and show that if 9, 7, 14, and 18 ar each written in the form of Formula A, then the value of $\phi(N)$ as give by Formula B will be 6 in each case.   The number of integers les than each of the numbers, N, and prime to it are also listed in Table 43

TABLE 43

VALUES OF N FOR WHICH $\phi(N) = 6$

N	Integers Less Than and Prime to N	Number of Such Integers, $b = \phi(N)$
$7^1 = 7$	1; 2; 3; 4; 5; 6	$7^0(7-1) = 6$
$3^2 = 9$	1; 2; 4; 5; 7; 8	$3^1(3-1) = 6$
$2 \cdot 7 = 14$	1; 3; 5; 9; 11; 13	$2^0(2-1) \cdot 7^0(7-1) = 6$
$2 \cdot 3^2 = 18$	1; 5; 7; 11; 13; 17	$2^0(2-1) \cdot 3^1(3-1) = 6$

The apparently trivial factor $2^0(2-1) = 1$ produces distinct solution when coupled with other numbers as in the solutions $N = 14$ and 18

For $\phi(N) = 12$, there are six solutions:

$$13^0(13-1); \quad 2^0(2-1) \cdot 13^0(13-1); \quad 3^0(3-1) \cdot 7^0(7-1);$$
$$2^0(2-1) \cdot 3^0(3-1) \cdot 7^0(7-1); \quad 2^1(2-1) \cdot 3^1(3-1);$$
$$2^1(2-1) \cdot 7^0(7-1).$$

The corresponding values of N are 13, 26, 21, 42, 36, and 28, and each of these integers has exactly 12 integers (unity included) less than itself with which it has no common factor except unity.

Care is required in solving III; the essential facts often escape us before they can be captured. It was previously stated that a number like $b = 14 = 2 \cdot 7$ cannot be put into the form $p_1^{a_1}(p_1 - 1)$ or a repeated product of several such p's. A few other impossible values are shown in Table 44.

TABLE 44

IMPOSSIBLE VALUES OF $\phi(N)$

14	62	90	122	152
26	68	94	124	154
34	74	98	134	158
38	76	114	142	170
50	86	118	146	174

If a given number b is: (1) twice a power of a prime, $2p^a$, and (2) p is greater than 3, and (3) if $2p^a + 1$ is composite, then b cannot be put into the form of Formula B. This is only one of many impossible forms. The formulation of some of these is left to the reader.†

It will be interesting and somewhat brain-wracking to work out an unbound set of rules as required in I and II. After the reader has done this he may wish to solve† the following five problems, where $b = \phi(N)$ is given and N is to be found: $b = 1$; 72; 144; 480; 3600 = $2^3 \cdot 3 \cdot 5^2 \cdot 11$.

R. D. Carmichael once tabulated all the numbers, N, for given values of b from 1 to 1000, which are solutions of $\phi(N) = b$. As might be expected, this involved a considerable amount of labor; for example, there are 47 values of N for which $\phi(N) = 960$. For b not in excess of 50, the greatest number of solutions is obtained from 48, which has 11. There are only 21 possible values of b below 50 that have solutions, so that the computation of a table of such solutions for b not exceeding this limit should not be very laborious and the reader may wish to try it.†

* * *

The integers less than a given number N which are prime to it may, of course, be either primes or composites. But in a few cases these numbers are all primes—namely, for $N = 2, 3, 4, 6, 8, 12, 18, 24,$ and 30. For example, the $\phi(18) = 6$ integers less than 18 and prime to it are 1, 5, 7, 11, 13, 17. This relation is remarkable in that these nine numbers are the only ones for which it holds; no integer larger than 30 can possess this property.

*   *   *

There are many striking relations involving the ϕ function, some of them of great complexity. A rather surprising one states that the *sum* of the integers less than n and prime to it is equal to $(n/2)[\phi(N)]$, provided n exceeds unity. To prove this, observe that if I is an integer prime to n, then $n-I$ must be another such integer. The sum of these two integers is n. But there are $[\phi(N)]/2$ *pairs* of these integers, hence the sum of all these pairs must be $n[\phi(N)/2]$ or $(n/2)[\phi(N)]$.

*   *   *

The equations $k \cdot \phi(x) = x+1$ and $k \cdot \phi(x) = x-1$ are interesting. Consider the former first. When $k = 1$, we have $\phi(x) = x+1$, and since $\phi(x)$ can never exceed x this is impossible. When $k = 2$, we have $2 \cdot \phi(x) = x+1$, which has the solution $x = 3$, besides others as shown in Table 45. When $k = 3$, there is a solution $x = 2$. But if there is another solution for this value of k it must be the product of at least 32 distinct prime factors!

TABLE 45

SOLUTIONS OF $k \cdot \phi(x) = x+1$

k	x	$x+1$	$\phi(x)$
1	No solution	—	—
2	3	2^2	2^1
2	$3 \cdot 5$	2^4	2^3
2	$3 \cdot 5 \cdot 17$	2^8	2^7
2	$3 \cdot 5 \cdot 17 \cdot 257$	2^{16}	2^{15}
2	$3 \cdot 5 \cdot 17 \cdot 353 \cdot 929$	$2^{18} \cdot 11 \cdot 29$	$2^{17} \cdot 11 \cdot 29$
2	$3 \cdot 5 \cdot 17 \cdot 257 \cdot 65537$	2^{32}	2^{31}
2	$3 \cdot 5 \cdot 17 \cdot 353 \cdot 929 \cdot 83623937$	$2^{36} \cdot 11^2 \cdot 29^2$	$2^{35} \cdot 11^2 \cdot 29^2$
2	Product of at least 7 different primes	—	—
3	2	3	1
3	Product of at least 32 distinct primes	—	—

Now consider $k \cdot \phi(x) = x-1$. When $k = 1$, then any prime, x, is a solution of the equation, since $\phi(x)$ is then always equal to $x-1$.

Formula B makes it clearly evident that when x is composite, $\phi(x)$ must differ from x by more than unity; hence, there cannot be a composite value of x satisfying $1 \cdot \phi(x) = x - 1$.

When k is greater than 1, x must, of course, be composite since, for a prime, $\phi(x)$ is exactly equal to $x - 1$.   But if x is composite it must be the product of at least seven distinct primes.   No solution is known, however.   It is suspected that a solution for a composite number x is impossible, but a proof of this involves difficulties of the same order as that for the hitherto undemonstrated fact that there are no odd perfect numbers.

When $k = 3$, a solution x must again contain at least 32 distinct prime factors.   These facts are summarized in Table 46.

TABLE 46

Solutions of $k \cdot \phi(x) = x - 1$

k	x	$x-1$	$\phi(x)$
1	Any prime	$x-1$	$x-1$
2	Must be product of at least 7 primes; no known solution	—	—
3	Must be product of at least 32 primes; no known solution	—	—

BIBLIOGRAPHY

Carmichael, R. D.   *Theory of Numbers and Diophantine Analysis*.   New York: Dover Publications, Inc., 1959.

————.   "Notes on the Simplex Theory of Numbers," *Bulletin of the American Mathematical Society*, **15** (1908–1909), 217.

————.   "A Table of Values of m Corresponding to Given Values of $\phi(m)$," *American Journal of Mathematics*, **30** (1908), 394.

————.   "Note on Euler's ϕ Function," *Bulletin of the American Mathematical Society*, **28** (1922), 109.

Dickson, L. E.   *History of the Theory of Numbers*.   3 vols.   New York: Chelsea Publishing Co., 1950.

Klee, V. L.   "On a Conjecture of Carmichael," *Bulletin of the American Mathematical Society*, **54** (1948), 53.

Lehmer, D. H.   "On Euler's Totient Function," *Bulletin of the American Mathematical Society*, **38** (1932), 745.

CHAPTER XIII

QUEER LOGS—
BACK TO THE PRIMITIVE

It is with a real thrill that one discovers that logarithms, which might be supposed to belong exclusively to the continuous domain, have a counterpart in the discrete domain of number theory. In $10^2 = 100$, 2 is the "log" of 100, and in $10^3 = 1000$, 3 is the log of 1000. For the same "base" 10, the log of some intermediate number, say 500, lies between 2 and 3; its value to five decimal places is 2.69897. It is difficult at first to conceive how integer counterparts of such decimal approximations can exist. Nevertheless, to a given modulus, any integer can be represented exactly by a power of a *suitable* integral base, the exponent or "logarithm" in every case being an integer. It is interesting to learn something about such logarithms—in number theory they are called "indices."

Suppose we select some arbitrary base such as 2 and see how to express all integers, modulo 13 as powers of 2. We have $2^{12} \equiv 1$, $2^1 \equiv 2$, $2^4 \equiv 3$, $2^2 \equiv 4$, $2^9 \equiv 5$, $2^5 \equiv 6$, $2^{11} \equiv 7$, $2^3 \equiv 8$, $2^8 \equiv 9$, $2^{10} \equiv 10, 2^7 \equiv 11, 2^6 \equiv 12$. This is a complete table, modulo 13 of indices and numbers to the base 2. There has been no repetition of index or number; thus a one-to-one correspondence exists between them. Is this always true? Let us select the base 3 instead. Then $3^1 \equiv 3$, $3^2 \equiv 9$, $3^3 \equiv 1$, $3^4 \equiv 3$, $3^5 \equiv 9$, $3^6 \equiv 1$, $3^7 \equiv 3$, $3^8 \equiv 9$, $3^9 \equiv 1$, $3^{10} \equiv 3$, $3^{11} \equiv 9$, $3^{12} \equiv 1$. Here, although the indices ranged from 1 to 12, only the integers (residues) 1, 3, and 9 were represented. For a "complete residue system" to a given modulus, only certain bases can be used; these are any one of the primitive roots of the modulus. It will be recalled that a primitive root, g, of a given prime modulus, p, is an integer for which the least exponent, e, in $g^e \equiv 1 \mod p$ is $p-1$. Thirteen has only the four primitive roots, 2, 6, 7, and 11, and the powers of each form a complete residue system as shown in Table 47. Any one of the four tables can be used for a problem in indices just as the common or natural bases 10 or e can be used for a problem in logarithms. But whereas any other base would serve for a logarithm problem, only one of the four primitive roots of 13 can serve for an indices problem.

TABLE 47

INDICES TABLES, MODULO 13

Number (or Residue)	Table A Primitive Root 2	Table B Primitive Root 6	Table C Primitive Root 7	Table D Primitive Root 11
1	12 (or 0)	12 (or 0)	12 (or 0)	12 (or 0)
2	1	5	11	7
3	4	8	8	4
4	2	10	10	2
5	9	9	3	3
6	5	1	7	11
7	11	7	1	5
8	3	3	9	9
9	8	4	4	8
10	10	2	2	10
11	7	11	5	1
12	6	6	6	6

To solve a problem in multiplication using logarithms, we add the logs of the numbers to be multiplied. A similar procedure is followed with indices. For a prime modulus, p, the greatest index for any number is $p-1$; therefore, if the sum of the indices, resulting from such a multiplication problem, exceeds $p-1$, multiples of $p-1$ can be discarded without affecting the solution.

We shall solve a simple problem in logarithms and one in indices, arbitrarily selecting the common logs, that is, to base 10 and the indices of the primitive root 11, modulo 13.

Solve $6 \cdot 8 \cdot 9 = x$ Solve $6 \cdot 8 \cdot 9 \equiv x$ mod 13

$\log_{10} 6 = 0.77815$ $\text{ind}_{11} 6 = 11$

$\log_{10} 8 = 0.90309$ $\text{ind}_{11} 8 = 9$

$\log_{10} 9 = 0.95424$ $\text{ind}_{11} 9 = 8$

Adding, $\log_{10} x = 2.63548.$ Adding, $\text{ind}_{11} x = 28 \equiv 4$ mod 12

$x = 432$ $x \equiv 3$ mod 13

The logarithm problem requires little explanation; we find x by looking up the anti-log of 2.63548. In the congruence problem, the index of x is 28, that is, $x \equiv 11^{28}$ mod 13. But since $11^{12} \equiv 1$ mod 13 by Fermat's theorem, we can drop multiples of 12 from the exponent, as that is equivalent to dividing by unity, thus leaving the result unchanged, modulo 13. Hence $x \equiv 11^4$ mod 13, and by the inverse operation in Table D analogous to finding the anti-log of 2.63548, we find the residue 3 corresponding to the index 4; or $6 \cdot 8 \cdot 9 \equiv 3$ mod 13.

In logarithms, we change from base a to base b by the formula:

$$\log_b N = \log_a N \cdot \log_b a.$$

Analogously,

$$\text{ind}_b N \equiv \text{ind}_a N \cdot \text{ind}_b a \quad \text{mod } (p-1).$$

By means of this formula we can find the indices of Table 47A, for instance, from the indices of Table 47B:

$$\text{ind}_2 N \equiv \text{ind}_6 N \cdot \text{ind}_2 6 \equiv (\text{ind}_6 N) \cdot 5 \quad \text{mod } 12.$$

Hence, the indices of the table utilizing 2 as base may be found from those using 6 as a base by multiplying the latter by 5. This gives 60, 25, 40, 50, 45, 5, 35, 15, 20, 10, 55, 30, congruent respectively to 12 (or 0), 1, 4, 2, 9, 5, 11, 3, 8, 10, 7, 6, modulo 12. These are the indices of Table A.

By means of the table of indices we can solve a power congruence such as $4 \cdot 5^x \equiv 9$ mod 13 in a manner analogous to that in which exponential equations are solved by logarithms. Taking indices, arbitrarily, to base 2, $\text{ind}_2 4 + x \cdot \text{ind}_2 5 \equiv \text{ind}_2 9$ (mod 12). Then, since $\text{ind}_2 5 = 9$, we have: $9x \equiv \text{ind}_2 9 - \text{ind}_2 4 \equiv 8 - 2 \equiv 6$ (mod 12). Then $3x \equiv 2$ (mod 4) (obtained by dividing both terms of the congruence and also the modulus, by 3). Finally $x \equiv 2$ (mod 4), so that $4 \cdot 5^2 = 100$ is congruent to 9 mod 13, 2 being the least value of x for which this is true. Other values would be $x = 6, 10, 14 \ldots (4K+2)$.

Many other types of problems can be solved by indices.

*   *   *

C. G. J. Jacobi, one of the mathematical luminaries of the early nineteenth century, constructed tables of residues and indices of all primes less than 1000, publishing them under the title *Canon Arithmeticus*. Allan Cunningham in his *Haupt-Exponents, Residue Indices, Primitive Roots and Standard Congruences* tabulated the *least* positive and the least negative primitive root of all primes to 25409. The *least* exponent, e, for which $b^e \equiv 1 \bmod p$, where b and p are given numbers, is called "the exponent to which b belongs mod p" or simply the "Haupt-Exponent of b mod p." The quotient of $p-1$ divided by the Haupt-Exponent is called the "residue-index." Thus since 3 is the least exponent, e, for which $9^e \equiv 1$ (mod 13), 3 is the Haupt-Exponent and 4 the residue index of 9 (mod 13).

It is frequently convenient to know the values of the Haupt-Exponents and the residue-indices of various bases to different moduli. An indication of what has been done in this direction may be obtained by referring to Cunningham's book mentioned above, wherein he tabulates, to all prime moduli up to 25409, both the residue index and the Haupt-Exponent for the bases 2, 3, 5, 6, 7, 10, 11, and 12. Reference to a similar table computed by Shanks for base 10 and prime moduli to 120000 has previously been made in Chapter X.

The author once calculated as a pastime the Haupt-Exponents of all integers from 1 to 100 for all prime moduli and their powers, less than 100. These are given in Table 48. Looking, for example, at the column headed 13, we find the Haupt-Exponents for the consecutive integers starting with unity. Thus, for the integer 9, the exponent is 3; for the integers 6 and 7, the exponent is 12, so that 6 and 7 are primitive roots of 13. For bases, "a," greater than 12, the same exponents apply as for those less than 12 to which the larger numbers are respectively congruent, modulo 13. For example,

$$9^3 \equiv 22^3 \equiv 35^3 \equiv 1,$$

all modulo 13. There are no entries in the table for bases which are not prime to the modulus, since in that case the remainder cannot be unity.

From Table 48 the *least* primitive root of the 24 primes from 3 to 97 may be obtained. They are listed in Table 49. It is rather remarkable that 2 appears as a primitive root so often—twelve times.

From Table 48 *composite* moduli for which Fermat's theorem holds for *any* selected base "a" can be easily obtained. For instance, suppose one wanted $17^{x-1} \equiv 1 \bmod x$, where x is a composite number. Look along the row for $a = 17$ and find any two numbers whose L.C.M. leaves a remainder of 1 when divided into the product of the two *column headings* under which these numbers are found. Thus along the line for $a = 17$, the numbers 4 and 2 under column headings

TABLE 48

Exponents to Which a Belongs, mod p and mod p^n

a	$p=$ 97	89	83	3^4	79	73	71	67	2^6	61	59	53	7^2	47	43	41	37	2^5	31	29	3^3	5^2	23	19	17	2^4	13	11	3^2	2^3	7	5	2^2	3	2	a
1	1	1	1	1	1	1	1	1	1	1	1	1	1	1	1	1	1	1	1	1	1	1	1	1	1	1	1	1	1	1	1	1	1	1	1	1
2	48	11	82	54	39	9	35	66	–	60	58	52	21	23	14	20	36	–	5	28	18	20	11	18	8	–	12	10	6	–	3	4	–	2	–	2
3	48	88	41	–	78	12	35	22	16	10	29	52	42	23	42	8	18	8	30	28	–	20	11	18	16	4	3	5	–	2	6	4	2	–	1	3
4	24	11	41	27	39	9	35	33	–	30	29	26	21	23	7	10	18	–	5	14	9	10	11	9	4	–	6	5	3	–	3	2	–	1	–	4
5	96	44	82	54	39	72	5	22	16	30	29	52	42	46	42	20	36	8	3	14	18	–	22	9	16	4	4	5	6	2	6	–	1	2	1	5
6	12	88	82	–	78	36	35	33	–	60	58	26	14	23	3	40	4	–	6	14	–	5	11	9	16	–	12	10	–	–	2	1	–	–	–	6
7	96	88	41	27	78	24	70	66	8	60	29	26	–	23	6	40	9	4	15	7	9	4	22	3	16	2	12	10	3	2	–	4	2	1	1	7
8	16	11	82	18	13	3	35	22	–	20	58	52	7	23	14	20	12	–	5	28	6	20	11	6	8	–	4	10	2	–	1	4	–	2	–	8
9	24	44	41	–	39	6	35	11	8	5	29	26	21	23	21	4	9	4	15	14	–	10	11	9	8	2	3	5	–	1	3	2	1	–	1	9
10	96	44	41	9	13	8	35	33	–	60	58	13	42	46	21	5	3	–	15	28	3	–	22	18	16	–	6	2	1	–	6	–	–	1	–	10
11	48	22	41	54	39	72	70	66	16	4	58	26	21	46	7	40	6	8	30	28	18	5	22	3	16	4	12	–	6	2	3	1	2	2	1	11
12	16	8	41	–	26	36	35	66	–	15	29	52	42	23	42	40	9	–	30	4	–	20	11	6	16	–	2	1	–	–	6	4	–	–	–	12
13	96	88	82	27	39	72	70	66	16	3	58	13	14	46	21	40	36	8	30	14	9	20	11	18	4	4	–	10	3	2	2	4	1	1	1	13
14	96	88	82	54	26	72	10	11	–	6	58	52	–	23	21	8	12	–	15	28	18	10	22	18	16	–	1	5	6	–	–	2	–	2	–	14
15	96	88	82	–	26	72	35	11	4	15	29	13	7	46	21	40	36	2	10	28	–	–	22	18	8	2	12	5	–	2	1	–	2	–	1	15
16	12	11	41	27	39	9	35	33	–	15	29	13	21	23	7	5	9	–	5	7	9	5	11	9	2	–	3	5	3	–	3	1	–	1	–	16
17	96	44	41	18	26	24	10	33	4	60	29	26	42	23	21	40	36	2	30	4	6	20	22	9	–	1	6	10	2	1	6	4	1	2	1	17
18	16	44	82	–	13	18	35	66	–	60	58	52	3	23	42	5	36	–	15	28	–	4	11	2	1	–	4	10	–	–	3	4	–	–	–	18
19	32	88	82	9	39	36	35	33	16	30	29	52	6	46	42	40	36	8	15	28	3	10	22	–	8	4	12	10	1	2	6	2	2	1	1	19
20	32	44	82	54	39	72	7	66	–	5	29	52	14	46	42	20	36	–	15	7	18	–	22	1	16	–	12	5	6	–	2	–	–	2	–	20
21	96	44	41	–	13	24	70	33	16	12	29	52	–	23	7	20	18	8	30	28	–	5	22	18	4	4	4	2	3	2	–	1	2	–	1	21
22	4	22	82	27	13	8	70	11	–	15	29	52	7	46	14	40	36	–	30	14	9	20	2	18	16	–	3	–	3	–	1	4	–	1	–	22
23	96	88	41	54	3	36	14	33	8	20	58	4	21	23	21	10	12	4	10	7	18	20	–	9	16	2	6	1	6	2	3	4	2	2	1	23
24	24	88	82	–	6	12	35	11	–	20	58	13	42	23	21	40	36	–	30	7	–	2	1	9	16	–	12	10	–	–	6	2	–	–	–	24
25	48	22	41	27	39	36	5	11	8	15	29	26	21	23	21	10	18	4	3	7	9	–	11	9	8	2	2	5	3	1	3	–	1	1	1	25
26	96	88	41	6	39	72	14	33	–	60	29	52	42	46	42	40	3	–	6	28	2	1	11	3	8	–	–	5	2	–	6	1	–	2	–	26
27	16	88	41	–	26	4	35	22	16	10	29	52	14	23	14	8	6	8	10	28	–	20	11	6	16	4	1	5	–	2	–	4	2	–	1	27
28	32	88	41	3	78	72	70	66	–	20	29	13	–	23	42	40	18	–	15	2	1	20	22	9	16	–	12	10	1	–	1	4	–	1	–	28
29	96	88	41	54	78	72	35	3	16	12	29	26	7	46	42	40	12	8	10	–	18	10	11	9	16	4	3	10	6	2	3	2	2	2	1	29
30	32	88	41	–	78	24	7	6	–	60	58	4	3	46	42	40	18	–	2	1	–	5	22	3	4	–	6	10	–	–	6	–	–	–	–	30
31	48	88	41	27	39	72	70	66	2	60	58	52	6	46	21	10	4	2	–	28	9	5	11	6	16	2	4	5	3	2	3	1	2	1	1	31
32	48	11	82	54	39	9	7	66	–	12	58	52	21	23	14	4	36	–	5	28	18	4	11	18	8	–	12	2	6	–	6	4	–	2	–	32
33	8	88	41	–	26	72	70	33	2	20	58	52	42	46	42	20	9	1	30	14	–	20	22	18	2	1	12	–	–	1	6	4	1	–	1	33
34	32	4	82	27	78	72	14	66	–	5	58	52	14	23	42	40	9	–	5	14	9	10	22	18	–	–	4	1	3	–	2	2	–	1	–	34
35	3	88	82	18	78	36	70	33	16	60	29	52	–	46	7	40	36	8	3	14	6	5	11	9	1	4	3	10	2	2	1	–	2	2	1	35
36	6	44	41	–	39	18	35	33	–	30	29	13	7	23	3	20	2	–	6	7	–	20	11	9	8	–	6	5	–	–	3	1	–	–	–	36
37	96	8	41	9	78	9	7	3	16	20	58	26	21	23	6	5	–	8	6	28	3	20	22	2	8	4	12	5	1	2	6	4	1	1	1	37
38	96	88	41	54	13	36	35	6	–	20	58	26	42	46	21	8	1	–	15	14	18	20	22	–	16	–	2	5	6	–	6	4	–	2	–	38
39	96	11	82	–	78	72	14	33	8	30	58	52	21	46	14	20	36	4	5	28	–	10	11	1	16	2	–	10	–	2	3	2	2	–	1	39
40	96	44	41	27	39	72	35	11	–	12	58	26	42	46	21	2	18	–	15	28	9	–	22	18	16	–	1	10	3	–	6	–	–	1	–	40
41	96	88	41	54	26	18	14	66	8	10	29	52	14	46	7	–	18	4	15	4	18	5	11	18	8	2	12	10	6	2	2	1	2	2	1	41
42	32	44	82	–	39	72	70	22	–	15	58	13	–	23	2	1	36	–	30	14	–	20	22	9	8	–	3	5	–	–	–	4	–	–	–	42
43	24	88	82	27	78	24	35	22	16	60	58	26	7	46	–	20	9	8	30	28	9	4	22	9	8	4	6	2	3	2	1	4	1	1	1	43
44	48	44	41	18	39	72	70	66	–	60	58	13	21	46	1	8	9	–	30	28	6	10	22	9	16	–	4	–	2	–	3	2	–	2	–	44
45	32	11	82	–	39	72	7	22	16	30	29	52	42	46	14	10	12	8	15	7	–	–	2	3	16	4	12	1	–	2	6	–	2	–	1	45
46	32	88	82	9	13	4	10	66	–	30	29	13	21	2	42	20	9	–	10	4	3	5	–	6	16	–	12	10	1	–	3	1	–	1	–	46
47	8	44	82	54	78	72	70	33	4	3	58	13	42	–	7	40	3	2	5	28	18	20	1	9	4	2	4	5	6	2	6	4	2	2	1	47

a	97	89	83	34	79	73	71	67	28	61	59	53	47	43	41	37	...	a
48																		48
49																		49
50																		50
51																		51
52																		52
53																		53
54																		54
55																		55
56																		56
57																		57
58																		58
59																		59
60																		60
61																		61
62																		62
63																		63
64																		64
65																		65
66																		66
67																		67
68																		68
69																		69
70																		70
71																		71
72																		72
73																		73
74																		74
75																		75
76																		76
77																		77
78																		78
79																		79
80																		80
81																		81
82																		82
83																		83
84																		84
85																		85
86																		86
87																		87
88																		88
89																		89
90																		90
91																		91
92																		92
93																		93
94																		94
95																		95
96																		96
97																		97
98																		98
99																		99
100																		100

5 and 3^2 respectively have an L.C.M. of 4, and 4 divided into $5 \cdot 3^2 = 45$ leaves a remainder of 1. Therefore $17^4 \equiv 1$ mod 45, and therefore $17^{44} \equiv 1$ mod 45 as required.

The reason for this rule is not difficult to understand. The table gives the least exponent e in $a^e \equiv 1$ mod p for every selection of a and p. If we find for a selected "a" that $a^{e_1} \equiv 1$ mod p_1 and $a^{e_2} \equiv 1$ mod p_2, then the L.C.M., e, of e_1 and e_2 may be used as an exponent in each congruence, so that $a^e \equiv 1$ mod p_1 and $a^e \equiv 1$ mod p_2. Then since p_1 and p_2 are prime to each other, the congruence must hold for the modulus $p_1 p_2$ so that $a^e \equiv 1$ mod $p_1 p_2$. The congruence will still hold for any exponent which is a multiple of e, say ke. If now e leaves a remainder of 1 when divided into $p_1 p_2$, we have $p_1 p_2 - 1$ exactly divisible by e, that is $p_1 p_2 - 1 = ke$. We have, finally $a^{ke} = a^{p_1 p_2 - 1} \equiv 1$ mod $p_1 p_2$, as required.

It may be noted that the composite modulus may consist of more than two primes. Thus, for $a = 41$, we can select 2, 1, and 2 headed by the primes 3, 5, and 7. The L.C.M. of 2, 1, and 2 is 2, which leaves a remainder of unity when divided into $3 \cdot 5 \cdot 7 = 105$. Therefore $41^2 \equiv 1$ mod 105 and also $41^{104} \equiv 1$ mod 105.

TABLE 49

Least Primitive Roots for Primes, 3 to 97

Prime $= p$	Least Primitive Root $= g$	Prime $= p$	Least Primitive Root $= g$	Prime $= p$	Least Primitive Root $= g$
3	2	29	2	61	2
5	2	31	3	67	2
7	3	37	2	71	7
11	2	41	6	73	5
13	2	43	3	79	3
17	3	47	5	83	2
19	2	53	2	89	3
23	5	59	2	97	5

*   *   *

If, for some given modulus, we group all those bases having like Haupt-Exponents, we obtain a peculiar relation. We find that the *number* of bases having a given Haupt-Exponent, e, is $\phi(e)$. Table 50 illustrates this property for the modulus 13.

TABLE 50

HAUPT-EXPONENTS, e, TO MODULUS 13

$$e =$$

1	2	3	4	6	12
$1^1 \equiv 1$	$12^2 \equiv 1$	$3^3 \equiv 1$	$5^4 \equiv 1$	$4^6 \equiv 1$	$2^{12} \equiv 1$
		$9^3 \equiv 1$	$8^4 \equiv 1$	$10^6 \equiv 1$	$6^{12} \equiv 1$
					$7^{12} \equiv 1$
					$11^{12} \equiv 1$

It is evident from the last column of Table 50 that a prime modulus, p, has $\phi(p-1) = \phi[\phi(p)]$ primitive roots.

*   *   *

Composite numbers, also, can have primitive roots. We called x a primitive root of a prime, p, if the Haupt-Exponent of x is $p-1 = \phi(p)$. If the modulus m is either *composite* or *prime*, we say that x is a primitive root of m if, in the congruence $x^{\phi(m)} \equiv 1 \bmod m$, $\phi(m)$ is the Haupt-Exponent of x. It can be shown that primitive roots of *composite* moduli can exist only when the modulus is a power of an odd prime, twice such a power, or for the trivial case $m = 4$, which has the single primitive root 3.

From the definitions given in Chapter XII we have that

$$\phi(p^n) = p^{n-1}(p-1)$$

and

$$\phi(2p^n) = \phi(2)\phi(p^n) = 1 \cdot p^{n-1}(p-1),$$

identical results. For a number like $49 = 7^2$ we have:

$$\phi(7^2) = 7^{2-1}(7-1) = 42.$$

Referring to the column headed 7^2 of Table 48, we find that the exponent 42 applies to the bases 3, 5, 10, 12, 17, 24, 26, 33, 38, 40, 45, 47 so that all of these integers are primitive roots of 49. There are 12 of them because of the property that the number of bases belonging to an exponent e is $\phi(e)$ and

$$\phi(42) = \phi(2) \cdot \phi(3) \cdot \phi(7) = 1 \cdot 2 \cdot 6 = 12.$$

*   *   *

There are many other interesting properties of primitive roots, only a few of which can be mentioned here.

1. The product of all the primitive roots of a prime greater than 3 leaves a remainder of unity when divided by the prime. Thus, the product of the primitive roots 2, 6, 7, and 11 of 13 is 924, which is congruent to 1 modulo 13.

2. If p is a prime and if $p-1$ is divisible by a square, then the sum of the primitive roots is exactly divisible by p; but if $p-1$ is not divisible by a square, then the sum of the primitive roots leaves a remainder of plus or minus one according as $p-1$ has an even or an odd number of prime factors. Since $13-1 = 12$, which is divisible by the square 4, we have $2+6+7+11 = 26$, which is divisible by 13. For the prime 11, however, since $11-1 = 10$ is not divisible by a square, and since 10 is composed of an even number of primes, the sum of the primitive roots of 11, $2+6+7+8 = 23$, leaves a remainder of $+1$ mod 11.

3. The integer 3 is always a primitive root of primes of the form $2^{2^n}+1$ (except for the prime 3, where $n = 0$). For example, 3 is a primitive root of 5, 17, 257, 65537, corresponding to $n = 1, 2, 3, 4$.

4. The integer 2 is a primitive root of all primes of the form $8n+3$ provided $4n+1$ is a prime. Thus for $n = 1$, both 11 and 5 are primes, hence 2 is a primitive root of 11. The next admissible value for n is 7, and 2 is a primitive root of 59.

5. The integer 2 is a primitive root of all primes of the form $4q+1$ provided q is a prime. For $q = 3$, $4q+1 = 13$, and 2 is a primitive root of 13. Also for $q = 7$, $4q+1 = 29$, which has 2 as a primitive root.

6. If 2^m+1 is a prime, p, every quadratic non-residue of p (see Chapter XIX) is a primitive root of p. Taking $m = 4$, $p = 17$, a prime, whose quadratic non-residues are 3, 5, 6, 7, 10, 11, 12, 14. Table 48 shows that these are all primitive roots of 17.

7. Every prime $2^{4n}+1$ has the primitive root 7. Taking $n = 1$, we have that 17 has the primitive root 7 as noted above.

8. If we have one primitive root, g, mod p, then each of the $\phi(p-1)$ numbers co-prime to $p-1$ may be used as exponents of g to obtain powers congruent, mod p, to the remaining primitive roots. For example, 3 is a primitive root of 17 and the $\phi(16) = 8$ numbers co-prime to 16 are 1, 3, 5, 7, 9, 11, 13, 15. Hence 3^1, 3^3, 3^5, 3^7, 3^9, 3^{11}, 3^{13}, and 3^{15}, congruent respectively to 3, 10, 5, 11, 14, 7, 12, 6, mod 17, are all primitive roots of 17.

BIBLIOGRAPHY

Cunningham, A. *Haupt-Exponents, Residue Indices, Primitive Roots.* London: F. Hodgson, 1922.

Jacobi, C. G. J. *Canon Arithmeticus.* Berlin, 1839.

Reid, L. W. *Elements of the Theory of Algebraic Numbers.* Baltimore: Johns Hopkins Press, 1946.

Shanks, W. "On the Number of Figures in the Period of the Reciprocal of Every Prime Number Below 20000," *Proceedings of the Royal Society of London,* **22** (1873), 200.

———. "Given the Number of Figures (Not Exceeding 100) in the Reciprocal of a Prime Number, to Determine the Prime Itself," *Proceedings of the Royal Society of London,* **22** (1873), 381.

———. "On the Number of Figures in the Reciprocal of Every Prime Between 20000 and 30000," *Proceedings of the Royal Society of London,* **22** (1873), 384.

Tchebycheff, P. L. *Theorie der Congruenzen.* Berlin, 1889.

CHAPTER XIV

THE ETERNAL TRIANGLE

PRACTICALLY everyone knows that $3^2 + 4^2 = 5^2$, the simplest application of the Pythagorean theorem, which states that the sum of the squares on the legs of a right-angled triangle is equal to the square on the hypotenuse. But comparatively few know 5, 12, and 13, which also satisfy the relation without being proportional to 3, 4, and 5. Still fewer people could give the sides of a third "Pythagorean triangle," dissimilar to the two mentioned, for example, 7, 24, and 25.

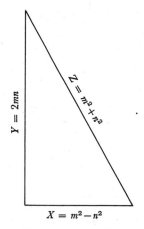

FIG. 3. PYTHAGOREAN TRIANGLE

Triangles with integral sides have been the subject of much recreational material. Finding two integers the sum of whose squares is a square integer, is but one of many interesting problems involving these figures. Except for the squares of 1 and 2, it is always possible to find at least one square which, added to a given square, yields a sum which is a square. It is to be noted, however, that this is not true for the hypotenuse; an integer must be of a certain type in order to be the hypotenuse of an integral right triangle.

The formulas that will give integral sides of a right-angled triangle

have been known since the time of Diophantus and the early Greeks.
They are:

$$\text{One leg:} \quad X = m^2 - n^2$$
$$\text{Second leg:} \quad Y = 2mn \qquad \text{(Formula 1)}$$
$$\text{Hypotenuse:} \quad Z = m^2 + n^2.$$

The numbers m and n are integers which may be *arbitrarily* selected.
Table 51 gives a few examples.

TABLE 51

"PYTHAGOREAN" OR INTEGRAL RIGHT TRIANGLES

Example	m	n	$X = m^2 - n^2$	$Y = 2mn$	$Z = m^2 + n^2$
1	2	1	3	4	5
2	3	2	5	12	13
3	5	2	21	20	29
4	9	6	45	108	117
5	5	3	16	30	34
6	4	3	7	24	25
7	6	1	35	12	37
8	18	17	35	612	613
9	9	8	17	144	145
10	4	1	15	8	17

The numbers m and n are sometimes called *generating* numbers.   If
we take *consecutive pairs* of integers for the values of m and n, we obtain
Table 52.   Here the larger leg, Y, and the hypotenuse, Z, are
consecutive integers.

TABLE 52

PYTHAGOREAN TRIANGLES WITH LEG AND HYPOTENUSE CONSECUTIVE

Generating Numbers		Sides of Pythagorean Triangle		
m	n	X	Y	Z
2	1	3	4	5
3	2	5	12	13
4	3	7	24	25
5	4	9	40	41
6	5	11	60	61
7	6	13	84	85

Suppose now we make the two legs, X and Y, of these triangles the generating numbers. We then obtain Table 53.

TABLE 53

PYTHAGOREAN TRIANGLES WITH HYPOTENUSE A SQUARE

Generating Numbers		Sides of Pythagorean Triangle		
m	n	X	Y	Z
4	3	7	24	$25 = 5^2$
12	5	119	120	$169 = 13^2$
24	7	527	336	$625 = 25^2$
40	9	1519	720	$1681 = 41^2$
60	11	3479	1320	$3721 = 61^2$
84	13	6887	2184	$7225 = 85^2$

Here the hypotenuse (not the square of the hypotenuse) is a perfect square. Only one side of a Pythagorean triangle *can* be a square.

Now select from Table 52 the values of Z and Y (instead of X and Y) as generating numbers. This gives us Table 54. Here the smallest side, X, is a square.

TABLE 54

PYTHAGOREAN TRIANGLES WITH SMALLEST SIDE A SQUARE

Generating Numbers		Sides of Pythagorean Triangle		
m	n	X	Y	Z
5	4	9	40	41
13	12	25	312	313
25	24	49	1200	1201
41	40	81	3280	3281

Now take for generating numbers the triangular numbers: 1, 3, 6, 10, 15, each of which is the sum of the consecutive integers starting from unity: $6 = 1+2+3$; $10 = 1+2+3+4$, etc. Here the side X is a perfect cube. Many other relations of this kind may be derived.

TABLE 55

PYTHAGOREAN TRIANGLES WITH SMALLEST SIDE A CUBE

Generating Numbers		Sides of Pythagorean Triangle		
m	n	X	Y	Z
6	3	27	36	45
10	6	64	120	136
15	10	125	300	325

*   *   *

Let us examine Formula 1 in a little more detail. If two numbers have a common factor, their product must have it as well as the sum or difference of powers of the numbers. Applying these facts to the formula, we find that if m and n contain a common factor, the three sides X, Y, Z contain this factor. Furthermore, if both m and n are even or both odd, the numbers X, Y, Z have at least the number 2 as a common factor. If it is desired to exclude those number sets X, Y, Z having a common factor, we select *either* m or n even and the other odd ("of unlike parity"), and without a common factor. The right-angled triangles with integral sides obtained with these limitations are called *primitive*, and only these need be found by the formula since any *non-primitive* can be obtained from a primitive by multiplying the respective sides by any desired integer.

To include *all* Pythagorean triangles, Formula 1 must be modified to:

$$X = K(m^2 - n^2)$$
$$Y = K(2mn) \qquad \text{(Formula 1A)}$$
$$Z = K(m^2 + n^2).$$

Without the factor K, some non-primitive triangles, such as 9, 12, 15, could not be obtained by Formula 1. But by Formula 1A, $K = 3$, $m = 2$, $n = 1$.

Formula 1 gives *all* primitive triangles but only those non-primitives whose sides have a highest common factor which is either a square or double a square. In particular, the formula gives solutions of non-primitive triangles whose sides have only the common factor 2. A remarkable transformation takes place when the common factor is twice a square. Then, by Formula 1A:

$$X = 2L^2(m^2 - n^2)$$
$$Y = 2L^2(2mn)$$
$$Z = 2L^2(m^2 + n^2).$$

These expressions can be transformed into Formula 1 as follows:

$$X = 2L^2(m^2 - n^2) = 2(Lm + Ln)(Lm - Ln) \qquad = 2MN$$
$$Y = 2L^2(2mn) \qquad = (Lm + Ln)^2 - (Lm - Ln)^2 = M^2 - N^2$$
$$Z = 2L^2(m^2 + n^2) = (Lm + Ln)^2 - (Lm - Ln)^2 = M^2 + N^2$$

where $M = Lm + Ln$ and $N = Lm - Ln$. These transformations are particularly striking when $L = 1$.

When K is a square, L^2, we have directly without any transformation:

$$X = L^2(m^2 - n^2) = m^2L^2 - n^2L^2$$
$$Y = L^2(2mn) = 2(mL \cdot nL)$$
$$Z = L^2(m^2 + n^2) = m^2L^2 + n^2L^2.$$

In Example 3 of Table 51, X, Y, and Z are relatively prime since $m = 5$, $n = 2$ have no common factor; one is even, and the other odd. In Example 4, the sides have the common factor 9 because m and n have the common factor 3. If we divide m and n by the common factor, the primitive triangle 5, 12, 13 results. In Example 5, we obtain a non-primitive triangle because, although m and n are relatively prime, they are of like parity—both odd—instead of one being even and one odd.

* * *

It may also be noted that in every triplet of integers for the sides of a primitive Pythagorean triangle, one of them is always divisible by 3 and one by 5. The product of the two legs is always divisible by 12, and the product of all three sides is always divisible by 60. These relations may be easily established by the reader.

* * *

We shall now find how, given an integer, we can find another, such that the sum of their squares is an integral square. The method of solution for odd and even integers is different.

1. When the given number A is odd:

Resolve A into any two factors. (If A is prime, these two factors are A itself and unity.) Equate the larger factor to $m+n$, the smaller to $m-n$, solve the two linear simultaneous equations in m and n, and substitute in the formulas to obtain X, Y, and Z. If primitive solutions are desired, the two factors must be taken relatively prime.

Take $A = 35$. Let $m+n = 7$, $m-n = 5$, whence $m = 6$, $n = 1$, with values of sides shown by Example 7 in Table 51. If we had taken $m+n = 35$, $m-n = 1$, we would have obtained a second solution as illustrated by Example 8.

Take $A = 17$. Here we *must* let $m+n = 17$, and $m-n = 1$, since 17 is a prime, giving the results shown in Example 9.

2. When the given number A is even:

Equate to $2mn$ and let m and n be any two integers which give the required product. If primitive solutions are desired, A must be divisible by 4 and the integers m and n must be taken relatively prime and of unlike parity. If A is not divisible by 4, a primitive solution is impossible.

Take $A = 8$. Then $2mn = 8$, $mn = 4$. Let $m = 4$, $n = 1$, resulting in the triplet 15, 8, 17 of Example 10.

Again, take $A = 12$. Then $mn = 6$. If we let $m = 6$, $n = 1$, we obtain the triplet of Example 7; if we let $m = 3$, $n = 2$, we get the triplet of Example 2.

* * *

Here are a very few of the many problems in Pythagorean triangles which have engaged the attention of many mathematicians throughout the centuries:

1. If A is a given integer, of how many *primitive* Pythagorean triangles may it be a leg?

2. If A is a given integer, of how many Pythagorean triangles, whether *primitive* or *non-primitive*, may it be a leg?

3. What form must an integer have in order to be the *hypotenuse* of a Pythagorean triangle, primitive or non-primitive, and of how many such triangles can it be a hypotenuse in each case?

4. If A is a given integer, of how many such triangles may it be *either* a leg or a hypotenuse?

5. Find a number, say the least, which can be the leg of a specified number of such triangles, for instance, 1000 of them.

6. Find a number which may be a hypotenuse alone, or again, either leg *or* hypotenuse of perhaps exactly 1,000,000 such triangles.

7. Find Pythagorean triangles whose *legs* differ by unity and derive formulas for obtaining these systematically. Find the first 100 such triangles.†

8. Find three or more Pythagorean triangles having equal areas.

9. Find the primitive Pythagorean triangle of minimum perimeter whose area just exceeds 1,000,000.†

10. Find the single primitive Pythagorean triangle each of whose three sides lies between 2000 and 3000.†

† Problems indicated by a dagger are solved in Chapter XXVI.

Then there are problems involving Pythagorean triangles whose areas have a given ratio; whose perimeter is a square; the sum of whose area and perimeter is a cube; whose area equals the hypotenuse; whose area increased by the square of the hypotenuse is a square; whose perimeter is a given number; almost *ad infinitum*.

It was natural during the course of the formulation of such problems to try to impose the apparently simple condition that the area of the Pythagorean triangle shall be a square, but here the mathematicians sought the unattainable. Fermat, the master, finally proved this impossible, that is, that $mn(m^2 - n^2)$ cannot be a square. One who has had some experience with Diophantine problems, of which the above is an example, but who had never met this area problem before, would be tempted to attack it with impunity, feeling that sooner or later some ingenious little trick will resolve it, as is so often the case. But in this instance, one gets enmeshed in unsuspected quicksands of numbers and would soon wander from his objective. It was into such a morass that Fermat flung that reassuring road of logic known as the method of infinite descent. It must be negotiated with care, however —on either side of the trail repose the bones of luckless mathematicians who essayed the path without due regard for its limitations.

Fermat's ingenious logic to *disprove* the possibility of a relation such as $mn(m^2 - n^2) = K^2$, a square, proceeds along this line: Assume that integers exist for which this relation is possible; m and n are then limited to certain forms. Substituting these forms for m and n and simplifying, an equation similar to the original one results, but for numbers, say p and q, smaller than m and n. The same process of reasoning may then be continued *indefinitely* for smaller and smaller integers. But since there are only a *finite* number of integers less than the finite integers m and n, this leads to an absurdity and proves the impossibility of the assumption. Refer to the proof of the impossibility of $x^4 + y^4 = z^4$ of Chapter XXIV for details of this method.

It is not evident why certain relations in mathematics can be proved directly, while others require such subtle reasoning as the method of infinite descent.

*   *   *

Returning to the problems previously enumerated, Examples 2 and 7 of Table 51 are two solutions of a Pythagorean triangle one of whose sides is 12. Examples 7 and 8 give two solutions for side 35. Examples 9 and 10 give two solutions for the number 17, in this case, one for a leg and the second for a hypotenuse.   The number 48 can be the leg of 10 distinct Pythagorean triangles, as shown in Figure 4.   Any number p^3q where p and q are odd primes, or $16p$ where p is an odd prime, has exactly 10 solutions; i.e., may be the leg of 10 Pythagorean triangles.   Thus, $3^3 \cdot 5 = 135$ or $16 \cdot 5 = 80$ have 10 solutions.   Table

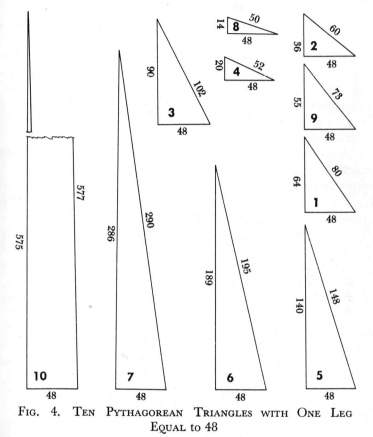

FIG. 4. TEN PYTHAGOREAN TRIANGLES WITH ONE LEG
EQUAL TO 48

6 gives the *least* number, N, which can be one side (either leg or hypotenuse) of a specified number, T, from 1 to 100, of Pythagorean triangles.

Usually the number N is a leg only; sometimes it is selected of such form as to be also the hypotenuse. This is done whenever such a selection will give a smaller value of N for a given T than if N were restricted to only a leg. All numbers cannot be hypotenuses, but any number that has at least one *prime* factor of the form $4x+1$ wil do. The column L shows the number of solutions where N is a leg only; the column H, where N is a hypotenuse also. Thus $L+H=T$ For example, the smallest number which may be the side of exactly two Pythagorean triangles is 5; in one case 5 is a side (the triple 5, 12, 13); in the second, a hypotenuse (the triplet 3, 4, 5). The actual values of the triplets are not listed.

Returning to the case where $T=10$, we have found that $48 = 16,$ is a solution, but since 48 contains only the odd prime factor 3, which is not of the form $4x+1$, it cannot be a hypotenuse. However, fo $N = 80 = 16 \cdot 5$, its odd prime factor is 5, which is of the form $4x+1$, and 80 may therefore be the hypotenuse of just one Pythagorean triangle (in the triplet 48, 64, 80). For $T = 29$, the least number 97 is the *leg* of 22 triangles and the hypotenuse of seven of them. Had we desired the *smallest* number which would be the *leg only* of 2' triangles, the answer would have been $2^{30} = 1073741824$, a numbe over a million times as large.

Table 57 gives the *least* numbers which can be the sides of the exac hundreds of triangles, while Table 58 is similar for exact half millions Try to visualize a nest of 5,000,000 right-angled triangles, all of whic have one side alike. Figures 5A, B, and C show a buzz saw and tw stars representing a total of 23 triangles, each having one side equal t 120. In 22 cases it is a leg; in one case a hypotenuse.

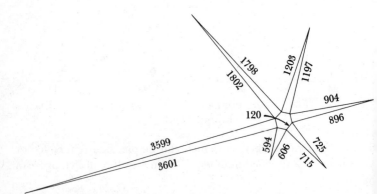

Fig. 5A. Pythagorean Triangles Having a Side Equal to 120

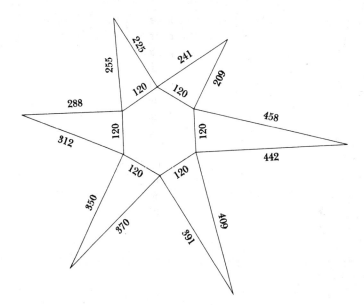

FIG. 5B. PYTHAGOREAN TRIANGLES HAVING A SIDE EQUAL
TO 120

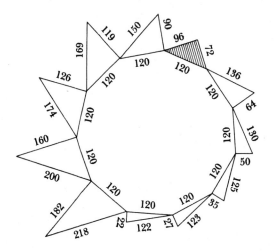

FIG. 5C. PYTHAGOREAN TRIANGLES HAVING A SIDE EQUAL
TO 120

TABLE 56

Least Number, N, Which May Be the Side of a Specified Number, T, 1 to 100, of Pythagorean Triangles

T	N	L	H	T	N	L	H
1	$3 = 3$	1	0	51	$2^4 \cdot 5^6 = 250000$	45	6
2	$5 = 5$	1	1	52	$2^4 \cdot 3^2 \cdot 7 = 1008$	52	
3	$2^4 = 16$	3	0	53	$2^4 \cdot 3^2 \cdot 5 = 720$	52	
4	$2^2 \cdot 3 = 12$	4	0	54	$2^4 \cdot 3 \cdot 5^2 = 1200$	52	
5	$3 \cdot 5 = 15$	4	1	55	$2^3 \cdot 3 \cdot 5^3 = 3000$	52	
6	$5^3 = 125$	3	3	56	$2^{19} \cdot 5 =$	55	
7	$2^3 \cdot 3 = 24$	7	0	57	$2^{12} \cdot 3^2 = 36864$	57	
8	$2^3 \cdot 5 = 40$	7	1	58	$2^7 \cdot 3 \cdot 7 = 2688$	58	
9	$3 \cdot 5^2 = 75$	7	2	59	$2^7 \cdot 3 \cdot 5 = 1920$	58	
10	$2^4 \cdot 3 = 48$	10	0	60	$2^6 \cdot 3^5 = 15552$	60	
11	$2^4 \cdot 5 = 80$	10	1	61	$2^{21} \cdot 3 =$	61	
12	$2^3 \cdot 3^2 = 72$	12	0	62	$2^3 \cdot 3^2 \cdot 7^2 = 3528$	62	
13	$2^2 \cdot 3 \cdot 7 = 84$	13	0	63	$2^{64} =$	63	
14	$2^2 \cdot 3 \cdot 5 = 60$	13	1	64	$2^3 \cdot 3^2 \cdot 5^2 = 1800$	62	
15	$2^{15} = 32768$	15	0	65	$3 \cdot 5^5 \cdot 13 = 121875$	49	1
16	$2^6 \cdot 3 = 192$	16	0	66	$2^{10} \cdot 3^3 = 27648$	66	
17	$2^4 \cdot 3^2 = 144$	17	0	67	$2^3 \cdot 3 \cdot 7 \cdot 11 = 1848$	67	
18	$2^{19} = 524288$	18	0	68	$2^3 \cdot 3 \cdot 5 \cdot 7 = 840$	67	
19	$2^7 \cdot 3 = 384$	19	0	69	$2^2 \cdot 3 \cdot 5^2 \cdot 7 = 2100$	67	
20	$2^7 \cdot 5 = 640$	19	1	70	$2^{24} \cdot 3 =$	70	
21	$3 \cdot 5^5 = 9375$	16	5	71	$2^3 \cdot 3 \cdot 5 \cdot 13 = 1560$	67	
22	$2^3 \cdot 3 \cdot 7 = 168$	22	0	72	$2^{15} \cdot 3^2 = 294912$	72	
23	$2^3 \cdot 3 \cdot 5 = 120$	22	1	73	$2^4 \cdot 3^3 \cdot 7 = 3024$	73	
24	$2^2 \cdot 3 \cdot 5^2 = 300$	22	2	74	$2^4 \cdot 3^3 \cdot 5 = 2160$	73	
25	$2^9 \cdot 3 = 1536$	25	0	75	$2^4 \cdot 5^9 =$	66	
26	$2^3 \cdot 5 \cdot 13 = 520$	22	4	76	$2^4 \cdot 3 \cdot 5^3 = 6000$	73	
27	$2^6 \cdot 3^2 = 576$	27	0	77	$2^9 \cdot 3 \cdot 5 = 7680$	76	
28	$2^{10} \cdot 3 = 3072$	28	0	78	$2^{79} =$	78	
29	$3 \cdot 5^2 \cdot 13 = 975$	22	7	79	$2^{16} \cdot 5^2 =$	77	
30	$2^{31} =$	30	0	80	$2^3 \cdot 5 \cdot 13 \cdot 17 = 8840$	67	1
31	$2^4 \cdot 3 \cdot 7 = 336$	31	0	81	$3 \cdot 5^{20} =$	61	2
32	$2^4 \cdot 3 \cdot 5 = 240$	31	1	82	$2^6 \cdot 3^2 \cdot 7 = 4032$	82	
33	$3 \cdot 5^8 =$	25	8	83	$2^6 \cdot 3^2 \cdot 5 = 2880$	82	
34	$2^2 \cdot 3 \cdot 5^3 = 1500$	31	3	84	$2^6 \cdot 3 \cdot 5^2 = 4800$	82	
35	$2^4 \cdot 5 \cdot 13 = 1040$	31	4	85	$2^{10} \cdot 3 \cdot 7 = 21504$	85	
36	$2^{37} =$	36	0	86	$2^{10} \cdot 3 \cdot 5 = 15360$	85	
37	$2^3 \cdot 3^2 \cdot 7 = 504$	37	0	87	$2^4 \cdot 3^2 \cdot 7^2 = 7056$	87	
38	$2^3 \cdot 3^2 \cdot 5 = 360$	37	1	88	$2^{30} \cdot 3 =$	88	
39	$2^3 \cdot 3 \cdot 5^2 = 600$	37	2	89	$2^4 \cdot 3^2 \cdot 5^2 = 3600$	87	
40	$2^2 \cdot 3 \cdot 7 \cdot 11 = 924$	40	0	90	$2^3 \cdot 3^2 \cdot 5^3 = 9000$	87	
41	$2^2 \cdot 3 \cdot 5 \cdot 7 = 420$	40	1	91	$2^4 \cdot 5^{11} =$	80	
42	$2^9 \cdot 3^2 = 4608$	42	0	92	$2^{19} \cdot 3^2 =$	92	
43	$2^4 \cdot 5^5 = 50000$	38	5	93	$2^9 \cdot 3^5 = 124416$	93	
44	$2^2 \cdot 3 \cdot 5 \cdot 13 = 780$	40	4	94	$2^4 \cdot 3 \cdot 7 \cdot 11 = 3696$	94	
45	$2^7 \cdot 3^3 = 3456$	45	0	95	$2^4 \cdot 3 \cdot 5 \cdot 7 = 1680$	94	
46	$2^{16} \cdot 3 = 196608$	46	0	96	$2^{97} =$	96	
47	$2^{10} \cdot 3^2 = 9216$	47	0	97	$2^7 \cdot 3^2 \cdot 7 = 8064$	97	
48	$2^7 \cdot 5^3 = 16000$	45	3	98	$2^4 \cdot 3 \cdot 5 \cdot 13 = 3120$	94	
49	$2^6 \cdot 3 \cdot 7 = 1344$	49	0	99	$2^7 \cdot 3 \cdot 5^2 = 9600$	97	
50	$2^6 \cdot 3 \cdot 5 = 960$	49	1	100	$2^{34} \cdot 3 =$	100	

TABLE 57

LEAST NUMBER, N, WHICH MAY BE THE SIDE OF A
SPECIFIED NUMBER, T, 100 TO 1000, OF PYTHAGOREAN TRIANGLES

T	N	L	H
100	$2^{34} \cdot 3 =$	100	0
200	$2^{10} \cdot 3^3 \cdot 5 = 138240$	199	1
300	$2^9 \cdot 3^2 \cdot 5^3 = 576000$	297	3
400	$2^{45} \cdot 3 \cdot 7 =$	400	0
500	$2^{19} \cdot 3 \cdot 5 \cdot 7 =$	499	1
600	$2^{601} =$	600	0
700	$2^{234} \cdot 3 =$	700	0
800	$2^{21} \cdot 3^6 \cdot 5 =$	799	1
900	$2^4 \cdot 3^2 \cdot 5^8 \cdot 7 =$	892	8
1000	$2^{10} \cdot 3^2 \cdot 5^3 \cdot 7 =$	997	3

TABLE 58

LEAST NUMBER, N, WHICH MAY BE THE SIDE OF A
SPECIFIED NUMBER, T, 500,000 TO 10,000,000, OF PYTHAGOREAN TRIANGLES

T	N	L	H
500000	$2^{19} \cdot 3^6 \cdot 5 \cdot 7^5 \cdot 11^3 \cdot 19 \cdot 23$	499999	1
1000000	$2^{9901} \cdot 5^{50}$	999950	50
1500000	$2^{180} \cdot 3^2 \cdot 5^{278} \cdot 7$	1499722	278
2000000	$2^{1000} \cdot 3^{14} \cdot 5 \cdot 7^{11}$	1999999	1
2500000	$2^{19} \cdot 3^6 \cdot 5^3 \cdot 7^5 \cdot 11^2 \cdot 19 \cdot 23 \cdot 31$	2499997	3
3000000	$2^{271} \cdot 3^6 \cdot 5^{426}$	2999574	426
3500000	$2^{19} \cdot 3^6 \cdot 5 \cdot 7^5 \cdot 11^3 \cdot 13 \cdot 19^3 \cdot 23$	3499996	4
4000000	$2^{6634} \cdot 3^{33} \cdot 7 \cdot 11$	4000000	0
4500000	$2^{19} \cdot 3^6 \cdot 5^5 \cdot 7^3 \cdot 11 \cdot 19 \cdot 23 \cdot 31 \cdot 43$	4499995	5
5000000	$2^{2325} \cdot 3^{119} \cdot 5 \cdot 7$	4999999	1
5500000	$2^{19} \cdot 3^5 \cdot 5^6 \cdot 7^3 \cdot 11 \cdot 19 \cdot 23$	5499994	6
6000000	$2^{1279} \cdot 3^9 \cdot 7^9 \cdot 11^6$	6000000	0
6500000	$2^{97} \cdot 3^8 \cdot 5^{116} \cdot 13^8$	6498020	1980
7000000	$2^{117} \cdot 3^{30} \cdot 5^{98} \cdot 7^2$	6999902	98
7500000	$2^{1230} \cdot 3^{74} \cdot 5^{11} \cdot 7$	7499989	11
8000000	$2^{79} \cdot 3^6 \cdot 5^{33} \cdot 7^6 \cdot 13 \cdot 17$	7999699	301
8500000	$2^{7210} \cdot 3^{65} \cdot 7 \cdot 11$	8500000	0
9000000	$2^{2722} \cdot 3^{1653}$	9000000	0
9500000	$2^{19} \cdot 3^9 \cdot 5^3 \cdot 7^6 \cdot 11^5 \cdot 13 \cdot 19 \cdot 23$	9499990	10
10000000	$2^{330} \cdot 3^{44} \cdot 5^5 \cdot 7^{15}$	9999995	5

Let us now find solutions of some of the problems previously given.
Suppose 60 is a given number and we wish to find in how many ways
it may be the leg of a *primitive* Pythagorean triangle.   Resolve 60 into
its elements, the product of powers of 3 primes, namely, $2^2 \cdot 3 \cdot 5$.

Then 60 may be the leg of $2^{3-1} = 4$ such triangles. Again, for $5040 = 2^4 \cdot 3^2 \cdot 5 \cdot 7$, there are 4 primes and $2^{4-1} = 8$ solutions. In general, if a number consists of n primes or their powers, it may be the leg of 2^{n-1} primitive Pythagorean triangles, with one exception: In case the given number is even but not divisible by 4, there is no solution; for example, $30 = 2 \cdot 3 \cdot 5$ cannot be the leg of a *primitive* Pythagorean triangle, nor can any number of the form $4x+2$.

* * *

To find the number of ways in which a given number, N, can be the *leg* of a Pythagorean triangle, whether primitive or non-primitive, a quite different formula is used.

If $N = 2^{a_0} p_1{}^{a_1} p_2{}^{a_2} \ldots p_n{}^{a_n}$, the number of ways N may be the leg of a Pythagorean triangle is

$$L = \frac{(2a_0-1)(2a_1+1)(2a_2+1)\ldots(2a_n+1)-1}{2}.$$

(Formula 2)

For $60 = 2^2 \cdot 3 \cdot 5$, double each exponent and add 1, except for the exponent of 2, where we subtract 1. Multiply the results together, subtract 1, and divide by 2. This gives:

$$\frac{(2\cdot2-1)(2\cdot1+1)(2\cdot1+1)-1}{2} = \frac{3\cdot3\cdot3-1}{2} = 13.$$

For $30 = 2 \cdot 3 \cdot 5$, the result is

$$\frac{(2\cdot1-1)(2\cdot1+1)(2\cdot1+1)-1}{2} = 4.$$

For $45 = 3^2 \cdot 5$, the answer is

$$\frac{(2\cdot2+1)(2\cdot1+1)-1}{2} = 7.$$

* * *

For Problem 3, only such numbers as can be put into the form $K(m^2+n^2)$ can be hypotenuses of Pythagorean triangles, primitive or otherwise. Any number which has at least one prime divisor of the form $4x+1$ can always be so expressed, such as 5, 10, 13, 15, etc. To be the hypotenuse of a *primitive* Pythagorean triangle, however, the value of K must be restricted to unity; also m and n must be co-prime integers of unlike parity.   For primitive triangles, only those integers *every one* of whose prime divisors is of the form $4x+1$ meet these requirements, such as 5, 13, 65, 85, etc.   No primes of the form $4x-1$ such as 3, 7, 11, 19, etc., may be factors of the number.   If a number N has a total of n distinct prime divisors and each is of the form $4x+1$, then N can be the hypotenuse of 2^{n-1} *primitive* Pythagorean triangles.   For example $65 = 5 \cdot 13$ may be the hypotenuse of $2^{2-1} = 2$ such triangles; $1105 = 5 \cdot 13 \cdot 17$ is the hypotenuse of $2^{3-1} = 4$ of them.   Numbers like 15, 21, and 39 will not do because at least one of the divisors, 3, is not of the required form.

If

$$N = 2^{a_0}\, p_1^{a_1}\, p_2^{a_2} \ldots p_n^{a_n}\, q_1^{b_1}\, q_2^{b_2} \ldots q_r^{b_r},$$

where the p's are primes of the form $4x-1$ and the q's those of the form $4x+1$, N cannot be the hypotenuse of even a single primitive triangle but may be the hypotenuse of

$$H = \frac{(2b_1+1)(2b_2+1)\ldots(2b_r+1)-1}{2} \qquad \text{(Formula 3)}$$

non-primitive ones.   Thus the same formula applies here as for the legs except that instead of all primes, only those of the form $4x+1$ are taken into account.

Let $N = 2^5 \cdot 3 \cdot 5 \cdot 7^5 \cdot 11^3 \cdot 13^2$.   Disregarding the primes 2, 3, 7, and 11 and considering the exponents of 5 and 13 only, we have:

$$H = \frac{(2 \cdot 1+1)(2 \cdot 2+1)-1}{2} = 7,$$

so that N may be the hypotenuse of only seven Pythagorean triangles. It may, however, be the *leg* of

$$\frac{(2 \cdot 5-1)(2 \cdot 1+1)(2 \cdot 1+1)(2 \cdot 5+1)(2 \cdot 3+1)(2 \cdot 2+1)-1}{2} = 15592$$

such triangles, making a total of 15599 ways in which it may be *either* leg or hypotenuse.   The number of *primitive* Pythagorean triangles of which N is a hypotenuse is zero, since not *every* prime divisor is of the form $4x+1$.

*   *   *

Problem 5 is the converse of Problem 2. From Formula 2 we get

$$2L+1 = (2a_0-1)(2a_1+1)(2a_2+1)\ldots(2a_n+1),$$

and this should make evident the reason for the following procedure: Given a number L, to obtain another number N, preferably the smallest, which may be the leg of L Pythagorean triangles. Resolve $2L+1$ into factors, $c_0, c_1, c_2, c_3, \ldots c_n$, not necessarily unlike nor prime. Find $a_0 = (c_0+1)/2$, $a_1 = (c_1-1)/2$, $a_2 = (c_2-1)/2$, $a_3 = (c_3-1)/2$, $\ldots a_n = (c_n-1)/2$. Then $N = 2^{a_0} p_1^{a_1} p_2^{a_2} p_3^{a_3}\ldots p_n^{a_n}$ is a solution where the primes p may be selected as one pleases. Generally, but not always, to obtain small solutions, resolve $2L+1$ into the first powers of primes like or unlike and apply decreasing values of the exponents $a_0, a_1, a_2, a_3 \ldots a_n$ to respectively increasing values of the primes $2, p_1, p_2, p_3 \ldots p_n$.

Example 1. Find a number N such that it may be the leg of 52 Pythagorean triangles. Here, $2L+1 = 105 = 7\cdot5\cdot3$. Let $a_1 = (7-1)/2 = 3$, $a_2 = (5-1)/2 = 2$, and $a_3 = (3-1)/2 = 1$; then any number, $N = p_1^3 p_2^2 p_3$, is a solution. If $p_1 = 3$, $p_2 = 5$, $p_3 = 7$, this gives $N = 3^3\cdot5^2\cdot7 = 4725$. If the primes 2, 3, and 5 are selected instead, this gives $N = 2^4\cdot3^2\cdot5 = 720$, the exponent of 2 having been increased by unity, because instead of $a_1 = 3$, we would have $a_0 = (7+1)/2 = 4$. Since 5 is one of the factors, N can also be a hypotenuse in one way, and if it were desired to exclude this possibility, 7 may be substituted for 5, giving $N = 2^4\cdot3^2\cdot7 = 1008$, the number indicated in Table 56 for $T = 52$. The smaller number 720 was not used because it may really be the *side* of 53 Pythagorean triangles, 52 of them with 720 as a leg and one with 720 as a hypotenuse. This is, in fact, the solution for $T = 53$.

A noteworthy point arises here in connection with the least solution. Resolving $2L+1$ into prime factors of the first power does not always result in the least solution even when the resulting exponents $a_0, a_1, a_2, a_3, \ldots a_n$ are assigned to the primes most favorably. Thus, for $L = 121$, $2L+1 = 243 = 3\cdot3\cdot3\cdot3\cdot3$, $a_1 = a_2 = a_3 = a_4 = 1$, $a_0 = (3+1)/2 = 2$, and $N = 2^2\cdot3\cdot5\cdot7\cdot11$ would appear to be the least solution. But if $2L+1$ were resolved into $9\cdot3\cdot3\cdot3$, then $a_0 = 5$, $a_1 = a_2 = a_3 = 1$, and $N = 2^5\cdot3\cdot5\cdot7$, which happens to be a smaller number. This will occur in rare instances when $2L+1$ is composed of many small primes. It will be possible then if $2L+1 = p_1 p_2 p_3\ldots p_k$ is the product of k primes all of the first degree, identical or different, with p_1 larger than or equal to p_2, p_2 larger than or equal to p_3, etc., and if $2^{(p_1 p_2 - p_1)/2}$ is smaller than P where P is the kth prime in the consecutive sequence of integers starting from 2. In the above example, $p_1 = p_2 = 3$; $k = 5$; $P = 11$, and 2^3 is smaller than 11.

Example 2. Let $L = 1000$. Then $2L+1 = 2001 = 29 \cdot 23 \cdot 3$, and $a_1 = 14$, $a_2 = 11$, $a_3 = 1$. The general solution is $p_1{}^{14} p_2{}^{11} p_3$; the minimum solution is $2^{15} \cdot 3^{11} \cdot 5$. If the required number may also be a hypotenuse, a much smaller solution can be obtained, as shown later and as indicated in Table 57.

*   *   *

The first part of Problem 6 is solved like Problem 5, except that the primes contributing to the required number of solutions must all have the form $4x + 1$. Powers of 2 or of primes having the form $4x - 1$ can be included *ad lib*, without affecting the result. Thus, for the least number which may be the hypotenuse of exactly 1000 Pythagorean triangles, the answer is $5^{14} \cdot 13^{11} \cdot 17$ (see Example 2 above). Of course, this number may also be a *leg* in 1000 Pythagorean triangles. Multiplying $5^{14} \cdot 13^{11} \cdot 17$ by any power of 2 or by primes of the form $4x - 1$ will not change the number of triangles of which the resulting number is a hypotenuse.

The second requirement of Problem 6, namely, to find a number which may be the *leg* or *hypotenuse* of a given number of Pythagorean triangles, is rather interesting, for by admitting just a few hypotenuse solutions, a much smaller answer can often be found than if the requirement were restricted to the leg only.

For

$$N = 2^{a_0} p_1{}^{a_1} p_2{}^{a_2} \ldots p_n{}^{a_n} q_1{}^{b_1} q_2{}^{b_2} \ldots q_r{}^{b_r}$$

we have, using Formulas 2 and 3,

$$
\begin{aligned}
2L+1 &= (2a_0-1)(2a_1+1)(2a_2+1)\ldots(2a_n+1) \\
&\quad \times (2b_1+1)(2b_2+1)\ldots(2b_r+1) \qquad \text{(Formula 4)} \\
2H+1 &= (2b_1+1)(2b_2+1)\ldots(2b_r+1)
\end{aligned}
$$

and if Q is the ratio of these two expressions and T the sum of L and H, we get, by eliminating L, that $(2H+1)(Q+1) = 2(T+1)$. Obviously $(2H+1)$ is always odd, hence $(Q+1)$ must be even and Q odd.

This suggests the following procedure: Let T be the required number of solutions which may be either leg or hypotenuse. Separate $2(T+1)$ into a pair of factors, A and B, where A is odd and B is even.

In general this will be possible in several ways each of which will furnish a *type* of solution. These factors then correspond to $(2H+1)$ and $(Q+1)$ respectively. Resolve A into factors $d_1 \geq d_2 \geq d_3 \ldots d_r$, and solve for $b_1 = (d_1-1)/2$, $b_2 = (d_2-1)/2 \ldots b_r = (d_r-1)/2$. These are the exponents to apply to primes q of the form $4x+1$. For least solutions, apply descending values of b_i to ascending values of q_i. From $B = Q+1$, find Q. Resolve Q into factors

$$c_0 \geq c_1 \geq c_2 \geq c_3 \ldots c_n$$

and solve for $a_0 = (c_0+1)/2$, $a_1 = (c_1-1)/2$, $a_2 = (c_2-1)/2$, $a_3 = (c_3-1)/2 \ldots a_n = (c_n-1)/2$. Apply the first of these, a_0, as an exponent to the prime 2 and the remainder $a_1, a_2 \ldots a_n$ as exponents to primes, p, of the form $4x-1$.

In case $Q = 1$, a_0 will be 1 and $a_1 = a_2 = \ldots a_n$ will be zero, and then $N = 2q_1^{b_1} q_2^{b_2} \ldots q_r^{b_r}$. This number will be the *side* (leg or hypotenuse) of exactly the same number of triangles as when $N = q_1^{b_1} q_2^{b_2} \ldots q_r^{b_r}$ (as can be verified by Formula 4). Hence if one is interested in *least* solutions, the former value may be disregarded and only the latter used. When $Q = 1$, $L = H$, so that there are the same number of Pythagorean triangles where N is a leg as where N is a hypotenuse.

Example 3. Find a number which may be the leg or hypotenuse of exactly 1000 Pythagorean triangles and find the least such number. Here $T = 1000$ and $2(T+1) = 2002$. The odd divisors $A = 2H+1$ of 2002 are given in Table 59, also the factors $d_1, d_2 \ldots d_r$ of these divisors and the corresponding exponents $b_1, b_2, \ldots b_r$. The value of $Q = B-1$ is also given, together with its factors $c_0, c_1, c_2, \ldots c_n$. Finally we obtain the exponents $a_0, a_1, a_2, \ldots a_n$ and then the solutions with the primes selected to give the smallest answers.

Solution 5 in Table 59 is the least, and since $2H+1$ is 7 in this case, $H = 3$ and there are three triangles where the number, $2^{10} \cdot 3^2 \cdot 5^3 \cdot 7$, is a hypotenuse, and the remainder, 997, where it is a leg. Compare this answer with $2^{15} \cdot 3^{11} \cdot 5$ of Example 2, which is a larger number because the minimum solution is restricted to a leg only.

In case $T+1$ is a power of 2, it has no odd divisors; consequently there cannot be any H solutions. As an example of such a case, we will find N, a number which may be the leg or hypotenuse of 63 Pythagorean triangles. Here $T = 63$ and

$$2(T+1) = 2 \cdot 64 = 1 \cdot 128 = (2H+1)(Q+1)$$

TABLE 59

NUMBERS WHICH MAY BE THE SIDE OF $T = 1000$ PYTHAGOREAN TRIANGLES

Type Number of Solution	Factor Pairs of $2(T+1)$	$A = 2H+1 =$ Odd Factor	Factors $d_1, d_2 \ldots d_r$ of A	Exponents $b_1, b_2 \ldots b_r$	$B-1 = Q$	Factors $c_0, c_1, c_2 \ldots c_n$ of Q	Exponents $a_0, a_1, a_2 \ldots a_n$	Smallest Solutions
1	1001·2	1001	13·11·7	6, 5, 3	1	1	1	$5^6 \cdot 13^5 \cdot 17^3$
2	77·26	77	11·7	5, 3	25	5·5	3, 2	$2^3 \cdot 3^2 \cdot 5^5 \cdot 13^3$
3	91·22	91	13·7	6, 3	21	7·3	4, 1	$2^4 \cdot 3 \cdot 5^6 \cdot 13^3$
4	143·14	143	13·11	6, 5	13	13	7	$2^7 \cdot 5^6 \cdot 13^5$
5*	7·286	7	7	3	285	19·5·3	10, 2, 1	$2^{10} \cdot 3^2 \cdot 5^3 \cdot 7$
6	11·182	11	11	5	181	181	91	$2^{91} \cdot 5^5$
7	13·154	13	13	6	153	17·3·3	9, 1, 1	$2^9 \cdot 3 \cdot 5^6 \cdot 7$

NUMBERS WHICH MAY BE THE SIDE OF $T = 1000000$ PYTHAGOREAN TRIANGLES

Type Number of Solution	Factor Pairs of $2(T+1)$	$A = 2H+1 =$ Odd Factor	Factors $d_1, d_2 \ldots d_r$ of A	Exponents $b_1, b_2 \ldots b_r$	$B-1 = Q$	Factors $c_0, c_1, c_2 \ldots c_n$ of Q	Exponents $a_0, a_1, a_2 \ldots a_n$	Smallest Solutions
1	1000001·2	1000001	9901·101	4950, 50	1	1	1	$5^{4950} \cdot 13^{50}$
2	9901·202	9901	9901	4950	201	67·3	34, 1	$2^{34} \cdot 3 \cdot 5^{4950}$
3*	101·19802	101	101	50	19801	19801	9901	$2^{9901} \cdot 5^{50}$

* This is the smallest solution.

whence $2H+1 = 1$ and $H = 0$, $Q = 127$ and $N = 2^{64}$ or $p_1{}^{63}$ where p_1 has the form $4x-1$. The first solution is the least. We may not assign the value 5 or any prime of the form $4x+1$ to p_1, since then there would be 63 hypotenuses and, in addition, 63 leg solutions, making a total of 126, double the quantity required.

Example 4. Find the minimum solution given $T = 1000000$. Table 59 also indicates the steps. Here there are 50 hypotenuse solutions.

The minimum solution here is $2^{9901} \cdot 5^{50}$, where 50 triangles have that number as a hypotenuse (since $2H+1 = 101$) and 999950 triangles have the number as a leg.

For 1000000 as a *leg* only, we have $2000001 = 666667 \cdot 3$, the first factor being a prime. The exponents are 333333 and 1, resulting in the number $p_1{}^{333333}p_2$ or $2^{333334} \cdot 3$ as the minimum solution. This is a very much larger number than $2^{9901} \cdot 5^{50}$.

*   *   *

Problem 7 imposes the condition that the *legs* of a Pythagorean triangle be consecutive integers. Obviously, the 3, 4, 5 triangle fulfills the condition; it so happens that *all three* sides are consecutive integers. No other such triangle can have all three sides consecutive integers because if $m^2-n^2 = X$, $2mn = X+1$, $m^2+n^2 = X+2$, then, by addition, $m^2 = X+1$, and by subtraction, $n^2 = 1$, which would make $2mn = m^2$ or $2n = m$. But $n = 1$, hence $m = 2$ and $X = 3$, resulting in the single solution 3, 4, 5.

For only the legs to be consecutive integers, either

$$m^2-n^2+1 = 2mn \quad \text{or} \quad 2mn+1 = m^2-n^2.$$

The first relation gives $(m-n)^2 = 2n^2-1$, the second $(m-n)^2 = 2n^2+1$. They can be combined into $(m-n)^2 = 2n^2 \pm 1$ so that $(m-n)^2-2n^2 = \pm 1$. An equation of this type, namely, a square minus k times another square equals ± 1, is called a Pell equation; it has acquired great celebrity among number-theory enthusiasts. A discussion of the Pell equation will be left for a later chapter; at present we will find by trial the values of n which make $2n^2 \pm 1$ a square. These values form the series 1, 2, 5, 12, 29, 70, 169, the plus and minus signs alternating, starting with the minus sign. The corresponding values of the resulting squares $(m-n)^2$, the values of m and the legs and hypotenuses of the first 10 Pythagorean triangles with consecutive legs are tabulated in Table 60.

TABLE 60

PYTHAGOREAN TRIANGLES WITH CONSECUTIVE LEGS

Order r	n	$2n \pm 1 = (m-n)^2$	$m-n$	m	$X = m^2 - n^2$	$Y = 2mn$	$Z = m^2 + n^2$
1	1	1	1	2	3	4	5
2	2	9	3	5	21	20	29
3	5	49	7	12	119	120	169
4	12	289	17	29	697	696	985
5	29	1681	41	70	4059	4060	5741
6	70	9801	99	169	23661	23660	33461
7	169	57121	239	408	137903	137904	195025
8	408	332929	577	985	803761	803760	1113689
9	985	1940449	1393	2378	4684659	4684660	6625109
10	2378	11309769	3363	5741	27304197	27304196	38613965

Various relationships may be observed among numbers in these columns. For example, the values of m are the same as those of n but displaced one step, so that $m_r = n_{r+1}$. The successive values of either m or n are obtained by taking twice the previous value and adding the one previous to that. Thus, $12 = 2 \cdot 5 + 2$; $29 = 2 \cdot 12 + 5$, etc.; or, in general, $n_r = 2n_{r-1} + n_{r-2}$. It will also be noted that the successive values of the hypotenuse are the alternate values of m or $Z_r = m_{2r}$.

More useful formulas may be derived for calculating X, Y, and Z directly without tabulating m and n. If instead of tabulating X and Y as above so that they alternately exceed one another, we list in a column only the smaller of the two legs,

Order	A	Z
1	3	5
2	20	29
3	119	169
4	696	985
5	4059	5741

heading this column A and listing the corresponding hypotenuses Z as before, then $A_r = 6A_{r-1} - A_{r-2} + 2$, and $Z_r = 6Z_{r-1} - Z_{r-2}$. For instance, in the fifth triangle $r = 5$ and $A_r = 4059$; $A_{r-1} = 696$; $A_{r-2} = 119$; and $4059 = 6 \cdot 696 - 119 + 2$. Similarly, $Z_r = 5741$; $Z_{r-1} = 985$; and $Z_{r-2} = 169$, whence $5741 = 6 \cdot 985 - 169$. The successive triangles can thus be rapidly calculated and the following check formula used: $A_r + A_{r-1} + Z_{r-1} + 1 = Z_r$, for example $4059 + 696 + 985 + 1 = 5741$.

The reader may wish to prove these three relations, and calculat the next 20 or so triangles with consecutive legs. The autho calculated the first 100 such triangles. The smaller leg and hypote nuse of the last one are given here for the reader's moral support i case he desires to calculate the triangles from the eleventh to th hundredth.† If his courage should fail en route, he may refer t Chapter XXVI and find all 100 of them.

A_{100} = 2166969314861378833054797972928630716401520276
86994653460816919923388459929696

Z_{100} = 30645573943232956180057972969833245887630954508753693529117371074705767728665

This figure, having legs each of which is represented by a 77-digi number, is almost an exact 45° isosceles right triangle. The differenc between either acute angle and 45° is, as one might suspect, fairl small, but if the sides of this differential angle were extended fa enough, we might expect a considerable divergence between then ultimately. An electron measures approximately $8 \cdot 10^{-14}$ inches i diameter. Now suppose we assumed the outer confines of measurabl space at a hundred billion light years, which is quite a distanc beyond the range of the 200-inch telescope on Mt. Palomar, or th new radio telescope at Big Pine, California. One light year is th distance traversed by light in one year at a velocity of 186,300 mile a second; it is therefore approximately $186300 \cdot 60 \cdot 60 \cdot 8765$ mile (there are 8765+ hours in a year). This is about 6 trillion = $6 \cdot 10^{12}$ miles. If the sides of the differential angle were extended t this ultima Thule of space (about $6 \cdot 10^{23}$ miles), an electron—or eve a hydrogen nucleus, which is only 1/2000 as large—would have to b subdivided, assuming that that were possible, into smaller sphere more numerous than there are drops of water on the earth before on of these infinitesimal particles could fit between the sides of the angle We had, therefore, best call the one-hundredth, a 45° isosceles righ triangle and let it go at that.

* * *

The rth leg and hypotenuse can be found *directly* in terms o r by formulas instead of "recurring" series, but such formulas ar impractical for calculating purposes since the computations are tedious. These formulas are:

$$A_r = \frac{(\sqrt{2}+1)^{2r+1}-(\sqrt{2}-1)^{2r+1}}{4}-\frac{1}{2}$$

$$Z_r = \frac{(\sqrt{2}+1)^{2r+1}+(\sqrt{2}-1)^{2r+1}}{2\sqrt{2}}.$$

Letting $r = 1$ and 2:

$$A_1 = \frac{(\sqrt{2}+1)^3-(\sqrt{2}-1)^3}{4}-\frac{1}{2} = 3$$

$$Z_1 = \frac{(\sqrt{2}+1)^3+(\sqrt{2}-1)^3}{2\sqrt{2}} = 5$$

$$A_2 = \frac{(\sqrt{2}+1)^5-(\sqrt{2}-1)^5}{4}-\frac{1}{2} = 20$$

$$Z_2 = \frac{(\sqrt{2}+1)^5+(\sqrt{2}-1)^5}{2\sqrt{2}} = 29.$$

The length of the computation for other values of A and Z, even for comparatively small values of r, rapidly increases.

A simple way to calculate the successive triangles with consecutive legs is by the rule that if m and n are the generators of such a triangle where $m > n$, then $2m+n$, m will generate another such triangle. Thus the generators of the 3, 4, 5 triangle are $m = 2$, $n = 1$; hence 5 and 2 will generate 21, 20, 29. The next set of generators are 12 and 5, which produce the triangle 119, 120, 169, and so on.

* * *

A much simpler problem is the determination of Pythagorean triangles where one leg and the *hypotenuse* are consecutive integers. For this condition either $m^2-n^2+1 = m^2+n^2$ or $2mn+1 = m^2+n^2$. The first equation cannot hold because n would be irrational. From the second, $m^2-2mn+n^2 = 1$. Then $(m-n)^2 = 1$ and $m = n+1$. Hence, whenever m and n are consecutive integers, the hypotenuse exceeds the even leg by unity and, of course, this is possible only in a primitive Pythagorean triangle.

* * *

The area of a Pythagorean triangle is evidently equal to $mn(m^2-n^2)$. In Problem 8 we are asked to find three such triangles with equal areas, requiring the solution in integers of:

$$mn(m^2-n^2) = pq(p^2-q^2) = tu(t^2-u^2).$$

This is a problem in Diophantine analysis and there are a number of methods for obtaining solutions. The three triangles of Figure 6 satisfy the relation.

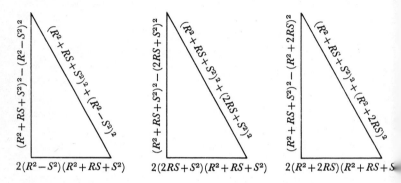

FIG. 6. PYTHAGOREAN TRIANGLES WITH EQUAL AREAS

This solution corresponds to:

$$m = r^2+rs+s^2 \qquad p = m = r^2+rs+s^2 \qquad t = r^2+2rs$$
$$n = r^2-s^2 \qquad q = 2rs+s^2 \qquad u = r^2+rs+s^2.$$

The common area is equal to $rs(2r+s)(r+2s)(r+s)(r^3-s^3)$.

If $r = 2$ and $s = 1$, this gives the triplet sets, $(40, 42, 58)$; $(24, 70, 74)$; $(15, 112, 113)$; for the sides of the Pythagorean triangles, each of which has an area of 840. If $r = 3$ and $s = 1$, the resulting triplets are $(105, 208, 233)$; $(120, 182, 218)$; $(56, 390, 394)$; each of which has an area of 10920.

Fermat used a simple method of obtaining two Pythagorean triangles with equal areas. If a and b are the two legs and c the hypotenuse of a Pythagorean triangle, so that $a^2+b^2 = c^2$, he used $m = c^2$ and $n = 2ab$ as the generators of a new Pythagorean triangle with legs: $m^2-n^2 = c^4-4a^2b^2 = (a^2-b^2)^2$ and $2mn = 4c^2ab$ and hypotenuse $m^2+n^2 = c^4+4a^2b^2$. Its area is $2c^2ab(c^4-4a^2b^2) = 2c^2ab(a^2-b^2)^2$. This triangle has the same area as the one obtained when the sides of triangle a, b, c are each multiplied by $2c(a^2-b^2)$.

This is easily proved: The two legs of the magnified triangle are $a \cdot 2c(a^2-b^2)$ and $b \cdot 2c(a^2-b^2)$, and the area is $2c^2ab(a^2-b^2)^2$, the same as above.

Taking $a = 4$, $b = 3$, $c = 5$, the generators become $m = 25$, $n = 24$, forming the triangle 49, 1200, and 1201. Multiplying 4, 3, and 5 by $2 \cdot 5 \cdot (4^2-3^2) = 70$, the magnified triangle becomes 280, 210, and 350. The area of both of these triangles is 29400.

The *smallest* area common to three *primitive* Pythagorean triangles is 13123110. These triangles have the following sides: 4485, 5852, 7373; 19019, 1380, 19069; 3059, 8580, 9109. Their respective generators are 77, 38; 138, 5; 78, 55.

Three Pythagorean triangles having equal areas can also be generated from four consecutive terms of an arithmetic progression. If a, b, c, d are four such terms, the generators, $m = ab$, $n = cd$ will form one triangle; $a(c-b)$, $c(c+b)$ will form the second; and the generators $d(c-b)$, $b(c+b)$ will form the third. Taking a, b, c, d as 1, 2, 3, 4 respectively, the generators become 2, 12; 1, 15; 4, 10; the corresponding three triangles have legs 140, 48; 224, 30; 84, 80, and each triangle has an area of 3360.

Here are a few sets of four Pythagorean triangles with equal area. The letters m and n are the generators of the triangle, so that the two legs are $k(m^2-n^2)$ and $k(2mn)$.

Area	1			2			3			4		
	m	n	k	m	n	k	m	n	k	m	n	k
341880	56	55	1	40	37	1	37	7	1	37	33	1
17957940	92	77	1	165	4	1	23	12	13	28	5	13
116396280	133	88	1	152	35	1	153	133	1	133	65	1
1071572040	232	155	1	301	40	1	301	279	1	319	301	1
1728483120	259	144	1	368	35	1	259	155	1	299	259	1

Problems 9 and 10 are left for the reader to solve.†

* * *

The following problem appeared in the *American Mathematical Monthly*: "Find a scheme for writing mechanically without computation, a series of integral right triangles having given one set." It was solved as follows: In $a^2+b^2 = c^2$, assume $c = b+1$. Then $a^2 = c^2-b^2 = b^2+2b+1-b^2 = 2b+1$, and since a^2 is an odd number, a must also be odd, say equal to $2n+1$, so that $a^2 = 4n^2+4n+1$, and

$b = (a^2 - 1)/2 = 2n^2 + 2n$. Then $c = b + 1 = 2n^2 + 2n + 1$. If n is selected as an integral power of 10, we can make a table, starting with the triangle 21, 220, 221 and inserting zeros, as shown in Table 61.

TABLE 61

PYTHAGOREAN TRIANGLES WRITTEN MECHANICALLY

n	$a = 2n+1$	$b = 2n^2+2n$	$c = 2n^2+2n+1$
10	21	220	221
10^2	201	20200	20201
10^3	2001	2002000	2002001
10^4	20001	200020000	200020001
10^5	200001	20000200000	20000200001
10^6	2000001	2000002000000	2000002000001

Similarly we could start with $n = 20$, twice an integral power of 10, whence

$$41^2 + 840^2 = 841^2,$$

and continue with

$$401^2 + 80400^2 = 80401^2, \text{ etc.}$$

Also starting with $a = 6n+9$, $b = 2n^2+6n$, and $c = 2n^2+6n+9$, there results, when n is an integral power of 10:

$$69^2 + 260^2 = 269^2,$$
$$609^2 + 20600^2 = 20609^2, \text{ etc.}$$

*   *   *

In 1643 Fermat wrote a letter to Mersenne asking for a Pythagorean triangle the sum of whose legs and whose hypotenuse were squares. If the sides are labeled X, Y, Z, this requires:

$$
\begin{aligned}
X + Y &= a^2 \\
Z &= b^2 \\
X^2 + Y^2 = Z^2 &= b^4.
\end{aligned}
\tag{1}
$$

The solution is an example of Fermat's famous method of infinite descent, except that instead of proving that the conditions are impossible, the method will show how from the least possible solution of a certain type of equation, other solutions may be found step by step until the required conditions are fulfilled. The method is ingenious.

Let

$$X - Y = e. \tag{2}$$

Combining (1) and (2) and solving for X and Y,

$$X = (a^2 + e)/2, \quad Y = (a^2 - e)/2$$

and

$$X^2 + Y^2 = (2a^4 + 2e^2)/4 = (a^4 + e^2)/2 = Z^2 = b^4,$$

whence

$$a^4 + e^2 = 2b^4 \quad \text{or} \quad 2b^4 - a^4 = e^2. \tag{3}$$

From the fundamental Pythagorean triangle formulas, we have: $X = m^2 - n^2$; $Y = 2mn$; $Z = m^2 + n^2 = b^2$. This last equation for Z is itself a Pythagorean triangle relation, requiring that:

$$m = r^2 - s^2; \quad n = 2rs; \quad b = r^2 + s^2. \tag{4}$$

From (1), $m^2 - n^2 + 2mn = a^2 = (m+n)^2 - 2n^2$ or $(m+n)^2 - a^2 = 2n^2$, that is, we must find two squares whose difference is twice a square. A general solution of $A^2 - B^2 = 2C^2$ is given by: $A = t^2 + 2u^2$; $B = t^2 - 2u^2$; $C = 2tu$, as may easily be verified. In this instance we have $A = (m+n)$; $B = a$; $C = n$, so that $m+n = t^2 + 2u^2$, $n = 2tu$, and therefore, $m = t^2 + 2u^2 - 2tu$. These values of m and n in terms of t and u are now equated with those in terms of r and s in (4) giving:

$$\begin{aligned} r^2 - s^2 &= t^2 + 2u^2 - 2tu \\ 2rs &= 2tu, \end{aligned} \tag{5}$$

and integral values of these quantities are required to satisfy both equations. From $rs = tu$ we have $r/t = u/s$. Let these fractions in lowest terms be equal to d/c. Then $r = kd$; $u = Ld$; $t = kc$; $s = Lc$. Substituting in (5) and combining terms, we have:

$$L^2(c^2 + 2d^2) - 2cdLk + k^2(c^2 - d^2) = 0,$$

and dividing by k^2,

$$(L/k)^2(c^2 + 2d^2) - 2cd(L/k) + (c^2 - d^2) = 0.$$

Solving by the quadratic formula for L/k we have

$$L/k = [cd \pm (2d^4 - c^4)^{1/2}]/(c^2 + 2d^2).$$

This requires that $2d^4 - c^4$ be a square, say V^2. Then

$$2d^4 - c^4 = V^2. \tag{6}$$

Now it will be noted that equation (6) has exactly the same form as equation (3) except that the quantities involved are smaller. We can, therefore, start with equation (6) and go through a similar analysis to an equation with still smaller values. But this cannot be continued indefinitely for finite quantities, so that ultimately, if there is a solution, the smallest one must be reached. This turns out to be $2 \cdot 1^4 - 1^4 = 1^2$. Here $d = c = V = 1$, and from these quantities we can work back to b, a, and e in equation (3). If our required conditions for X, Y, Z are met, we have a solution; if not we let $b = d_1$, $a = c_1$, $e = V_1$ and proceed similarly for new values of b, a, e until the required solution is found.

Before substituting values, let us summarize our results:

(1) V, c, and d are any numbers satisfying the equation $2d^4 - c^4 = V^2$, such as 1, 1, 1.

(2) $L = cd \pm V$ (3) $m = r^2 - s^2$
$\quad k = c^2 + 2d^2$ $\quad n = 2rs$
$\quad r = kd$ $\quad b = r^2 + s^2$
$\quad s = Lc$

(4) $X = m^2 - n^2$ (5) $X + Y = a^2$
$\quad Y = 2mn$ $\quad X - Y = e$.
$\quad Z = b^2$

Assuming first, therefore, that $d = c = V = 1$, we have

$$L/k = (1 \pm 1)/3 = 0/3 \quad \text{or} \quad 2/3.$$

The value $L = 0$ must be discarded, but for $L = 2$, $k = 3$, we have $r = kd = 3$, $s = Lc = 2$; $m = 5$, $n = 12$; $X = -119$, $Y = 120$, $Z = 169 = 13^2$. Unfortunately we cannot accept the value of -119 for the side of a Pythagorean triangle. Proceeding, however, to solve for b, a, and e, we have $r^2 + s^2 = b = 13$; $X + Y = a = 1$, and $X - Y = e = -239$. Thus equations (3) and (6) are satisfied by $2 \cdot 13^4 - 1^4 = (-239)^2$.

Starting all over again, $d_1 = 13$; $c_1 = 1$; $V_1 = -239$. Then $L/k = (13 \cdot 1 \pm 239)/(1 + 2 \cdot 13^2) = 252/339 = 84/113$ or $(-226)/339 = -2/3$. Take $L = -2$, $k = 3$; then $r = 39$, $s = -2$, whence $m = r^2 - s^2 = 1517$, $n = -156$; $X = 2276953$, $Y = -473304$. Since Y is negative we must again discard the values associated with it and try $L = 84$, $k = 113$ instead. Then $r = 1469$, $s = 84$; $m = 2150905$, $n = 246792$;

$$X = m^2 - n^2 = 4565486027761$$
$$Y = 2mn = 1061652293520$$

and

$$Z = b^2 = 4687298610289 = 2165017^2.$$

Also

$$X + Y = a^2 = 2372159^2 = 5627138321281.$$

It seems difficult to believe that these are the *smallest* three numbers satisfying the given condition but such indeed is the case.   As may be surmised, a second solution would yield numbers which, representing feet or inches, would result in a triangle whose legs would project some little distance beyond the confines of the Milky Way.

*   *   *

The perimeter of a Pythagorean triangle is

$$K(m^2 - n^2) + K(2mn) + K(m^2 + n^2) = K(2m^2 + 2mn)$$
$$= 2Km(m+n).$$

To find sets of such triangles with equal perimeters requires a number which can be put in the form $2Km(m+n)$ in several ways.   This looks deceptively easy but such numbers are not too small nor too easy to find.   Here are the generators, m, n, and the perimeter, p, of five sets of three *primitive*, Pythagorean triangles, the perimeters in each triplet being the same:

Perimeter,	1		2		3	
$p = 2m(m+n)$	m	n	m	n	m	n
14280	60	59	68	37	84	1
72930	187	8	165	56	143	112
81510	195	14	165	82	143	142
92820	170	103	182	73	210	11
103740	182	103	190	83	210	37

In these five sets, the triangles are primitive but if non-primitive triangles may be used, a triplet having as small a perimeter as 120 exists.   These three triangles have respective sides of (20, 48, 52), (45, 24, 51), and (40, 30, 50).

*   *   *

Four primitive Pythagorean triangles having a common perimeter have also been found.   Only seven such quads exist for a perimeter less than 1000000 so they are quite rare.   The smallest of these perimeters is 317460; the corresponding generators are (286, 269), (330, 151), (370, 59), (390, 17); and the three sides of these four triangles are (153868, 9435, 154157), (99660, 86099, 131701), (43660, 133419, 140381), (13260, 151811, 152389). Can the reader find the other six?†

*   *   *

The primitive Pythagorean triangle whose sides are 693; 1924; and 2045 has an area of 666666.

*   *   *

There are many Pythagorean triangles whose area utilizes 9 or 10 different digits. Using generators 149 and 58, the area is 162789354; using 224 and 153, the area is 917358624. For all 10 digits, generators 666 and 5 produce 1476958230; generators 406 and 279 produce 9854271630.

*   *   *

Any pair of Pythagorean triangles are related in a curious way. If A, B, C and a, b, c are respectively the legs and hypotenuses of two such triangles, then $(C+c)^2 - (A+a)^2 - (B+b)^2 = D^2$, a square. Furthermore

$$Cc - Aa - Bb = 2E^2 \qquad Cc - Ab - aB = J^2$$
$$Cc + Aa + Bb = 2F^2 \qquad Cc + Ab + aB = K^2$$
$$Cc - Aa + Bb = 2G^2 \qquad Cc + Ab - aB = L^2$$
$$Cc + Aa - Bb = 2H^2 \qquad Cc - Ab + aB = M^2.$$

*   *   *

The square of any complex number yields the legs of a Pythagorean triangle. Thus $(2+i)^2 = 3+4i$, and $3^2+4^2 = 5^2$. Again

$$(3+2i)^2 = 5+12i \quad \text{and} \quad 5^2+12^2 = 13^2.$$

In general,

$$(a+bi)^2 = (a^2-b^2)+2abi \quad \text{and} \quad (a^2-b^2)^2+(2ab)^2 = (a^2+b^2)^2.$$

It will be recalled that $i = \sqrt{-1}$, $i^2 = -1$, $i^3 = -i$, and $i^4 = +1$.

By this method, two squares can be found whose sum is an nth power. Take $a = 2$, $b = 1$, then

$$(2+i)^3 = 8+12i+6i^2+i^3 = 2+11i \quad \text{and} \quad 2^2+11^2 = 5^3.$$

Again $(3+2i)^4 = 81+216i+216i^2+96i^3+16i^4 = -119-120i$ and $119^2+120^2 = 13^4$. And generally, x^2+y^2 can be made equal to z^n by expanding $(a+bi)^n$ by the binomial theorem and using the coefficients of the real and imaginary terms for x and y. The value of z will then turn out to be a^2+b^2. Such being the case, we can select *any* z (provided of course it is expressible as the sum of two squares) and *any* n and then find $x^2+y^2 = z^n$. Thus for $z = 13 = 3^2+2^2$ and $n = 3$, we can find two squares whose sum is equal to $13^3 = 2197$ by expanding $(3+2i)^3$. The coefficients of the real and imaginary terms are the required numbers, x, y, in this case 9 and 46, so that $9^2+46^2 = 13^3$.

BIBLIOGRAPHY

Anema, A. S. "Pythagorean Triangles with Equal Perimeters," *Scripta Mathematica*, **15** (1949), 89.

Barlow, P. *Theory of Numbers*. London: J. Johnson & Co., 1811.

Block, D., and Umansky, H. L. "Pythagorean Variations," *Scripta Mathematica*, **15** (1949), 244.

Carmichael, R. D. *Theory of Numbers and Diophantine Analysis*. New York: Dover Publications, Inc., 1959.

Cheney, W. F., and Rosenbaum, J. "Solution to Problem: Show That There Is Just One Right-Triangle Whose Three Sides Are Relatively Prime Integers Between 2000 and 3000," *American Mathematical Monthly*, **41** (1934), 393.

Christie, R. W. D. "Problem: Prove That $(\sum p_n)^2+(\sum p_n+1)^2 = (p_{2n}+q_{2n})^2 = q_{2n+1}^2$ Where $\sum p_n$ Signifies the Sum of the Even Convergents of $p^2-2q^2 = \pm 1$," *Mathematical Gazette*, **1** (1896–1900), 394.

Dickson, L. E. *History of the Theory of Numbers*. 3 vols. New York: Chelsea Publishing Co., 1950.

———. *Introduction to the Theory of Numbers*. New York: Dover Publications, Inc., 1957.

Ginsburg, J. "Complex Numbers as Generators of Pythagorean Triangles," *Scripta Mathematica*, **13** (1947), 105.

———. "Triplets of Equiareal Rational Triangles," *Scripta Mathematica*, **20** (1954), 219.

Gruber, M. A., *et al.* "Solution to Problem: Find the First Six Sets of Values in Which the Sum of Two Consecutive Integral Squares Is a Square," *American Mathematical Monthly*, **4** (1897), 24.

Hopkins, G. H. "Solution to Problem: [Find Two Consecutive Integral Squares Whose Sum Is a Square]," *Mathematical Questions from the Educational Times*, **12** (1869), 104.

Licks, H. E. *Recreations in Mathematics*. New York: D. Van Nostrand, 1921.

Loyd, S. *Cyclopedia of Puzzles.* New York: Lamb Publishing Co., 1914.

———. *Mathematical Puzzles of Sam Loyd,* ed. by Martin Gardner. 2 vols. New York: Dover Publications, Inc., 1959–1960.

Martin, A. "Solution to Problem: [Find Two Consecutive Integral Squares Whose Sum Is a Square]," *Mathematical Questions from the Educational Times,* **14** (1871), 89.

———. "Solution to Problem: [Find Two Consecutive Integral Squares Whose Sum Is a Square]," *Mathematical Questions from the Educational Times,* **16** (1872), 107.

———. "Solution to Problem: [Find Two Consecutive Integral Squares Whose Sum Is a Square and Find the Eightieth Such Set]," *Mathematical Questions from the Educational Times,* **20** (1874), 42.

———. "Rational Right-Triangles Nearly Isosceles," *The Analyst,* **3** (1876), 47.

———. "Solution to Problem: [Integral Right-Triangles Whose Legs Differ by Unity]," *Mathematical Visitor,* **1** (1879), 55.

Miksa, F. L. "Pythagorean Triangles with Equal Perimeters," *Mathematics,* **24** (1950), 52.

———. "Table of Primitive Pythagorean Triangles Whose Areas Contain All (10) Digits," *Scripta Mathematica,* **20** (1954), 231.

Moessner, A. "If—Then," *Scripta Mathematica,* **18** (1950), 164.

Ozanam, J. *Recreations in Science and Natural Philosophy.* London: T. Tegg, 1884.

Putnam, K. S. "Solution to the Problem: [Pythagorean Triangles Whose Legs Differ by Unity]," *Mathematical Visitor,* **1** (1879), 122.

Shedd, C. L. "Another Triplet of Equiareal Triangles," *Scripta Mathematica,* **11** (1945), 273.

———. "Equiareal Triangles," *Scripta Mathematica,* **16** (1950), 293.

Uspensky, J. V., and Heaslet, M. A. *Elementary Number Theory.* New York: McGraw-Hill Book Co., 1939.

Vinogradov, I. M. *Elements of Number Theory.* New York: Dover Publications, Inc., 1954.

Whitlock, W. P., Jr. "An 'Impossible' Triangle," *Scripta Mathematica,* **9** (1943), 189.

Wilkinson, T. T. "Problem: [Rule for Finding Integral Right-Triangles Whose Legs Differ by a Given Number]," *Mathematical Questions from the Educational Times,* **20** (1874), 20.

Willey, M., and Kennedy, E. C. "Solution to Problem: [Find a Scheme for Writing Mechanically an Unlimited Number of Pythagorean Triangles]," *American Mathematical Monthly,* **41** (1934), 330.

CHAPTER XV

ON THE SQUARE

THERE IS something about a square! Note its perfection and symmetry. All its sides are equal, its angles are neither stupidly obtuse nor dangerously acute. They are just right. The square has many beautiful geometric properties. Readers may recall how any rectangle can be converted by straightedge and compass into a square by

FIG. 7. A SQUARE

finding the "mean proportional" between the sides of the rectangle. Then there is the famous Pythagorean theorem: "The sum of the *squares* on the arms of a right-angled triangle is equal to the *square* on the hypotenuse."

We shall not concern ourselves here with the geometric properties of squares; instead we shall examine this regular quadrilateral from a numerical viewpoint. A square number is one of the integers in the series $1, 4, 9, 16, 25\ldots$. It is not very difficult to see the relation between consecutive members of this series. Thus 3, added to the first square, gives the second; 5 added to the second square gives the third, etc. Generalizing, we see that if to the square of x, twice x plus one is added, the next succeeding square is obtained, that is, $x^2 + (2x+1) = (x+1)^2$. For example, $5^2 + 2 \cdot 5 + 1 = 6^2$.

135

If we know the value of a certain square the next one is thus easily obtained.   Knowing $18^2 = 324$, we have

$$19^2 = 18^2 + 2 \cdot 18 + 1 = 324 + 36 + 1 = 361.$$

By another rule, the square of a number ending in 5, such as 35, may be written immediately by multiplying together the first digit, 3, and the next consecutive integer, 4, and affixing 25 after the product so that the answer is 1225.   Similarly $65^2 = 6 \cdot 7$ and 25 = 4225.   Also $15^2 = 1 \cdot 2$ and 25 = 225, etc.   For more than two digits, $115^2 = 11 \cdot 12$ and 25 = 13225.

*   *   *

From the familiar algebraic relations,

$$(a+b)^2 = a^2 + 2ab + b^2$$

and

$$(a-b)^2 = a^2 - 2ab + b^2,$$

we have the special cases,

$$(a+1)^2 = a^2 + 2a + 1$$

and

$$(a-1)^2 = a^2 - 2a + 1.$$

Thus, knowing $60^2 = 3600$, it is easy to find

$$61^2 = (60+1)^2 = 60^2 + 2 \cdot 60 + 1 = 3600 + 120 + 1 = 3721,$$

a mental addition.   Similarly,

$$59^2 = (60-1)^2 = 60^2 - 120 + 1 = 3600 - 120 + 1 = 3481.$$

A little more difficult is

$$(a \pm 2)^2 = a^2 \pm 4a + 4.$$

Thus

$$62^2 = (60+2)^2 = 3600 + 4 \cdot 60 + 4 = 3844,$$

and

$$58^2 = (60-2)^2 = 3600 - 4 \cdot 60 + 4 = 3364.$$

*   *   *

The squares ending in zero are of course easy to memorize; we now have a short method for finding those ending in 5 and for those which are one or two more or less than a known square. This covers the interval between squares pretty well. Thus, for the squares between 70 and 80, we can *think* as follows and write the result with little or no computation:

$$70^2 = 4900$$
$$71^2 = (70+1)^2 = 70^2+2\cdot70+1 = 5041$$
$$72^2 = (70+2)^2 = 70^2+4\cdot70+4 = 5184$$
$$73^2 = (75-2)^2 = 75^2-4\cdot75+4 = 5625-300+4 = 5329$$
$$74^2 = (75-1)^2 = 75^2-2\cdot75+1 = 5625-150+1 = 5476$$
$$75^2 = 7\times8 = 56 \quad \text{and} \quad 25 = 5625$$
$$76^2 = (75+1)^2 = 75^2+2\cdot75+1 = 5625+150+1 = 5776$$
$$77^2 = (75+2)^2 = 75^2+4\cdot75+4 = 5625+300+4 = 5929$$
$$78^2 = (80-2)^2 = 80^2-4\cdot80+4 = 6400-320+4 = 6084$$
$$79^2 = (80-1)^2 = 80^2-2\cdot80+1 = 6400-160+1 = 6241$$
$$80^2 = 6400, \text{ etc.}$$

With a little practice it is easy to memorize the squares of integers from 1 to 100. This is a particularly effective remedy against insomnia.

Another method perhaps even simpler depends upon the familiar algebraic formula:

$$(a+b)(a-b) = a^2-b^2.$$

By transposing, we get:

$$(a+b)(a-b)+b^2 = a^2.$$

Assume a^2 is to be found; then select b so that either $a+b$ or $a-b$ become convenient multipliers (ending in zero, for example). Thus

$$47^2 = (\ 47+\ 3)(\ 47-\ 3)+\ 3^2 = \ 50\cdot44\ +\ \ 9 = \ 2209$$
$$96^2 = (\ 96+\ 4)(\ 96-\ 4)+\ 4^2 = 100\cdot92\ +\ 16 = \ 9216$$
$$113^2 = (113+13)(113-13)+13^2 = 126\cdot100+169 = 12769$$
$$\quad\ \ = (113+\ 3)(113-\ 3)+\ 3^2 = 116\cdot110+\ \ 9 = 12769$$
$$179^2 = (179+21)(179-21)+21^2 = 200\cdot158+441 = 32041.$$

*   *   *

Within limited ranges very simple methods can often be used for obtaining the squares of numbers. For squares between 40 and 60, add algebraically to 25 the excess or deficiency from 50, and annex the square of the excess or deficiency to the result. Thus for 54^2, the excess is 4; add to 25, giving 29. Annex the square of the excess, 16, to 29, and 2916 is the square of 54. Similarly for 57, we have $25 + 7 = 32$ and $7^2 = 49$ so that $57^2 = 3249$. If the square of the excess has only one digit, make it two digits by prefixing a zero; thus $53^2 = 25 + 3$ and 09 = 2809. For 46^2, the deficiency is 4, and $25 - 4$ and 4^2 gives 2116, and for 48^2 we have $25 - 2$ and 04, giving 2304.

This simple method is credited to Professor James McGiffert of Rensselaer Polytechnic Institute. The reason for the rule is readily shown. We have that

$$(50 \pm x)^2 = 2500 \pm 100x + x^2 = (25 \pm x)100 + x^2.$$

Multiplying $(25 \pm x)$ by 100 leaves the units and tens spaces of the product empty, and these are then filled by the square of x expressed as a two-digit number. Nothing in this formula precludes x exceeding 10 but then x^2 has more than two digits and the rule is not quite so simple. Thus for 63^2 we have $25 + 13$ and 13^2, giving 38 and 169, or 3969, and $36^2 = 25 - 14$ and 14^2, giving 11 and 196, or 1296.

Numbers from 20 to 29 can be placed within the range of the simple rule by remembering that the square of a number is one-quarter of the square of its double. For 28^2, find 56^2 by the rule and divide by 4. Similarly, even numbers from 82 to 98 can be brought within the range of the rule by dividing by 2, applying the rule, and multiplying the answer by 4. Thus for 82^2, we have $41^2 = 25 - 9$ and $9^2 = 1681$, which when multiplied by 4 gives 6724.

We have a similar rule for numbers from 90 to 110.

$$(110 \pm x)^2 = 10000 \pm 200x + x^2 = (100 \pm 2x)100 + x^2$$
$$= (100 \pm x \pm x)100 + x^2.$$

This too is applicable to all numbers but is most convenient for squares between 90 and 110. Thus for 104^2 we have $104 + 04$ and $04^2 = 10816$, and $109^2 = 109 + 09$ and $09^2 = 11881$. Similarly $97^2 = 97 - 3$ and $3^2 = 94$ and 3^2, giving 9409; and $94^2 = 94 - 6$ and 6^2, giving 8836.

There are many other rules of this kind which most people, including the author, forget almost immediately after learning them.

*   *   *

Peter Barlow published a table of the squares of the first 10000 integers. It is very useful for number-theory enthusiasts and is available in a modern reprinted edition. Barlow's original work was

dated July 1, 1814.   As early as 1781 a table of squares to 25400 had
been published by a Dr. Hutton.

A perusal of such a table reveals some rather interesting properties
of squares.   For example, they all end in 0, 1, 4, 5, 6, and 9 and never
in 2, 3, 7, or 8.   In number-theory parlance, each of the first set of
numbers is a *quadratic residue* of 10; each of the latter a *non-residue*.
Thus one has a test at sight for a *necessary* but not a *sufficient* requirement for a square.   Numbers ending in 0, 1, 4, 5, 6, or 9 are not
necessarily squares, but no integer can be a square unless it ends in
one of these digits.

A more exclusive test is to examine the two-digit endings of squares,
the "*quadratic residues of 100.*"   There are 22 such, and a square
greater than 9 must terminate in one of the two-digit endings shown
in Table 62.

TABLE 62

Two-Digit Square Termini

00	21	41	64	89
01	24	44	69	96
04	25	49	76	
09	29	56	81	
16	36	61	84	

This information is very useful in studying certain *forms* of numbers.
Frequently we wish to ascertain whether a square added to or subtracted from a certain number yields a square sum or remainder.
The two-digit termini rapidly exclude the impossible cases.   If we
want to find a square, x^2, such that $5581 - x^2$ is a square, the table
shows that x^2 must end only in 00, 25, 56, or 81.   (The answer turns
out to be $x^2 = 4356 = 66^2$, and $5581 - 4356 = 1225 = 35^2$.)

The two-digit termini 00 and 44 of a square are the only possible
ones with like digits.   Squares may of course end with any even
number of zeros.   However, no square can end in more than 3
fours and $38^2 = 1444$ is the least square with such an ending.   There
is quite an interval to the next one: $462^2 = 213444$.   After that
comes $538^2 = 289444$ and $962^2 = 925444$.   In general, $500x \pm 38$ is
a number whose square ends in 3 fours.   Here x may be any integer
including zero.

*   *   *

Many readers of this book are no doubt familiar with the rule given above for single-digit endings of squares but there is another condition less well known that a square must fulfill. Unless the sum of the digits of a number add to 1, 4, 7, or 9, it cannot be a square. This is proved as follows: All numbers to the modulus 9 must leave remainders of either 0, 1, 2, 3, 4, 5, 6, 7, or 8; that is, all numbers are of the form: $9a$; $9a \pm 1$; $9a \pm 2$; $9a \pm 3$; $9a \pm 4$. The squares of these numbers, to the modulus 9, leave remainders or residues, respectively, of 0, 1, 4, 9, 7. However, a number when divided by 9 leaves the same remainder as does the sum of its digits (see Chapter VIII), hence the rule. A remainder, zero, may be called a remainder of 9; obviously the sum of the digits of a number cannot be zero, unless the number is itself zero.

*   *   *

Squares and their properties have always attracted mathematicians and there have been attempts to make almost every conceivable kind of relation into a square. Every odd integer greater than unity and every multiple of 4, starting with 8, can be expressed in at least one way as the difference of two square integers. However, twice an odd integer cannot be expressed as the difference of two integer squares. To solve $x^2 - y^2 = A$ where A is given, set $x+y$ equal to any divisor of A larger than its square root, and set $x-y$ equal to the complementary divisor. Both divisors must be even or both odd, that is, "of like parity." Then solve the resulting equation for x and y.

*   *   *

Chapter XIV described the requirements for an integer to be the hypotenuse, H, of a Pythagorean triangle: $H = K(m^2 + n^2)$. This is equivalent to $2^{a_0}QP$ where a_0 may be any integer including zero, Q the product of powers of primes of the form $4x - 1$, and P the product of powers of primes of the form $4x + 1$. If at least one prime of the form $4x + 1$ is present, P can always be expressed as the sum of two integral squares, $m^2 + n^2$; and equating $2^{a_0}Q$ to K, we have the requisite form for H (actually K may be *any* integer). An allied problem is to find the requirements for an integer to be the sum of two integral squares. To meet this requirement, Q must be replaced by Q^2, so that in order for an integer to be the sum of two integral squares, it must have the form $2^{a_0} Q^2 P$. (In this instance $K = 2^{a_0} Q^2$ is either a square or twice a square, not just *any* integer, a more severe restriction than before.) As an example, $2^7 \cdot 3^4 \cdot 5 \cdot 7^2 \cdot 13^3$ may be written $2^7 (3^2 \cdot 7)^2 (5 \cdot 13^3)$, which has the required form. Later in this chapter we shall see how to write this number as the sum of two squares.

A number $N = 2^{a_0} p_1^{2a_1} p_2^{2a_2} \ldots p_n^{2a_n} q_1^{b_1} q_2^{b_2} \ldots q_r^{b_r}$, where the p's are primes of the form $4x - 1$ and the q's those of the form $4x + 1$, is the hypotenuse of

$$[(2b_1 + 1)(2b_2 + 1) \ldots (2b_r + 1) - 1]/2$$

Pythagorean triangles but is the sum of two *unequal* squares neither of which is zero in only

$$(b_1 + 1)(b_2 + 1) \ldots (b_r + 1)/2 \qquad \text{(Formula 1)}$$

ways if the numerator of this fraction is even, and

$$[(b_1 + 1)(b_2 + 1) \ldots (b_r + 1)/2] - 1/2 \qquad \text{(Formula 2)}$$

ways if the numerator is odd.

Thus $N = 2^7 \cdot 3^4 \cdot 5 \cdot 7^2 \cdot 13^3$ is the hypotenuse of

$$[(2 \cdot 1 + 1)(2 \cdot 3 + 1) - 1]/2 = 10$$

Pythagorean triangles but the sum of two squares in only

$$(1 + 1)(3 + 1)/2 = 4$$

ways. Only the exponents of the primes 5 and 13 were used; the other primes were disregarded.

The qualification "unequal squares" above is to be noted. Any integer $2x^2$ which is twice a square can be written $x^2 + x^2$, the sum of two squares. If equal squares are permitted, this adds a solution to the number given by Formula 2, or yields a solution where otherwise there would be none. (Formula 2 applies here rather than Formula 1, because for twice a perfect square, $2x^2$, all the exponents of its odd prime factors are even and the product of each of these exponents increased by one is therefore odd, requiring the use of the formula having the odd numerator.) Thus in $2 \cdot 5^2 \cdot 13^2$, Formula 2 indicates $[(2 + 1)(2 + 1)/2] - 1/2$, or only 4 solutions, but $5^2 \cdot 13^2 + 5^2 \cdot 13^2$ is a fifth one. Again, $2 \cdot 3^2 = 18$ gives no solution by Formula 2 because 18 has no divisor of the form $4x + 1$, but one solution is of course $3^2 + 3^2$.

This additional solution for twice a square can be included as part of Formula 2 by modifying the formula to:

$$(b_1+1)(b_2+1)\ldots(b_n+1)/2-[(-1)^{a_0}]/2.$$

Whenever the exponent a_0 of 2 is odd, then N is twice a square, the minus 1/2 of Formula 2 becomes plus 1/2 and adds another solution; whenever a_0 is even, the original number, N, cannot be twice a square and the minus 1/2 remains unchanged and does not add another solution.

Jacobi gave an elegant rule for the number of ways in which a number can be the sum of two squares: Four times the excess of the number of divisors of the form $4x+1$ over that of the form $4x-1$. However, this rule (1) counts zero as a square, (2) counts the squares of both positive and negative numbers, and (3) counts which of the two squares comes first, so that $(\pm3)^2+(\pm4)^2$ is counted as eight solutions. Formulas 1 and 2 are easier to apply and yield the results ordinarily understood by the "sum of two squares."

TABLE 63

POWERS OF A PRIME, $N = 4x+1 = 5$ AS SUM OF TWO SQUARES

N^a	Number of Ways of Expressing N^a as Sum of Two Squares		Solution
	In Any Manner	Relatively Prime	
5	1	1	1^2+2^2
5^2	1	1	3^2+4^2
5^3	2	1	5^2+10^2; 2^2+11^2
5^4	2	1	15^2+20^2; 7^2+24^2
5^5	3	1	25^2+50^2; 10^2+55^2; 38^2+41^2
5^6	3	1	75^2+100^2; 35^2+120^2; 44^2+117^2
5^7	4	1	50^2+275^2; 125^2+250^2; 190^2+205^2; 29^2+278^2
5^8	4	1	175^2+600^2; 375^2+500^2; 220^2+585^2; 336^2+527^2
5^9	5	1	250^2+1375^2; 950^2+1025^2; 625^2+1250^2; 145^2+1390^2; 718^2+1199^2
5^{10}	5	1	875^2+3000^2; 1875^2+2500^2; 1100^2+2925^2; 1680^2+2635^2; 237^2+3116^2

In Chapter XIV mention was made of the curious fact that every prime of the form $4x+1$ can always be expressed as the sum of two *relatively* prime squares and that in only one way. This unique representation is also true of a power of a prime or the double of either the prime or its power. Examples are: $5 = 1^2+2^2$; $2 \cdot 5 = 1^2+3^2$; $5^3 = 2^2+11^2$; $2 \cdot 5^3 = 9^2+13^2$. No number, prime or composite, of the form $4x-1$ can be expressed as the sum of two squares.

Formulas 1 and 2 reveal in an interesting manner the number of ways in which a power of a single prime of the form $4x+1$ may be expressed as the sum of two squares. We use these formulas alternately according as the power is odd or even. Selecting 5, the smallest prime of the requisite form, we have Table 63.

It is to be noted that in each case there is only a single representation where the squares are *relatively prime*, indicated in heavy type. This is always true of primes, their powers, and the doubles of these quantities.

$$* \qquad * \qquad *$$

The fact that the product of the sum of two squares by another sum of two squares always reproduces the sum of two squares is a truly remarkable relation. From $5 = 2^2+1^2$ and $13 = 3^2+2^2$, we have $5 \cdot 13 = 65 = 8^2+1^2$ or 7^2+4^2. This comes from the algebraic identity:

$$(a^2+b^2)(c^2+d^2) = (ac+bd)^2+(ad-bc)^2$$
$$= (ac-bd)^2+(ad+bc)^2. \quad \text{(Formula 3)}$$

If, in the original product, the two factors are alike, we have:

$$(a^2+b^2)(a^2+b^2) = (a^2+b^2)^2 = (a^2-b^2)^2+(2ab)^2,$$
$$\text{(Formula 4)}$$

which is the sum of two squares as before but this time in only a single way. For instance,

$$(3^2+2^2)(3^2+2^2) = 13^2 = (3^2-2^2)^2+(2 \cdot 3 \cdot 2)^2 = 5^2+12^2.$$

Observe the startling fact that Formula 4 is the Pythagorean triangle relation of Formula 1 in Chapter XIV.

If in the original product of Formula 3, $c = d = 1$, we have

$$2(a^2+b^2) = (a+b)^2+(a-b)^2, \quad \text{(Formula 5)}$$

again the sum of two squares and again in only one way. For example:

$$2(3^2+1^2) = (3+1)^2+(3-1)^2 = 20.$$

The sum of two squares can also be a cube. From Formula 4 we have $(a^2+b^2)^2 = (a^2-b^2)^2+(2ab)^2$. Multiplying both sides of the equation by (a^2+b^2) and using Formula 3, we have

$$(a^2+b^2)^3 = [(a^2-b^2)^2+(2ab)^2](a^2+b^2) = (a^3+ab^2)^2+(-a^2b-b^3)^2$$

or also

$$(a^3-3ab^2)^2+(3a^2b-b^3)^2.$$

If we take $a = 2$, $b = 1$ and substitute in these last two results we find $10^2+5^2 = 5^3$ and $2^2+11^2 = 5^3$. Thus the sum of the squares of (a^3+ab^2) and $(-a^2b-b^3)$ or of (a^3-3ab^2) and $(3a^2b-b^3)$ is a cube. In a similar way formulas for two squares whose sum is any nth power may be developed.

*   *   *

We can now undertake the seemingly formidable task of expressing the number, $2^7\cdot3^4\cdot5\cdot7^2\cdot13^3$, as the sum of two squares. The numbers 5 and 13 are primes of the form $4x+1$; hence we know that each can be expressed as the sum of two squares. The method of doing so when the prime is large is by no means easy. Allan Cunningham in his extensive table, *Quadratic Partitions*, showed this resolution, among others, for all primes of the requisite form not greater than 100,000. In the case of 5 and 13, we know by inspection that $5 = 2^2+1^2$ and $13 = 3^2+2^2$. Then by Formula 3:

$$5\cdot13 = (2^2+1^2)(3^2+2^2) = (6+2)^2+(4-3)^2 = 8^2+1^2,$$

or also

$$(6-2)^2+(4+3)^2 = 4^2+7^2.$$

Call these Solutions 1 and 2. Now let us rewrite the original number so that all powers with even exponents are in a group. Then $2^7\cdot3^4\cdot5\cdot7^2\cdot13^3$ becomes $(2^6\cdot3^4\cdot7^2\cdot13^2)(2\cdot5\cdot13)$. By Formula 5 we can express $2\cdot5\cdot13$ as the sum of two squares since we already have $5\cdot13$ so expressed. Using Solution 1 and Formula 5, we have $2(5\cdot13) = 9^2+7^2$. Similarly Solution 2 results in 11^2+3^2.

The remainder of the product $2^6 \cdot 3^4 \cdot 7^2 \cdot 13^2$ is a square since the exponents of the primes are all even. So we may write,

$$2^6 \cdot 3^4 \cdot 7^2 \cdot 13^2 = (2^3 \cdot 3^2 \cdot 7 \cdot 13)^2,$$

and multiplying this square by each term of the sum $9^2 + 7^2$, we have finally for Solution 1:

$$2^7 \cdot 3^4 \cdot 5 \cdot 7^2 \cdot 13^3 = (2^3 \cdot 3^2 \cdot 7 \cdot 13 \cdot 9)^2 + (2^3 \cdot 3^2 \cdot 7 \cdot 13 \cdot 7)^2$$

or

$$5580731520 = (58968)^2 + (45864)^2 = 3477225024 + 2103506496.$$

The second solution due to $11^2 + 3^2$ is:

$$2^7 \cdot 3^4 \cdot 5 \cdot 7^2 \cdot 13^3 = (2^3 \cdot 3^2 \cdot 7 \cdot 13 \cdot 11)^2 + (2^3 \cdot 3^2 \cdot 7 \cdot 13 \cdot 3)^2$$

or

$$5580731520 = (72072)^2 + (19656)^2 = 5194373184 + 386358336.$$

Formula 1 tells us that there should be a total of four solutions because the exponents of the primes 5 and 13, the only ones of the form $4x+1$, are $a_1 = 1$ and $a_2 = 3$, and substituting in the formula we have $(1+1)(3+1)/2 = 4$. Find the other two ways of expressing 5580731520 as the sum of two squares.†

*   *   *

The square of *any* integer can be expressed as the sum of two squares if the solution is not restricted to integers, and there are an infinite number of ways in which a given square may be expressed as the sum of two fractional squares. Of course, the solutions must be rational numbers, that is, the numerators and denominators of the fractions must be integers. Suppose we wanted two squares whose sum is 3^2, a square which does *not* have a prime divisor of the form $x+1$. Two solutions are $(9/5)^2$, $(12/5)^2$ and $(15/13)^2$, $(36/13)^2$, but we can find as many as we please as follows:

From $X^2 + Y^2 = Z^2$, we have $(X^2/Z^2) + (Y^2/Z^2) = 1$, and if ^{2} is our given square, we multiply through by it and obtain

$$(A^2 X^2/Z^2) + (A^2 Y^2/Z^2) = A^2.$$

† Problems indicated by a dagger are solved in Chapter XXVI.

Substituting the Pythagorean triangle relations of Chapter XIV, we obtain $A(m^2-n^2)/(m^2+n^2)$ and $2mnA/(m^2+n^2)$ as the fractions, the sum of whose squares is A^2. For $m = 2$, $n = 1$, and $m = 3$, $n = 2$, we obtain the two solutions given above.

Since solutions are not restricted to integers, m and n may also be fractions and then more simple formulas result, namely:

$$A(M^2-1)/(M^2+1),\quad 2MA/(M^2+1).$$

Here M may be any rational fraction. With the given square A^2 equal to 16, take for example $M = 2/3$; then

$$4(-5/9)/(13/9) = -20/13$$

and

$$(2[2/3]4)/(13/9) = 48/13,$$

are the two fractions the sum of whose squares is 16.

If we want two fractions whose squares add to unity, we have simply $(M^2-1)/(M^2+1)$ and $2M/(M^2+1)$.

*   *   *

It is possible to have three integral squares, X, Y, Z, so that their sum in pairs is also a square. For example, $44^2+240^2 = 244^2$; $44^2+117^2 = 125^2$; and $240^2+117^2 = 267^2$. Thus the box whose dimensions are $44 \times 117 \times 240$ has faces with integral diagonals. These numbers are rather few and far between; the next set are

$$828^2+3120^2 = 3228^2;\quad 828^2+2035^2 = 2197^2;$$
$$2035^2+3120^2 = 3725^2.$$

The general formulas are:

$$X = 2mn(3m^2-n^2)(3n^2-m^2)$$
$$Y = 8mn(m^4-n^4)$$
$$Z = (m^2-n^2)(m^2+n^2+4mn)(m^2+n^2-4mn).$$

The two triplets above come from $m = 2$, $n = 1$ and $m = 3$, $n =$ respectively.

*   *   *

Another striking fact about squares is that any integer can be expressed as the sum of no more than four squares. The proof this theorem is not simple. Many integers can be expressed with smaller number of squares. Obviously all squares are "sums" of single square, and we have seen that $2^{a_0} Q^2 P$, where P is the product of primes of the form $4x+1$, can be expressed as the sum of two squares. All other integers can be expressed as the sum of only three squares except the special integers of the form $4^a(8x+7)$, such as 7, 28, 60, 92, etc. These require four squares.

* * *

An elegant branch of number theory deals with "Quadratic Residues" or remainders of squares. These will be discussed in Chapter XIX.

* * *

There is a class of integers known as automorphic numbers for whose squares the last x digits are the same as those of the number itself. Thus for $x = 1$, any number ending in 5 has its square ending in 5; for $x = 2$, any number ending in 25 has its square ending in 25; for $x = 3$, any number ending in 625 has its square ending in the same three digits. Another kind of solution for $x = 1, 2, 3$, is 6, 76, or 376; the squares of numbers having these endings end similarly. Endings of automorphic numbers have been calculated to many places—the last 16 digits of the only possible ones in the scale of 10 are 6259918212890625 and 3740081787109376. There are also the two rather trivial cases of numbers ending in zeros or in zeros followed by a terminate 1, such as 000 or 0001, whose squares end in the same digits.

Numbers may be automorphic in some other scale than 10. In the scale whose radix is 6, the last seven digits of automorphic numbers must be either 1350213 or 4205344. To be automorphic for n digits in the scale whose radix is p, we must have, $x^2 \equiv x \bmod p^n$.

* * *

There are many noteworthy relations involving squares and their digits. The four-digit square 2025 is still a square, 3136, when each of its digits is increased by unity. The two-digit square 25 possesses the same property.

By reversing the digits of 65, we obtain 56, and $65^2 - 56^2 = 33^2$; the only two-digit relationship of this type.

Table 64 lists squares containing all nine digits not repeated, and Table 65 lists squares using the ten digits in this manner. Actually 8 entries could be made in Table 64 and 87 in Table 65.

TABLE 64

SQUARE NUMBERS CONTAINING THE NINE DIGITS UNREPEATED

$11826^2 = 139854276$	$19629^2 = 385297641$	$25059^2 = 627953481$
$12363^2 = 152843769$	$20316^2 = 412739856$	$25572^2 = 653927184$
$12543^2 = 157326849$	$22887^2 = 523814769$	$25941^2 = 672935481$
$14676^2 = 215384976$	$23019^2 = 529874361$	$26409^2 = 697435281$
$15681^2 = 245893761$	$23178^2 = 537219684$	$26733^2 = 714653289$
$15963^2 = 254817369$	$23439^2 = 549386721$	$27129^2 = 735982641$
$18072^2 = 326597184$	$24237^2 = 587432169$	$27273^2 = 743816529$
$19023^2 = 361874529$	$24276^2 = 589324176$	$29034^2 = 842973156$
$19377^2 = 375468129$	$24441^2 = 597362481$	$29106^2 = 847159236$
$19569^2 = 382945761$	$24807^2 = 615387249$	$30384^2 = 923187456$

TABLE 65

SQUARE NUMBERS CONTAINING ALL TEN DIGITS UNREPEATED

$32043^2 = 1026753849$	$45624^2 = 2081549376$
$32286^2 = 1042385796$	$55446^2 = 3074258916$
$33144^2 = 1098524736$	$68763^2 = 4728350169$
$35172^2 = 1237069584$	$83919^2 = 7042398561$
$39147^2 = 1532487609$	$99066^2 = 9814072356$

Here are a few relations taken from the flyleaf of an old Bible showing the difference of two squares equal to a number containing all the nine digits used once only.

TABLE 66

DIFFERENCE OF TWO SQUARES CONTAINING THE NINE DIGITS

$$11113^2 - 200^2 = 11313 \cdot 10913 = 123458769$$
$$31111^2 - 200^2 = 31311 \cdot 30911 = 967854321$$
$$11117^2 - 200^2 = 11317 \cdot 10917 = 123547689$$
$$11356^2 - 2000^2 = 13356 \cdot 9356 = 124958736$$
$$12695^2 - 6017^2 = 18712 \cdot 6678 = 124958736$$
$$16260^2 - 11808^2 = 28068 \cdot 4452 = 124958736$$
$$12372^2 - 300^2 = 12672 \cdot 12072 = 152976384$$

Note that the first squares in the first two examples are reversals of each other as is also true of one of the factors.

It is not known why the computer used these particular combinations of digits, but in fact any odd number exceeding unity, and a even numbers which are multiples of 4 except 4 itself, can be expresse as the *difference* of two squares. It would have been better perhaps to express the numbers whose digits are in regularly ascending or descending order as the difference of two squares. This the present writer has done below:

$$123456789 = 3^2 \cdot 3607 \cdot 3803 = 61728395^2 - 61728394^2$$
$$= 20576133^2 - 20576130^2 = 6858715^2 - 6858706^2$$
$$= 18917^2 - 15310^2 = 18133^2 - 14330^2$$
$$= 11115^2 - 294^2.$$
$$987654321 = 3^2 \cdot 17^2 \cdot 379221 = 493827161^2 - 493827160^2$$
$$= 164609055^2 - 164609052^2$$
$$= 54869689^2 - 54869680^2 = 29048665^2 - 29048648^2$$
$$= 9682911^2 - 9682860^2 = 3227705^2 - 3227552^2$$
$$= 1708889^2 - 1708600^2 = 570015^2 - 569148^2$$
$$= 191101^2 - 188560^2.$$

It is interesting to note that the nine digits can be permuted in $9! = 362880$ ways. One-quarter of these, or 90720 integers, are of the form $4x + 2$, such as numbers ending in 02, 06, 10, 14, . . .98, and are therefore not expressible as the difference of two squares. With the integers 1 and 4 there are 90722 numbers in all not so expressible. This leaves 272158 numbers involving all nine digits used once only which *can* be expressed as the difference of two squares; the table in the old Bible, therefore, was far from complete and had little claim to distinction.

* * *

Squares and tables of squares are of great use in factoring numbers. For instance, since any prime of the form $4x + 1$ can be expressed as the sum of two squares, the product of two such primes can be expressed as the sum of two squares in either of two ways, as shown by Formula 3. Hence:

1. If an odd number can be expressed as the sum of two squares in two ways, we know it must be composite and there are means for obtaining its factors (see Chapter XXI). If the two squares are not co-prime, we know immediately that their common factor is a divisor of the number.

2. If an odd number can be expressed as the sum of two *relatively prime* squares in only a single way, it must be a prime or its power. It may be that the number is also expressible as the sum of two

squares having a common factor, in which case the number cannot be a prime or its square but must be some higher power of the prime. The common factor is itself a power of the prime.

3. If an unknown number is of the form $4x+1$, and if it cannot be expressed as the sum of two squares in even a single way, it is composite and contains an even number of prime factors, each of the form $4x-1$.

4. If the unknown number is of the form $4x-1$, it cannot be expressed as the sum of two squares in any case, and therefore the method of square sums is inapplicable for testing whether or not the number is a prime.

Let us examine the number 221. Subtracting squares from it, starting with 196, we obtain immediately the remainder 25, so that $221 = 196 + 25 = 14^2 + 5^2$. Continuing, we find also that $221 - 121 = 100$ so that $221 = 11^2 + 10^2$. This proves definitely that 221 is composite since it is the sum of two squares in two ways. We shall defer to Chapter XXI the method of finding the actual factors.

Now take the number 229. Subtracting squares, we find immediately that $229 = 15^2 + 2^2$; but continuing, we need go only to 11^2, which leaves a remainder just under half the number, before it is ascertained that no other two squares add to 229. Hence 229 is surely a prime.

The number 77, when tested in this manner, proves not to be expressible as the sum of two squares, although it is of the form $4x+1$. Hence, 77 is composite, and composed of an even number of factors of the form $4x-1$, in fact, 7 and 11.

If we wish to examine 223, it is noted that it is of the form $4x-1$; hence it is futile to attempt to express this number as the sum of two squares, and other means of factoring it must be resorted to.

Of course, this method would not be used for numbers as small as those in the above examples. Suppose, however, we wish to factor 16000001. This resolution was necessary in computing the numbers which may be one side of 8000000 Pythagorean triangles, as shown in Table 58 of Chapter XIV ($T = 8000000$ and $2T+1$ must be resolved into factors). The available factor tables by Lehmer go to only 10000000; the method of the sum of two squares was therefore resorted to. It so happens that 16000001 is immediately observed to be the sum of the two squares $(4000)^2 + 1^2$; hence if two other squares can be found adding to this same sum, the number is composite and its factors can be found. The table of two-digit square termini shows that only squares ending in 00, 01, 25, and 76 leave two-digit square endings when subtracted from 16000001. However, the three-digit square termini of numbers can be used—there are of course more than 22 of them. The number of trials is thus reduced considerably, and utilizing a table of squares we find in only a few minutes that $16000001 - 1049^2$ is a square, so that

$$16000001 = 4000^2 + 1^2 = 1049^2 + 3860^2.$$

The game is up; the number is in our power and within a few minutes we find that it is the product of 229 and 69869. Looking up these latter numbers in the factor tables (we could have used the same method for them as above), we find that 229 is prime and that 69869 can be further resolved into 641 and 109, finally yielding $16000001 = 229 \cdot 641 \cdot 109$.

* * *

In Chapter XIV we found formulas for the form of two squares whose sum is a square. There are also formulas for the form of three or more integral squares whose sum is an integral square. Thus one way of solving $x^2 + y^2 + z^2 = w^2$ is by:

$$x = p^2 + q^2 - r^2$$
$$y = 2pr$$
$$x = 2qr$$
$$w = p^2 + q^2 + r^2.$$

Here p, q, and r need not necessarily be rational. Table 67 gives a few results using these formulas:

TABLE 67

Square Equal to the Sum of Three Squares

p	q	r	x	y	z	w	Sum of Three Squares = a Square
1	1	1	1	2	2	3	$1^2 + 2^2 + 2^2 = 3^2$
$\sqrt{2}/2$	$3\sqrt{2}/2$	$\sqrt{2}$	3	2	6	7	$3^2 + 2^2 + 6^2 = 7^2$
1	2	2	1	4	8	9	$1^2 + 4^2 + 8^2 = 9^2$
2	3	4	−3	16	24	29	$3^2 + 16^2 + 24^2 = 29^2$

* * *

A curious relation among squares states that the sum of $(n+1)$ consecutive squares, beginning with the square of $n(2n+1)$, is equal to the sum of the squares of the next n consecutive integers.

Tabulating a few values, we have Table 68.

TABLE 68

LIKE SUMS OF CONSECUTIVE SQUARES

n	
1	$3^2 + 4^2 = 5^2$
2	$10^2 + 11^2 + 12^2 = 13^2 + 14^2$
3	$21^2 + 22^2 + 23^2 + 24^2 = 25^2 + 26^2 + 27^2$
4	$36^2 + 37^2 + 38^2 + 39^2 + 40^2 = 41^2 + 42^2 + 43^2 + 44^2$
5	$55^2 + 56^2 + 57^2 + 58^2 + 59^2 + 60^2 = 61^2 + 62^2 + 63^2 + 64^2 + 65^2$

There are many formulas for consecutive squares whose sum is a single square. Table 69 gives a few examples.

TABLE 69

SUM OF CONSECUTIVE SQUARES A SQUARE

$$1^2 + 2^2 + 3^2 + \ldots + 24^2 = 4900 = 70^2$$
$$18^2 + 19^2 + 20^2 + \ldots + 28^2 = 5929 = 77^2$$
$$25^2 + 26^2 + 27^2 + \ldots + 50^2 = 38025 = 195^2$$
$$38^2 + 39^2 + 40^2 + \ldots + 48^2 = 20449 = 143^2$$
$$456^2 + 457^2 + 458^2 + \ldots + 466^2 = 2337841 = 1529^2$$
$$854^2 + 855^2 + 856^2 + \ldots + 864^2 = 8116801 = 2849^2$$

In addition to consecutive squares whose sum is a square, we can have numbers in other arithmetic progressions the sum of whose squares is a square, such as

$$2^2 + 5^2 + 8^2 + 11^2 + 14^2 + 17^2 + 20^2 + 23^2 + 26^2 = 48^2.$$

In passing, we might mention some remarkable relations among consecutive cubes whose sum is a cube, such as:

$$3^3 + 4^3 + 5^3 = 6^3$$
$$6^3 + 7^3 + 8^3 + \ldots + 69^3 = 180^3$$
$$1134^3 + 1135^3 + 1136^3 + \ldots + 2133^3 = 16830^3.$$

*   *   *

Three squares may be in arithmetic progression, but four or more cannot. The proof of this last fact is difficult. To find three squares X^2, Y^2, Z^2 in arithmetic progression, we must have $Y^2 - X^2 = Z^2 - Y^2$, or $2Y^2 = X^2 + Z^2$. If $X = p - q$ and $Z = p + q$, then $X^2 + Z^2 = 2(p^2 + q^2)$. Then $Y^2 = p^2 + q^2$, which is the fundamental Pythagorean triangle relation given in Chapter XIV. Therefore, $p = m^2 - n^2$; $q = 2mn$; $Y = m^2 + n^2$; $X = m^2 - n^2 - 2mn$; $Z = m^2 - n^2 + 2mn$. (If instead we make $p = 2mn$; $q = m^2 - n^2$; Y and Z remain unchanged but X becomes $2mn - (m^2 - n^2)$ and the two results can be combined by writing $X = \pm [m^2 - n^2 - 2mn]$.) Table 70 shows a few square triplets in arithmetic progression.

TABLE 70

THREE SQUARES IN ARITHMETIC PROGRESSION

m	n	X	Y	Z	X^2	Y^2	Z^2	Common Difference
2	1	∓ 1	5	7	1	25	49	24
3	2	∓ 7	13	17	49	169	289	120
4	1	± 7	17	23	49	289	529	240
4	3	∓ 17	25	31	289	625	961	336
5	2	± 1	29	41	1	841	1681	840

The mathematician Frenicle neatly described the formulas for numbers whose squares are in arithmetic progression by saying that the middle one, Y, is the hypotenuse of a Pythagorean triangle; the smallest, X, is the difference; and the largest, Z, the sum of the legs of such a triangle, giving $Y = m^2 + n^2$; $X = m^2 - n^2 - 2mn$; $Z = m^2 - n^2 + 2mn$ as before.

Some problems require three squares, not necessarily integral, in arithmetic progression when the common difference d is given. This requires: $Y^2 - X^2 = d = (m^4 + 2m^2n^2 + n^4) - (m^4 + n^4 + 4m^2n^2 - 4m^3n - 2m^2n^2 + 4mn^3) = 4mn(m^2 - n^2)$. Rational solutions in integers or fractions may be impossible and even when possible may be very difficult to obtain. It will be noted from Table 70 that the common difference, when the squares are integers, is always divisible by 24; this is a necessary condition for integral solutions.

For a given d, as 240, we must find m and n in $240 = 4mn(m^2 - n^2)$, or $60 = mn(m^2 - n^2)$. The values $m = 4$, $n = 1$ found by trial satisfy the equation and lead to a solution.

If d is not a multiple of 24, a solution in integers is impossible but one in fractions may sometimes be obtained. Thus for $d = 5$,

$$5 = 4mn(m^2 - n^2).$$

Find if possible a solution to:

$$5K^2 = 4MN(M^2 - N^2),$$

then

$$5 = 4(M/\sqrt{K})(N/\sqrt{K})[(M/\sqrt{K})^2 - (N/\sqrt{K})^2]$$

and the values $m = M/\sqrt{K}$ and $n = N/\sqrt{K}$ will lead to rational fractional solutions X, Y, Z as required. The irrational quantity $\sqrt{K}$ will always vanish in X, Y, Z since it always appears to the second degree. A solution of $5 \cdot K^2 = 4MN(M^2 - N^2)$, found by trial, is $5 \cdot 12^2 = 4 \cdot 5 \cdot 4(5^2 - 4^2)$. Then $m = 5/\sqrt{12}$ and $n = 4/\sqrt{12}$, substituted in the formulas for X, Y, Z, give $X = -31/12$, $Y = 41/12$, $Z = 49/12$, whence

$$(1681/144) - (961/144) = (2401/144) - (1681/144) = (720/144) = 5,$$

that is, $961/144$, $1681/144$, $2401/144$ are the squares in arithmetic progression that have a common difference of 5.

* * *

The Ladies' Diary for 1739–1740 contained a curious problem which the reader should now have no difficulty in solving. The problem deals with three Dutchmen and their wives who went marketing for pigs.

The men's names were Henry, Ely, and Cornelius; the women's Gertrude, Catherine, and Anna. Each person bought as many pigs as he or she paid dollars for each pig and each man spent 63 dollars more than his wife. Henry bought 23 more pigs than Catherine, and Ely 11 more than Gertrude. What was the name of each man's wife?†

A similar problem deals with five mothers and their daughters. Each of the 10 women bought as many yards of cloth as she paid cents per yard, and each mother spent $4.05 more than her daughter. Mrs. Robinson spent $2.88 more than Mrs. Evans, who spent about one-fourth as much as Mrs. Jones. Mrs. Smith spent most of all. Mrs. Brown bought 63 yards more than Bessie, one of the girls. Anna bought 48 yards more than Mary and spent $29.12 more than Emily. The Christian name of the other girl was Ada. Now what was her surname?†

It is reported that when this problem was once submitted to

Sydney, Australia, evening newspaper which ran a special column for such "intellect sharpeners," it was rejected on the grounds of being childish and because the newspaper only published problems capable of solution!

*　　*　　*

An ancient problem, discussed by the Arabs in the Middle Ages and closely allied to the one about Captain John Smith and his progeny, described in Problem 59 of Chapter XXV, concerns "congruent" numbers. A number k is called congruent if integers x and y exist such that both x^2+ky^2 and x^2-ky^2 are squares. The expression x^2-ky^2 may also be a negative square as it is always possible to obtain a positive solution from such a negative one. No certain method for ascertaining the congruence of a given number is known even in these modern times when mighty analytic tools are at our disposal. It is also difficult to find a solution even when we know that k is congruent. For values of k less than 100 and containing no square factor, only the 36 values 5, 6, 7, 13, 14, 15, 21, 22, 23, 29, 30, 31, 34, 37, 38, 39, 41, 46, 47, 53, 55, 61, 62, 65, 69, 70, 71, 77, 78, 79, 85, 86, 87, 93, 94, and 95 are possible. The exception was made for square factors, because if $x^2+ky^2 = u^2$ and $x^2-ky^2 = v^2$ have solutions when k has no such square factor, they will also have solutions for a new constant $K = kL^2$ by writing $L^2x^2+kL^2y^2 = L^2u^2$ and $L^2x^2-kL^2y^2 = L^2v^2$, that is $(Lx)^2+Ky^2 = (Lu)^2$ and $(Lx)^2-Ky^2 = (Lv)^2$. Thus kL^2 is a congruent number if k is. Fourteen additional integers less than 100 containing squares are thus congruent: 20, 24, 28, 45, 52, 54, 56, 60, 63, 80, 84, 88, 92, and 96. The remaining 49 integers, among which are 1 and 2, are incongruent. Thus $x^2+y^2 = u^2$ and $x^2-y^2 = v^2$ are impossible and also $x^2+2y^2 = u^2$ and $x^2-2y^2 = v^2$.

Proofs exist that a prime $8x+3$ or the product of two such primes is incongruent; this is also true of the double of a prime $8x+5$ or twice the product of two such primes. A prime k is also incongruent if no number m exists, smaller than one-half k, such that either m^2+1 or m^2-2 is divisible by k.

An example of a solution for the smallest congruent number 5 is $1^2+5\cdot12^2 = 49^2$ and $41^2-5\cdot12^2 = 31^2$. A smaller solution: $2^2+5\cdot1^2 = 3^2$ and $2^2-5\cdot1^2 = -1^2$ can be obtained if a negative square is permitted in the second equation. From such a negative solution positive ones can always be obtained as described later.

The next set of values satisfying $x^2 + 5y^2 = u^2$, $x^2 - 5y^2 = v^2$ are $x = 3344161$; $y = 1494696$; $u = 4728001$; and $v = 1494696$. The third smallest set is not so small:

$$x = 654686219104361;$$
$$y = 178761481355556;$$
$$u = 767067390499249;$$

and

$$v = 518493692732129.$$

When it was required to find three squares in arithmetic progression having a given common difference d, we found that this led to the equation $dK^2 = 4MN(M^2 - N^2)$. Suppose d is a prime. Then M, N, and K may be taken relatively prime, for if they have a common factor it can be cancelled. Since $M^2 - N^2$, M and N are relatively prime, two of these three factors must be squares, and the third d times a square so as to correspond to the left-hand side of the equation. For the assumption that N is a square, p^2; $M^2 - N^2$ a square, q^2; and $M = dr^2$; we obtain by substituting the values of N and M in $M^2 - N^2 = q^2$, the result $d^2r^4 - p^4 = q^2$. Then

$$(dr^2 + p^2)(dr^2 - p^2) = q^2.$$

Each factor on the left must be (1) a square or (2) twice a square since p, q, r are relatively prime and therefore the G.C.D. of these factors cannot exceed 2. In the former instance this leads to $dr^2 + p^2 = u^2$; $dr^2 - p^2 = v^2$, which can be written as:

$$p^2 + dr^2 = u^2$$
$$p^2 - dr^2 = -v^2.$$

We have therefore arrived at the result that d must be a congruent number. We have already found that if $d = 5$, then $p = 2$; $r = 1$ $u = 3$; $v = 1$. Then

$$N = p^2 = 2^2; \quad M = 5r^2 = 5 \cdot 1^2;$$
$$M^2 - N^2 = q^2 = u^2v^2 = 3^2 \cdot 1^2.$$

Then $5K^2 = 4 \cdot 5 \cdot 4 \cdot 3^2$, whence $K = 12$, and as before the value $M/\sqrt{k} = 5/\sqrt{12}$ and $N/\sqrt{K} = 4/\sqrt{12}$ substituted in the formula for three squares in arithmetic progression lead to the solution $(31/12)^2$, $(41/12)^2$, and $(49/12)^2$, whose common difference is 5.

Mention was made previously of the fact that when $x^2 - ky^2 = -v^2$

another solution can be found with a positive square v^2. This is obtained from the following general rule applying to all congruent numbers. To solve:

$$X^2 + abY^2 = Z^2$$
$$X^2 - abY^2 = W^2,$$

first find a solution of the auxiliary equations:

$$ax^2 + by^2 = nz^2$$
$$ax^2 - by^2 = \pm nw^2.$$

Then $X = n(z^4 + w^4)/2$ and $Y = 2xyzw$.

As an example, let $a = 1$, $b = 5$, $n = 1$, whence $x^2 + 5y^2 = z^2$ and $x^2 - 5y^2 = \pm w^2$. By trial we have $2^2 + 5 \cdot 1^2 = 3^2$ and $2^2 - 5 \cdot 1^2 = -1^2$ so that $x = 2$, $y = 1$, $z = 3$, $w = 1$. Then $X = (3^4 + 1^4)/2 = 41$; $Y = 2 \cdot 2 \cdot 1 \cdot 3 \cdot 1 = 12$, whence $41^2 + 5 \cdot 12^2 = 49^2$ and $41^2 - 5 \cdot 12^2 = +31^2$, where now the square on the right-hand side of the second equation is positive. We can proceed again and find $X_1 = (49^4 + 31^4)/2 = 3344161$, and $Y_1 = 2 \cdot 41 \cdot 49 \cdot 31 = 1494696$, etc.

The congruent numbers 47, 53, and 61 each require a 15-digit number as the minimum value of x in the dual equations; 79 requires a 17-digit number. The minimum values of x, y, u, and v in $x^2 + 101y^2 = u^2$ and $x^2 - 101y^2 = v^2$ are:

$$x = 2015242462949760001961$$
$$y = 118171431852779451900$$
$$u = 1628124370727269996961$$
$$v = 2339148435306225006961.$$

Further discussion of this interesting aspect of congruent numbers must be abandoned here. If the reader can find three rational squares in arithmetic progression (integral ones are impossible) whose common difference is 23, he will have obtained a very good grasp of the subject.†

*   *   *

An unsolved problem, although much work has been done within the last few years, is the determination of the number of unlike squares into which a rectangle may be divided. It is not sufficient that the sum of the areas of the squares equals that of the rectangle, for any integer can be expressed as the sum of no more than four integer squares. Squares are required which can be *geometrically* assembled into a rectangle, and, in particular, a square. Thus the number 78, corresponding to the rectangle whose sides are 6 and 13, for instance, is equal to $7^2 + 5^2 + 2^2$, but squares of these dimensions cannot be placed together, without cutting, to form a rectangle of the given dimensions. The number 78 is also equal to $8^2 + 3^2 + 2^2 + 1^2$ and $6^2 + 5^2 + 4^2 + 1^2$, but neither group of squares can be assembled into a 6-by-13, a 3-by-26, or a 2-by-39 rectangle. Only certain rectangles, that is, composite numbers, can be separated into unlike squares. What are the characteristics of such composite numbers?

FIG. 8A. TWENTY-EIGHT DIFFERENT SQUARES ASSEMBLED INTO A SQUARE

When this decomposition was found possible it required no fewer than nine unlike squares to make it. It is an unsolved question whether a rectangle can be separated into fewer than nine different squares. Again, until quite recently, no *square* had been found which could be separated into *different* squares, but then 1015^2 was discovered, which can be decomposed into the following 28 squares:

$$2^2 + 18^2 + 22^2 + 37^2 + 38^2 + 39^2 + 41^2 + 43^2 + 49^2 + 67^2$$
$$+ 72^2 + 80^2 + 85^2 + 103^2 + 116^2 + 154^2 + 164^2 + 175^2 + 178^2$$
$$+ 192^2 + 200^2 + 207^2 + 215^2 + 222^2 + 230^2 + 247^2 + 422^2 + 593^2.$$

It is quite a feat to assemble squares of the given dimensions into a single square measuring 1015 on a side. Figure 8A shows how this is accomplished.

Another solution for this 1015 square, again involving 28 pieces, is obtained from the squares of 13; 16; 17; 23; 30; 43; 47; 84; 92; 93; 119; 120; 142; 163; 165; 167; 177; 183; 188; 199; 215; 219; 261; 270; 280; 363; 372; and 382.

The square measuring 608 on a side can be decomposed into 26 smaller dissimilar squares. The solution of this problem and the assembly of the 28-piece square having a side of 1015 are left to the reader.

The square measuring 175 on a side, total area 30625, can be decomposed into 24 dissimilar squares. As far as the writer knows, this is the smallest number of dissimilar squares into which a square can be decomposed. Starting counterclockwise from the upper left, the nine border squares are 55^2, 56^2, 64^2, 33^2, 35^2, 43^2, 51^2, 81^2, and 39^2. With this as a clue, the reader should not have too much difficulty fitting in the remaining 15 squares: 1^2, 2^2, 3^2, 4^2, 5^2, 8^2, 9^2, 14^2, 16^2, 18^2, 20^2, 29^2, 30^2, 31^2, and 38^2.

A quite remarkable square measures 4920 on a side, has an area of 24206400, and can be decomposed into 38 dissimilar squares. There are 11 border squares: 1348^2, 1440^2, 2132^2, 840^2, 922^2, 1026^2, 1130^2, 1177^2, 1587^2, 893^2, 1092^2, reading counterclockwise from the upper left. The remaining squares have sides of 47, 82, 104, 108, 120, 164, 173, 199, 217, 240, 244, 256, 281, 287, 310, 420, 454, 527, 534, 584, 615, 627, 692, 694, 758, 900, and 984. The square is illustrated in Figure 8B.

The number 1056 is a rectangle which may be decomposed into nine different squares having sides as indicated in Figure 8C. Can the reader reassemble these into a rectangle?†

A somewhat different problem is the decomposition of a square into the least number of squares some of which may be alike. Again, it is not sufficient that the numerical sum of the squares add to a square; the smaller squares must be capable of being assembled geometrically into a square. The square measuring 13 on a side may be divided into a number of smaller squares some of which are alike. For

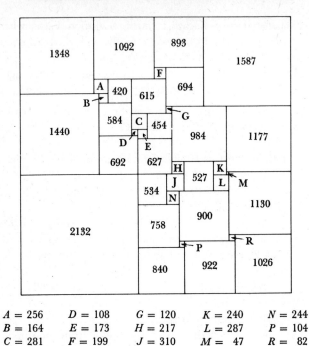

$A = 256$	$D = 108$	$G = 120$	$K = 240$	$N = 244$
$B = 164$	$E = 173$	$H = 217$	$L = 287$	$P = 104$
$C = 281$	$F = 199$	$J = 310$	$M = 47$	$R = 82$

FIG. 8B. THIRTY-EIGHT DIFFERENT SQUARES ASSEMBLED INTO A SQUARE

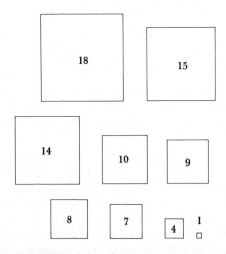

FIG. 8C. NINE SQUARES TO BE ASSEMBLED INTO A RECTANGLE

example, a square measuring 12 on a side and 25 unit squares can be so assembled; also, $1 \cdot 10^2 + 7 \cdot 3^2 + 6 \cdot 1^2$. The first solution requires 26 squares, the second $1 + 7 + 6 = 14$ squares. What is the least number of squares?†

* * *

Factorials lead to a difficult question involving squares. If we look at the column headed $(n-1)! + 1$ of Table 22 in Chapter VII, it will be noted that 25 and 121 are squares, that is, $4! + 1 = 25 = 5^2$ and $5! + 1 = 121 = 11^2$. It is also true that $7! + 1 = 5041 = 71^2$. What in general are the solutions of $x! + 1 = Y^2$ besides the three values of $x = 4, 5, 7$? The equation has been investigated up to $x = 1020$ and no other solution found. If any such squares exist they must be enormous numbers; even 100! has 158 digits, and factorial 1020 has over 2600.

* * *

Speaking of squares, the square of the sum of the first n consecutive integers is equal to the sum of the cubes of these integers, that is, $(1 + 2 + 3 + \ldots n)^2 = 1^3 + 2^3 + 3^3 + \ldots n^3$ and since $1 + 2 + 3 + \ldots n$ is an arithmetic progression whose sum is $n(n+1)/2$, it follows that $1^3 + 2^3 + 3^3 + \ldots n^3 = [n(n+1)/2]^2$. On the other hand, the sum of the *squares* of consecutive integers is given by

$$1^2 + 2^2 + 3^2 + \ldots n^2 = n(n+1)(2n+1)/6.$$

* * *

The late Dr. Jekuthiel Ginsburg of Yeshiva College observed that 6 has the divisors, 1, 2, 3, 6, which have 1, 2, 2, and 4 divisors, respectively. Then $(1 + 2 + 2 + 4)^2 = 1^3 + 2^3 + 2^3 + 4^3$. Again 30 has the divisors 1, 2, 3, 5, 6, 10, 15, 30, the number of whose divisors is 1, 2, 2, 2, 4, 4, 4, 8. Hence

$$(1 + 2 + 2 + 2 + 4 + 4 + 4 + 8)^2$$
$$= 1^3 + 2^3 + 2^3 + 2^3 + 4^3 + 4^3 + 4^3 + 8^3 = 729.$$

* * *

Another relation of a somewhat different type is

$$2(1 + 2 + \ldots n)^4 = (1^5 + 2^5 + \ldots n^5) + (1^7 + 2^7 + \ldots n^7).$$

* * *

A triangular number is a number of the form $a(a+1)/2$. Using the notation: $\sum_1^n a(a+1)/2$ to represent the sum of n numbers of this form, with "a" taking on integral values from 1 to n we get:

$$3\left[\sum_1^n a(a+1)/2\right]^3 = \sum_1^n [a(a+1)/2]^3 + 2\sum_1^n [a(a+1)/2]^4.$$

If $n = 3$, then $3(1+3+6)^3 = 1^3+3^3+6^3+2(1^4+3^4+6^4) = 3000$. If $n = 4$, then

$$3(1+3+6+10)^3 = 1^3+3^3+6^3+10^3+2(1^4+3^4+6^4+10^4) = 24000,$$

and so on.

*   *   *

Here are a few more square curiosities:

$$12345678987654321 = (111111111)^2$$
$$278886^2 = 77777400996$$
$$278887^2 = 77777958469.$$

*   *   *

It is not difficult to find a number of squares whose sum is equal to the sum of other squares, for example, $4^2+5^2+6^2 = 8^2+3^2+2^2$. More noteworthy are such relations which hold *simultaneously* for several powers; thus

$$1^n+4^n+5^n+5^n+6^n+9^n = 2^n+3^n+3^n+7^n+7^n+8^n,$$

which holds for $n = 1, 2, 3$. Such a relation is called a "multigrade." The symbol $\overset{n}{=}$ is used to indicate the range of powers for which such a multigrade holds; the "trigrade" above, in abbreviated form, would be written $1, 4, 5, 5, 6, 9 \overset{3}{=} 2, 3, 3, 7, 7, 8$. This saves writing the exponent for each power. More remarkable yet are the pentagrades $0, 5, 6, 16, 17, 22 \overset{5}{=} 1, 2, 10, 12, 20, 21$; and $1, 11, 13, 33, 35, 45 \overset{5}{=} 3, 5, 21, 25, 41, 45$. If we add the respective terms of these two series we get $1, 16, 19, 49, 52, 67 \overset{5}{=} 4, 7, 31, 37, 61, 64$. Other pentagrades are $1, 5, 10, 18, 23, 27 \overset{5}{=} 2, 3, 13, 15, 25, 26$; and $1, 6, 7, 17, 18, 23 \overset{5}{=} 2, 3, 11, 13, 21, 22$. Becoming more literal, we have also $a, (a+4b+c), (a+b+2c), (a+9b+4c), (a+6b+5c), (a+10b+6c) \overset{5}{=} (a+b), (a+c), (a+6b+2c), (a+4b+4c), (a+10b+5c),$

$(a+9b+6c)$. Finally there is 1, 13, 28, 70, 82, 124, 139, 151 $\stackrel{7}{=}$ 4, 7, 34, 61, 91, 118, 145, 148.

Sometimes the relationship holds only for even powers. Thus 1, 2, 31, 32, 55, 61, 68 $\stackrel{2n}{=}$ 17, 20, 23, 44, 49, 64, 67 for $n = 1, 2, 3, 4, 5$.

We can become quite selective in our choice of the terms. Thus 43, 61, 67 $\stackrel{2}{=}$ 47, 53, 71; also 127, 149, 151 $\stackrel{2}{=}$ 131, 139, 157; also 281, 281, 1181, 1181 $\stackrel{3}{=}$ 101, 641, 821, 1361 involve only primes.

Again we can have the sum of the squares be a square; thus in 1, 14, 24, 27, 52, 57, 63, 74 $\stackrel{2}{=}$ 5, 10, 20, 31, 48, 61, 67, 70, the sum of the squares is 130^2, but the sum of the first powers is, of course, *not* a square. Another example is 27, 30, 40, 53, 76, 87, 93, 98 $\stackrel{2}{=}$ 28, 33, 39, 50, 73, 86, 96, 99, where the sum of the squares is 194^2.

* * *

Sums of powers of digits, equal to sums of like powers of other digits, serve as generators of powers whose sum is the same as that of these powers with the digits reversed. Thus, starting with

$$4^2+5^2+6^2 = 8^2+3^2+2^2,$$

we can combine in any manner the digits on the right- and left-hand side of the equal sign and obtain, for example, 48, 53, and 62. These numbers, with the digits reversed, are 84, 35, and 26. Then $48^2+53^2+62^2 = 84^2+35^2+26^2$. Continuing, we may also use 48, 52, 63; 43, 58, 62; 43, 52, 68; 42, 58, 63; 42, 53, 68. The sum of the squares of each of these triplets is the same as the sum of the squares when the digits are reversed. There are a total of $3 \times 2 \times 1 = 3! = 6$ permutations and therefore 6 equations can be written.

This relation, too, can hold for several powers. Thus from 8, 5, 3, 2 $\stackrel{2}{=}$ 7, 6, 4, 1 as a generator, we can obtain $4 \times 3 \times 2 \times 1 = 4! = 24$ ways in which the right- and left-hand digits can be associated to form equations having the digit-reversal property. Two examples are 87, 56, 34, 21 $\stackrel{2}{=}$ 12, 43, 65, 78; and 86, 54, 31, 27 $\stackrel{2}{=}$ 72, 13, 45, 68.

If some of the terms in the generator are zero, the relations can still hold. Thus 1, 3, 5, 9 $\stackrel{2}{=}$ 4, 6, 8, 0, from which one of the 24 possible equalities is 10, 54, 96, 38 $\stackrel{2}{=}$ 01, 45, 69, 83. Even the familiar $3^2+4^2 = 5^2+0^2$ produces $35^2+40^2 = 04^2+53^2$ or $30^2+45^2 = 54^2+03^2$.

These relations originate from the fact that if

$$x_1{}^2+x_2{}^2+ \ldots x_n{}^2 = y_1{}^2+y_2{}^2+ \ldots y_n{}^2$$

(some of these terms may be zeros), then

$$(10x_1+y_1)^2 + (10x_2+y_2)^2 + \ldots (10x_n+y_n)^2$$

is equal to

$$(10y_1+x_1)^2 + (10y_2+x_2)^2 + \ldots (10y_n+x_n)^2,$$

and the equality will still hold if the y terms are permuted in any manner with the x terms, since the order in which the terms of the generating series is written does not affect their sum.

Continuing for higher powers, the trigrade 1, 4, 5, 5, 6, 9 $\overset{3}{=}$ 3, 2, 3, 7, 8, 7 serves as a generator for 6! = 720 equalities, one of which is 13, 42, 53, 57, 68, 97 $\overset{3}{=}$ 79, 86, 75, 35, 24, 31.

By more complicated generators, we can get three- and four-digit trigrades having the digit-reversal property. Thus 132, 223, 241, 243, 312, 314, 332, 423 $\overset{3}{=}$ 324, 233, 413, 213, 342, 142, 322, 231; also 1234, 2455, 2565, 3346, 4541, 5322, 5432, 6653 $\overset{3}{=}$ 3566, 2345, 2235, 1454, 6433, 5652, 5542, 4321.

Becoming even more selective, we can obtain palindromic (reading the same forwards and backwards) multigrades having the digit-reversal property by digit *pairs*. Thus 13031, 42024, 53035, 57075, 68086, 97079 $\overset{3}{=}$ 31013, 24042, 35053, 75057, 86068, 79097.

Starting with the generators 1, 5, 6 $\overset{2}{=}$ 2, 3, 7 and 2, 4, 9 $\overset{2}{=}$ 1, 6, 8, we can form the palindromic bigrade 1221, 5445, 6996 $\overset{2}{=}$ 2112, 3663, 7887. Using a third generator 2, 2, 5 $\overset{2}{=}$ 1, 4, 4 and combining it with the previous two, we get the six-digit palindromic bigrade 122221, 542245, 695596 $\overset{2}{=}$ 211112, 364463, 784487. A *double* palindromic trigrade, this time of seven digits, is 1030301, 6030306, $\overline{61}\overline{31}\overline{30}6$, $\overline{11}\overline{13}\overline{13}\overline{11}$ $\overset{3}{=}$ 3010103, 2070702, $\overline{10}\overline{09}\overline{09}\overline{10}$, $\overline{91}\overline{51}\overline{50}9$ $\overset{3}{=}$ 2010102, 3090903, 9070709, $\overline{10}\overline{15}\overline{15}\overline{10}$. Here, however, some terms are palindromic only in digit-*pairs*, as indicated by the overline.

The terms of these multigrades can also be "polygonal" or "pyramidal" numbers (see Chapter XVIII). A triangular number, mentioned previously, is a polygonal number; it has the form $n(n+1)/2$. When $n = 1, 19, 28$, we get the triangular numbers 1, 190, 406 respectively. These and additional triangular numbers form the trigrade 1, 190, 406, 1770, 2145, 4095, 5353 $\overset{3}{=}$ 3, 105, 780, 1035, 2926, 3655, 5356. A tetragrade of triangular numbers is 1, 325, 496, 3570, 3828, 9045, 12561, 16653, 19701 $\overset{4}{=}$ 3, 171, 903,

2211, 6441, 6786, 14365, 15400, 19900. "Heptagrades" of order 7 have also been made.

Then there are multigrades whose terms, n, represent the *order* of a triangular number, rather than its value. Thus $1, 4, 6, 7 \overset{2}{=} 2, 3, 5, 8$. Substituting these numbers in the formula for a triangular number: $n(n+1)/2$, we get $1, 10, 21, 28 = 3, 6, 15, 36$. Another example is $5, 8, 10, 11 \overset{2}{=} 6, 7, 9, 12$ for which the corresponding triangles are $15, 36, 55, 66 = 21, 28, 45, 78$. If we add the two bigrades we get $6, 12, 16, 18 \overset{2}{=} 8, 10, 14, 20$, which has a similar property. Using the symbol $2, T$ to represent bigrades with the triangle property, the last bigrade above could be written $6, 12, 16, 18 \overset{2,T}{=} 8, 10, 14, 20$. The sum of the triangular numbers in this case is 406.

If we use the symbols S_1, S_2, S_T respectively for (1) the sum of the terms on one side of the multigrade, (2) the sum of their squares, and (3) the sum of the corresponding triangular numbers, we can apply these symbols to $1-2-3+4 \overset{2,T}{=} 5-6-7+8 \overset{2,T}{=} 9-10-11+12\ldots$, where $S_1 = 0$, $S_2 = 4$, $S_T = 2$.

* * *

Still more tricks can be performed by these equalities. In 123789, $561945, 642864 \overset{2}{=} 242868, 323787, 761943$, the first digit in each can be dropped and the equality will still hold, for both the first and second powers. Thus $23789, 61945, 42864 \overset{2}{=} 42868, 23787, 61943$. We can continue this process, one digit at a time, until only one digit is left: $9, 5, 4 \overset{2}{=} 8, 7, 3$. We could also start by dropping the units digit to get $12378, 56194, 64286 \overset{2}{=} 24286, 32378, 76194$ and continuing to drop digits from the right until $1, 5, 6 \overset{2}{=} 2, 3, 7$ remain.

Then we can drop the second and third digits simultaneously and obtain $1789, 5945, 6864 \overset{2}{=} 2868, 3787, 7943$. Again dropping the new second and third digits, we end with $19, 55, 64 \overset{2}{=} 28, 37, 73$.

There seemingly is no end to the ingenuity that has been displayed in finding these relationships. But *vita brevis, ars longa*.

BIBLIOGRAPHY

Ball, W. W. R. *Mathematical Recreations and Essays*. New York: Macmillan Co., 1939.

Barlow, P. *Tables of Squares, Cubes, etc.* Chicago: Charles T. Powner Co., 1948.

Barlow, P. *Theory of Numbers.* London: J. Johnson & Co., 1811.

Bastien, L. "[Congruent Numbers]," *L'Intermédiaire des Mathématiciens*, **22** (1915), 231.

Collins, M. "A Tract on the Possible and Impossible Cases of Quadratic Duplicate Equalities in the Diophantine Analysis," *British Association for the Advancement of Science*, **25** (1855), Notes and Abstracts, 2.

Cunningham, A. "On Finding Factors," *Messenger of Mathematics*, **20** (1890), 37.

Dickson, L. E. *History of the Theory of Numbers.* 3 vols. New York: Chelsea Publishing Co., 1950.

Draughton, H. W. "Solution to Problems: Find Nine Integral Numbers in Arithmetic Progression the Sum of Whose Squares Is a Square; Find Nine Integral Square Numbers Whose Sum Is a Square," *American Mathematical Monthly*, **2** (1895), 129.

Gérardin, A. "[Congruent Numbers]," *L'Intermédiaire des Mathématiciens*, **22** (1915), 52.

Gloden, A. "Multigrade Prime-Number Identities," *Scripta Mathematica*, **16** (1950), 125.

———. "On Piza's Bigrades," *Scripta Mathematica*, **21** (1955), 193.

———. "Remarkable Multigrades," *Scripta Mathematica*, **21** (1955), 200.

Goldberg, M. "The Squaring of Developable Surfaces," *Scripta Mathematica*, **18** (1952), 17.

Goormaghtigh, R. "Identities with Digits in Reversed Order," *Scripta Mathematica*, **17** (1951), 19.

Hart, D. S. "Consecutive Square Numbers Whose Sum Is a Square," *Mathematical Magazine*, **1** (1883), 119.

Heath, R. V. "Sums Equal to Products," *Scripta Mathematica*, **9** (1943), 190.

———. "Bigrade Identities with a Special Condition," *Scripta Mathematica*, **18** (1952), 68.

Hollcraft, T. R. "On Sums of Powers of n Consecutive Integers," *Bulletin of the American Mathematical Society*, **59** (1953), 526.

Iyer, R. V. "Multigrades with Palindromic Numbers as Elements," *Scripta Mathematica*, **20** (1954), 220.

Kaprekar, D. R., and Iyer, R. V. "Identities with Digits in Reversed Order," *Scripta Mathematica*, **16** (1950), 160.

———. "Reversible Tarry-Escott Identities," *Scripta Mathematica*, **17** (1951), 146.

Khatri, M. N. "'Graphs' of Identities," *Scripta Mathematica*, **21** (1955), 202.

Kraitchik, M. *Recherches sur la Théorie des Nombres.* Vol. I. Paris: Gauthier-Villars et Cie., 1924.

Lehmer, D. N. *Factor Tables for the First Ten Million.* New York: Hafner Publishing Co., 1956.

Loyd, S. *Cyclopedia of Puzzles.* New York: Lamb Publishing Co., 1914.

Marenholz, M. "Mathematical Quintuplets," *Scripta Mathematica*, **7** (1940), 159.

Martin, A. "Some Curious Properties of Numbers," *Mathematical Magazine*, **1** (1883), 69.

Moessner, A. "Curious Identities," *Scripta Mathematica*, **6** (1939), 180.

———. "Arithmetic Operations on Multigrade Identities," *Scripta Mathematica*, **19** (1953), 282.

Piza, P. A. "Sums of Powers of Triangular Numbers," *Scripta Mathematica*, **16** (1950), 127.

———. "Telescoped Identities," *Scripta Mathematica*, **21** (1955), 90.

Steinhaus, H. *Mathematical Snapshots*. New York: Oxford University Press, 1960.

Stone, A. H., *et al.* "Problem for Solution: [Fitting Together Twenty-eight Squares to Form a Square]," *American Mathematical Monthly*, **47** (1940), 48.

———. "Solution to Problem: [Fitting Together Twenty-eight Squares to Form a Square]," *American Mathematical Monthly*, **47** (1940), 570.

Thebault, V. "Number Pleasantries," *Scripta Mathematica*, **12** (1946), 218.

White, W. F. *Scrap Book of Elementary Mathematics*. Chicago: Open Court Publishing Co., 1910.

CHAPTER XVI

FAREY TAILS

CHAPTER X dealt with certain properties of decimal fractions. The common fraction too has recreational properties. It will be recalled from arithmetic that a common or "vulgar" fraction is one having integers for its numerator and denominator. When the denominator exceeds the numerator, the fraction is called "proper."

Suppose we list all the proper common-fractions in their lowest terms in order of magnitude up to some arbitrarily assigned limit—say with denominator not exceeding 7. We have the 17 fractions: 1/7, 1/6, 1/5, 1/4, 2/7, 1/3, 2/5, 3/7, 1/2, 4/7, 3/5, 2/3, 5/7, 3/4, 4/5, 5/6, 6/7. This is called a Farey series.

John Farey was a somewhat versatile man who lived in the Napoleonic era. He was a surveyor who collected rocks and minerals and found time to write articles in the *Philosophical Magazine* on such diverse subjects as geology, music, decimal coinage, carriage wheels, comets—and Farey series! He did not consider his discovery particularly important, little realizing that his name would go down in mathematical lore because he had found something which had entirely escaped such acute observers as Fermat and Euler. One must report with regret, however, that once again the man whose name was given to a mathematical relation was not the original discoverer so far as the records go. One C. Haros apparently anticipated Farey by fourteen years, but this fact was unknown to the mathematician Cauchy, who attributed the discovery to Farey, and others repeated Cauchy's statement. Anyway, "Farey series" sounds better than "Haros series." Who knows—perhaps some Arabian mathematician anticipated Haros by a thousand years.

It seems almost unbelievable that these relations had not been investigated prior to 1816 when John Farey first observed them. The discovery was made while perusing the lengthy tables of decimal quotients compiled by that Henry Goodwyn mentioned in Chapter X of this book. Farey's revelation was eagerly seized upon by contemporary mathematicians, and it was not long before the theory of such fractions had been pretty thoroughly expounded. Some of it is fairly elementary, and some, as is so often the case with the Queen of Mathematics, involves rather recondite thinking.

Certain questions immediately present themselves in contemplating a series such as the one given above:

1. How many such fractions are there, and can their number be expressed as a function of the number selected, namely 7?

2. Is there any relation between adjoining fractions?

The second of these questions is easily answered by an inspection of the series. Apparently the numerator of any fraction is obtained by adding the numerators of the fractions on each side of it and similarly for the denominators. The result must be reduced to lowest terms. Thus in the triplets 3/5, 2/3, 5/7, arbitrarily selected from the series, we have $(3+5)/(5+7) = 8/12 = 2/3$. This rule enables us to find successive terms of the series if we know only the first two. These two, for denominators not exceeding 7, must obviously be 1/7 and 1/6. Let the third fraction be x/y, so that 1/7, 1/6, x/y form a triplet. Then, by the rule, $(1+x)/(7+y) = 1/6$. It does not necessarily follow that $1+x = 1$ and $7+y = 6$, for the fraction may have been reduced to produce 1/6. But if z is the greatest common factor of numerator and denominator, then

$$1+x = z \cdot 1$$

and

$$7+y = z \cdot 6.$$

Then $x = z-1$, $y = 6z-7$. Since y cannot exceed 7, z must be 2, $x = 1$, and $y = 5$, and the third fraction is 1/5. For the triplet 1/3, 2/5, x/y, we have $1+x = 2z$, $3+y = 5z$, whence $x = 2z-1$ and $y = 5z-3$. Here it would appear that z might be either 1 or 2 whereas $z = 2$ is the only correct value. There is a rule for settling this ambiguity.

If n is the order of a Farey series (in the example above, $n = 7$), and if a/b, a'/b', x/y are three terms of the series, then $a+x = za'$ and $b+y = zb'$, where z is the *greatest* integer equal to or smaller than $(n+b)/b'$. The greatest integer equal to or smaller than $(7+3)/5$ is 2. In the first case for the triplet 1/7, 1/6, x/y, we had $z \leq (7+7)/6$, or $z = 2$.

Taking 5/7, 3/4, x/y, we have $z \leq (7+7)/4$, whence $z = 3$ and $5+x = 3 \cdot 3$; $7+y = 3 \cdot 4$, so that $x = 4$, $y = 5$ and the fraction succeeding 3/4 is 4/5.

The *number* of fractions of order n is obtained as follows: Since the fractions are all in lowest terms, it follows that for a given denominator b, the number of numerators is the number of integers less than b and prime to it, namely $\phi(b)$. This reasoning may be used for *any* integer from 2 to n; consequently, the number of fractions N in the Farey series of order n is equal to $\phi(2)+\phi(3)+\phi(4)+\ldots+\phi(n)$. If $n = 7$, we have

$$N = \phi(2)+\phi(3)+\phi(4)+\phi(5)+\phi(6)+\phi(7)$$
$$= 1+2+2+4+2+6 = 17$$

as found. The value of N increases rapidly as n increases, and when $n = 100$, $N = 3043$, that is, there are that many irreducible common fractions with numerator and denominator not exceeding 100.

The reader may wish to prove the relations existing between adjacent numerators or denominators of a Farey series and the rule for finding the value of z. The proofs are not too easy.

Another property of Farey series is that the fractions equidistant from $1/2$ are complementary, that is, their sum is unity. Since $\phi(x)$ is always even except for $x = 1$ and 2, it follows that

$$N = \phi(2)+\phi(3)+\ldots+\phi(n)$$

is always odd, so that there are always an odd number of terms in a Farey series and the middle term is always $1/2$.

Still another property is that the difference between consecutive fractions is equal to the reciprocal of the product of their denominators.

*   *   *

There is a remarkable formula involving the ϕ function and the constant π, the ratio of the circumference to the diameter of a circle. It can be demonstrated that the sum,

$$\phi(1)+\phi(2)+\phi(3)+\ldots+\phi(n),$$

is approximated by the expression $3n^2/\pi^2$, the approximation becoming more and more accurate as the value of n increases. Except for the first term, which in fact may be disregarded without appreciably affecting the result, this sum represents the number of terms, N, in a Farey series of order n. Since we know the value of π to any desired degree of accuracy (it has been calculated to 100000 places of decimals), this means that we can find approximately the number of terms in a Farey series without evaluating separately $\phi(1)$, $\phi(2)$, $\phi(3) \ldots \phi(n)$.

Thus for $n = 100$ we would have

$$N = (3 \cdot 100^2)/\pi^2 = 3039.6355\ldots,$$

whereas the true value is 3043.

J. J. Sylvester tabulated the number of terms, N, in a Farey series for denominators not exceeding n where n ranges from 1 to 500, and compared this with the value of $3n^2/\pi^2$. Remembering that the accuracy increases as n increases, the excerpt of his table shown in Table 71 should prove of interest.

TABLE 71

NUMBER OF TERMS IN FAREY SERIES

n	$\phi(n)$	$N = \sum \phi(n) - 1 = $ $\phi(2) + \phi(3) + \ldots + \phi(n)$	$3n^2/\pi^2$
1	1	0	.30
2	1	1	1.22
3	2	3	2.74
4	2	5	4.86
5	4	9	7.60
6	2	11	10.94
7	6	17	14.90
8	4	21	19.46
9	6	27	24.62
10	4	31	30.40
15	8	71	68.39
25	20	199	189.98
50	20	773	759.91
100	40	3043	3039.64
200	80	12231	12158.54
300	80	27397	27356.72
400	160	48677	48634.17
500	200	76115	75990.89

Investigators have invented many other series derived from Farey series and discussed their properties at great length.

BIBLIOGRAPHY

Bell, E. T. *The Last Problem.* New York: Simon and Schuster, 1961.
Dickson, L. E. *History of the Theory of Numbers.* 3 vols. New York: Chelsea Publishing Co., 1950.

Farey, J.   "On a Curious Property of Vulgar Fractions," *London, Edinburgh and Dublin Philosophical Magazine*, **47** (1816), 385.

Glaisher, J. W. L.   "On a Property of Vulgar Fractions," *London, Edinburgh and Dublin Philosophical Magazine* (Fifth Series), **7** (1879), 321.

Hardy, G. H.   "An Introduction to the Theory of Numbers," *Bulletin of the American Mathematical Society*, **35** (1929), 778.

Shanks, D., and Wrench J. W., Jr.   "Calculation of π to 100,000 Decimals," *Mathematics of Computation*, **16** (1962), 76.

Sylvester, J. J.   "On the Number of Fractions Contained in Any Farey Series of Which the Limiting Number Is Given," *London, Edinburgh and Dublin Philosophical Magazine* (Fifth Series), **15** (1883), 251.

CHAPTER XVII

ROUND THE PERIMETER

ONE OF THE fascinating things about mathematics is the fact that wholly unrelated fields are often linked in the most unexpected ways. Who would suppose that number theory can determine which regular polygons can be inscribed in a circle by straightedge and compass and which cannot? Fermat, discussing the integers $2^{2^n}+1$, which posterity calls "Fermat numbers," little dreamed how closely their theory was linked with inscribed polygons. It took the acumen of Gauss to do that.

Nothing that Fermat ever stated he had proved has ever been disproved. About Fermat numbers he had only an opinion, and he stated he could find no satisfactory proof of his belief. He thought that $2^{2^n}+1$ is always a prime, whereas this has been demonstrated only for $n = 0, 1, 2, 3, 4$. The corresponding numbers are 3, 5, 17, 257, 65537. When $n = 5$, however, the Fermat number F_5 has the factors 641 and 6700417, and it is remarkable that a man of Fermat's genius, who could produce the factors of a number like 100895598169 with the facility of a magician drawing rabbits out of a hat, should have missed the small factor 641 of F_5. No better warning can be given the amateur than this error of a genius, to resist the temptation to draw conclusions from data only instead of from rigid proof. What makes Fermat's erroneous conclusion the more remarkable is the fact that for the values of n greater than 4, *every one* of the numbers, F_n, whose character has been determined to date, is composite so that there is cause to wonder whether almost the exact opposite of his conclusion may not be true and whether perhaps someone may yet demonstrate that *only* when n is an integer smaller than 5 is F_n a prime.

The verification that 641 is a divisor of $2^{32}+1$ is easily demonstrated by congruences, but of course Gauss who invented them wasn't even born when Fermat was meditating these matters. Without the theory of congruences, the verification of divisibility for the large values of n would be altogether impossible.

It is difficult to grasp the significance of a number like

$$F_{73} = 2^{2^{73}} + 1$$

for which one factor has already been found. This number is so large that if printed in ordinary type, all the books in all the libraries in the entire world could not contain it. It is not difficult to demonstrate the truth of this statement. For $2^{10} = 1024 =$ approximately $1000 = 10^3$, and by calling 2^{10} one thousand, we are being conservative in our calculation. Hence $2^{70} = 10^{21}$ approximately and 2^{73} is close to 10^{22}. Then F_{73} equals approximately $2^{10^{22}} = 2^{10 \cdot 10^{21}}$. But since $2^{10} = 10^3$ approximately, $2^{10 \cdot 10^{21}} = (10^3)^{10^{21}} = 10^{3 \cdot 10^{21}}$, so that F_{73} has approximately $3 \cdot 10^{21}$ digits. Now assume that every book in the world has 1000 pages, and that each page has 100 lines and that every line can hold 100 letters or numbers. This is far above the capacity of the average book. Then assume that there are one million libraries in the world and that each library contains one hundred million volumes. Then the number of letters or numbers in all of these volumes is $1000 \cdot 100 \cdot 100 \cdot 1000000 \cdot 100000000 = 10^{21}$, and about three times that number of digits is in the number F_{73}.

This has been expressed another way. Using figures one millimeter square in size, the line which would contain the number would be $2700 \cdot 10^{12}$ kilometers long and could be wound around the earth at the equator sixty billion times. A person writing one digit a second and working 10 hours per day and 360 days per year would take 200000 billion years to write the number. And if the entire population of the earth, estimated at $2\frac{1}{2}$ trillion ($25 \cdot 10^{11}$), were put to the task, it would take about 80000 years. Utilizing one square millimeter per digit, an area over five times that of the earth would be required to write the number.

Even F_{36} contains over twenty trillion digits.

Table 72 contains the "latest" (1961) data on the factors of Fermat numbers.

*   *   *

As long ago as 1770 the blind mathematician Euler had proved that if a and b are co-prime, then every factor of $a^{2^n} + b^{2^n}$ is either the number 2 or of the form $2^{n+1} K + 1$. A Fermat number is a special case of this general theorem where $a = 2$ and $b = 1$. Over 100 years later, in 1878, Lucas proved that every prime divisor of $2^{2^n} + 1$ must

TABLE 72

Prime Factors of Fermat Numbers, $F_n = 2^{2^n} + 1$

n	Character	Factors in Power Form	Factors as Integers
0	Prime	—	3
1	,,	—	5
2	,,	—	17
3	,,	—	257
4	,,	—	65537
5	Composite	$(2^7 \cdot 5 + 1)(2^7 \cdot 52347 + 1)$	$641 \cdot 6700417$*
6	,,	$(2^8 \cdot 3^2 \cdot 7 \cdot 17 + 1)(2^8 \cdot 5 \cdot 52562829149 + 1)$	$274177 \cdot 67280421310721$*
7	,,	2 or 3 factors, none smaller than 2^{32}	(?)
8	,,	(?)	(?)
9	,,	$(2^{16} \cdot 37 + 1) \cdot (?)$	$2424833 \cdot (?)$
10	,,	$(2^{12} \cdot 11131 + 1) \cdot (?)$	$45592577 \cdot (?)$
11	,,	$(2^{13} \cdot 3 \cdot 13 + 1)(2^{13} \cdot 7 \cdot 17 + 1) \cdot (?)$	$319489 \cdot 974849 \cdot (?)$
12	,,	$(2^{14} \cdot 7 + 1)(2^{16} \cdot 397 + 1)(2^{16} \cdot 7 \cdot 139 + 1) \cdot (?)$	$114689 \cdot 26017793 \cdot 63766529 \cdot (?)$
13	,,	Composite. No factor smaller than 2^{35}	(?)
15	,,	$(2^{21} \cdot 3 \cdot 193 + 1) \cdot (?)$	$1214251009 \cdot (?)$
16	,,	$(2^{19} \cdot 1575 + 1) \cdot (?)$	$825753601 \cdot (?)$
18	,,	$(2^{20} \cdot 13 + 1) \cdot (?)$	$13631489 \cdot (?)$
23	,,	$(2^{25} \cdot 5 + 1) \cdot (?)$	$167772161 \cdot (?)$
36	,,	$(2^{39} \cdot 5 + 1) \cdot (?)$	$2748779069441 \cdot (?)$
38	,,	$(2^{41} \cdot 3 + 1) \cdot (?)$	$6597069766657 \cdot (?)$
73	,,	$(2^{75} \cdot 5 + 1) \cdot (?)$	$1888945593147858085478841 \cdot (?)$

* Completely factored.

be of the form $2^{n+2}L+1$.   Referring to Table 72, it will be noted that 641, a factor of F_5, is equal to $2^{5+2} \cdot 5 + 1$, and the other factor, $6700417 = 2^{5+2} \cdot 52347 + 1$.   For F_7, $2^{2^7}+1$, which has been found to be composite but whose factors are unknown, each of its prime divisors is of the form $2^9 \cdot K + 1$, and the divisors of F_8, $2^{2^8}+1$, are of the form $2^{10} \cdot K + 1$.   It is also known that F_n is prime if, and only if, $3^{(F_n-1)/2} \equiv -1 \bmod F_n$.

*   *   *

Although the Fermat numbers are noteworthy in themselves, they have a remarkable geometric application.   Before discussing this it will be advisable to review a little elementary geometry.   Most readers probably know how to bisect a line or an arc of a circle, and it is clear that by repeated bisections one can divide an arc into 2, 4, 8, ..., 2^n equal parts.   It will also be recalled that an angle other than a multiple and a few sub-multiples of 90° cannot be trisected by straightedge and compass alone; indeed, the trisection of an angle has been one of the will-o'-the-wisps of the centuries.

A regular hexagon can be easily inscribed in a circle by laying off the radius as a chord exactly six times around the circumference as in Figure 9, and an inscribed equilateral triangle can be formed by connecting alternate vertices of this hexagon.

An inscribed square can be formed by connecting, in order, the extremities of two mutually perpendicular diameters.   By continually

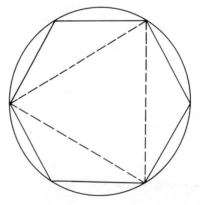

FIG. 9.   INSCRIBED TRIANGLE OR HEXAGON

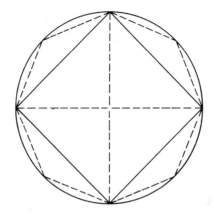

FIG. 10. INSCRIBED SQUARE OR OCTAGON

bisecting the arcs of Figure 9, regular polygons of 12, 24, 48...$2^n \cdot 3$ sides may be constructed. Similarly, from the square, an octagon may be formed, or any regular 2^n-gon.

Readers may recall from elementary geometry that a pentagon can be constructed by straightedge and compass. It is done as follows: In a circle of unit radius (Figure 11) AC and BD are mutually perpendicular diameters. E is the midpoint of AO and $EF = EB$.

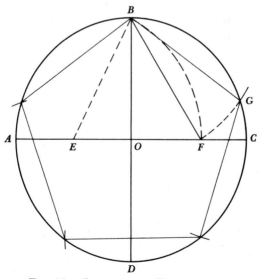

FIG. 11. INSCRIBING A PENTAGON

With B as center and a radius equal to BF, an arc is drawn intersecting the circumference in G. Then BG is a side of the pentagon. The proof of this construction is given in most geometry books.

As an indication of how lines may represent expressions involving square roots, mentioned in the subsequent discussion, the length of the side of the pentagon will be found in such terms. It is easy to show that $(BG)^2$ is $(5-\sqrt{5})/2$. For $BO = 1$ (in a unit circle), $EO = 1/2$, and therefore $EB = \sqrt{1+1/4} = \sqrt{5}/2$, whence $EF = \sqrt{5}/2$ and $OF = \sqrt{5}/2 - 1/2$. Then $(BG)^2 = (BF)^2$ (the line, not the arc) $= (BO)^2 + (OF)^2 = 1 + (\sqrt{5}/2 - 1/2)^2 = (5-\sqrt{5})/2$.

Thus polygons of $2^n \cdot 5$ sides can also be constructed by straightedge and compass. Try as we may, however, we cannot inscribe a regular 7- or 9-sided polygon in a circle using only these instruments.

A 15-sided regular polygon and therefore any $2^n \cdot 15$-sided one can also be inscribed in a circle because we know how to inscribe 3- and 5-sided ones and because 3 and 5 are co-prime integers. In Chapter V it was found that for two given co-prime integers, p and q, it is always possible to find two others, a and b, such that $pa - qb = 1$. Then $a/q - b/p = 1/pq$. If 5 and 3 are the given integers, then $a = 2$ and $b = 3$ and $2/3 - 3/5 = 1/15$. Hence, if a regular pentagon and an equilateral triangle are inscribed in a circle, twice the arc subtended by the side of the triangle exceeds three times the arc subtended by the side of the pentagon by $1/15$ of the circumference

It may also be well at this point to see how a product or quotien is constructed graphically. The expression db/c is easily constructed because, letting $db/c = x$, we have $c/d = b/x$. If we draw any two intersecting lines as in Figure 12, and lay off from the point of intersection the lengths c and d on one of them and the length b on the other, then a line through the terminus of d parallel to the line joining the extremities of the segments c and b will determine the required segment x. Sometimes one of the quantities is disguised, as in th

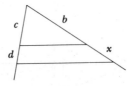

Fig. 12.   Finding the Fourth Proportional

problem: To construct the product mn, the lengths m and n being given. Here an arbitrary unit length must be decided upon and then we have

$$mn/1 = x \quad \text{and} \quad 1/m = n/x.$$

Segments 1, m, and n are laid off as before and x found.

If we wish to construct $\sqrt{pq}$, we have $x^2 = pq$, so that x is the mean proportional between p and q. This is found by laying off the lengths p and q (Figure 13), drawing a semicircle on their sum as a

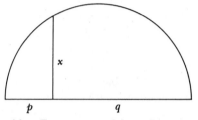

FIG. 13. FINDING THE MEAN PROPORTIONAL

diameter and erecting a perpendicular where the segments join. This perpendicular is the required length x. To construct simply $\sqrt{p}$, we interpret this as $x = \sqrt{p \cdot 1}$ or $x^2 = p \cdot 1$. Here we lay off the unit and the length p and find x as before.

More complicated expressions such as $\sqrt{p + \sqrt{pq}} + r - \sqrt{s}$ can be constructed similarly with straightedge and compass. For example, the side of a pentagon in a circle of unit radius is equal to $\sqrt{(5 - \sqrt{5})/2}$, and the construction of Figure 11 shows the length BG, which is the geometric equivalent of this expression.

We are now ready for Gauss's brilliant and recondite reasoning by which he showed that using straightedge and compass only, a polygon can be inscribed in a circle only if the number of its sides is (1) a prime of the form $2^{2^u} + 1$, or (2) the product of such primes (all different), or (3) the product of a power of 2 and one or more of such primes. The construction of regular polygons of 2^n; $2^n \cdot 3$; $2^n \cdot 5$; and $2^n \cdot 15$ sides had been known since the time of the Greeks, but no one suspected before Gauss that polygons of any other number of sides could be constructed by straightedge and compass. The way had to be paved by numerous theorems in algebra.

The steps—considerably abbreviated—leading to Gauss's conclusions are approximately as follows:

1. A quantity can be constructed by straightedge and compass if it can be expressed by a finite number of square roots. Thus

$$x = [\sqrt{a + \sqrt{c + ef}} + \sqrt{d + \sqrt{b}}]/(\sqrt{a} + \sqrt{b}) + (p + \sqrt{q})/\sqrt{r}$$

can be so solved.

2. There exist equations that have solutions—roots—consisting only of such quantities, and for specified unlike roots there is only one equation of lowest degree satisfied by these roots and by no others. This lowest-degree equation is called irreducible because it cannot be resolved into two or more factors wherein the variable appears with only integral exponents.

3. The degree of the irreducible equation satisfied by expressions composed of a finite number of square roots only is always a power of 2, and if an irreducible equation is not of degree 2^h, its solutions cannot be expressions containing a finite number of square roots only.

4. The roots of the equation $x^n - 1 = 0$, when plotted with reference to two mutually perpendicular lines, where points on one represent real numbers and points on the other imaginary numbers, lie on the circumference of a circle whose center is the intersection of these two lines and whose radius is unity. The points representing the roots are spaced at n equal intervals around the circumference.

5. The roots of the equation $x^n - 1 = 0$ can be constructed by straightedge and compass for a composite number $n = pq$ if the roots of $x^p - 1 = 0$ and $x^q - 1 = 0$ can be so constructed. For if $n = pq$, the product of two relatively prime integers, then two integers a and b can always be found such that $ap - bq = 1$ or $a/q - b/p = 1/qp$ whence the circle can be divided into pq parts. Therefore, in considering the possibility of dividing a circle into n equal parts, n may be taken prime.

6. Since we know how to bisect an arc by straightedge and compass, and since this may be done repeatedly, a circle can be divided into 2, 4, 8...2^a equal parts. Hence if we can divide a circle into n equal parts when n is odd (prime or composite), we can divide it into $2^a \cdot n$ equal parts.

7. If we divide the equation $x^p - 1 = 0$, where p is a prime, by the

factor $x-1$ corresponding to the only real root $x = 1$, we obtain an equation

$$(x^p - 1)/(x - 1) = x^{p-1} + x^{p-2} + x^{p-3} + \ldots + 1 = 0,$$

whose roots are the complex roots of the original equation. This result, called the cyclotomic equation, because its roots are on the circumference of a circle, is irreducible.

8. Since the cyclotomic equation is irreducible, it is solvable by square roots only if it is of degree 2^h, that is, $p - 1 = 2^h$ or $p = 2^h + 1$.

9. If $p = 2^h + 1$ is to be a prime, h must be a power 2^u of 2, since otherwise, h has at least one *odd* factor e so that $h = ef$ and $p = 2^h + 1 = (2^f)^e + 1$, which always has the factor $2^f + 1$ and is therefore never a prime.

10. Hence a circle can be divided by straightedge and compass into n equal parts only if n is of the form:

$$2^{a_0}(2^{2^{a_1}} + 1)(2^{2^{a_2}} + 1) \ldots (2^{2^{a_n}} + 1),$$

where each of the quantities in parenthesis is a prime of the first power and where $a_1, a_2, \ldots a_n$ are all different positive integers.

From Table 72 it may be seen that the only known primes of the form $2^{2^n} + 1$ are $3; 5; 17; 257;$ and $65537;$ and therefore the number of regular polygons with an odd number of sides theoretically constructable by straightedge and compass is the combination of these five integers taken any number at a time, or $2^5 - 1 = 31$. The number of sides in these polygons is shown in Table 73.

TABLE 73

REGULAR POLYGONS WITH ODD NUMBER OF SIDES
CONSTRUCTABLE BY STRAIGHTEDGE AND COMPASS

Order	Number of Sides in Polygon
1	$3 = 3$
2	$5 = 5$
3	$15 = 3 \cdot 5$
4	$17 = 17$
5	$51 = 3 \cdot 17$
6	$85 = 5 \cdot 17$

TABLE 73—*continued*

Order	Number of Sides in Polygon
7	$255 = 3 \cdot 5 \cdot 17$
8	$257 = 257$
9	$771 = 3 \cdot 257$
10	$1285 = 5 \cdot 257$
11	$3855 = 3 \cdot 5 \cdot 257$
12	$4369 = 17 \cdot 257$
13	$13107 = 3 \cdot 17 \cdot 257$
14	$21845 = 5 \cdot 17 \cdot 257$
15	$65535 = 3 \cdot 5 \cdot 17 \cdot 257$
16	$65537 = 65537$
17	$196611 = 3 \cdot 65537$
18	$327685 = 5 \cdot 65537$
19	$983055 = 3 \cdot 5 \cdot 65537$
20	$1114129 = 17 \cdot 65537$
21	$3342387 = 3 \cdot 17 \cdot 65537$
22	$5570645 = 5 \cdot 17 \cdot 65537$
23	$16711935 = 3 \cdot 5 \cdot 17 \cdot 65537$
24	$16843009 = 257 \cdot 65537$
25	$50529027 = 3 \cdot 257 \cdot 65537$
26	$84215045 = 5 \cdot 257 \cdot 65537$
27	$252645135 = 3 \cdot 5 \cdot 257 \cdot 65537$
28	$286331153 = 17 \cdot 257 \cdot 65537$
29	$858993459 = 3 \cdot 17 \cdot 257 \cdot 65537$
30	$1431655765 = 5 \cdot 17 \cdot 257 \cdot 65537$
31	$4294967295 = 3 \cdot 5 \cdot 17 \cdot 257 \cdot 65537$

Any power of 2 may be combined with any one of these 31 numbers to represent the number of sides in a geometrically constructable even-sided polygon. There are only 24 such polygons, either odd- or even-sided with sides not exceeding 100; 37 with sides not exceeding 300; 52 with sides not exceeding 1000, and only 206 with sides not exceeding 1000000. The 24 polygons with sides not exceeding 100 are given in Table 74.

Although theoretically polygons with the number of sides given in Table 73 can be constructed by straightedge and compass, the practical accomplishment of this feat is far from easy. Even for only the 17-sided polygon, the analysis and construction are rather involved and many pages are required for the exposition of a 257-sided one. Professor Hermes of Lingen devoted ten years of his life to the regular polygon of 65537 sides!

TABLE 74

REGULAR POLYGONS CONSTRUCTABLE BY STRAIGHTEDGE AND COMPASS

Order	Number of Sides	Order	Number of Sides
1	3	13	30
2	4	14	32
3	5	15	34
4	6	16	40
5	8	17	48
6	10	18	51
7	12	19	60
8	15	20	64
9	16	21	68
10	17	22	80
11	20	23	85
12	24	24	96

The side of a regular 17-sided polygon or heptadecagon may be found as follows (Figure 14):

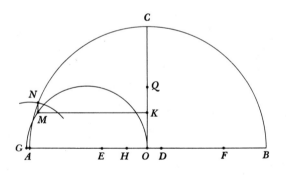

FIG. 14.   INSCRIBING A HEPTADECAGON

On the radius OC of a semicircle, find the midpoint Q, and on the diameter AB, perpendicular to this radius, lay off from the center O the distance $OD = 1/8$ of the radius.   Lay off DF and DE each equal to DQ, and EG and FH equal respectively to EQ and FQ.   Lay off OK, the mean proportional between OH and OQ, and through K draw KM parallel to AB, meeting the semicircle described on OG in M.   Draw MN parallel to OC, cutting circle O in N.   The arc AN

is 1/17 of a circumference.   This construction was invented by one John Lowry in 1819 and his proof required nine pages in the *Mathematical Repository* for that year.

*   *   *

Gauss was so proud of his discovery showing the relation between prime Fermat numbers and inscriptible polygons that he wished to have a heptadecagon inscribed on his tombstone.   For some reason this request was not granted, but one such is engraved on the side of a monument to him in Braunschweig, Germany, his birthplace.

*   *   *

Not content with examining numbers of the form $2^{2^n}+1$, mathematicians have investigated $10^{2^n}+1$; but up to $n=6$, the only primes found have been 11 and 101 corresponding to $n=0$ and 1, respectively.

*   *   *

It had once been conjectured that $2+1$, 2^2+1, $2^{2^2}+1$, $2^{2^{2^2}}+1$, etc., are all primes.   However, $2^{2^{16}}+1$, is composite, having the factor $2^{19}\cdot1575+1=825753601$.   Conjectures are treacherous in number theory.

BIBLIOGRAPHY

Ball, W. W. R.   *Mathematical Recreations and Essays*.   New York: Macmillan Co., 1939.

Carmichael, R. D.   "Fermat Numbers $F_n=2^{2^n}+1$," *American Mathematical Monthly*, **26** (1919), 137.

Klein, F.   *Famous Problems of Elementary Geometry*.   New York: Dover Publications, Inc., 1956.

Kraitchik, M.   *Recherches sur la Théorie des Nombres*.   Paris: Gauthier-Villars et Cie., 1924.

Paxson, G. A.   "The Compositeness of the Thirteenth Fermat Number," *Mathematics of Computation*, **15** (1961), 420.

Robinson, R. M.   "Mersenne and Fermat Numbers," *Proceedings of the American Mathematical Society*, **5** (1954), 842.

Selfridge, J. L.   "Factors of Fermat Numbers," *Mathematical Tables and Other Aids to Computation*, **7** (1953), 274.

Young, J. W. A.   *Monographs on Topics of Modern Mathematics*.   New York: Dover Publications, Inc., 1955.

CHAPTER XVIII

BALL GAMES

ANYONE who has visited a bowling alley knows that the 10 pins are set up in a triangular array. Pool players use a triangular frame in which to store the 15 balls of that game when they are not in use. Fifteen and 10 are triangular numbers. The number of discs, spheres, counters, or similar objects that can be arranged in an equilateral-triangular pattern is termed a triangular number (see Figure 15). Evidently such a number is the sum of consecutive

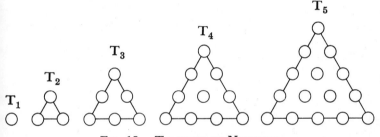

FIG. 15.   TRIANGULAR NUMBERS

integers starting from unity; thus $15 = 1+2+3+4+5$. The first triangular number T_1 is unity, $T_2 = 3$, $T_3 = 6$, etc., as seen in Figure 15. The sum of the arithmetic series $1, 2, 3, 4, \ldots r$ is $r(r+1)/2$, which accordingly is the value of T_r.

Counters or balls may also be placed in square arrays as shown in Figure 16. These of course are called "square numbers" and

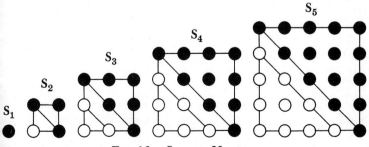

FIG. 16.   SQUARE NUMBERS

follow the series 1, 4, 9, 16, 25.... It can be seen from the arrangement of the black and white circles that the first and second triangular numbers 1 and 3 together form the second square number 4; the second and third triangular numbers 3 and 6 form the third square number 9; and in general if S_r is the rth square number, $S_r = T_r + T_{r-1}$. This can be demonstrated as follows: Since

$$T_r = r(r+1)/2$$

and

$$T_{r-1} = (r-1)(r-1+1)/2 = (r-1)r/2,$$

we have by addition

$$T_r + T_{r-1} = r(r+1+r-1)/2 = r^2,$$

which is obviously equal to S_r.

Taking a few examples, we have:

$T_r =$	1	3	6	10	15	21	28	36	45...
$T_{r-1} =$		1	3	6	10	15	21	28	36...
$T_r + T_{r-1} = S_r =$	1	4	9	16	25	36	49	64	81...

*   *   *

The pupils of Pythagoras used to chant an incantation to numbers, which they invested with personalities and qualities. Thus "Bless us, divine number, who generatest gods and men! O holy *tetraktys*, that contains the root and source of the eternally flowing creation," was their tribute to the number 4. And yet out of such mumbo-jumbo emerged the beginnings of number theory. Uspensky and Heaslet in their book *Elementary Number Theory* say, "...so the ancient number mysticism thrives even now under the guise of numerology—a fact that would make one despair of mankind had not, on the other hand, the human spirit produced sublime creations of which the theory of numbers is one."

But in Pythagoras's day, odd numbers were still "masculine" and even ones "feminine," well-deserved appellations, no doubt, testifying to the characteristic orneryness of the male and the essentially sweet and even temper of the female! The number 1 was the source of all numbers, and 2 the first female number. Three was the first male number and the sum or union of $2+3 = 5$ stood for marriage (see Chapter III). Even among numbers the female preceded the male. The number 8 held the secret of love since it added male potency 3 to marriage 5. The Greeks always had a word for it.

The Pythagorean was an esoteric cult and consequently it lost a good deal of its original virility by withdrawing from worldly but necessary affairs. Readers may be familiar with the story of the merchant who asked Pythagoras what he could teach him. "I will teach you to count," said the geometer. "I know that already," replied the merchant. "How do you count?" asked the originator of $3^2+4^2 = 5^2$. The merchant began, "One, two, three, four..." "Stop," cried the sage, "what you take to be four is ten, or a perfect triangle, and our symbol."

The Chinese apparently originated the representation of numbers in simple geometric patterns. This was about 500 years before the time of Pythagoras, so apparently they knew a few things about numbers long before the Greeks. They used a horizontal bar (-) or a series of such bars for the male principle of odd numbers and combinations of two horizontal bars (--) for the female principle. An old

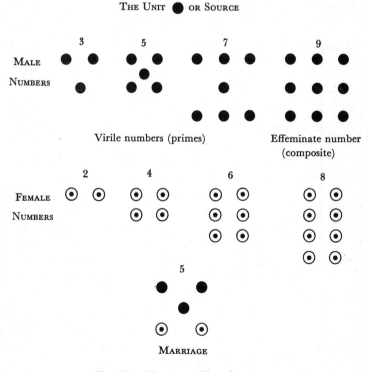

FIG 17. NUMBERS HAD SEX

TABLE 75

Polygonal Numbers

Number	RANK				
	1	2	3	4	5
Triangle	○				
Square	○				
Pentagon	○				
Hexagon	○				
Hepta-gon	○				
Octagon	○				

Chinese text written no later than 1000 B.C. indicated odd or male numbers as white circles and even or female ones as black.

An odd composite number was not a properly masculine one. True masculine qualities require stern indivisibility such as only primes possessed. Hence odd composites such as 9 or 15 were "effeminate." But the number 3, an odd prime, was considered a fitting mate to feminine 2 to consummate marriage, 5. The sex number patterns shown in Figure 17 remind one of the chromosome arrangements pictured in biology texts.

* * *

Since circles can be placed in either a triangular or a square array, it is natural to inquire about pentagonal, hexagonal, etc., arrays. Table 75 shows the first five *ranks* of the polygonal numbers, p_n^r, from triangular to octagonal, and Table 76 indicates the number of units in each of these polygons and gives also the formula for the n-gon for the ranks from 1 to 8 and for rank r.

TABLE 76

Polygonal Numbers, (p_n^r)

Name	No. of Sides = n	Set No. s = n−2	Rank = r								
			1	2	3	4	5	6	7	8	r
Triangular	3	1	1	3	6	10	15	21	28	36	$\dots r(r+1)/2$
Square	4	2	1	4	9	16	25	36	49	64	$\dots r^2$
Pentagonal	5	3	1	5	12	22	35	51	70	92	$\dots r(3r-1)/2$
Hexagonal	6	4	1	6	15	28	45	66	91	120	$\dots r(2r-1)$
Heptagonal	7	5	1	7	18	34	55	81	112	148	$\dots r(5r-3)/2$
Octagonal	8	6	1	8	21	40	65	96	113	176	$\dots r(3r-2)$
. . .											
n-gonal	n	$n-2$	1	n	$3(n-1)$	$2(3n-4)$	$5(2n-3)$	$3(5n-8)$	$7(3n-5)$	$4(7n-12)$	$(r/2)[(r-1)n-2(r-2)]$*

* In terms of r and s this becomes $r(rs-s+2)/2$.

* * *

There is a simple test for determining whether a number is an *n*-gon. All we need do is to multiply the unknown by $8(n-2)$ and add $(n-4)^2$ to the product. If the result is a square, then the number is an *n*-gon; otherwise it is not. Thus to ascertain if 45 is a hexagon, multiply by $8(6-2)$, giving 1440, and add $(6-4)^2$, giving 1444, which is the square of 38. To find the rank of this *n*-gon add $(n-4)$ to the root of the square and divide the sum by twice $(n-2)$. Thus $38+(6-4) = 40$, which, divided by twice 4, is 5 as the rank and 45 is the fifth hexagon as shown in Table 76.

This is proved as follows: Table 76 shows that the *n*-gon of rank *r* is equal to $(r/2)[(r-1)n-2(r-2)]$, and if we multiply this result by $8(n-2)$ and add $(n-4)^2$, the result is an exact square whose root *R* is $2rn-4r-n+4$. Solving for the rank *r*, we have

$$r = [R+(n-4)]/2(n-2),$$

as given in the rule above.

For given *n*-gons, for instance those from 3 to 8, we can thus find and tabulate for ready reference the multipliers and addends for the test and the expression for the rank. These are given in Table 77.

TABLE 77

TEST FOR *n*-GON

n	Multiplier	Addend	Rank *r*
3	8	1	$(R-1)/2$
4	16	0	$R/4$
5	24	1	$(R+1)/6$
6	32	4	$(R+2)/8$
7	40	9	$(R+3)/10$
8	48	16	$(R+4)/12$

A very simple negative test for a *triangular* number is to add together the digits of the unknown number, then the digits of the sum, and so on until only one digit remains. If this digit is 2, 4, 5, 7, or 8, the number is not triangular; otherwise it may or may not be. Testing 79, we have $7+9 = 16$, $1+6 = 7$, so that 79 is not a triangle. Again for 54, $5+4 = 9$, so that 54 is not excluded by this test. But by the positive test, $54 \cdot 8+1 = 433$, which is not a square, and therefore 54 cannot be a triangle.

*   *   *

Just as any square number can be derived from the sum of two triangular numbers, so a pentagonal number can be derived from the sum of the square of the same rank and the triangle of the preceding rank. Figure 18 illustrates these results. Symbolically, referring to the formulas for the rth rank of triangular numbers T, square numbers S, and pentagonal numbers P, we have

$$S_r + T_{r-1} = P_r \quad \text{or} \quad (r-1)r/2 + r^2 = r(3r-1)/2.$$

In general, any n-gonal number is equal to the sum of the $(n-1)$-gonal number of the same rank and the *triangular* number of the previous rank.

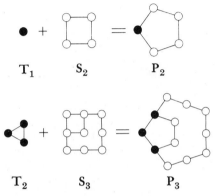

$\mathrm{T}_1 \qquad \mathrm{S}_2 \qquad\qquad \mathrm{P}_2$

$\mathrm{T}_2 \qquad \mathrm{S}_3 \qquad\qquad \mathrm{P}_3$

FIG. 18.   ADDITION OF POLYGONAL NUMBERS

All sorts of relationships among the various polygonal numbers can be found in an elementary manner by algebra; the corresponding geometric patterns are frequently entertaining. A few of these relations in pictures and symbols are shown in Figure 19.

* * *

The cubes 1; 8; 27; 64; 125... are related to triangular numbers. The sum of r consecutive cubes starting from unity is equal to the square of the rth triangular number. For $r = 4$, we have

$$1^3 + 2^3 + 3^3 + 4^3 = 100,$$

which is the square of the fourth triangular number 10. In general,

$$1^3 + 2^3 + 3^3 + \ldots + r^3 = [r(r+1)/2]^2 = (1+2+3+\ldots+r)^2.$$

* * *

Eight triangles increased by unity produce a square because

$$8r(r+1)/2 + 1 = 4r^2 + 4r + 1 = (2r+1)^2.$$

This interesting relation is the basis of the method of finding numbers which are simultaneously square and triangular. For if we can find a square X^2 such that, when multiplied by 8 and increased by 1, the

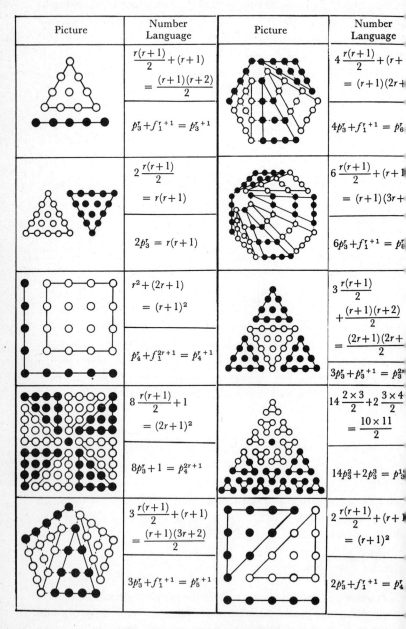

Fig. 19. Polygonal Numbers

result is also a square, then X^2 must also be a triangle. This requires the solution of $8X^2 + 1 = Y^2$, a Pell equation, described in Chapter XXII. The first seven sets of solutions of this equation are given in Table 78, the values of X^2 being simultaneously square and triangular.

TABLE 78

NUMBERS SIMULTANEOUSLY SQUARE AND TRIANGULAR

Solution of Pell Equation $8X^2 + 1 = Y^2$		Triangular Number $= X^2$	$n =$ Side of Triangle	$X =$ Side of Square
$8 \cdot 1^2 + 1 =$	3^2	1	1	1
$8 \cdot 6^2 + 1 =$	17^2	36	8	6
$8 \cdot 35^2 + 1 =$	99^2	1225	49	35
$8 \cdot 204^2 + 1 =$	577^2	41616	288	204
$8 \cdot 1189^2 + 1 =$	3363^2	1413721	1681	1189
$8 \cdot 6930^2 + 1 =$	19601^2	48024900	9800	6930
$8 \cdot 40391^2 + 1 =$	114243^2	1631432881	57121	40391

The general value of X in this Pell equation is given later in this chapter.

* * *

Polygonal numbers are only one group of a class of numbers called "figurate." The first or "linear" group of figurate numbers are simply the terms of an arithmetic progression starting from 1. If d is the common difference between terms of the progression, then $1, 1+d, 1+2d, \ldots 1+(r-1)d$ are the successive terms from 1 to r of this linear group. Letting $d = 1$ and 2, respectively, $1, 2, 3, 4, 5, \ldots (r-1)$ and $1, 3, 5, 7, 9 \ldots (2r-1)$ are two sets in this group. In the sth such set, $d = s$, and the series becomes, $1, 1+s, 1+2s, 1+3s \ldots 1+(r-1)s$. The symbol $f_{1,s}^r$ can be used to represent the linear group of the figurate numbers, where 1 represents the group number (or dimension), m, of the figurate number, s the number of the set, and r the rank in the set. Thus $f_{1,2}^5 = 9$ and $f_{1,1}^4 = 4$.

If we form a new series from the *sums* of the terms in each of the above series, starting from unity, we get $1, 3, 6, 10, 15 \ldots r(r+1)/2$ and $1, 4, 9, 16, 25 \ldots r^2$. The sth series would be $1, 2+s, 3+3s, 4+6s \ldots r(rs-s+2)/2$.

These series are no longer arithmetic progressions. It will be noticed that these are the polygonal numbers of Table 76 with $s = n-2$.

The terms of these sum-series are called "plane figurate numbers"; in such numbers the dimension $m = 2$. Thus all plane figurate numbers can be symbolized by $f_{2,s}^r$ corresponding to the notation, p_{n-2}^r.

Thus $f_{2,2}^4 = p_4^4 = 16$, $f_{2,1}^7 = p_3^7 = 28$, $f_{2,s}^5 = p_{n-2}^5 = 10s+5 = 10n-15$. In general an n-gonal number is equal to the sum of an arithmetic progression whose first term is unity and whose common difference, d, is $n-2$. For example, the hexagonal numbers, where $n = 6$, are the sums of an arithmetic series, the difference between adjacent terms of which is $6-2 = 4$. The Pythagoreans called each term of the arithmetic series a "gnomon."

The polygonal number series can similarly be summed to form "solid" three-dimensional figurate numbers, where $m = 3$. Such numbers are also called "pyramidal numbers." They are symbolized by $f_{3,s}^r$ or P_{n-2}^r for the sth pyramid of rank r. Table 79 for pyramidal numbers corresponds to Table 76 for polygonal numbers. Referring to Table 79, $f_{3,5}^6 = P_7^6 = 196$.

The name "pyramidal numbers" might imply that a pyramidal number of symmetrical objects, such as balls, could be assembled into

TABLE 79

PYRAMIDAL NUMBERS P_n^r

Name of Base	Sides in Base $= n$	Set No. $s = n-2$	1	2	3	4	5	6	7	8	r
											Rank $= r$	
Triangle	3	1	1	4	10	20	35	56	84	120	...$r(r+1)(r+2)/6$
Square	4	2	1	5	14	30	55	91	140	204	...$r(r+1)(2r+1)/6$
Pentagon	5	3	1	6	18	40	75	126	196	288	...$r^2(r+1)/2$
Hexagon	6	4	1	7	22	50	95	161	252	372	...$r(r+1)(4r-1)/6$
Heptagon	7	5	1	8	26	60	115	196	308	456	...$r(r+1)(5r-2)/6$
Octagon	8	6	1	9	30	70	135	231	364	540	...$r(r+1)(2r-1)/2$
...											
n-gon	n	$n-2$	1	$n+1$	$2(2n-1)$	$10(n-1)$	$5(4n-5)$	$7(5n-7)$	$28(2n-3)$	$12(7n-11)$	$[r(r+1)/6][(r-1)n-(2r-5)]$*

* In terms of r and s this becomes $r(r+1)(rs-s+3)/6$.

a uniform symmetrical pyramid, but this is possible only for pyramids with triangular or square bases. In all other cases the layers, consisting of a polygonal number of balls, do not uniformly fill all of the space. For example, with a hexagonal base of only 2 spheres on a side or a total of 6, there is room in the center for an additional sphere not counted in the hexagonal number 6 of rank 2, and for rank 4, there is room for 9 more balls in the base than is taken up by the 28 spheres of that rank. Table 75 makes this clear.

However, with triangular and square bases, balls can be piled into a uniform pyramid; the total number of balls is a pyramidal number. A square-based pyramid with 5 balls along each side would use $f_{2,2}^5 = P_4^5 = 1+4+9+16+25 = 55$ balls.

A pyramidal number P_n^r can be conveniently obtained from the corresponding polygonal number p_n^r by the formula:

$$P_n^r = (r+1)(2p_n^r+r)/6.$$

The reader may wish to verify this relation for the polygonal and pyramidal numbers of Tables 76 and 79. For example:

$$p_6^7 = 91 \quad \text{and} \quad P_6^7 = (7+1)(2\cdot91+7)/6 = 252.$$

Just as any n-gonal number is the sum of the $(n-1)$-gon of the same rank and the triangular number of the previous rank, so any n-gonal pyramidal number is the sum of the $(n-1)$-gonal pyramid of the same rank and the *triangular* pyramid (tetrahedron) of the previous rank.

TABLE 80

FOURTH-DIMENSIONAL FIGURATE NUMBERS $f_{4,s}^r$

Generating Polygon	Set No. = s	Rank = r								
		1	2	3	4	5	6	7	8	r
Triangle	1	1	5	15	35	70	126	210	330	...$r(r+1)(r+2)(r+3)/4!$
Square	2	1	6	20	50	105	196	336	540	...$r(r+1)^2(r+2)/12$
Pentagon	3	1	7	25	65	140	266	462	750	...$r(r+1)(r+2)(3r+1)/4!$
Hexagon	4	1	8	30	80	175	336	588	960	...$r^2(r+1)(r+2)/6$
Heptagon	5	1	9	35	95	210	406	714	1170	...$r(r+1)(r+2)(5r-1)/4!$
Octagon	6	1	10	40	110	245	476	840	1380	...$r(r+1)(r+2)(6r-2)/4!$
...										
$(s+2)$-gon	s	1	$(s+4)$	$5(s+2)$	$5(3s+4)$	$35(s+1)$	$14(5s+4)$	$42(3s+2)$	$30(7s+4)$	$r(r+1)(r+2)(rs-s+4)/4!$

For example, the hexagonal pyramid, P_6^7 of rank 7 is 252, which is the sum of the pentagonal pyramid 196 of rank 7 and the tetrahedron 56 of rank 6. Generally:

$$P_n^r = P_{n-1}^r + P_3^{r-1}$$

for pyramids, and

$$p_n^r = p_{n-1}^r + p_3^{r-1}$$

for polygons.

Polygonal numbers can be illustrated by polygonal designs on a plane and pyramidal numbers by pyramids. Although we cannot conceive of fourth- or higher-dimensional patterns corresponding to the sums of the pyramidal numbers, we can consider them at least analytically. The series formed by summing the rank numbers of the respective pyramidal series produce fourth-dimensional figurate numbers $f_{4,s}^r$. These are tabulated in Table 80.

Finally, we can generalize this procedure to obtain the m-dimensional figurate numbers:

$$f_{m,s}^r = (rs+m-s)(r+m-2)!/m!(r-1)!$$

With this single formula we can find any figurate number of whatever dimension, m, set number, s, and rank, r.

When $s = 1$, corresponding to the *first* set, we have

$$f_{m,1}^r = (r+m-1)(r+m-2)!/m!(r-1)! = (r+m-1)!/m!(r-1)!$$
$$= r(r+1)(r+2)\ldots(r+m-1)/m!$$
$$= (m+1)(m+2)(m+3)\ldots(r+m-1)/(r-1)!$$

This the reader may recognize as the binomial coefficients, also the combination of $(r+m-1)$ things taken either m or $(r-1)$ at a time.

A whole series of tables could be made up for m-dimensional figurate numbers corresponding to Tables 76, 79, and 80 for dimensions 2, 3, and 4. If these were all assembled, they would form a three-dimensional *table* of figurate numbers.

*   *   *

Additional recreational aspects of figurate numbers are problems requiring them to fulfill stated conditions.

1. Thus it may be required to find a square number which can represent the number of balls in a pyramid with a square base, in other words P_4^r must be a square. There is only one such, for $r = 24$, namely $1^2+2^2+3^2+\ldots+24^2 = 4900 = 70^2$.

2. The only solutions to a square number of balls in a triangular-based pyramid or tetrahedron, P_3^r, are $2^2 = 1+3$ and

$$140^2 = 1+3+6+10+\ldots+1176.$$

3. No triangular number can be a cube, a fourth power, or a fifth power.

4. No pyramidal numbers can be cubes or fifth powers, and except for the examples given above, they cannot even be squares.

5. Triangular numbers may be squares, however, as Table 78 shows. They can be found from the series $0, 1, 6, 35, 204\ldots u_n$, where $u_n = 6u_{n-1} - u_{n-2}$. Each term is six times the previous term, diminished by the one before that. Squares of these numbers are simultaneously square and triangular.

A formula resembling the one for the Pythagorean triangle with consecutive sides, of Chapter XIV, may be used instead of this series, for numbers which are simultaneously triangular and square:

$$\{[(1+\sqrt{2})^{2x} - (1-\sqrt{2})^{2x}]/4\sqrt{2}\}^2.$$

As x takes on the values $1, 2, 3\ldots$, we obtain the solutions $1, 6, 35$ as before, but of course it is a much more cumbersome formula to use than the previous one.

6. The triangular number 6 is the only one besides unity with fewer than 660 digits whose square is a triangular number. This condition requires that the number X of Table 78 be a triangular number.

7. The triangular numbers 55, 66, and 666 are the only ones with fewer than 30 digits consisting of a repeated digit only.

8. Find triangular numbers whose sum and difference are also triangular. A few solutions are given in Table 81.

TABLE 81

PAIRS OF TRIANGULAR NUMBERS
WHOSE SUM AND DIFFERENCE ARE TRIANGULAR

1st No. $F =$ $x(x+1)/2$	2nd No. $S =$ $y(y+1)/2$	Sides of Triangle x	y	Sum $=$ $F+S =$ $Z(Z+1)/2$	Diff. $=$ $F-S =$ $V(V+1)/2$	Sides of Triangle Z	V
21	15	6	5	36	6	8	3
171	105	18	14	276	66	23	11
990	780	44	39	1770	210	59	20
3741	2145	86	65	5886	1596	108	56
2185095	1747515	2090	1869	3932610	437580	2804	935

9. Find m-gonal numbers which are n-gonal. We have already found triangles which are squares. Triangular numbers which are pentagonal are 1, 210, and 40755.

10. The product of three consecutive triangular numbers, $p_3^{r-1} \cdot p_3^r \cdot p_3^{r+1}$, is a square only if $2r+1 = 3u$, where

$$u = 1, 3, 17, \ldots u_n = 6u_{n-1} - u_{n-2}.$$

If $u = 3$, then $r = 4$, and the product of the third, fourth, and fifth triangular numbers, 6, 10, and 15, is equal to the square 900. When $u = 17$, then $r = 25$ and

$$p_3^{24} \cdot p_3^{25} \cdot p_3^{26} = 300 \cdot 325 \cdot 351 = 34222500 = 5850^2.$$

*   *   *

Despite the elementary nature of many theorems and problems involving figurate and polygonal numbers, other relations arise in this subject which require far from elementary means for their demonstration. Thus every integer is either a triangular number, the sum of two such numbers, or at most the sum of three triangular numbers; every integer is the sum of at most four squares; and in general every integer is the sum of at most m m-gonal numbers. Although cubes and biquadrates (fourth powers) do not belong to the class of numbers that were discussed above, it may be noted that every integer is the sum of at most 9 cubes or 19 biquadrates.

Table 76 for pentagonal numbers shows that they follow the sequence: 1; 5; 12; 22; 35..., and the general formula $r(3r-1)/2$. Numbers included in $r(3r \pm 1)/2$ are called "generalized" pentagonal numbers and follow the sequence 1; 2; 5; 7; 12; 15; 22; 26; 35; 40.... These generalized pentagonal numbers appear in a celebrated formula discovered by Euler. The sum of all of the divisors of a number N is sometimes symbolized as $S(N)$ (see Chapter III). Euler's formula states that

$$\begin{aligned} S(N) - S(N-1) - S(N-2) + S(N-5) + S(N-7) - S(N-12) \\ - S(N-15) + S(N-22) + S(N-26) - S(N-35) \\ - S(N-40) + \ldots = 0. \end{aligned}$$

The sequence of signs in pairs after the first term and the use of the generalized pentagonal numbers are obvious. A little explanation of the number of terms in a particular case is required. Continue only so long as the integer within a parenthesis is not negative, and interpret $S(0)$, which would otherwise be meaningless, as equal to N. For example, take $N = 15$ and we have:

$$S(15) - S(14) - S(13) + S(10) + S(8) - S(3) - S(0) = 0.$$

The divisors of 15 are 1; 3; 5; 15, whose sum is 24. The divisors of 14 are 1; 2; 7; 14, whose sum happens again to be 24. Continuing similarly, we have $S(13) = 14$; $S(10) = 18$; $S(8) = 15$; $S(3) = 4$; $S(0) = 15$, and $24 - 24 - 14 + 18 + 15 - 4 - 15 = 0$.

The number 15 happened to be pentagonal; let us try another integer such as 27, which is not, where $S(0)$ does not occur:

$$S(27) - S(26) - S(25) + S(22) + S(20) - S(15) - S(12)$$

$$+ S(5) + S(1) = 40 - 42 - 31 + 36 + 42 - 24 - 28 + 6 + 1 = 0.$$

When one considers the apparent irrelevancy between sums of divisors and polygonal numbers, this formula is truly remarkable.

BIBLIOGRAPHY

Barlow, P. *Theory of Numbers.* London: J. Johnson & Co., 1811.

Danzig, T. *Number: The Language of Science.* New York: Macmillan Co., 1954.

Dickson, L. E. *History of the Theory of Numbers.* 3 vols. New York: Chelsea Publishing Co., 1950.

Hall, H. S., and Knight, S. R. *Higher Algebra.* New York: Macmillan Co., 1932.

Hogben, L. *Mathematics for the Million.* New York: W. W. Norton & Co., 1951.

Lucas, E. *Récréations Mathématiques.* Paris: Gauthier-Villars et Cie., 1882.

Uspensky, J. V., and Heaslet, M. A. *Elementary Number Theory.* New York: McGraw-Hill Book Co., 1939.

CHAPTER XIX

THEOREMA AUREUM

"THEOREMA AUREUM"—the golden theorem, and the "Gem of the Higher Arithmetic"—such were Karl Friedrich Gauss's enthusiastic appellations for the law of quadratic reciprocity. They were well deserved—it is indeed a gem among number-theory laws.

The law of quadratic reciprocity, also known as "Legendre's Law of Quadratic Reciprocity," was first clearly enunciated by A. M. Legendre, although the famous Euler had made references to this property of primes many years previously. Legendre was unable to present a flawless proof and it remained for the great Gauss to do so. He succeeded in obtaining seven distinct proofs of it, the first when he was only nineteen, and stimulated no doubt by his efforts, other investigators have discovered additional proofs so that no less than fifty are now extant.

Gauss, without knowing of the work of either Euler or Legendre, discovered the law by observation. He required a year to prove it completely. "It tortured me," he says, "for the whole year and eluded the most strenuous efforts before, finally, I got the proof explained in the fourth section of the *Disquisitiones Arithmeticae*"—his magnum opus.

Before we can understand even the statement of the law we must learn something about quadratic residues—remainders of squares—and the special notations applying to them.

If I say to you, "Find a square, such that when divided by 11 it leaves a remainder of 2," you know exactly what is wanted. Reaching for the nearest piece of paper and a pencil, you write down a few squares and mentally divide by 11, feeling that in only a few trials one with the requisite remainder will be found. You might even have a table of squares in your bookcase and referring to it try the first 20 or so squares before becoming convinced that none of them leaves a remainder of 2. This doesn't seem quite right because you have an "intuitive" feeling that it should be possible to obtain any remainder from 0 up to 10 when you divide by 11. However, if you examine the remainders you will find only 0, 1, 3, 4, 5, 9 and never 2, 6, 7, 8, or 10.

That all numbers cannot be remainders of squares for a given modulus is easily demonstrated using the number 11 as such a modulus. Every positive integer must be of one of the forms $11x$, $11x \pm 1$, $11x \pm 2$, $11x \pm 3$, $11x \pm 4$, $11x \pm 5$, and consequently, its square must be of one of the forms: $121x^2$, $(121x^2 \pm 22x + 1)$, $(121x^2 \pm 44x + 4)$, $(121x^2 \pm 66x + 9)$, $(121x^2 \pm 88x + 16)$, $(121x^2 \pm 110x + 25)$. These expressions are, respectively, congruent to 0, 1, 4, 9, 5, 3 mod 11. Consequently, only these integers are *quadratic residues* (remainders), modulo 11, whereas 2, 6, 7, 8, and 10, which are never remainders when a square is divided by 11, are *quadratic non-residues* of 11.

Table 82 shows the quadratic residues and non-residues of all odd primes from 3 to 29. It will be noted that there is always the same number of residues as non-residues for any one prime.

In general an integer r is a quadratic residue of m if a square, x^2, exists such that $x^2 \equiv r$ mod m. (If the modulus m is composite, quadratic residues not prime to it are usually excluded; thus 6 is not considered a quadratic residue of 15 even though $9^2 \equiv 6$ mod 15.) For simplicity, further discussion will be confined to odd prime moduli.

A knowledge of quadratic residues is required to solve second-degree congruences such as $2x^2 - 5x \equiv 7$ mod 23 or to demonstrate that such a congruence is impossible. Quadratic residues can be applied very elegantly to the factoring of numbers as explained in Chapter XXI. Mention of them has already been made in connection with Mersenne's numbers and primitive roots.

There is a simple means of ascertaining whether a number r is a quadratic residue of a prime p. If $r^{(p-1)/2} \equiv +1$ mod p, then r is such a residue; if $r^{(p-1)/2} \equiv -1$, it is a non-residue. The right-hand member of the congruence *will* be either plus or minus one (never any other integer), hence r is or is not a quadratic residue of p according as $r^{(p-1)/2}$ is congruent to plus or minus one, modulo p. The Legendre symbol $(r|p)$ whose value is either plus or minus one compactly represents the "quadratic character" of r with respect to the *prime p*. When $r = 2$ and $p = 11$, $2^{(11-1)/2} = 2^5 \equiv -1$ mod 11, hence 2 is a quadratic non-residue of 11, that is, $(2|11) = -1$. But for $r = 3$, $3^5 = 243 \equiv +1$ mod 11, hence 3 *is* a quadratic residue, so that $(3|11) = +1$.

It is easy to prove the validity of this test. For if r *is* a quadratic

TABLE 82

Quadratic Residues and Non-Residues

Prime	Residue	Non-Residue
3	1	2
5	1, 4	2, 3
7	1, 2, 4	3, 5, 6
11	1, 3, 4, 5, 9	2, 6, 7, 8, 10
13	1, 3, 4, 9, 10, 12	2, 5, 6, 7, 8, 11
17	1, 2, 4, 8, 9, 13, 15, 16	3, 5, 6, 7, 10, 11, 12, 14
19	1, 4, 5, 6, 7, 9, 11, 16, 17	2, 3, 8, 10, 12, 13, 14, 15, 18
23	1, 2, 3, 4, 6, 8, 9, 12, 13, 16, 18	5, 7, 10, 11, 14, 15, 17, 19, 20, 21, 22
29	1, 4, 5, 6, 7, 9, 13, 16, 20, 22, 23, 24, 25, 28	2, 3, 8, 10, 11, 12, 14, 15, 17, 18, 19, 21, 26, 27

residue of p, a square x^2 exists such that $r \equiv x^2$ mod p, and raising both sides of the congruence to the $(p-1)/2$ power, we have:

$$r^{(p-1)/2} \equiv (x^2)^{(p-1)/2} \equiv x^{p-1},$$

and x^{p-1} is always congruent to 1 mod p by Fermat's theorem.

This test, although conclusive, may involve much labor when modulus and residue are large, hence more practical ones are required. Gauss's Golden Theorem, the Law of Quadratic Reciprocity, is such a test; it enables one to determine whether an odd prime p is a quadratic residue of another, q, by ascertaining whether q is a quadratic residue of p. The law states that $(p|q) = (q|p)$ except when both p and q are of the form $4x-1$, in which case $(p|q) = -(q|p)$. For instance, to ascertain the quadratic character of 3 with respect to the prime 13, we have $(3|13) = (13|3)$ since 3 and 13 are *not* both of the form $4x-1$. Since the symbol $(13|3)$ implies the congruence $x^2 \equiv 13$ mod 3, it can be simplified to $x^2 \equiv 1$ mod 3, by dropping multiples of 3, so that $(13|3)$ is the same as $(1|3)$. However, 1 *is* a quadratic residue of 13, hence $(13|3) = +1$, and therefore $(3|13) = +1$, so that 3 is a quadratic residue of 13, in fact $4^2 \equiv 3$ mod 13.

Again, since both 29 and 1193 are of the form $4x+1$, we have $(29|1193) = (1193|29) = (4|29)$. (Multiples of 29 are dropped from 1193.) Obviously $(4|29) = +1$, since 4 itself is *the* square that leaves 4 as a remainder when divided by 29. Therefore $(29|1193) = +1$, but the actual finding of the square which will leave a remainder of 29 when divided by 1193 is a more difficult matter and will be discussed later. Can the reader find it?†

The product of two residues or two non-residues is a residue (to the same modulus of course); the product of a residue and a non-residue is a non-residue. Thus if $(r|p) = +1$, $(s|p) = -1$, and $(t|p) = -1$, then $(rs|p) = -1$, $(st|p) = +1$, etc. For if $(r|p) = +1$ and $(s|p) = -1$, then $r^{(p-1)/2} \equiv 1$ and $s^{(p-1)/2} \equiv -1$ mod p, whence $(rs)^{(p-1)/2} \equiv -1$ mod p, etc.

We can apply this to another example of the reciprocity law. The integers 19 and 31 are both of the form $4x-1$, hence $(19|31) = -(31|19) = -(12|19)$. Now $-(12|19)$ may be written

$$-(3|19)(4|19) = -(3|19) \cdot (+1)$$

† Problems indicated by a dagger are solved in Chapter XXVI.

since 4 is a square.   Continuing, $-(3|19) = --(19|3) = +(1|3) = +1$, so that 19 is a quadratic residue of 31.   The square 81 is the solution, but of course the above was only a test and not a method of finding the solution.

*   *   *

Of greater generality and interest than determining the value of $(p|q)$ in a particular instance is the finding of a large class of primes for which some given integer is always a quadratic residue.   For example, -1 is always a quadratic residue of *every* prime of the form $4x + 1$, and 2 is a quadratic residue of every prime of either the form $8x + 1$ or $8x - 1$.   These two rules together with the law of quadratic reciprocity can be elegantly expressed as follows:

Mathematical Expression	*Meaning*
(a) $(-1|p) = (-1)^{(p-1)/2}$	Minus one is a quadratic residue of all primes, p, of the form $4x + 1$, and of no others.
(b) $(2|p) = (-1)^{(p^2-1)/8}$	The prime 2 is a quadratic residue of all primes, p, of the form $8x \pm 1$, and of no others.
(c) $(p|q)(q|p) = (-1)^{(p-1)(q-1)/4}$	The quadratic character of the prime p with respect to the prime q is the same or opposite to the quadratic character of q with respect to p according as at least one or neither of these primes is of the form $4x + 1$.

Suppose we wanted to find the form for that class of primes of which 10 is a quadratic residue.   Then $(10|p) = (2|p)(5|p)$, and 10 will be a quadratic residue of p if $(2|p)$ and $(5|p)$ are either both positive or both   negative.   First   assume   both   positive.   Now $(2|p) = +1$ holds only when $p = 8x \pm 1$ by (b) above, and $(5|p) = (p|5)$ since 5 is of the form $4x + 1$.   The quadratic residues of 5 are 1 and -1, hence p must be of the form $5y \pm 1$.   To be simultaneously of the form $8x \pm 1$ and $5y \pm 1$, it develops that p must be one of the forms $40x \pm 1$ or $40x \pm 9$, and therefore 10 is a quadratic residue of any prime of these four forms, for example, 41, 79, 89, or 31.

For $(2|p) = -1$ and $(5|p) = -1$, the first expression is satisfied if p is of the form $8x \pm 3$, and since $(5|p) = (p|5) = -1$, the second is satisfied for $p = 5y \pm 2$, since the quadratic non-residues of 5 are 2 and 3; i.e., ± 2. Then for p to be simultaneously of the form $8x \pm 3$ and $5y \pm 2$, it develops that p must be of the form $40x \pm 3$ or $40x \pm 13$. Finally, then, 10 is a quadratic residue of all primes of the eight forms: $40x \pm 1$, $40x \pm 3$, $40x \pm 9$, $40x \pm 13$, and of no others.

Use was made of this fact in Chapter XI in finding factors of numbers of the form $10^z - 1$, where z is a prime. We have

$$10^{(p-1)/2} \equiv 1 \mod p$$

for the eight forms of p given above, so that whenever $(p-1)/2$ is also a prime, z, then $10^z - 1$ will be divisible by p. This is true only for $p = 40x - 1$, $40x + 3$, $40x - 13$ as in the other cases $(p-1)/2$ is composite. Hence:

$$10^{20x-1} \equiv 1 \mod 40x - 1$$
$$10^{20x+1} \equiv 1 \mod 40x + 3$$
$$10^{20x-7} \equiv 1 \mod 40x - 13.$$

If $x = 2$, then $20x + 1 = 41$, $40x + 3 = 83$, both primes, and therefore $10^{41} \equiv 1 \mod 83$.

* * *

The proof of the quadratic reciprocity law is too recondite for us here, but it is so ingenious that the steps leading to the conclusion may at least be stated. The reader is referred to a modern number-theory text for the complete proof.

1. If multiples $1m$, $2m$, $3m \ldots [(p-1)/2]m$ of any integer, m, not divisible by the prime, p, be taken, and if among the least *positive* residues mod p of these numbers there are an even number of them exceeding $p/2$, then m is a quadratic residue of p; if an odd number, m is a non-residue. This is known as Gauss's lemma, and if r is the number of such positive residues we can state the lemma compactly as $(m|p) = (-1)^r$.

For example, take $p = 13$ and $m = 3$. Then $(p-1)/2 = 6$ and we write the six multiples,

$$3, 6, 9, 12, 15, 18.$$

The positive residues, mod 13 of these multiples are:

$$3, 6, 9, 12, 2, 5,$$

and two of them, namely 9 and 12, exceed $p/2$. Then, since 2 is an even number, the integer $m = 3$ is a quadratic residue of 13. Had there been five residues exceeding $p/2$, m would have been a non-residue since 5 is an odd number.

2. From this it follows that if p and q are two primes, and r and s are the respective number of least positive residues, mod p and mod q exceeding $p/2$ and $q/2$ respectively, in the series

$$1q, 2q, 3q \ldots [(p-1)/2]q, \quad \text{and}$$
$$1p, 2p, 3p \ldots [(q-1)/2]p, \quad \text{then}$$
$$(p|q)(q|p) = (-1)^r(-1)^s = (-1)^{r+s}.$$

3. The sum $r+s$ is odd only when both p and q are of the form $4x-1$, and therefore $(p|q)(q|p) = -1$ only under this condition. From this follows the quadratic reciprocity law as previously stated. The proof of Step 3 is what so tortured Gauss.

*　　*　　*

An interesting property of primitive roots enters into the theory of quadratic residues. The even powers of any primitive root are residues and the odd ones are non-residues of any prime p. For instance, 2 is a primitive root of 13, and 2^2, 2^4, 2^6, 2^8, 2^{10}, and 2^{12}, which are respectively congruent to 4, 3, 12, 9, 10, and 1, are quadratic residues of 13. On the other hand, 2^1, 2^3, 2^5, 2^7, 2^9, and 2^{11}, congruent respectively to 2, 8, 6, 11, 5, 7, are non-residues.

*　　*　　*

After it has been ascertained that a number is a quadratic residue of a given prime, the actual finding of a square leaving the requisite remainder is often difficult. Here are a few rules which apply in special cases.

1. Solution of $x^2 \equiv -1 \bmod p = 4n+1$:

$$x \equiv \pm[(p-1)/2]!$$

2. Solution of $x^2 \equiv a \bmod p = 4n+3$:

$$x \equiv \pm a^{n+1}.$$

3. Solution of $x^2 \equiv a \bmod p = 8n+5$:

$$x \equiv \pm[(4a)^{n+1}]/2.$$

4. Solution of $x^2 \equiv a \bmod p = 8n+1$:

There is no direct solution unless $a = \pm 2$.

Solution of $x^2 \equiv \pm 2 \bmod p = 8n+1$.

Let g be a primitive root of p. Then

$$x \equiv g^n \pm g^{7n} \bmod p.$$

* * *

An ingenious practical method for solving *any* quadratic congruence depends on the method of excludents. To solve $x^2 \equiv b \bmod p$ is the same as to solve the equation: $b + py = x^2$, where some multiple py of p must be found which when added to b gives a square. Even for fairly large values of b and p, the values of y to be tried can be sufficiently restricted so that in comparatively few trials a solution is obtained. If the terms in the above equation are referred to some arbitrary small modulus, E, not all values of y, modulo E, will make $b + py$, and therefore x^2, a quadratic residue of E as would be necessary since x^2 is a square. These values of y may then be excluded.

Suppose we wish to solve $x^2 \equiv 33 \bmod 97$ or its equivalent $33 + 97y = x^2$, having of course first tested the congruence by the reciprocity law and convinced ourselves that it is possible. For the arbitrary modulus 5, the left-hand side of the equation becomes $3 + 2y$. To modulo 5, y might be 0, 1, 2, 3, or 4; and $3 + 2y$ would then be congruent to 3, 0, 2, 4, or 1. But if $b + py$ is to be a square, it must be congruent to one of the quadratic residues of 5, namely, 0, 1, or 4; therefore, the values of y which make $3 + 2y$ equal 2 or 3 must be excluded. Thus y can be congruent only to 1, 3, or 4, modulo 5. Therefore it is unnecessary to try any values of y of the form $5z$ or $5z + 2$. Similarly, to the arbitrary small modulus 7, y can be only of the form $7z + 1$, $7z + 3$, $7z + 4$, or $7z + 5$; and $7z$, $7z + 2$, and $7z + 6$ must be excluded. Similar excludents can be found modulo 8, 9, 11, 13, etc. (primes or their powers), but for so small a modulus as 97 the two excludents 5 and 7 sufficiently restrict y.

Furthermore, values of y in excess of $p/4$ need never be tried, for if there is a solution x, then $p - x$ is another solution (x^2 is congruent to $p - x]^2 \bmod p$, so that either x or $p - x$ is less than $p/2$ and x^2 or $p - x]^2$ less than $p^2/4$). Therefore py must be less than $p^2/4$ or y less than $p/4$. We list, therefore, the consecutive integers, starting from unity, for values of y not exceeding 24 and delete any which are of the forms $5z$ or $5z+2$, leaving 1, 6, 11, 16, 21, 3, 8, 13, 18, 23, 4, 9, 14, 19, 24. From these we delete any numbers which are of the form $7z$, $7z+2$, or $7z+6$, leaving 1, 3, 4, 8, 11, 18, 19, 24. The second value 3 gives a solution since $33+97 \cdot 3 = 324 = 18^2$. A second solution is obtained from $97-18 = 79$.

Convenient lists of excludents for small moduli have been tabulated, and with their aid one can rapidly solve quadratic congruences for fairly large moduli. The excludent method for the above problem may not have appeared very effective. But to solve, for example, the congruence $x^2 \equiv 29 \bmod 1193$, discussed earlier in this chapter, the number of values of y to try can be reduced from 298 to only 4, using 5, 7, 8, 9, 11, and 13 as excludents. To further reduce labor, one can obtain or make a set of stencils with holes punched at assigned intervals for different moduli. By superimposing these stencils and noting where the holes coincide, numbers which are simultaneously of several forms can be readily identified. And with the aid of a digital computer, millions of numbers can be examined rapidly without human intervention.

*   *   *

It is frequently necessary to obtain a number of *small* quadratic residues of given modulus. Such residues are of considerable aid in factoring the modulus or determining that it is a prime. The method of carrying out this factorization will be described in Chapter XXI. but the way to obtain a few small residues of an unknown number will be explained here as the method is ingenious and easy to understand Suppose we wanted to obtain at least five quadratic residues, each smaller than 250, of the number $N = 135287$. We find first the smallest square n^2 larger than N, in this case $368^2 = 135424$. Then $n^2 - N = 137$, so that 137 is a quadratic residue of 135287 since 368^2 leaves that remainder when divided by 135287. We follow a similar procedure for 369^2, 370^2, etc., the successive residues being easily obtained without subtraction by adding $2n+1$ to the first residue and two more than the previous addend to each succeeding residue. This gives Table 83.

Negative residues are similarly obtained, continuing the table for as long as we please. Since it was decided to find only five residues less than 250, the table need not be very long. Of course, every number in the residue column is a quadratic residue; the problem is t

TABLE 83

QUADRATIC RESIDUES OF $N = 135287$

n	Residue = R = $n^2 - N$	Residue Factored	n	Residue = R = $n^2 - N$	Residue Factored
368	137	137	367	-598	$-2 \cdot 13 \cdot 23$
369	874	$2 \cdot 19 \cdot 23$	366	-1331	$-11 \cdot (11^2)$
370	1613	1613	365	-2062	$-2 \cdot 1031$
371	2354	$11 \cdot 107$	364	-2791	-2791
372	3097	$19 \cdot 163$	363	-3518	$-2 \cdot 1759$
373	3842	$2 \cdot 17 \cdot 113$	362	-4243	-4243
374	4589	$13 \cdot 353$	361	-4966	$-2 \cdot 13 \cdot 191$
375	5338	$2 \cdot 17 \cdot 157$	360	-5687	$-47 \cdot (11^2)$

find residues below our set limit of 250. We see that 137 is the only residue in the list less than this limit. However, it is clear that if a residue has a square factor, that factor may be suppressed and the remainder will still be a residue because the quadratic character of a square with respect to any modulus is always plus one. For instance, a residue $R = a^2b$, with respect to the modulus N, can be written $(a^2|N)(b|N) = +1(b|N) = (b|N)$. Applying this rule we find that -11 and -47 are also residues. Extending this principle, we know that the product of any number of quadratic residues is a quadratic residue, and by judicious combination of them we may be able to drop square factors. Thus $11 \cdot 107$ and -11 may be so combined, producing -107 as an additional residue, and $2 \cdot 19 \cdot 23$ and $-2 \cdot 13 \cdot 23$ yield $-13 \cdot 19 = -247$, barely under the limit. To find still more residues less than 250 it would be necessary to extend the table.

In most investigations only those quadratic residues which are prime to the modulus are of interest; hence all numbers in the residue column must be tested for this restriction unless one knows in advance that the modulus is a prime. To test whether two numbers are relatively prime, their greatest common divisor is found by the method explained in arithmetic or algebra books. If this greatest common divisor turns out to be unity, the two numbers are of course relatively prime.

*   *   *

From what has been said before, we would expect quadratic residues and non-residues to be equally divided in a sequence of numbers. But if p is a prime of the form $4x - 1$, there are more residues than non-residues in the sequence 1, 2, 3...$(p-1)/2$. For example, if $p = 19$, the sequence 1, 2, 3, 4, 5, 6, 7, 8, 9 contains six quadratic residues: 1, 4, 5, 6, 7, 9.

BIBLIOGRAPHY

Bell, E. T. *Men of Mathematics*. New York: Simon and Schuster, 1937.

Dickson, L. E. *Introduction to the Theory of Numbers*. New York: Dover Publications, Inc., 1957.

Lehmer, D. N. *Factor Stencils*. Washington, D.C.: Carnegie Institution of Washington, 1939.

————. "A Photo-Electric Number Sieve," *American Mathematical Monthly*, **40** (1933), 401.

Mathews, G. B. *Theory of Numbers*. New York: Chelsea Publishing Co., 1961.

Reid, L. W. *Elements of the Theory of Algebraic Numbers*. Baltimore: Johns Hopkins Press, 1946.

Uspensky, J. V., and Heaslet, M. A. *Elementary Number Theory*. New York: McGraw-Hill Book Co., 1939.

Vinogradov, I. M. *Elements of Number Theory*. New York: Dover Publications, Inc., 1954.

CHAPTER XX

AMONG THE HIMALAYAS

Inseparably woven into the fabric of number theory, nay, the very weft of the cloth, are the ubiquitous primes. Almost every investigation includes them; they are the elementary building blocks of our number edifice. From the humble 2, the only even prime, and 1, the smallest of the odd primes, they rise in an unending succession aloof and irrefrangible. Well-nigh unscalable peaks such as $(10^{23} - 1)/9$ and the once peerless 39-digit $2^{127} - 1$ have finally yielded to the assaults of men determined to learn their secret and have been proved primes. Nowadays one cannot mention a number as the largest known prime because overnight a larger one will have been found. As far as the author knows, $2^{9941} - 1$ is the largest at this writing. This prime has 2993 digits. The Illiac II digital computer at the University of Illinois required 85 minutes to make 3/4 billion multiplications and additions to verify that this number is a prime; by hand it would require 80 men working together for 1000 years.

What other giants now proudly rearing their heads into the unknown will finally be brought within the ken of our knowledge as primes or composites? How about the unknown members of that mountain chain of "repunit" numbers from $(10^{37} - 1)/9$ to $(10^{97} - 1)/9$ containing those peaks where 10 has the exponent 47; 59; 67; 71; 73; 83; and 89? And what about prime exponents beyond 100?

Since the dawn of mathematical history, primes have remained beyond the pale of any law attempting to classify them. Men have pored over the meager tables of primes available, vainly seeking a relation between the nth prime and its value—some order to the sequence of primes. Ever and anon, only defeat has met their efforts. During the last century some of the great mathematical leaders have directed the heavy artillery of analysis at these impregnable fortresses. Methods were brought into the discrete domain, previously applicable only in the continuous domain, sometimes revealing startling results. For example, there are approximation formulas giving to an astonishing degree of accuracy the number of primes within a given range.

Tantalizingly, however, the degree of accuracy does not increase as the range increases, a result often met with elsewhere, but oscillates in a haphazard, altogether unpredictable manner.

As numbers get larger, the probability of their having divisors increases and one might suppose therefore that perhaps some limit is approached beyond which a number cannot be a prime. However, Euclid proved in a most elementary manner that the number of primes is infinite. This proof has an almost universal appeal because of its conciseness and simplicity.

Assume that the number of primes is *not* infinite and let p be the largest prime. Then the number $N = 2 \cdot 3 \cdot 5 \cdot 7 \ldots p$, consisting of the product of *all* the primes in their natural order from 2 to p, is divisible by each of these primes. Then $N+1$ is divisible by none of these primes, since each of them when divided into $N+1$ leaves unity as a remainder. Hence, either of two possibilities exists:

1. $N+1$, if composite, is divisible by a prime larger than p.
2. $N+1$ is divisible by no number smaller than itself, that is $N+1$ is a prime.

In the latter case, it appears that $N+1$, a much larger number than p, is a prime; in the former, that a prime divisor of $N+1$ is greater than p. In either case this admits of the existence of a prime larger than p, which was assumed the largest prime. Our assumption thus being contradicted by each of the only two possibilities, it follows that it must be untenable and therefore there cannot be a prime, p, which is the largest prime.

*   *   *

Eratosthenes, one of the early Greeks, invented a simple way of finding and listing primes. Write down all the integers in their natural order. Starting from 2, cross off every second number, leaving 2 uncrossed, continuing as long as one pleases. Starting from 3, cross off every third number, excluding 3. Then start all over again from the first uncrossed number after 3, namely, 5, and cross off every fifth number. Repeat for the next uncrossed number, crossing off every seventh number, etc. A number must be counted each time whether it was crossed off before or not. The remaining uncrossed numbers are the primes:

1, 2, 3, 4̸, 5, 6̸, 7, 8̸, 9̸, 1̸0̸, 11, 1̸2̸, 13, 1̸4̸, 1̸5̸, 1̸6̸, 17, 1̸8̸, 19, 2̸0̸, 2̸1̸, 2̸2̸, 23, 2̸4̸, 2̸5̸

The arrangement above shows how a table of primes not exceeding 25 may be formed by this rule.

Again, imagine a long strip of paper on which all the integers are printed in their natural order. Suppose it is run through a stamping machine which punches out every second number after 2 and continues to another machine which punches out every third number after 3, etc. The remaining unpunched numbers would constitute a table of primes.

Table 84 lists the first 5600 primes from 1 to 55079. This is the arrangement given in Lehmer's list of primes to 10000000.

Prodigious indeed is the labor that has been expended on tables of primes. There is something sublime in reading of these efforts, expended for their own sake, unsullied by all lucrative hope or desire. L. E. Dickson in the second volume of his *History* expresses the sentiments that animate the authors of such immense labors. It "fitted in with his conviction that every person should aim to perform at some time in his life some serious useful work for which it is highly improbable that there will be any reward whatever other than his satisfaction therefrom."

There is a record dating back to the year 1202 that one Leonardo Pisano gave a table of the primes from 11 to 97 and a table of the composite numbers from 12 to 100. In 1603, Pietro Cataldi published a factor table to 800 and a list of primes to 750. The computers followed one another closely after that, pushing over onward to larger and larger limits. A brief list of the more important calculators and their range of computation is given in Table 85.

Contemplating such efforts within the frame of a world troubled by war and ceaseless unrest, it seems that the men who spent so large a part of their lives in this kind of work must have found the secret to an inner peace and happiness that all men crave but that no exigent clamorer for worldly goods can ever attain. The hopes and ensuing frustrations of life are also portrayed in such toil. Consider, for example, the labors of Antonio Felkel, who in 1776 calculated the prime factors of all numbers to 2000000. The first part of the table to 408000 had no purchasers, and all but a few copies of the entire edition were used for cartridges in the Turkish war! The imperial treasury at Vienna, which had furnished the funds for printing, retained the manuscript of the balance of the table. When subsequently he was unable to obtain his manuscript, Felkel recalculated the factors of the numbers from 408000 to 2856000.

TABLE 84 — List of Primes*

	1	2	3	4	5	6	7	8	9	10	11	12	13	14	15	16	17	18	19	20	21	22	23	24	25	26	27	28
		541	1223	1987	2741	3571	4409	5279	6133	6997	7919	8831	9733	0657	1657	2553	3499	4519	5401	6361	7369	8313	9425	0357	1383	2307	3321	4281
																												2
																												317
1	1	47	29	93	49	83	21	81	43	43	27	39	39	63	63	77	37	37	33	11	93	41	29	59	91	43	27	29
2	3	57	31	97	53	85	23	97	51	01	27	47	43	67	81	79	23	53	27	17	01	41	35	69	97	49	33	37
3	5	65	37	2003	57	93	41	09	63	13	33	49	49	73	89	89	37	49	39	21	17	55	41	89	401	67	39	29
4	7	69	49	2003	77	607	47	35	73	27	37	61	67	91	99	601	53	71	43	27	19	67	47	95	07	69	57	71
6	11	71	59	93	89	11	61	57	97	43	51	63	69	709	701	11	67	57	51	39	31	61	47	407	19	69	61	73
7	13	77	77	97	91	17	63	33	99	57	63	67	81	11	17	17	77	61	61	43	43	79	57	11	33	81	63	75
8	17	87	79	17	97	31	65	35	205	63	93	67	87	17	19	19	91	63	67	47	49	83	65	31	39	91	99	77
9	19	93	89	29	03	51	85	51	11	69	95	925	803	29	31	31	97	95	75	53	67	401	69	41	81	97	417	91
10	23	95	89	37	03	51	85	81	17	69	8009	925	803	35	45	39	615	621	95	61	71	401	71	45	93	409	31	407
11	29	29	91	53	19	45	93	87	21	103	17	29	11	39	77	41	19	27	511	81	77	37	77	43	91	501	47	15
12	31	601	97	55	33	59	507	93	29	11	39	35	17	37	79	47	27	33	07	83	83	57	89	45	93	11	49	19
13	37	07	303	69	35	73	15	99	35	09	55	41	29	41	83	55	33	35	29	89	89	61	89	53	95	21	53	21
14	41	13	301	99	43	75	17	409	47	21	59	63	35	47	93	67	43	65	33	91	91	73	501	57	503	29	55	39
15	43	19	19	111	51	91	19	51	59	31	69	63	47	53	801	77	69	67	41	97	97	87	07	59	97	41	57	35
16	47	31	19	87	57	97	23	17	71	51	81	83	51	99	13	85	79	39	47	509	509	503	31	09	21	85	31	69
17	53	41	21	89	57	701	31	31	71	77	17	11	59	831	17	89	81	53	51	07	73	507	41	21	23	501	37	73
18	59	43	27	99	79	709	37	37	77	77	23	13	61	37	25	03	609	57	19	603	79	11	43	23	29	11	39	81
19	61	47	99	111	87	19	39	41	87	93	47	09	901	47	35	45	11	59	29	07	81	23	53	43	41	41	49	99
20	67	55	409	13	903	01	61	67	99	207	61	07	07	55	39	67	21	85	41	19	97	27	59	49	59	51	57	509
1	71	59	73	29	903	33	85	43	301	11	17	13	87	61	53	89	25	03	41	51	609	21	71	27	601	41	61	17
2	73	61	77	31	11	35	91	49	11	11	23	19	07	61	59	705	21	05	29	69	23	23	77	51	11	49	67	27
3	79	73	85	37	17	39	97	77	17	19	31	41	07	67	65	43	25	13	41	73	27	31	85	63	13	49	65	35
4	83	77	99	41	27	61	21	77	29	19	47	49	23	85	67	65	49	21	45	75	57	41	97	65	27	51	67	47
5	89	85	409	43	39	71	21	603	29	29	61	59	29	89	87	75	51	25	71	85	59	55	603	77	59	73	81	51
6	97	91	27	55	57	69	37	37	43	43	67	67	87	901	97	79	57	29	79	609	69	61	09	27	99	613	99	51
7	101	701	37	79	57	39	39	501	53	47	71	67	907	903	903	99	59	31	49	23	81	81	61	19	601	19	605	73
8	05	03	39	203	63	93	49	05	59	59	79	67	07	09	09	809	51	37	61	27	23	87	81	41	11	27	09	93
9	07	09	47	13	69	803	49	07	59	85	91	103	0007	09	23	09	59	47	67	57	27	97	87	63	13	31	23	611
30	09	27	47	47	71	21	51	19	61	85	209	09	37	39	27	23	65	51	71	59	57	617	97	77	17	39	27	23
1	13	33	51	21	23	23	57	27	67	307	19	27	39	39	33	41	81	57	79	69	69	61	99	07	47	29	29	59
2	27	39	55	31	3001	25	63	31	73	11	21	31	39	57	39	99	89	67	85	81	81	71	709	31	61	33	33	71
3	31	43	59	37	11	31	75	37	79	33	31	33	37	65	41	93	99	71	27	85	85	87	17	31	65	41	35	77
4	37	51	71	39	19	47	91	57	89	51	35	51	61	71	55	95	807	73	31	707	707	93	27	45	71	49	63	83
5	39	57	81	43	23	53	91	57	97	57	37	57	61	87	59	95	29	85	35	15	15	701	39	49	83	51	71	01
6	49	61	87	51	37	55	703	63	421	43	43	57	95	1005	69	907	31	815	37	29	29	701	51	45	7001	27	77	97
7	51	75	87	61	41	77	21	65	27	63	63	73	99	11	81	11	41	21	49	47	47	13	53	47	37	39	89	709
8	57	79	89	73	61	77	23	73	61	65	65	75	79	19	61	17	61	37	61	61	61	19	55	49	37	41	89	35
9	63	81	93	75	67	803	33	623	61	69	87	99	79	57	73	25	75	75	61	81	81	31	65	55	39	21	719	45
40	67	97	99	83	73	907	49	07	59	85	99	203	95	59	07	23	79	79	73	807	807	43	77	77	51	27	41	63
1	73	809	511	87	79	907	59	11	73	411	93	09	103	59	11	85	85	81	91	89	89	49	95	75	51	27	45	67
2	79	11	21	89	89	11	59	41	81	33	93	97	11	71	23	901	901	89	91	91	91	73	801	89	57	39	47	81
3	91	23	23	97	109	17	87	47	91	53	311	209	33	85	41	03	03	79	97	807	807	87	13	807	67	41	53	83
4	95	27	43	309	19	23	93	51	521	29	17	09	39	87	49	07	07	97	803	27	27	95	19	09	73	51	61	93
5	97	35	49	11	21	31	93	53	29	51	29	27	41	113	71	79	13	97	09	37	37	03	41	47	87	59	67	809
6	99	53	59	33	37	55	99	59	47	57	53	41	51	17	73	79	21	923	23	39	39	603	53	73	803	83	73	21
7	99	59	83	41	63	31	99	69	53	77	63	41	59	19	97	01	31	29	59	51	51	61	61	75	17	87	801	47
8	211	59	67	59	63	59	801	81	63	87	69	77	63	19	3001		33		59	63	63	59	67	79	21	807	13	51

* Reprinted with permission from D. N. Lehmer, *Factor Stencils*, 2nd ed., Carnegie Institution of Washington, 1939, pp. 14–15.

TABLE 84 —continued

	29	30	31	32	33	34	35	36	37	38	39	40	41	42	43	44	45	46	47	48	49	50	51	52	53	54	55	56
	2	2	2	2	2	3	3	3	3	3	3	3	3	3	3	4	4	4	4	4	4	4	4	5	5	5	5	5
1	5391	6399	7449	8499	9443	0559	1601	2609	3613	4649	5759	6781	7813	8921	9971	1081	2073	3051	4201	5307	6447	7527	8611	9665	0785	1805	2919	3993

	29	30	31	32	33	34	35	36	37	38	39	40	41	42	43	44	45	46	47	48	49	50	51	52	53	54	55	56	
51	13	91	47	53	59	91	99	13	57	59	77	09	71	19	31	603	57	61	41	53	93	49	23	47	29	61	41	41	1
2	19	93	53	49	71	121	73	19	59	07	93	13	77	39	43	09	69	69	53	59	97	73	39	53	41	63	55	47	2
3	31	903	61	9009	103	23	203	49	201	201	99	21	93	45	45	11	71	91	69	69	7017	79	57	59	43	60	503	59	3
4	35	27	63	17	09	39	33	81	27	27	307	37	431	61	77	17	77	711	73	87	41	91	67	77	47	76	07	65	4
5	39	21	67	27	97	47	69	61	27	27	13	39	47	61	85	21	89	87	93	93	51	109	207	207	49	87	27	77	5
6	43	47	97	17	103	51	03	79	13	51	19	57	49	99	91	27	08	21	89	943	57	19	21	21	61	91	57	81	6
7	51	93	8001	31	13	53	33	81	57	57	19	61	49	503	609	41	71	53	97	49	59	21	93	27	61	433	61	83	7
8	69	55	19	23	13	59	59	91	67	67	43	63	63	09	93	47	43	59	55	55	37	31	27	31	07	53	99	601	8
9	81	59	27	27	19	77	33	99	79	79	51	69	61	11	37	51	45	77	39	79	113	57	11	63	13	89	61	07	9
60	99	81	31	33	35	81	57	203	91	91	73	79	501	21	37	59	67	81	39	21	11	79	89	63	21	89	41	23	60
1	6003	87	57	59	39	83	61	11	311	311	435	97	57	41	53	69	85	85	61	41	23	79	77	87	57	501	609	29	1
2	17	7011	63	63	37	93	61	23	17	17	51	23	57	51	31	81	81	87	47	89	37	83	87	91	73	11	99	29	2
3	21	17	81	77	39	213	47	47	23	25	25	41	69	65	19	93	85	89	69	6021	43	97	311	311	79	29	17	67	3
4	29	31	87	29	81	47	89	87	27	27	27	501	71	59	77	701	701	93	87	49	43	221	21	21	39	41	17	73	4
5	41	43	97	31	41	53	53	301	39	39	67	65	39	71	89	29	09	57	55	51	49	39	29	29	61	43	29	79	5
6	85	59	109	47	57	37	13	11	61	61	69	89	03	79	11	13	19	45	51	61	49	47	33	33	73	53	33	13	6
7	99	61	21	47	39	41	63	23	73	23	73	93	11	19	43	71	27	89	27	73	59	71	41	411	79	61	39	21	7
8	107	67	31	73	69	47	11	19	85	27	75	01	17	33	19	77	29	91	69	21	89	81	17	17	91	29	33	67	8
69	1	207	91	91	81	53	87	33	19	27	93	37	39	59	25	89	33	97	85	93	207	81	69	63	97	71	53	27	69
70	11	11	201	201	35	307	303	301	507	507	93	71	707	71	29	93	43	307	77	49	39	71	29	63	81	97	717	87	70
1	71	27	11	07	307	31	43	13	47	07	97	47	13	19	87	51	45	69	19	53	21	39	35	23	87	39	19	99	1
2	77	43	19	91	13	27	49	403	07	21	527	81	53	27	801	09	55	13	91	35	311	09	13	27	61	31	31	35	2
3	77	91	29	31	19	41	13	49	13	31	11	11	73	31	13	13	67	27	39	41	37	13	27	31	71	21	39	07	3
4	85	97	77	45	25	45	19	13	91	23	21	29	19	33	19	43	69	29	39	61	69	39	41	59	79	29	33	77	4
5	97	53	89	83	77	57	23	27	25	37	37	37	37	59	25	51	93	63	85	47	43	79	49	59	97	71	57	79	5
6	203	71	89	91	87	71	57	67	37	47	97	49	93	61	67	51	93	71	31	53	49	97	503	77	77	79	73	79	6
7	09	91	91	97	89	77	53	61	403	91	523	61	23	69	41	79	97	87	39	71	83	83	03	83	87	83	93	99	7
8	27	39	307	11	19	81	33	69	11	21	27	71	29	91	73	87	29	91	41	73	93	87	87	87	91	609	17	77	8
9	37	97	09	33	49	37	25	13	29	23	37	89	99	99	09	95	45	97	79	301	303	407	33	411	97	27	21	61	9
80	49	53	49	45	49	93	41	27	37	37	41	91	47	821	23	41	41	40017	85	09	17	09	33	17	37	31	813	19	80
1	51	71	19	69	69	57	43	57	47	47	55	19	65	29	53	83	55	13	53	53	53	13	81	81	57	21	09	41	1
2	61	77	49	97	87	87	59	95	95	47	57	33	67	29	79	79	23	27	51	73	57	39	87	87	69	57	99	59	2
3	67	81	59	33	91	91	91	505	501	69	35	49	91	41	53	93	49	57	63	301	63	87	91	91	83	69	73	73	3
4	81	85	87	47	49	511	29	21	13	93	95	63	61	59	59	59	55	87	79	01	91	87	07	07	79	83	85	85	4
89	99	99	301	303	403	17	503	29	21	93	93	717	707	91	63	81	43	89	09	17	87	97	91	91	79	807	03	79	89
90	209	307	09	07	27	17	41	57	21	603	709	89	13	57	51	55	55	101	91	09	31	97	93	93	91	13	97	83	90
1	309	37	49	09	17	17	77	67	73	17	13	81	33	69	1011	23	61	19	27	27	31	27	627	09	19	17	917	5001	1
2	21	61	11	11	23	31	59	95	71	71	39	93	93	91	17	99	19	59	37	37	59	33	51	47	49	37	23	09	2
3	39	67	23	29	39	31	61	69	71	31	77	99	903	37	39	61	29	23	39	49	49	39	85	49	49	61	27	21	3
4	47	97	47	25	17	47	87	603	89	77	61	47	17	37	51	59	73	29	59	81	63	41	71	71	69	79	39	49	4
5	57	07	63	31	29	67	69	13	603	729	39	81	85	29	57	71	13	59	81	99	71	63	83	83	63	83	51	57	5
6	71	31	61	35	41	73	77	07	07	31	17	85	61	37	51	79	19	71	85	59	89	89	23	23	69	89	59	73	6
9	87	37	83	37	57	73	89	99	47	47	77	99	903	53	77	89	49	79	93	41	21	89	41	25	89	901	87	79	9
100	93	31	37	37	57	83	605	601	53	53	79	811	17	53	77	71	49	89	93	41	21	93	41	41	97	03	03	79	100

TABLE 85

Factor Tables and Lists of Primes

Author	Year	Limit of Factor Table		List of Primes
L. Pisano	1202		100	97
P. Cataldi	1603		800	750
F. van Schooten	1657			10000
J. H. Rahn	1659		24000	
T. Brancker	1668		100000	
J. G. Kruger	1746			100999
J. H. Lambert	1770			102000
A. F. Marci	1772			400000
A. Felkel	1776		408000	
A. Felkel	1785		2856000	
L. Chernac	1811		1020000	
J. C. Burckhardt	1814	1000000 to	2000000	
J. C. Burckhardt	1816	2000000 to	3000000	
J. C. Burckhardt	1817	1 to	1000000	
Z. Dase	1862	7000000 to	8000000	
Z. Dase and H. Rosenberg	1863	8000000 to	9000000	
J. P. Kulik	1867	1 to	100000000	
J. Glaisher	1879	3000000 to	4000000	
J. Glaisher	1880	4000000 to	5000000	
J. Glaisher	1883	5000000 to	6000000	
D. N. Lehmer	1909	1 to	10000000	
D. N. Lehmer	1914			1 to 10000000

The mathematician Lambert promised immortality to the man who would produce a factor table to 1000000, and C. F. Hindenburg, among others thus urged, completed such a table. But Burckhardt, Glaisher, Kulik, and the mathematical prodigy Dase probably performed the most useful work, and it is upon their efforts that the modern tables are based. Accessible to American readers is the splendid *Factor Table of the First Ten Million* and the *List of Prime Numbers from 1 to 10006721* of D. N. Lehmer.

The work of Kulik, the factor table to 100000000, almost surpasses comprehension. This man spent twenty years of his life on it unassisted and alone! One shares the thrill of D. N. Lehmer, when reading in the introduction to his *Factor Tables* the description of his examination at the Vienna Royal Academy, of the first of the eight volumes of manuscript that contains Kulik's results. And again, although the gods mock man and his puny labors, we learn that

Volume 2, running from 12642600 to 22852800, is missing. What careless custodian, what heedless dusting woman, what furtive student was responsible for the loss?

* * *

There are a number of interesting formulas which yield primes for many successive values of the variable, but which must all sooner or later give composite numbers. A favorite example given to students to warn them against the danger of hastily drawing conclusions by common instead of mathematical induction is the remarkable formula, x^2+x+41. As x assumes successive values from zero to 39, the function yields primes, but when $x = 40$, the resulting number 1681 is composite. The list of 40 successive primes, and the subsequent irregular sequence, are so striking as to merit a place here. See Table 86.

TABLE 86
FORMULA FOR PRIMES
$$x^2+x+41$$

x	x^2+x+41	Kind*	x	x^2+x+41	Kind*
0	41	P	26	743	P
1	43	P	27	797	P
2	47	P	28	853	P
3	53	P	29	911	P
4	61	P	30	971	P
5	71	P	31	1033	P
6	83	P	32	1097	P
7	97	P	33	1163	P
8	113	P	34	1231	P
9	131	P	35	1301	P
10	151	P	36	1373	P
11	173	P	37	1447	P
12	197	P	38	1523	P
13	223	P	39	1601	P
14	251	P	40	1681	C
15	281	P	41	1763	C
16	313	P	42	1847	P
17	347	P	43	1933	P
18	383	P	44	2021	C
19	421	P	45	2111	P
20	461	P	46	2203	P
21	503	P	47	2297	P
22	547	P	48	2393	P
23	593	P	49	2491	C
24	641	P	50	2591	P
25	691	P	51	2693	P

P = prime, C = Composite.

TABLE 86—*continued*

x	x^2+x+41	Kind*	x	x^2+x+41	Kind*
52	2797	P	77	6047	P
53	2903	P	78	6203	P
54	3011	P	79	6361	P
55	3121	P	80	6521	P
56	3233	C	81	6683	C
57	3347	P	82	6847	C
58	3463	P	83	7013	P
59	3581	P	84	7181	C
60	3701	P	85	7351	P
61	3823	P	86	7523	P
62	3947	P	87	7697	C
63	4073	P	88	7873	P
64	4201	P	89	8051	C
65	4331	C	90	8231	P
66	4463	P	91	8413	C
67	4597	P	92	8597	P
68	4733	P	93	8783	P
69	4871	P	94	8971	P
70	5011	P	95	9161	P
71	5153	P	96	9353	C
72	5297	P	97	9547	P
73	5443	P	98	9743	P
74	5591	P	99	9941	P
75	5741	P	100	10141	P
76	5893	C			

* P = prime, C = Composite.

An indication of the exceptional character of this formula is the fact that in case there is another integer b which yields primes for $b-1$ successive values of x in x^2+x+b, then b must exceed 1,250,000,000 and there is at most one such integer.

But $x^2-79x+1601$ is even more remarkable. It gives primes for 80 consecutive values of x from zero to 79 and there are only five values between zero and 100 for which the function is composite.

Formulas for primes and the values of the variable not exceeding 100 for which they fail to give primes are shown in Table 87. It will be seen that the formula $x^2-79x+1601$ is by far the best one since it gives composite numbers for only five values of x.

Other formulas of this type are x^3+x^2+17, which yields primes for $x = -14, -13, \ldots +10$, and $x^2-2999x+2248541$, which yields primes for the 80 consecutive values of x between 1460 and 1539 inclusive. Simpler formulas are x^2+x+11 and x^2+x+17.

TABLE 87

Formulas for Primes

Formula $= f(x)$	Values of $x < 100$ Making $f(x)$ Composite	Number of Values of x Making $f(x)$ Composite
$x^2 - 79x + 1601$	80, 81, 84, 89, 96	5
$x^2 + x + 41$	40, 41, 44, 49, 56, 65, 76, 81, 82, 84, 87, 89, 91, 96	14
$2x^2 + 29$	29, 30, 32, 35, 39, 50, 57, 58, 61, 63, 65, 72, 74, 76, 84, 87, 88, 89, 91, 92, 94, 95, 97, 99	24
$6x^2 + 6x + 31$	29, 30, 31, 34, 36, 41, 44, 51, 55, 59, 61, 62, 64, 66, 69, 76, 80, 84, 86, 87, 88, 92, 93, 97, 99	25
$3x^2 + 3x + 23$	22, 23, 27, 30, 38, 43, 44, 45, 46, 49, 51, 55, 56, 59, 62, 66, 68, 69, 70, 78, 85, 87, 88, 89, 91, 92, 95, 96	28

*   *   *

Primes may be in arithmetic progression for a limited number of terms. It will be recalled that in an arithmetic progression, the difference between consecutive terms is a constant. A few examples of such primes are given in Table 88.

TABLE 88

Primes in Arithmetic Progression

(1)	(2)	(3)	(4)	(5)	(6)
7	107	7	47	71	199
37	137	157	257	2381	409
67	167	307	467	4691	619
97	197	457	677	7001	829
127	227	607	887	9311	1039
157	257	757	1097	11621	1249
		907	1307	11931	1459
					1669
					1879
					2089

*   *   *

Primes can even be palindromic (reading the same backward as forward) and be in arithmetic progression. Four such sets of four primes are: (13931, 14741, 15551, 16361), (10301, 13331, 16361, 19391), (70607, 73637, 76667, 79697), (94049, 94349, 94649, 94949). The respective common differences are 810; 3000; 3030; and 300.

* * *

Although the number of primes is infinite, one can easily find intervals of any desired length in the natural sequence of integers in which there are no primes. The formula $1 \cdot 2 \cdot 3 \ldots n + A$ may be used for this purpose. The integer n may have any value we please, for instance, a billion. As A takes on the values 2, 3, 4, ... n, the resulting 999999999 successive integers starting from $1,000,000,000! + 2$ are divisible respectively by 2, 3, 4, ... n, and there cannot therefore be any primes in this interval. Of course, $1,000,000,000! + A$ are a pretty formidable set of numbers; nevertheless they fulfill the required conditions.

Taking n equal to only 7, we have $n! = 5040$; and 5042, 5043, 5044, 5045, 5046, and 5047 are all composite numbers. It so happens that 5041 is also composite, and beyond 5047 we can continue with 5048, 5049, and 5050, but this cannot be determined by formula, as is the case with the six integers from 5042 to 5047.

* * *

Table 89 shows the number of primes within certain assigned limits as obtained by actual count and by means of one of the remarkable approximation formulas mentioned previously. This formula is denoted by $\int_2^x dt/\ln t$ and is called the "logarithmic integral of x," also the "integral logarithm of x" abbreviated "Li(x)." To readers unacquainted with the "integral" symbol we may say that "Li(x)" is equal approximately to the sum of n terms of the series:

$$x \left[\frac{1}{\ln x} + \frac{1!}{(\ln x)^2} + \frac{2!}{(\ln x)^3} + \frac{3!}{(\ln x)^4} + \cdots + \frac{(n-1)!}{(\ln x)^n} \right]$$

provided x and n are large numbers. "Ln x" or "ln t" represent the logarithm of x or t to the base e. This is the modern notation for $\log_e x$ or $\log_e t$. Do not confuse ln x and Li(x).

Table 89 verifies the statement made at the beginning of this chapter that the degree of accuracy does not either continuously increase or decrease but varies in an apparently haphazard way. It may be noted from the table that Li(x) is always *larger* than N and this has been verified for millions of instances. Yet the importance of conclusions based on rigorous demonstrations, not on mere induction, is again demonstrated here. It has been proved that for sufficiently large values of x, Li(x) is *smaller* than N in an infinite number of instances, but values of x for which this is so are far beyond the range of existing factor tables. On the other hand, there are also an infinite number of instances where Li(x) is larger than N.

There is another formula giving remarkably accurate results for the number of primes N in the interval between A and $A+b$ provided A is large and b small. It is: $N = b/\ln A$. If $A = 10000000$ and $b = 5000$, this gives $N = 5000/7 \ln 10 = (5000/7) \log_{10} e = 310.21$. Actually there are 305 such primes.

TABLE 89

PRIMES WITHIN ASSIGNED INTERVALS

Interval x	No. of Primes, N, in this Interval	Li(x) $= \int_2^x \dfrac{dt}{\ln t}$	Discrepancy Li(x) $- N$
50000	5134	5167	33
100000	9593	9630	37
200000	17985	18036	51
300000	25998	26087	89
400000	33861	33923	62
500000	41539	41606	67
600000	49099	49173	74
700000	56544	56645	101
800000	63952	64037	85
900000	71275	71362	87
1000000	78499	78628	129
1500000	114156	114263	107
2000000	148934	149055	121
2500000	183073	183245	172
3000000	216817	216971	154
4000000	283147	283352	205
5000000	348514	348638	124
6000000	412850	413077	227
7000000	476649	476827	178
8000000	539778	540000	222
9000000	602490	602676	186
10000000	664579	664918	339
100000000	5761455	5762209	754
1000000000	50847534	50849235	1701

E. Meissel actually calculated the number of primes less than a billion and found 50847479 such integers. The correct number is 50847534.

Several investigators have obtained exceedingly ingenious approximation formulas, and the graph, Figure 20, shows a comparison of

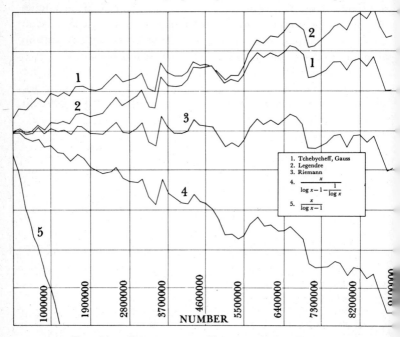

FIG. 20. DEVIATIONS IN FORMULAS FOR PRIMES

their result for numbers up to 9000000. Table 90 gives the names of these discoverers and their results.

TABLE 90

APPROXIMATION FORMULAS FOR NUMBER OF PRIMES BETWEEN
ZERO AND x

Number	Discoverer	Formula
1	Tchebycheff, Gauss	$\text{Li}(x) = \displaystyle\int_{2}^{x} dt/\ln t$
2	Legendre	$x/(\ln x - 1.08366)$
3	Riemann	$\text{Li}(x) - \frac{1}{2}\text{Li}(x^{1/2})$
4		$x/(\ln x - 1 - 1/\ln x)$
5		$x/(\ln x - 1)$

Riemann's graph touches or crosses the zero or "no deviation" axis no less than 19 times in the interval between 1 and 9000000.

The ratio of the circumference to the diameter of a circle, π, frequently enters into relations having nothing to do with a circle. Certain problems in probability often involve this constant. One of these states that if two people each write down a number at random, the probability that these two numbers are prime to one another is $6/\pi^2$. Thus two persons might each write 1000 numbers and then compare results to find how many pairs were relatively prime. This number divided by 1000 would be equated to $6/\pi^2$, and the value of π might be so calculated to a reasonable degree of accuracy. The reader may wish to try this experiment. Of course, 10000 trials instead of 1000 will give a better approximation!

A more simple but not so accurate expression for the number of primes, N, less than some given number, x, is $x/\ln x$. Roughly, one might say that the odds are $\ln x$ to 1 that a large number x is not a prime.

*   *   *

There are scores of provocative theorems about primes which observation seems to indicate are true but whose proofs have so far defied all efforts. The reader who can demonstrate any of these will surely find a place in the mathematical Valhalla and drink toasts with the shades of Fermat and Gauss.

Conjectures and Unsolved Problems about Primes

1. Prove Goldbach's conjecture that every even integer is the *sum* of two primes. For example: $12 = 5+7$; $18 = 7+11$; $100 = 3+97$.

2. It has been conjectured that every even integer is the difference of two primes in infinitely many ways. Is this true? For example: $12 = 19-7$ or $29-17$ or $23-11$.

3. In particular, the even integer 2 can be so expressed and therefore there must be an infinite number of pairs of primes differing by 2—twin primes as they are called. For example: 5, 7; 11, 13; 17, 19; 29, 31; 10006427, 10006429; 999999999959, and 999999999961; 1000000009649, 1000000009651.

4. Every even integer is the difference of two *consecutive* primes in an infinitude of ways. For example: $6 = 29-23$; $37-31$; $53-47$; $99929-99923$. Also, $10 = 23-13$; $41-31$; $71-61$; $99971-99961$.

5. Are there infinitely many primes of the form x^2+1? For example: 1^2+1; 2^2+1; 4^2+1; 6^2+1; 10^2+1.

6. Does there exist at least one prime between consecutive triangular or square numbers? This is true below the limit of 9000000.

7. Find a prime greater than a given prime or the prime which follows a given prime.

8. Compute directly the nth prime, when n is given.

9. Find the number of primes not greater than a given number.

10. Every prime of the form $4x-1$ is the sum of a prime of the form $4x+1$ and double a prime of this latter form.

11. Between n^2 and n^2-n and also between n^2 and n^2+n, there exists at least one prime.

12. There are at least four primes between the squares of consecutive primes greater than 3.

Rules about Primes (with Exceptions)

1. Goldbach found from observation that every odd number seems to be either a prime or the sum of a prime and twice a square. Thus $21 = 19+2$ or $13+8$ or $3+18$. It is stated that up to 9000, the only exceptions to his statement are $5777 = 53 \cdot 109$ and $5993 = 13 \cdot 641$, which are neither primes nor the sum of a prime and twice a square.

2. *Primes* can be expressed as the sum of a prime and twice a square (other than 0^2). Thus $37 = 29+8 = 19+18 = 5+32$. Exceptions, however, up to 9000 are the primes 17; 137; 227; 977; 1187; and 1493 as they cannot be so expressed.

3. In 1848 de Polignac conjectured that every odd number is the sum of a prime and a power of 2. Thus $107 = 43+2^6 = 103+2^2$. He claimed verification for this fact up to 3 million, later admitting that 959 could not be so expressed. The present author tried 509; 977; and 877 haphazardly and these integers are certainly also exceptions. Can the reader find any others? Something must be wrong with this conjecture.*

4. Up to 10000 at least, every even number is the sum of a prime and a power; this is also true of every odd number except 1549. Thus $856 = 127+9^3$ and $977 = 761+6^3$.

* * *

* In fact, it has been proved that there are an *infinite* number of odd numbers *not* so expressible. See *Mathematics*, **34** (1960–1961), 316.

The following miscellaneous results about primes are of interest:

It has been verified up to 6 million, and proved subsequently, for the general case, that there is at least one prime between x and $2x - 2$ provided x exceeds 3. This is known as Bertrand's Postulate.

As recently as 1937 it was shown that provided an odd number is "sufficiently large" it can be expressed as the sum of three primes.

*　　*　　*

If an integer of the form $4x + 1$ can be expressed as the sum of two squares in exactly one way and if, furthermore, these squares are co-prime, then the integer in question is a prime or the square of a prime. If the integer is not too large this is sometimes a rapidly effective way of ascertaining whether it is a prime.

Wilson's theorem that $(p - 1)! + 1 \equiv 0 \bmod p$ if and only if p is a prime may be repeated here.

A number can sometimes be proved a prime by means of Fermat's theorem. We know that $a^{p-1} \equiv 1 \bmod p$ if p is a prime, but the congruence can also hold for a composite modulus. With a prime modulus there *may* be a lower exponent for which the congruence holds (in case a is not a primitive root of p, for example), but for a composite modulus N, the congruence *must* hold for a lower exponent than $N - 1$. We know also that for every exponent e smaller than p for which $a^e \equiv 1 \bmod p$, e must divide $p - 1$ so that only divisors of $p - 1$ need be taken as exponents in order to verify whether or not the congruence holds for given values of p and a. If, therefore, *no* aliquot divisor f of $N - 1$ makes $a^f \equiv 1 \bmod N$ (a is any convenient low base such as 2 or 3), then N must be a prime. If an aliquot divisor of $N - 1$ does make $a^f \equiv 1 \bmod N$, then N may be prime or composite. (Of course it may be as difficult to find factors of $N - 1$ as of N.) Therefore, if low bases such as 2 or 3 do not turn out to belong to $N - 1$, indicating that this base is a primitive root of N, thus indicating that N is a prime, Fermat's theorem as a method of testing whether N is a prime cannot be used (see Chapter VI). D. H. Lehmer has used modifications of this method, however, and achieved brilliant results with extremely large numbers.

It is evident that if a^{N-1} is not congruent to 1 mod N, then N is surely composite although its factors still remain unknown.

*　　*　　*

E. V. Lucas, the French mathematician, used the series 4; 14; 194; 37634; ...$u_n = u_{n-1}^2 - 2$, obtained by squaring a term and then subtracting 2 to get the next term. He tested the primality of Mersenne's numbers by this series. D. H. Lehmer modified Lucas's test to the relatively simple form: "If, and only if, $2^n - 1$ divides the $(n-1)$th term of the series, then $2^n - 1$ is a prime, otherwise it is composite." Thus, $2^3 - 1$ is a factor of 14, hence $2^3 - 1 = 7$ is a prime. See Chapter III for the large primes calculated by a digital computer using Lucas's test.

*   *   *

There are an infinite number of palindromic primes. Here are a few: 101, 131, 151, 181, 313, 353, 727, 757, 787, 797, 919, 929... 79997, 91019, 93139, 93739, 94049...98389, 98689...1818181, 7878787, 7272727, 3535353.

*   *   *

Uspensky and Heaslet in their *Elementary Number Theory* say:

"Of necessity we must confine ourselves in regard to the fascinating problem of the distribution of primes to mere statements of facts. Their proofs belong to the analytical theory of numbers, a very vast and very difficult branch of our science in which properties of numbers are investigated by methods involving transcendental notions such as continuity, etc." With their words we will conclude this chapter.

BIBLIOGRAPHY

Ball, W. W. R. *Mathematical Recreations and Essays.* New York: Macmillan Co., 1939.

Bell, E. T. *The Last Problem.* New York: Simon and Schuster, 1961.

Crocker, R. "A Theorem Concerning Prime Numbers," *Mathematics,* **34** (1960–1961), 316.

Dickson, L. E. *History of the Theory of Numbers.* 3 vols. New York: Chelsea Publishing Co., 1950.

————. *Introduction to the Theory of Numbers.* New York: Dover Publications, Inc., 1957.

Gillies, D. B. "Computer Discovers New Prime Number," *Science News Letter,* **83** (May 11, 1963), 291.

Glaisher, J. *Factor Tables for the Sixth Million.* London: Taylor and Francis, 1883.

Hardy, G. H.   "An Introduction to the Theory of Numbers," *Bulletin of the American Mathematical Society*, **35** (1929), 778.

———, and Wright, E. M.   *An Introduction to the Theory of Numbers*. Oxford: Clarendon Press, 1954.

Hurwitz, A.   "New Mersenne Primes," *Mathematics of Computation*, **16** (1962), 249.

Lehmer, D. N.   *Factor Tables for the First Ten Million*. New York: Hafner Publishing Co., 1956.

Mapes, D. C.   "Fast Method of Computing the Number of Primes Less Than a Given Limit," *Mathematics of Computation*, **17** (1963), 179.

Martin, A.   "Prime Numbers in Arithmetical Progression," *School Science and Mathematics*, **13** (1913), 793.

Mathews, G. B.   *Theory of Numbers*. New York: Chelsea Publishing Co., 1961.

National Bureau of Standards.   "National Bureau of Standards Western Automatic Computer," Technical News Bulletin, **37** (Oct., 1953), 145.

Ore, O.   *Number Theory and Its History*. New York: McGraw-Hill Book Co., 1948.

Reid, C.   "Perfect Numbers," *Scientific American*, **188** (March, 1953), 84.

Starke, E. P.   "Palindromes in Progression," *Mathematics*, **29** (1955), 110.

Uspensky, J. V., and Heaslet, M. A.   *Elementary Number Theory*. New York: McGraw-Hill Book Co., 1939.

Van Der Pol, B.   "Radio Technology and Theory of Numbers," *Journal of the Franklin Institute*, **255** (June, 1953), 476.

———.   "An Addendum and Corrections to 'Radio Technology and Theory of Numbers,'" *Journal of the Franklin Institute*, **256** (Sept., 1953), 265.

Vinogradov, I. M.   *Elements of Number Theory*. New York: Dover Publications, Inc., 1954.

Wright, W. C.   *Wright vs. Eratosthenes*. Boston: G. H. Ellis Co., 1915.

CHAPTER XXI

RESOLUTION

THERE IS probably no more absorbing pursuit in all of number theory than the resolution of a number into its prime factors. The methods that have been used are as varied as they are ingenious, but, like poison-ivy cures, no one of them is a specific. One method might resolve a 10-digit number in 3 or 4 steps; the same method may require 50 or more steps for a 6-digit number.

It is often surprising to the neophyte to learn that there is no simple direct means of finding the divisors of a number. Factoring is quite unlike division in this respect. In division we are given a dividend and a divisor; in factoring we know only the dividend and have no universal practical rule for determining even whether there are any divisors other than the number itself and unity.

It is interesting to hear the opinion of the layman about how he would attempt to factor a number—for instance, 221. Generally he would try the integers 2, 3, 4, 5, 6, 7 . . . in succession, and if asked how far he would go with this process, the reply is generally given that all divisors up to half the number should be tried—in this case up to 111. But in fact only prime divisors need be tried, for if a number has a composite divisor, a prime factor of that divisor must also divide the number. Furthermore, no prime divisor larger than the *square root* of the number need be tried, for if there *is* a larger divisor the resulting quotient will be a smaller divisor.

For 221, the square root is less than 15 and only the prime divisors 2, 3, 5, 7, 11, and 13 need be considered. The first three integers can be ruled out immediately (2 and 5 are not divisors since the number is odd and does not end in 5; 3 is not a divisor since the sum of the digits is not divisible by 3); 7 and 11 do not divide 221, and finally 13 divides 221 with a quotient of 17.

Even less well known than the square-root limit is the fact that if the smallest prime divisor of a number is greater than its *cube* root, then the number has only one other divisor, of necessity also a prime. A little consideration will show why this must be so: since the smaller divisor, d, of a number, N, is *greater* than $N^{1/3}$, the larger divisor, D, is *less* than $N^{2/3}$. If D has an aliquot divisor, it must be less than the square root of $N^{2/3}$, hence it must be less than $N^{1/3}$. But this contradicts the hypothesis that the smallest divisor is greater than $N^{1/3}$. Hence D has *no* aliquot divisor and must be a prime. Consequently, N has only the two aliquot, prime divisors, d and D.

Although these limitations considerably reduce the number of divisors to be tried, it would be impractical to use them alone for even a 4- or 5-digit number. To test 33029, all primes up to and including 181, the largest prime just under the square root of the number, would have to be tried, and there are 42 such integers. Within the range of a table of squares—Barlow's goes to 100000000—the method of Chapter XV, to ascertain in how many ways the number can be expressed as the sum of two squares, can often be used expeditiously. Thus, since 33029 is of the form $4x+1$, it is a prime or the square of a prime if expressible as the sum of two squares in one way only, and if these two squares turn out to be co-prime. If the two squares are *not* co-prime their common divisor is also a divisor of the original number. To distinguish between a prime and its square, test by taking the square root so as to see if the root is an integer. If a number of the form $4x+1$ is *not* expressible as the sum of two squares, it is composite and contains an even number of prime factors of the form $4x-1$. Prime factors of the form $4x+1$ may or may not be present. None of the factors of either form can be determined by the method of the sum of two squares.

If expressible as the sum of two squares in more than one way, the number is again composite. If the two squares are co-prime in only one of these ways, the number is a cube or a higher power of a single prime; if more than one representation exists where the two squares are co-prime, the number is the product of at least two primes. When the two squares are not co-prime, their greatest common divisor is a divisor of the number under consideration.

The 22 two-digit termini of squares listed in Chapter XV limit the squares to be subtracted from 33029 to those ending only in 00; 04; 25; 29. Furthermore the squares to be tested must lie within the range from unity to just under half the number or 16384. There are 36 such squares, and it so happens that the first one less than 16384, namely, 16129, leaves the square remainder 16900 so that $33029 = 130^2 + 127^2$. No other square subtracted from 33029 leaves a square remainder, hence 33029 is a prime (since extracting the square root shows it is not a square).

When a number is the sum of two relatively prime squares in two or more ways, it is composite and is readily factored as follows: If $N = a^2 + b^2 = c^2 + d^2$, then

$$N = (ac+bd)(ac-bd)/(a+d)(a-d) \quad \text{or also}$$
$$(ac+bd)(ac-bd)/(c+b)(c-b). \qquad \text{(Formula 1)}$$

These expressions are always integers and express N as the product of two integers. In Chapter XV we found that $16000001 = 4000^2 + 1^2 = 1049^2 + 3860^2$. Then $a = 4000$, $b = 1$, $c = 1049$, $d = 3860$, and

16000001

$$= (4000 \cdot 1049 + 3860)(4000 \cdot 1049 - 3860)/(1049+1)(1049-1)$$
$$= (4199860 \cdot 4192140)/(1051 \cdot 1048) = 229 \cdot 69869.$$

It is easy to verify that 229 is a prime. To investigate 69869 we try to express it also as the sum of two squares since it is of the form $4x+1$. Since the number ends in 69, only squares ending in 00, 25, 44, and 69 can leave square remainders. In only a few trials we find that $68644 = 262^2$ leaves the square remainder 225 and that $56644 = 238^2$ leaves the square remainder 13225, so that $69869 = 262^2 + 15^2 = 238^2 + 115^2$. Factoring by Formula 1, as before, $69869 = 109 \cdot 641$ and finally $16000001 = 229 \cdot 109 \cdot 641$.

This method can be used not only when the number to be factored is the sum of two squares but also when it is of the form $x^2 + ky^2$. We have:

$$(x^2+ky^2)(m^2+kn^2) = (xm+kyn)^2 + k(xn-ym)^2$$
$$= (xm-kyn)^2 + k(xn+ym)^2,$$

which states that the product of numbers whose form is a square plus k times another square has the same form as each factor. For instance, $(2^2+5\cdot3^2)(3^2+5\cdot4^2) = 66^2+5\cdot1^2 = 54^2+5\cdot17^2$.

Reversing this process, if $N = a^2 + kb^2 = c^2 + kd^2$ then

$$N = k(ad+bc)(ad-bc)/(a+c)(a-c) \quad \text{or also}$$
$$(ad+bc)(ad-bc)/(d+b)(d-b), \qquad \text{(Formula 2)}$$

which resembles the previous result.

*   *   *

The "excludent" method of factoring numbers is often very effective. It facilitates the determination of the ways, if any, in which a number can be expressed in the quadratic form $x^2 + ky^2$, after which the method just described enables the factors to be found.

When $k = 4$, 2, and -2 in $x^2 + ky^2$, the corresponding forms $x^2 + 4y^2$, $x^2 + 2y^2$, and $x^2 - 2y^2$ represent among them all odd integers. The first form represents integers of the form $8x + 1$ or $8x + 5$; the second, those of the form $8x + 1$ or $8x + 3$; and the last, integers of the form $8x + 1$ or $8x + 7$. If the number 45677 is to be tested, we use the quadratic form $x^2 + 4y^2$ since the number is of the form $8x + 5$. Then $y = [(45677 - x^2)/4]^{1/2}$, and y must be smaller than 107. But to avoid the tedium of trying all values of x, an exclusion method similar to that described in Chapter XIX can be used.

We must solve $45677 - 4y^2 = x^2$. Taking the small excludent-modulus, 5, we have $2 - 4y^2 \equiv x^2$ mod 5 so that only those values of y which make $2 - 4y^2$ one of the quadratic residues of 5, namely, 1 or 4, need be considered. This excludes all values of y of the form $5z$, $5z + 1$, or $5z + 4$, since the respective remainders of $2 - 4y^2$ are then 2, 3, 3, which are quadratic non-residues of 5. The forms $5z + 2$ and $5z + 3$ are retained, since they make $2 - 4y^2$ congruent to 1 or 4 respectively. Continuing with the excludents 7, 8, 9, and 11 (primes or their powers), only 7, 17, 23, 27, 53, 67, and 77 remain, so that the 107 trials have been reduced to only 7 by comparatively little work. The value 17 gives $45677 - 4 \cdot 17^2 = 211^2$, and no other value of y leaves a square remainder, hence 45677 is a prime.

Again, suppose the given number N is 36661, which is of the form $8x + 5$. We therefore seek solutions of $x^2 + 4y^2 = 36661$ and find by the excludent method that $36661 = 169^2 + 4 \cdot 45^2 = 119^2 + 4 \cdot 75^2$. Here $a = 169$, $b = 45$, $c = 119$, and $d = 75$, whence, by Formula 2,

$$N = (169 \cdot 75 + 45 \cdot 119)(169 \cdot 75 - 45 \cdot 119)/288 \cdot 50 = 61 \cdot 601,$$

and 36661 is the product of these two prime factors.

Tables of excludents have also been made up for these congruences, conveniently and rapidly to eliminate forms of y, and stencils have been made to facilitate finding the requisite forms thereafter.

Perhaps the reader would like to test his grasp of this method by factoring (a) 23449; (b) 394831; (c) 16503593; and (d) 18000001.†

* * *

† Problems indicated by a dagger are solved in Chapter XXVI.

The use of quadratic residues is probably the most powerful means so far discovered for factoring a really large number. Chapters XIX and XXII explain how to obtain small quadratic residues of a number. The method of factoring from this information depends on the fact that if R is a quadratic residue of the number D which is to be decomposed, it is also a quadratic residue of every prime factor of D. One can, therefore, calculate and tabulate once and for all those primes (below some practical limit) which have a given R as a quadratic residue. If a number of quadratic residues of D are known, one can refer to the primes corresponding to each residue (listed for convenience on individual residue cards) and find those primes which are common to all the residues. These are the only possible prime divisors of D, and if a dozen or so small residues are known, this generally so restricts the number of primes which may be possible divisors as to readily factor a 9- or 10-digit number. If no prime is found common to all the residue lists, this demonstrates that D is a prime.

A neater way than to search each residue card for primes common to all of them is to punch holes in the card at positions assigned to each prime. The superimposed residue cards—factor stencils as they are called—will then admit light through the holes corresponding to the possible prime divisors of D. If no hole shows, then D is prime provided the stencil records primes to at least the square root of D.

Figure 21 is a facsimile of a standard Hollerith card used in business machines for tabulating data. It has 800 cells to each of which is assigned one prime. The card is perforated in those cells corresponding to the primes which have 29 as a quadratic residue. The 800th

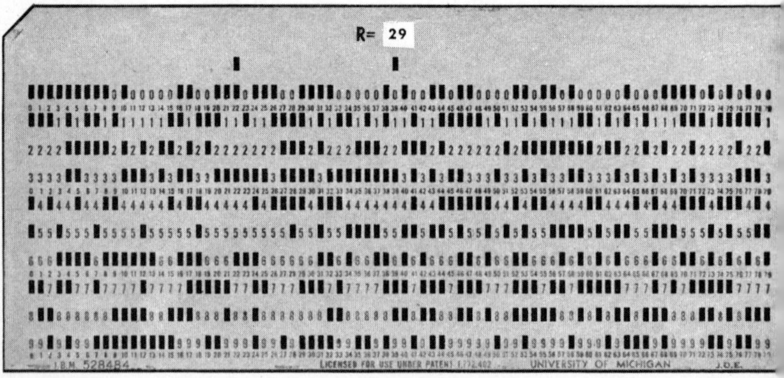

Fig. 21. A Factor Stencil

prime in the natural sequence of integers is 6131, which is the square root of 37589161. Thus factor stencils each of which contains only 800 cells are sufficiently large to factor numbers up to almost forty million.

The stencils have been made up for positive and negative residues not exceeding 250 and containing no square factors. The limitation in the size of the standard Hollerith card has been overcome by using seven cards of different colors for one residue, thus giving 5600 cells or 5600 primes. The 5600th prime is 55079, whose square is 3033696241, so that at this stage of the development of the stencils, numbers within that range can be factored with their aid. It is even possible to go beyond this limit provided the smallest prime divisor of the unknown does not exceed 55079.

Through the courtesy of Dr. J. D. Elder of the University of Michigan the writer is in possession of a set of the smaller stencils suitable for factoring numbers up to 37589161 and has derived much pleasure from their use.

*   *   *

The methods just given are elegant and powerful. Other methods may be easier to grasp and apply, but they are generally of limited application because the labor, except in the most favorable cases, may be prohibitive. Fermat used the following: Let N be the number to be factored and r^2 the smallest square just exceeding it, so that $N = r^2 - A_0$. If A_0 is a square, then N has been expressed as the difference of two squares and can therefore be factored. If not, we have this series of identities:

$$\begin{aligned}
N = r^2 - A_0 &= (r+1)^2 - (A_0 + 2r + 1) \\
&= (r+2)^2 - (A_0 + 2r + 1 + 2r + 3) \\
&= (r+3)^2 - (A_0 + 2r + 1 + 2r + 3 + 2r + 5) \\
&\quad \cdots \cdots \cdots \cdots \cdots \cdots \cdots \cdots \cdots \cdots \cdots \\
&= (r+n)^2 - A^2 = (r+n+A)(r+n-A).
\end{aligned}$$

In words: We add $2r+1$ to A_0; if the result is a square, we have expressed N as the difference of two squares; if the result is not a square, we add $2r+3$, then $2r+5$, $2r+7$, etc., successively, until the result is a square A^2, whence $N = (r+n+A)(r+n-A)$.

·Suppose $N = 340663$. Then $r^2 = 344569 = 587^2$ is the smallest square just exceeding 340663, and the difference $A_0 = 3906$ is not a square. Adding $2r+1 = 1175$ to 3906, the result 5081 is not a square.   Adding $2r+3 = 1177$ to 5081, the result 6258 is not a square. Continuing, we add 1179; 1181; and 1183; the last result 9801 is 99^2, and this occurred after only five additions.   Hence

$$340663 = (587+5+99)(587+5-99) = 691 \cdot 493.$$

The second factor is composite and equal to $17 \cdot 29$ so that finally $340663 = 17 \cdot 29 \cdot 691$.   Fermat by this method factored

$$2027651281 = 44021 \cdot 46061$$

in only 11 additions, compared to 4580 divisions by the odd primes up to 44021.   But this was a favorable case, probably devised on purpose to show the power of his method and much smaller numbers might require an impractical amount of labor.

A cruder method sometimes yielding rapid results is to add squares $1^2, 2^2, 3^2 \ldots x^2$ to the number N until the result y^2 is a square.   Then $N+x^2 = y^2$ and $N = (y+x)(y-x)$.   The squares to be added can be limited by using the two or more digit endings of squares.   Suppose 10541 is to be factored.   A table of squares shows that the next larger square is $10609 = 103^2$, but since the difference between these numbers ends in 8 it obviously will not do.   The next square $10816 = 104^2$ gives a difference of 75, which is not a square, but the following one $11025 = 105^2$, gives a difference of 484, which is the square of 22.   Hence $10541 + 22^2 = 105^2$ and

$$10541 = 105^2 - 22^2 = (105+22)(105-22) = 127 \cdot 83.$$

Again taking $N = 119143$, only seven squares exceeding this number need be tried and it is found that $119143 = 123904 - 4761 = 352^2 - 69^2 = (352+69)(352-69) = 421 \cdot 283$, these last two factors being themselves prime.

Since any odd integer in excess of unity can be represented as the difference of two squares, we must ultimately arrive at a square if we add squares to an unknown odd number.   But if the unknown should happen to be a prime, then it may take many steps before the sum is a square so that this method had best be abandoned if results are not obtained within a reasonable number of trials.   Thus, even for so small a number as 9839, one would have to exhaust almost half of Barlow's table of squares before finding that $9839 + 4919^2 = 4920^2$ or $9839 = (4920+4919)(4920-4919) = 9839 \cdot 1$, and that consequently 9839 is a prime.

Another manner of factoring often very effective is the method of remainders: Let N be the unknown. Find the largest square, a^2, not exceeding $(N-1)/2$ and let $(N-1)/2 - a^2 = r$. Place $a \cdot a$ in one column and $2r+1$ in a second. Then continue consecutively in the first column with $(a+1)(a-1)$, $(a+2)(a-2)$, etc., and in the second column with $2r+3$, $2r+9$, $2r+19$, $2r+33$, etc., obtained by adding 2 to the number heading the column and increasing the amount added each time by 4. That is, we add successively 2, 6, 10, 14, 18... to obtain the next number in the column. Test whether either number in the first column has a factor in common with the corresponding number in the second, and if so, this factor divides N.

For example, let $N = 142397$. Then $(N-1)/2 = 71198$. The largest square not exceeding this number is $70756 = 266^2$, so that $a = 266$ and $r = 71198 - 70756 = 442$. The two columns formed as above give:

n	$(a+n) \cdot (a-n)$	$(2r+1) + 2n^2$	Difference
0	$266 \cdot 266$	885	
			2
1	$267 \cdot 265$	887	
			6
2	$268 \cdot 264$	893	
			10
3	$269 \cdot 263$	903	
			14
4	$270 \cdot 262$	917	

We find that 131 divides 262 and 917, hence it divides 142397, the quotient being 1087.

This method can be algebraically described as follows: Since $(N-1)/2 = a^2 + r$, we have $N = 2a^2 + 2r + 1$

$$= 2(a+1)(a-1) + (2r+1+2)$$
$$= 2(a+2)(a-2) + (2r+1+2+6)$$
$$= 2(a+3)(a-3) + (2r+1+2+6+10)$$
$$\dots\dots\dots\dots\dots\dots\dots\dots\dots\dots$$
$$= 2(a+n)(a-n) + [2r+1+2+6+10+ \dots (4n-2)]$$
$$= 2(a+n)(a-n) + [(2r+1) + 2n^2] = N.$$

If therefore a number can be found that divides both the expression in the bracket and either $(a+n)$ or $(a-n)$, that number must divide N.

Let us try this method to factor 16000001. Here $(N-1)/2 = 8000000$, the largest smaller square, a^2, being $2828^2 = 7997584$. Then $r = 8000000 - 7997584 = 2416$, and our columns become:

n	$(a+n)\cdot(a-n)$	$(2r+1)+2n^2$	Difference
0	$2828\cdot2828$	4833	
			2
1	$2829\cdot2827$	4835	
			6
2	$2830\cdot2826$	4841	
			10
3	$2831\cdot2825$	4851	
			14
4	$2832\cdot2824$	4865	
			18
5	$2833\cdot2823$	4883	
			22
6	$2834\cdot2822$	4905	

We find that 2834 and 4905 have a greatest common divisor, 109, and therefore 109 is a divisor of 16000001. The G.C.D. is obtained by subtracting multiples of one of the numbers from multiples of the second until a difference is obtained which is readily separated into its prime factors and ascertaining whether any of these divide both original numbers. See any algebra text for complete details. In this case $4905 = 5\cdot981 = 5\cdot9\cdot109$, and 109 divides 2834, but 5 and 9 do not, so that 109 is the G.C.D. of 2834 and 4905. In only seven trials, therefore, we have factored the large number, 16000001.

That one does not always fare so luckily with this method even for much smaller numbers is demonstrated by the number 7031. Here $(N-1)/2 = 3515$, $a^2 = 59^2 = 3481$ and $r = 3515 - 3481 = 34$.

n	$(a+n)(a-n)$	$(2r+1)+2n^2$
0	$59\cdot59$	69
1	$60\cdot58$	71
2	$61\cdot57$	77
$\cdots$	$\cdots$	$\cdots$
20	$79\cdot39$	869

It takes 20 trials to find that 79 and 869 have the common factor 79 and that $7031 = 79\cdot89$.

By the method of *adding* squares we would have had in one trial that the square exceeding 7031 is 7056, the excess 25 being a square and $7031 = 84^2 - 5^2 = (84+5)(84-5) = 89 \cdot 79$. This demonstrates that one should not become too enthusiastic over any of these methods; another Fermat or Gauss still remains to be born to discover a general procedure that will go straight to the heart of any decomposition.

* * *

Dr. D. H. Lehmer of the University of California and his father Dr. D. N. Lehmer invented a remarkable factoring machine by which the prodigious labor of factoring large numbers has been considerably abridged. By its use, numbers have been factored which might otherwise have required the lifetime labor of several human computers. The great unconquered factor

$$1537228672093301419 = (2^{62} - 2^{31} + 1)/3$$

of $2^{93} + 1$ was set up on the machine and in three seconds the mechanism stopped, an indication that the quarry was in sight. A short computation gave the two factors 529510939 and 2903110321. Since $2^{93} + 1 = (2^{31})^3 + 1 = (2^{31}+1)(2^{62} - 2^{31} + 1)$, the complete factorization of $2^{93} + 1$ became known, since previous computers had found that $2^{31} + 1 = 3 \cdot 715827883$.

In the machine there are a set of 15 identical gears each having 100 teeth and mounted rigidly on a common central drive shaft. Meshing with these at diametrically opposite points are two sets of driven gears, each member of which has a different prime number of teeth and each rotating independently around an individual center. There are thus 30 driven gears corresponding to the 30 odd primes from 3 to 127. Holes in a circle concentric with the center are drilled in each gear, the number equalling the number of teeth (Figure 22). Suppose the driven gears are set to the zero or initial position by passing a long pin through one hole in each gear of the set. Then it is obvious that no other set of holes will be in line since the number of holes in each gear is prime to the number in any other gear. If the pin is now withdrawn, a beam of light can be made to shine through the holes in alignment, but as the gears start to rotate at different speeds this alignment will be lost and will not again recur at the initial position for perhaps thousands or millions of revolutions of the driving gears. By plugging certain holes, alignments which might otherwise take place are prevented.

The beam of light after passing through one series of driven gears is reflected by two prisms into the second set and then impinges on a

PLATE A. *Dr. Lehmer's Factoring Machine*

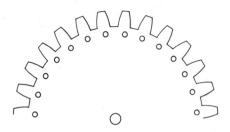

FIG. 22.   GEAR OF FACTORING MACHINE

photoelectric cell.   After suitable amplification, the electric current generated by the light beam is effective in stopping the driving mechanism.   When there is an alignment of open holes, signalizing a solution, a ray of light falls for only one ten-thousandth of a second on the sensitive "eye" of the cell and after being amplified 729000000 times, is strong enough to energize a relay to stop the motor.   The number of revolutions the machine has made is read from a cyclometer and a short computation then enables the factors to be found.

It will be recognized from this description, that the factoring machine is a device for rapidly obtaining a number which is simultaneously of many different forms, so as to confine within practical limits the number of possible divisors of a given number.

The description of the difficulties encountered in constructing this machine and overcoming practical obstacles to its successful operation make as fascinating reading as any adventure story.   The ray of light was so feeble an impulse and the time it had to speak to the photocell in passing was so short that every part of the machine had to be constructed with great accuracy and very delicately adjusted. And with an energy multiplication of 729000000, the amplifier was so sensitive that a slight jar, an infinitesimal variation in electric current, the turning off of an electric appliance, or even an impatient word by an attendant would send it off into a temperamental fit.

The late Dr. D. N. Lehmer, father of the inventor, who had the soul of a poet as well as that of a mathematician, vividly described* some of the birth pangs of the machine and its brilliant subsequent performance:

> The amplifier was placed in another room, separated from the whirling gears by a heavy brick wall, and was enclosed in a coffin

---

* D. N. Lehmer, "Machine Performs Difficult Mathematical Calculations," *News Service Bulletin*, Vol. III, No. 3, Carnegie Institution of Washington, 1939.

of celotex. This made things go a little better, but it was still subject to what seemed a perfectly unpredictable series of "jitters." It would run happily and sweetly for a few minutes and then suddenly become incoherent. Then it would suddenly pull itself together and behave in an entirely rational manner for another quarter of an hour before having another tantrum. And all without any appreciable change in environment.

Doctors were called in, but nothing could be inferred from the symptoms. To be sure, it was asking a good deal of a machine to work steadily with a magnification of over seven hundred million to one. It was like trying to write a smooth flowing hand with a pen ten thousand miles long, while all the time a mischievous imp was jogging at your elbow. And what was the imp, and how were we to lay hands on him?

Searching for the "Imp"

Days of futile adjustments and readjustments went by. There seemed to be nothing organically wrong; just a case of nerves. Nevertheless, it was an interesting and important case and the young doctor in charge was unwilling to give the patient up. At last it occurred to him to use a stethoscope. He installed a loud speaker and "listened in." Instantly the hiding place of the "imp" was discovered. There was a short-wave radio fan operating in a station in the immediate neighborhood. So long as he was quiet all went well. When he came on the air, the amplifier went into a spasm; the electric "eye" saw red.

There is no accounting for tastes and if the machine wanted to be temperamental on the subject of radio, there was nothing to be done about it except to screen the amplifier from this interesting but undesirable disturbance, or, to find a time when the radio operator was not playing with his machine. One could hope, of course, that the congruence machine had been giving him as much trouble as he had been giving it. At any rate, until the rival machine could be located, and a truce patched up, there was nothing to do but to wait until the ether was quiet before asking the machine any important arithmetical questions.

Attacking Giants

On the ninth of October, however, just after discovery of the "imp," the machine was set to do some real work in the Theory of Numbers. A time of day was selected when the radio man was not busy, and the machine was set to find the factors of the great unconquered factor 1537228672093301419 of $2^{93} + 1$, a number known by a very powerful test to be composite.

To resolve this number into its factors by the usual methods of computation would take the most skilled expert a lifetime of unremitting labor. In about three seconds the "eye" of the machine at the side of the whirling wheels gave the signal and the machine came to a stop. It was thought, of course, that the "imp" was on the air again. But, upon examination, it was found that this immense "binary" of nineteen digits had been decomposed into two prime factors, 529510939 and 2903110321.

This was in October 9 about noon. I got word of it as soon as the mail could reach me (at Berkeley) and arranged my affairs to go to Pasadena, where the machine had been constructed, and see what it was like. I arrived on the evening of October 17, and found that a small party had been staged. Professor Bell, Professor Wolfe, and Professor Ward had been invited by my son to see the machine attack another historic giant, the invincible large factor 3011347479614249131 of the number, $2^{95} + 1$, the symbol which represents 39614081257132168796771975169.

My son had necessary but not sufficient evidence that this number is a prime. To make sure, he must study the factors of the number less one. This number has the small factors, 2, 3, 5, and 19. Besides these it has the factor, 5283065753709209, which had been proved to be composite, but the factors of which were unknown.

To attack it my son determined to take advantage of the fact that he had found an expression of it as a square plus seven times another square. If he could find another such representation, from these two he could find the factors directly.

The matter was put up to the machine to find another representation of this enormous number as a square plus seven times another square. He had already set the holes in the gears for the solution of this problem and the only thing needful was to get a quiet time and let the machine run.

Stepping Out into the Unknown

It was a tense group that watched the machine being put through preliminary paces to see if it would be disturbed by outside forces. The zero point is always a solution and he turned the machine backward for five minutes and then drove it forward again to see if it would miss the zero point. It sprung the trap promptly on going through and all seemed propitious. "Here we step out into the unknown," said my son, as he threw on the power.

I confess that I walked the floor in the deepest anxiety. Was the machine going to prove temperamental, and was the radio "imp" going to jog its elbow? It had 10000000 numbers to report on and as the wheels whirled around, minute after minute, I could not believe but that the "eye" of the machine had relaxed its vigilance for a moment.

Suddenly, after about fifteen minutes of steady grind the hum died away into silence. With bated breath we read the dials and handed over the result to Dr. Wolfe, an expert computer, to see if the correct solution had really been found. In a few minutes we were assured that it was right and the machine was set to the task of finding the other solution.

It hummed quietly along, this time for twenty-five minutes, and again threw itself out of gear. It was another solution all right and in a few minutes we were in possession of the factors: 59957 and 88114244437. The first was easily found to be a prime, but the second was in doubt. This my son and I settled the next day, finding that it was prime also.

It would have surprised you to see the excitement in the group of professors and their wives, as we gathered around a table in the laboratory to discuss, over our coffee, the mysterious and uncanny powers of this curious machine. We all agreed that it would be unsportsmanlike to use it on small numbers such as can be handled by factor tables and factor stencils, but for the numbers that lie, as it were, in other galaxies than ours, outside the range of ordinary telescopes, so to say, there is as yet nothing to be compared with this device.*

The *News Service Bulletin*, Vol. III, No. 3, of the Carnegie Institution of Washington, from which this interesting description is taken, continues as follows:

This machine constructed at the laboratories of the Robert Burt Company, Pasadena, California, by the inventor, Derrick Henry Lehmer, is the first attempt ever made to apply the magic of the photoelectric cell to this problem of the study of remote numbers.

It is proposed to use it, first of all, in clearing up certain outstanding factorizations of numbers of the form $2^n + 1$ and of $10^n + 1$, numbers which have so far baffled the efforts of mathematicians.

Besides these problems there are also others, for the solution of which the machine is peculiarly adapted. One of these has to do with generalizations suggested by a formula proposed by Leonard Euler, a Swiss mathematician of the eighteenth century.

Euler suggested that the expression $n^2 - n + 41$ represents a prime number for every value of n. Although this formula gives a series of values that is remarkably rich in primes, nevertheless, it is consistently true only for all values up to and including 40. When $n = 41$, for example, the expression is equivalent to the number 1681, which is a composite number.

The work of examining the series which this formula produces will be greatly facilitated through use of the congruence machine. There are other time-honored formulae which mathematicians, working in the Theory of Numbers, have propounded, to the checking of which this machine, in due course, will also be set.

* Modern digital computers far surpass this machine.

The thrill of stepping into the unknown number realms to search for divisors was also whimsically described by Dr. Lehmer in an article entitled "Hunting Big Game in the Theory of Numbers," which appeared in *Scripta Mathematica*, Vol. 1, No. 3, March, 1933. No one reading Dr. Lehmer's account can help being infected with his enthusiasm as he reads with bated breath how 9999000099990001, a factor of $10^{20}+1$, fell under the assault of his son's original bicycle-sprocket-and-chain contraption. They stalked their prey for two hours, amidst the ominous clicking of electrical contacts as a pin on each of a number of chains opened one of several parallel circuits. And then—success—the simultaneous opening of all the contacts and the stopping of the machine. Their game bagged, the factors were found to be 1676321 and 5964848081.

In speaking of the then largest known prime,

$$2^{127}-1 = 170141183460469231731687303715884105727,$$

Dr. Lehmer said, "A light year of light years would have to be applied a light year of times to reach this remote star."

By extensions of Fermat's theorem, the Lehmers discovered several ingenious methods for resolving numbers far surpassing astronomical proportions. Suppose N is a number whose nature is to be determined. If for some base b, N divides $b^{N-1}-1$ but is prime to $b^{(N-1)/p}-1$ where p is a prime divisor of $N-1$, then every prime divisor of N is of the form $px+1$. Let us call this Theorem A.

Wishing to factor $2^{73}+1$, and having previously known the two factors 3 and 1753, it remained to investigate the quotient

$$N = (2^{73}+1)/3\cdot 1753 = 1795918038741070627.$$

It was found that to the arbitrarily selected base $b = 3$, $3^{N-1}-1$ was divisible by N. The divisor 811 of $N-1$ was also known and it was found that $3^{(N-1)/811}-1$ was prime to N. Therefore all prime divisors of N had to be of the form $811x+1$. There were a few other limitations on the value of N that need not be gone into here, and then the factoring machine disposed of all possibilities and determined N to be a prime.

The factors of $2^{95}+1$ were also investigated by the machine. Since $2^{95}+1 = (2^5)^{19}+1 = (2^{19})^5+1$, the number must be divisible by 2^5+1 and by $2^{19}+1$. It had also previously been known to be divisible by 2281. Hence it remained to investigate:

$$N = (2^{95}+1)(2+1)/(2^{19}+1)(2^5+1)\cdot 2281 = 3011347479614249131.$$

(The factor [2+1] must be included with the numerator because, although each binomial in the denominator divides $2^{95}+1$, their product does not, but their lowest common multiple does. Multiplying the numerator by the highest common factor, [2+1], of the two binomials insures that their product divides the complete numerator.) The number $(N-1)$ had the divisors $2 \cdot 3 \cdot 5 \cdot 19 \cdot 5283065753709209$, the character of the last factor M being unknown. Investigation revealed that -7 is a quadratic residue of this number and, therefore, that it can be represented at least once in the form x^2+7y^2. The factoring machine found two such representations:

$$M = 40923451^2+7 \cdot 22704112^2 = 66855539^2+7 \cdot 10779628^2.$$

Then, by the method described previously in this chapter, and using Formula 2, it was found that

$$5283065753709209 = 59957 \cdot 88114244437.$$

Factor tables showed the first of these numbers to be a prime and the second, p, was proved prime by means of Theorem A and the prime factor 2489947 of $M-1$.

For the base 3, it was found that $3^{N-1}-1$ was divisible by N but $3^{(N-1)/p}-1$ was prime to N and, therefore, all possible divisors of N had to be of the form $88114244437x+1$. The machine easily disposed of the comparatively limited possibilities and showed N to be a prime and thus $2^{95}+1$ was finally factored into

$$3 \cdot 11 \cdot 2281 \cdot 174763 \cdot 3011347479614249131.$$

In a similar manner

$$N = (2^{85}-1)/(2^{17}-1)(2^5-1) = 9520972806333758431$$

was tested. It was found that $N-1$ was divisible by 257, and Theorem A was satisfied for the base 3. The machine proved N to be a prime and therefore $2^{85}-1 = 31 \cdot 131071 \cdot N$.

The reader may have wondered how divisors of $N-1$ such as 257 above were obtained so readily. Another ingenious theorem applies here: If p and q are primes, then

$$[(a^{pq}-1)(a-1)/(a^p-1)(a^q-1)]-1$$

is divisible by every prime factor of $a^{p-1}-1$ not dividing a^q-1. For example, in $N = (2^{85}-1)/(2^{17}-1)(2^5-1)$, we have $p = 17$, $q = 5$, and $2^{16}-1$ has the divisors 2^8+1 and 2^8-1. The former is the prime 257 which does not divide $2^5 - 1$. Therefore $N - 1$ is divisible by 257.

By such processes of attrition, the Mersenne number $2^{79} - 1$, previously known to possess the lone factor 2687, was completely subjugated and an additional star was placed next to the name of Lehmer in its niche among the immortals.

BIBLIOGRAPHY

Barlow, P. *Tables of Squares, Cubes, etc.* Chicago: Charles T. Powner Co., 1948.

———. *Theory of Numbers.* London: J. Johnson & Co., 1811.

Carnegie Institution of Washington. "Machine Performs Difficult Mathematical Calculations," News Service Bulletin, **III, 3** (1933), 19.

Dickson, L. E. *History of the Theory of Numbers.* 3 vols. New York: Chelsea Publishing Co., 1950.

Lehmer, D. N. *Factor Stencils.* Washington, D.C.: Carnegie Institution of Washington, 1939.

———. "A Photo-Electric Number Sieve," *American Mathematical Monthly,* **40** (1933), 401.

———. "Some New Factorizations of $2^n \pm 1$," *Bulletin of the American Mathematical Society,* **39** (1933), 105.

———. "Hunting Big Game in the Theory of Numbers," *Scripta Mathematica,* **1** (1933), 229.

Uspensky, J. V., and Heaslet, M. A. *Elementary Number Theory.* New York: McGraw-Hill Book Co., 1939.

CHAPTER XXII

THE PELLIAN

IT WAS the fourteenth of October, the year 1066. "The men of Harold stood well together, as was their wont, and formed sixty and one squares, with a like number of men in every square thereof, and woe to the hardy Norman who ventured to enter their redoubts; for a single blow of a Saxon war-hatchet would break his lance and cut through his coat of mail.... When Harold threw himself into the fray the Saxons were one mighty square of men, shouting the battle cries, 'Ut!' 'Olicrosse!' 'Godemite!'"

The ill-fated Saxons presumably had 61 phalanxes each containing a square number of men, and the addition of Harold to their ranks enabled them to rearrange themselves into one solid square. We are to find the minimum number of men in his army. In the unimaginative but precise language of mathematics we have $61x^2 + 1 = y^2$ or $y^2 - 61x^2 = 1$.

Can the reader find the number of men, y^2, in the Saxon horde?†

The equation $x^2 - Dy^2 = 1$ is known as the "Pellian Equation," apparently because Pell neither first discussed nor first solved it! Fermat, that arch instigator of troublesome problems to plague posterity, proposed this equation to the English mathematicians in one of those frequent hands-across-the-sea gestures of his day. Fermat's countryman Frenicle had calculated the least solutions of $x^2 - Dy^2 = 1$ for all permissible values of D up to 150 and suggested that the English mathematician Wallis extend it to 200 or at least solve $x^2 - 151y^2 = 1$ and $x^2 - 313y^2 = 1$, hinting that the latter equation was perhaps beyond Wallis's ability. Lord Brouncker, Wallis's associate, replied that it had taken him only an hour or two to find $126862368^2 - 313(7170685)^2 = -1$ and that

$$x = 2 \cdot 7170685 \cdot 126862368$$

gave the desired solution of $x^2 - 313y^2 = +1$. Wallis also solved the problem and gave

$$1728148040^2 - 151(140634693)^2 = 1.$$

† Problems indicated by a dagger are solved in Chapter XXVI.

The mathematician Euler erroneously attributed Brouncker's method of solving the equation to Pell, and although history has unearthed the error, the equation is now irrevocably Pell's instead of rightfully the Fermat equation.   Pell's relation to the problem is the very remote one of having revised someone's translation of someone else's algebra—the author who first published Wallis and Brouncker's solution to Fermat's problem.   On such foundations does fame often rest.

Historical evidence shows that this problem had already received attention more than 400 years before the beginning of the Christian era.   To Archimedes is credited the famous cattle problem on which a great deal of pleasurable but useless time has been spent.   Stupendous feats of calculation have been performed and the answers have not yet been completely computed nor is it likely that they ever will be.

THE CATTLE PROBLEM OF ARCHIMEDES

Compute O friend, the host of the oxen of the sun, giving thy mind thereto, if thou hast a share of wisdom.   Compute the number which once grazed upon the plains of the Sicilian Isle Trinacia [Sicily itself] and which were divided according to color into four herds, one milk white, one black, one yellow and one dappled.   The number of bulls formed the majority of the animals in each herd and the relations between them were as follows:... [The first 7 conditions given below are then described.]

If thou canst give, O friend, the number of bulls and cows in each herd, thou art not unknowing nor unskilled in numbers, but still not yet to be counted among the wise.   Consider however, the following additional relations between the bulls of the sun:... [Conditions 8 and 9 are given below.]   When thou hast then computed the totals of the herds, O friend, go forth as conqueror, and rest assured that thou art proved most skilled in the science of numbers.

The problem stripped to its mathematical essentials is to find the numbers W, X, Y, Z of white, black, spotted, and yellow bulls and the numbers w, x, y, z of cows of the corresponding colors subject to the conditions:

(1) $W = \dfrac{5}{6} X + Z$ (2) $X = \dfrac{9}{20} Y + Z$

(3) $Y = \dfrac{13}{42} W + Z$ (4) $w = \dfrac{7}{12} (X + x)$

(5) $x = \dfrac{9}{20} (Y + y)$ (6) $y = \dfrac{11}{30} (Z + z)$

(7) $\quad z = \dfrac{13}{42}(W+w)$ (8) $W+X = $ a square number

(9) $Y+Z = $ a triangular number

The first seven equations are easy to satisfy, giving the answers:

$$
\begin{aligned}
W &= 10366482\,k & w &= 7206360\,k \\
X &= 7460514\,k & x &= 4893246\,k \\
Y &= 7358060\,k & y &= 3515820\,k \\
Z &= 4149387\,k & z &= 5439213\,k
\end{aligned}
$$

where k is any arbitrary positive integer. When $k = 1$, the least set of answers satisfying the first seven conditions is obtained and the total number of cattle is 50389082. According to the ancient manuscript stating the conditions of this problem, the animals grazed on the island of Sicily, whose area is 6358400 acres and therefore large enough to have easily fed the creatures.

Condition 8 requires that $W+X = 17826996\,k$ be a square number, which is easily satisfied. Since $17826996\,k$ can be factored into $4 \cdot 4456749\,k$ and the larger factor has no square divisor, it follows that k must equal $4456749\,t^2$. Then

$$ W+X = 4(4456749)^2 t^2 = 79450446596004\,t^2 $$

is a perfect square, but unfortunately, $Y+Z = 51285802909803\,t^2$ is not a triangular number. Triangular numbers, it will be recalled from Chapter XVIII, have the form $n(n+1)/2$ so that we must solve

$$ 51285802909803\,t^2 = n(n+1)/2. $$

By multiplying both sides of the equation by 8 and then adding unity, the result is:

$$ 410286423278424\,t^2+1 = 4n^2+4n+1 = (2n+1)^2. $$

If we let $2n+1 = u$ we have

$$ u^2-410286423278424\,t^2 = 1, $$

the Pell equation.

The method of continued fractions described later is used to solve this equation but let the reader try to imagine the work involved in finding the period of $\sqrt{410286423278424}$, and then the computation of the corresponding convergents. Yet in 1889, undaunted by what lay before them, A. H. Bell, a civil engineer, and two friends formed the Hillsboro, Illinois, Mathematical Club and started the computation. They spent four years at the job, computing 32 of the left-hand and 12 of the right-hand digits of the 206531-digit number t. This value of t is:

3455590635455937050630380296361 7*****252058980100.

Each of the numbers satisfying the first seven conditions must be multiplied by $k = 4456749\ t^2$ resulting finally in the following:

W = white bulls = 15965108046711445314355261943 70*****
385150341800

X = black bulls = 11489713877282899997123598218 24*****
899825178600

Y = spotted bulls = 11331927544386380771195558792 02*****
921175894000

Z = yellow bulls = 6390346482309028650085596761 83*****
635296026300

w = white cows = 11098298923733190397239602158 24*****
914059564000

x = black cows = 75359414205454262639814429119589*****
238562645400

y = spotted cows = 54146089457145667802361994210 6*****
608963318000

z = yellow cows = 83767688241852443869222198410 7*****
116422113700

Total cattle = 77602714064868182695302328332 09*****
719455081800

$W+X$ = a square
number = 27454821923994345311478860161 94*****
284975520400

$\sqrt{W+X}$ = 1656949665133506668.....357460163020

$Y+Z$ = a triangular
number, T = 17722274026695409421281155553 85*****
556471920300

$\sqrt{8T+1}$ = 3765344502347205884.....363134961201

Each set of asterisks represents 206502 digits and each line containing asterisks has a total of either 206544 or 206545 digits. Each set of dots represents 103242 digits and each of the two lines containing dots has a total of 103273 digits. Assuming that 10 typed digits occupy an inch of space, each of the 206545-digit numbers would be about 1/3 of a mile long, and to print completely the 13 numbers above would require a volume of over 2000 pages. A sphere with a radius equal to the distance from the earth to the Milky Way could contain only a part of the animals even if they were the smallest microbes—nay, even were they electrons. And it is doubtful whether 1000 men working for another 1000 years could finish Bell's computation. However, a modern digital computer could probably do the job in a reasonable length of time.

After reading the above paragraphs, the reader need hesitate no longer to start on the problem of Harold and his Saxon warriors—the answers are much smaller.

*   *   *

The Hindus, as long ago as 800 A.D., knew how to solve the Pell equation, but it remained for the great mathematician Lagrange to give a complete and elegant analysis of it 110 years after Fermat first proposed the problem to Messrs. Wallis and Brouncker. The latter two had only partly answered Fermat's questions. Lagrange's work is one of the outstanding achievements in the theory of numbers. Brahmagupta, a Hindu, said in about 650 A.D., "A person who can within a year solve the equation $x^2 - 92y^2 = 1$ is a mathematician." For those days he would indeed have had to be one, since $x = 1151$, $y = 120$ is the least solution.

*   *   *

It is interesting to note how, from one solution of $x^2 - Dy^2 = \pm 1$, an infinite number of solutions may be found. If p and q are the least values satisfying the equation $x^2 - Dy^2 = 1$, then $x^2 - Dy^2 = 1 = p^2 - Dq^2$. If we raise the right-hand member to the nth power, it is still equal to unity since $1^n = 1$. Then

$$x^2 - Dy^2 = (p^2 - Dq^2)^n = 1,$$

or, factoring,

$$(x + \sqrt{D}\,y)(x - \sqrt{D}\,y) = (p + \sqrt{D}\,q)^n(p - \sqrt{D}\,q)^n.$$

Equating the factors with the same sign:

$$x + \sqrt{D}\,y = (p + \sqrt{D}\,q)^n,$$
$$x - \sqrt{D}\,y = (p - \sqrt{D}\,q)^n.$$

Solving for x and y we obtain the general formulas:

$$x = [(p+q\sqrt{D})^n+(p-q\sqrt{D})^n]/2, \qquad \text{(Formula 1)}$$
$$y = [(p+q\sqrt{D})^n-(p-q\sqrt{D})^n]/2\sqrt{D}, \qquad \text{(Formula 2)}$$

and as n takes on the successive values $1, 2, 3 \ldots$ there result as many different solutions as we please.

If we take as an example, $x^2-2y^2 = 1$, the least solution is $3^2-2\cdot2^2 = 1$ so that $p = 3$ and $q = 2$. Additional solutions are obtained from

$$x = [(3+2\sqrt{2})^n+(3-2\sqrt{2})^n]/2,$$
$$y = [(3+2\sqrt{2})^n-(3-2\sqrt{2})^n]/2\sqrt{2}.$$

When $n = 1$, this gives $x = 3$, $y = 2$, the first solution; when $n = 2$, we have $x = 17$, $y = 12$, and $17^2-2\cdot12^2 = 1$, the second solution; for $n = 3$, $x = 99$, $y = 70$, and $99^2-2\cdot70^2 = 1$ is the third solution. It can be seen that the values of x and y increase very rapidly as n increases.

In a similar way, solutions of $x^2-Dy^2 = -1$ may be found except that here the exponent n must always be odd—equal to $2m-1$, for instance. For $D = 2$, the equation $x^2-2y^2 = -1$ has, as least solution, $p = 1$, $q = 1$. Then

$$x = [(1+\sqrt{2})^{2m-1}+(1-\sqrt{2})^{2m-1}]/2,$$
$$y = [(1+\sqrt{2})^{2m-1}-(1-\sqrt{2})^{2m-1}]/2\sqrt{2}.$$

When $m = 1$, we obtain $x = 1$, $y = 1$ as the first solution. When $m = 2$, $x = 7, y = 5$, and $7^2-2\cdot5^2 = -1$ is the second solution; for $m = 3$, $x = 41$, $y = 29$, and $41^2-2\cdot29^2$ is the third solution, and so on.

The labor of calculating the least solution of the equation $x^2-Dy^2 = \pm 1$, although often considerable, presents no real difficulty and many computers have tabulated the results to high values of D. In such a tabulation, D need contain no square factor since a square can be combined with y. Thus there is no need to tabulate the solution of $x^2-52y^2 = 1$, since we may write this as $x^2-13(2y)^2 = 1$, and solutions of $X^2-13Y^2 = 1$ when Y is even will give the desired result. In Brahmagupta's problem, $x^2-92y^2 = 1$, the equation $x^2-23y^2 = 1$ will yield the desired result when y is even.

There is no relation between the value of D and the magnitude of the numbers p and q which solve the equation. For some given D,

TABLE 91

LEAST SOLUTION OF THE PELL EQUATION, $x^2 - Dy^2 = 1$

D	x	y	D	x	y
2	3	2	54	485	66
3	2	1	55	89	12
5	9	4	56	15	2
6	5	2	57	151	20
7	8	3	58	19603	2574
8	3	1	59	530	69
10	19	6	60	31	4
11	10	3	61	1766319049	226153980
12	7	2	62	63	8
13	649	180	63	8	1
14	15	4	65	129	16
15	4	1	66	65	8
17	33	8	67	48842	5967
18	17	4	68	33	4
19	170	39	69	7775	936
20	9	2	70	251	30
21	55	12	71	3480	413
22	197	42	72	17	2
23	24	5	73	2281249	267000
24	5	1	74	3699	430
26	51	10	75	26	3
27	26	5	76	57799	6630
28	127	24	77	351	40
29	9801	1820	78	53	6
30	11	2	79	80	9
31	1520	273	80	9	1
32	17	3	82	163	18
33	23	4	83	82	9
34	35	6	84	55	6
35	6	1	85	285769	30996
37	73	12	86	10405	1122
38	37	6	87	28	3
39	25	4	88	197	21
40	19	3	89	500001	53000
41	2049	320	90	19	2
42	13	2	91	1574	165
43	3482	531	92	1151	120
44	199	30	93	12151	1260
45	161	24	94	2143295	221064
46	24335	3588	95	39	4
47	48	7	96	49	5
48	7	1	97	62809633	6377352
50	99	14	98	99	10
51	50	7	99	10	1
52	649	90	101	201	20
53	66249	9100	102	101	10

the values of p and q may be quite small; for the succeeding value, they may be exceedingly large. Table 91 illustrates these variations. The number x in $x^2 - 1620y^2 = 1$ has only 3 digits; in $x^2 - 1621y^2 = 1$ it has 76.

TABLE 92

LEAST SOLUTIONS OF THE PELL EQUATION, $x^2 - Dy^2 = 1$
(LARGE VALUES)

D	x	y
1515	506	13
1516	334949171001860160500111 891352199	8602591618573944625072398763290
1546	3802792051	9671580
1597	519711527755463096224266 385375638449943026746249	1300498608879077225030950464390867152083622910 0
1598	1599	40
1620	161	4
1621	629810181249373234303497 450009145781552994230866 705141285735231016966512 5001	156429324369979112128445 583345098338627552043874 824108399177922442751050 500
9781	476253760754326696229155 514206437758064174686478 459207091331165051639277 866110462913256334048166 314000750317798423947886 553290523568954482295429 78234993801	481555989037307915758858 176980967932471259067113 218060716438458121121697 033150997478138226408634 091745993475126174622767 474943622729435256180363 7330579140

The *Canon Pellianus* computed by C. F. Degen and published in 1817 gave the solution of $y^2 - Cx^2 = 1$ for all non-squares, C, not exceeding 1000. This has been corrected and extended by many investigators, and in addition, the solutions for special values of D with many digits in the equation $x^2 - Dy^2 = 1$, have been computed. An interesting book devoted exclusively to this subject, its history, theory, and tables of solutions from $D = 1501$ to 2012 is E. E. Whitford's *The Pell Equation*.

* * *

The number 48 has the peculiar property that if unity is added to it, the sum is a square, 49, and if unity is added to its half, 24, the result, 25, is also a square. What other numbers have this property? If b

is the number, then $b+1 = x^2$ and $b/2+1 = y^2$. Eliminating b, we have $x^2-2y^2 = -1$, a Pell equation. From the least solution $x = 1$, $y = 1$, $b = 0$, we can obtain others as before, Table 93 giving the first 9 such numbers b exhibiting the property required.

TABLE 93

SOLUTION OF $x^2 - 2y^2 = -1$

x	y	x^2	y^2	$b = 2y^2-2 =$ x^2-1
1	1	1	1	0
7	5	49	25	48
41	29	1681	841	1680
239	169	57121	28561	57120
1393	985	1940449	970225	1940448
8119	5741	65918161	32959081	65918160
47321	33461	2239277041	1119638521	2239277040
275807	195025	76069501249	38034750625	76069501248
1607521	1136689	2584123765441	1292061882721	2584123765440

In Chapter XIV we discussed Pythagorean triangles whose legs m^2-n^2 and $2mn$ differed by unity. This requires that $m^2-n^2-2mn = \pm 1$. Then $(m-n)^2-2n^2 = \pm 1$, a Pell equation. The successive triangles whose legs differ by unity are derived alternately from $(m-n)^2-2n^2 = +1$ and $(m-n)^2-2n^2 = -1$. From $1^2-2\cdot 1^2 = -1$ we have $n = 1$, $m-n = 1$, $m = 2$ to which correspond the legs $m^2-n^2 = 3$ and $2mn = 4$ of the triangle $3^2+4^2 = 5^2$. From $3^2-2\cdot 2^2 = +1$ we have $n = 2$, $m-n = 3$, $m = 5$ to which correspond the legs $m^2-n^2 = 21$ and $2mn = 20$ of the triangle $20^2+21^2 = 29^2$.

Since the general values of x and y in the Pell equation $x^2-2y^2 = \pm 1$ are

$$x = [(1+\sqrt{2})^r+(1-\sqrt{2})^r]/2$$

and

$$y = [(1+\sqrt{2})^r-(1-\sqrt{2})^r]/2\sqrt{2}$$

we can find the general values of $m = x+y$ and $n = y$ respectively. Then, solving for $X = m^2-n^2 = x^2+2xy$, $Y = 2mn = 2xy+2y^2$, $Z = m^2+n^2 = x^2+2xy+2y^2$, which are the sides of a Pythagorean triangle, we finally obtain:

$$X_r = \frac{(\sqrt{2}+1)^{2r+1}-(\sqrt{2}-1)^{2r+1}}{4}+\frac{1}{2}(-1)^r,$$

$$Y_r = \frac{(\sqrt{2}+1)^{2r+1}-(\sqrt{2}-1)^{2r+1}}{4}-\frac{1}{2}(-1)^r,$$

$$Z_r = \frac{(\sqrt{2}+1)^{2r+1}+(\sqrt{2}-1)^{2r+1}}{2\sqrt{2}},$$

the formulas given in Chapter XIV for the sides of a Pythagorean triangle with consecutive legs.

* * *

Did you ever dream, perhaps after eating not wisely but too well, of crawling along tortuous passageways and finally emerging into celestial worlds of Maxfield Parrish architecture? Even so does one feel who, after encountering "convergents," "partial quotients," and "continued fractions," issues forth into the beautiful Diophantine realm of the Pellian where quadratic surds flourish in periodic chains.

The rules involving continued or "chain" fractions are tedious and difficult to remember, but the results obtained with them, such as the solution of the Pell equation, are so entertaining as to be ample justification for their existence and for their description here. A simple continued fraction has the form:

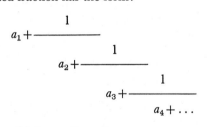

For convenience this is usually written:

$$a_1+\frac{1}{a_2+}\frac{1}{a_3+}\frac{1}{a_4+}\cdots$$

In recent years it has sometimes also been represented by

$$(a_1, a_2, a_3, a_4 \ldots).$$

Any number can be written as a *simple* chain fraction—"simple" because the numerators are unity. When the number is rational, that is, expressible as the quotient of two integers, the chain terminates; when irrational, the chain repeats its terms periodically. This last is markedly unlike the expression of an irrational number as a decimal—such a number does not repeat at periodic intervals a sequence of the decimal places that have already been found. Thus $\sqrt{3}$, an irrational number, is equal to $1.732051\ldots$ and there is no periodic recurrence of any sequence of digits.

Using continued fractions, the rational number

$$40/17 = 2 + \frac{1}{2+} \frac{1}{1+} \frac{1}{5}.$$

The irrational number

$$\sqrt{19} = 4 + \frac{1}{2+} \frac{1}{1+} \frac{1}{3+} \frac{1}{1+} \frac{1}{2+} \frac{1}{8+} \frac{1}{2+} \frac{1}{1+} \frac{1}{3+} \frac{1}{1+} \frac{1}{2+} \frac{1}{8+} \frac{1}{2+} \cdots$$

Also

$$\sqrt{2} = 1 + \frac{1}{2+} \frac{1}{2+} \frac{1}{2+} \frac{1}{2+} \cdots$$

Even mathematicians often avoid chain fractions and take long circuitous routes around and over rather than through the subterranean depths where the convergent goblins gambol. We too, will not tarry but hurry through, only occasionally risking a joust with an unavoidable goblin.

One might ascribe the reluctance to use continued fractions to dealing with denominators which never stay put. Thus, in the expression for 40/17, the sum of the first two terms, $2\frac{1}{2}$, is larger than 40/17 because it lacks the increment due to the fraction 1/1 in its denominator; the sum of $2 + \frac{1}{2+} \frac{1}{1} = 2\frac{1}{3}$ on the other hand is smaller than 40/17 because the fraction 1/1 lacks the increment 1/5 in its denominator which would make the part added to the denominator in $2 + \frac{1}{2}$ smaller and the total result larger than $2\frac{1}{3}$. Steady now!

If we were given either of the numbers 40/17 or $\sqrt{19}$, how would we proceed to express them as continued fractions? That is one problem.

Again, when a number is rational, its continued fraction has only a finite number of terms and one can arrive at the original number by simplifying the continued fraction, starting from the right-hand end of the series. On the other hand, an irrational number such as $\sqrt{19}$ has a never-ending continued fraction and one cannot start at the right-hand end of the series and proceed to simplify. It is therefore convenient to consider the sum of only a finite number of these terms starting with the first. Such a sum, called a *convergent*, is a rational number and is an approximation to the true value of the irrational one. Obtaining this convergent, after the irrational number has been expressed as a periodic chain fraction, is a second problem.

Either of these two problems is tedious to solve and a number of comparatively simple rules are available for abridging the computation. But why should one go to all this trouble in any case? It is because of certain relations among convergents which, remarkably, serve to solve first and second degree Diophantine equations such as $119x - 32y = 1$ or $X^2 - 13y^2 = 1$. This is another instance of apparently unrelated subjects in mathematics actually being linked in unsuspected and beautiful ways. To appreciate the power of these tools let the reader try to solve in integers the comparatively simple second-degree equation:

$$x^2 - 211y^2 = 1,$$

before continuing.†

By continually adding to the denominators of the denominators in a continued fraction we obtain at each step an expression which is alternately greater and less than the true value of the number, ultimately reaching the exact value for a rational expression but never quite doing so for an irrational one, although at each step we "converge" upon the true value ever more closely.

To convert 119/32 to a continued fraction, perform the division, giving $3\frac{23}{32}$. Then invert 23/32 to 32/23, again performing the division and obtaining $1\frac{9}{23}$. Proceeding in this manner, $23/9 = 2\frac{5}{9}$,

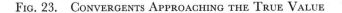

FIG. 23. CONVERGENTS APPROACHING THE TRUE VALUE

$9/5 = 1\frac{4}{5}$, $5/4 = 1\frac{1}{4}$, $4/1 = 4$.   The whole-number parts of each quotient are the denominators a_1, a_2, a_3, ... of the continued fraction, the operation stopping when the quotient is an integer.   Then $a_1 = 3$, $a_2 = 1$, $a_3 = 2$, $a_4 = 1$, $a_5 = 1$, $a_6 = 4$.

$$119/32 = 3 + \frac{1}{1} + \frac{1}{2} + \frac{1}{1} + \frac{1}{1} + \frac{1}{4}.$$

Since 119/32 is a rational expression, an integral quotient must always result after a finite number of divisions.   Had we started with 32/119, there would have resulted $a_1 = 0$, $a_2 = 3$, $a_3 = 1$, $a_4 = 2$, $a_5 = 1$, $a_6 = 1$, $a_7 = 4$, whence

$$32/119 = \frac{1}{3} + \frac{1}{1} + \frac{1}{2} + \frac{1}{1} + \frac{1}{1} + \frac{1}{4}.$$

Now for the convergents.   These can be evaluated by summing up the first one, two, three... terms of the continued fraction, giving 3/1, 4/1, 11/3, 15/4, 26/7, 119/32, respectively.   They are alternately less and greater than 119/32, but each convergent is closer to the true value than the previous one.   A much simpler method for finding the nth convergent p_n/q_n from the previous two convergents and the a's is by use of the formulas:

$$p_n = a_n p_{n-1} + p_{n-2} \qquad \text{(Formula 3)}$$
$$q_n = a_n q_{n-1} + q_{n-2}. \qquad \text{(Formula 4)}$$

For instance, the fourth convergent, 15/4, above, is obtained from $a_4 = 1$, $p_3 = 11$, $q_3 = 3$, $p_2 = 4$, $q_2 = 1$ so that

$$p_4 = 1 \cdot 11 + 4 = 15$$
$$q_4 = 1 \cdot 3 \; + 1 = \; 4.$$

The first and second convergents, p_1/q_1 and p_2/q_2, cannot of course be obtained in terms of previous convergents.   Instead we have in *every* case, the relation:

$$q_1 = 1, \quad p_1 = a_1, \quad q_2 = a_2, \quad p_2 = a_2 a_1 + 1$$

and the first two convergents are always

$$a_1/1 \quad \text{and} \quad (a_1 a_2 + 1)/a_2.$$

The evaluation of the a's, p's, and q's so as to express a common fraction as a continued fraction and as a series of converging fractions can then be conveniently tabulated as indicated by Table 94.

Express 426/359 as a continued fraction and as a series of converging fractions. First find the a's by division as before. Then use Formulas 3 and 4 to make Table 94.

TABLE 94

CONVERSION OF 426/359 INTO A CONTINUED FRACTION

n	1	2	3	4	5	6	7
a_n	1	5	2	1	3	1	4
p_n	1	6	13	19	70	89	426
q_n	1	5	11	16	59	75	359

whence

$$426/359 = 1 + \frac{1}{5} + \frac{1}{2} + \frac{1}{1} + \frac{1}{3} + \frac{1}{1} + \frac{1}{4}$$

and the convergents are

1/1, 6/5, 13/11, 19/16, 70/59, 89/75, 426/359.

* * *

The conversion of a quadratic surd $\sqrt{D}$ into a continued fraction and then into a series of converging fractions is somewhat longer, but the converging fractions will yield the precious solution to the Pell equation, well worth the extra effort. The convergents p_n/q_n are calculated from $a_1, a_2, a_3, \ldots$ by the same formulas as for rational fractions but the a's are defined differently and their evaluation requires another series of formulas involving two additional quantities P and Q defined as follows:

$$P_1 = 0$$
$$Q_1 = 1$$
a_1 is the integral part of $\sqrt{D}$
$$P_2 = a_1$$
$$Q_2 = D - a_1^2$$
$$P_n = a_{n-1}Q_{n-1} - P_{n-1} \qquad \text{(Formula 5)}$$
$$Q_n = (D - P_n^2)/Q_{n-1} \qquad \text{(Formula 6)}$$
a_n is the integral part of $(a_1 + P_n)/Q_n$.

For convenience, Formulas 3 and 4 are repeated here:

$$p_n = a_n p_{n-1} + p_{n-2}$$
$$q_n = a_n q_{n-1} + q_{n-2}$$
$$q_1 = 1, \; p_1 = a_1, \; q_2 = a_2, \; p_2 = a_2 a_1 + 1.$$

To express $\sqrt{23}$ in this manner we carry out these rules and obtain Table 95.

TABLE 95

CONVERSION OF $\sqrt{23}$ INTO A CONTINUED FRACTION

n	1	2	3	4	5	6	7	8	9	10
P_n	0	4	3	3	4	4	3	3	4	4
Q_n	1	7	2	7	1	7	2	7	1	7
a_n	4	1	3	1	8	1	3	1	8	1
p_n	4	5	19	24	211	235	916	1151	10124	11275
q_n	1	1	4	5	44	49	191	240	2111	2351

Thus

$$\sqrt{23} = 4 + \frac{1}{1+} \frac{1}{3+} \frac{1}{1+} \frac{1}{8+} \frac{1}{1+} \frac{1}{3+} \frac{1}{1+} \frac{1}{8+} \frac{1}{1+} \cdots \frac{1}{a_n+}$$

We are now finally ready to reap the reward for minding our p's and q's so carefully. The a's, P's, and Q's were but means to an end and like chaff will be blown away so that only the nutritious kernels p/q may remain. Two very important relations in chain fractions are:

$$p_n q_{n-1} - p_{n-1} q_n = (-1)^n \qquad \text{(Formula A)}$$
$$p_n^2 - D q_n^2 = (-1)^n Q_{n+1}. \qquad \text{(Formula B)}$$

By means of Formula A the linear equation $ax - by = \pm 1$ is solved; by Formula B the solution of the Pell equation $x^2 - Dy^2 = \pm 1$ is obtained. To solve the linear equation, express a/b as a continued fraction. The numerator, p_{n-1} of the next to the last convergent, $(p_{n-1})/(q_{n-1})$ then has the value y; the denominator, q_{n-1}, has the value x. The last convergent p_n/q_n is of course a/b, where $p_n = a$ and $q_n = b$.

Suppose we wish to solve $119x - 32y = 1$ in integers. We have already expanded $119/32$ as a continued fraction and found that the fifth, or next to the last, convergent is $26/7$. Hence $p_{n-1} = y = 26$, $q_{n-1} = x = 7$ so that $119 \cdot 7 - 32 \cdot 26 = (-1)^6 = +1$.

Additional solutions are obtained by assigning any integral values to K in $x = 7+32K$; $y = 26+119K$. For instance, when $K = 1$, $x = 39$, $y = 145$, and $119 \cdot 39 - 32 \cdot 145 = 1$.

Had we started with $32x - 119y = 1$, we would have found in the expansion of $32/119$ that $p_{n-1} = 7 = y$, $q_{n-1} = 26 = x$, and $32 \cdot 26 - 119 \cdot 7 = (-1)^7 = -1$. To obtain the desired solution with plus one, we multiply each term by minus one and obtain

$$32(-26) - 119(-7) = +1.$$

Remembering that $-26 + 119K$ is the general solution for x and $-7 + 32K$ is that for y, we can obtain positive solutions. When $K = 1$, $x = 93$, $y = 25$, and $32 \cdot 93 - 119 \cdot 25 = 1$.

To solve $ax - by = -1$ we would proceed similarly.

*   *   *

Returning now to Formula B, we can verify this relation by Table 95. For instance, for $n = 2$, $p_2 = 5$, $q_2 = 1$, $Q_3 = 2$, and $5^2 - 23 \cdot 1^2 = +2$. Again for $n = 5$, $p_5 = 211$, $q_5 = 44$, $Q_6 = 7$, and $211^2 - 23 \cdot 44^2 = -7$. When $Q_{n+1} = +1$, we obtain the famous Pell equation,

$$p_n^2 - Dq_n^2 = (-1)^n(1) \qquad \text{(Formula C)}$$

or more simply

$$x^2 - Dy^2 = (-1)^n = \pm 1,$$

where n is that value of the subscript such that Q_{n+1} equals unity. The number D is assumed to have no square divisor other than unity since, if originally present, such a square divisor can be removed by including it as part of y^2.

Table 95 shows that the a's, P's, and Q's repeat periodically after an a_n which is double a_1. *This is always true.* The corresponding Q term, Q_n, is then *always* unity. For example, $a_5 = 8$, which is double $a_1 = 4$, therefore a_6 is the same as a_2, a_7 as a_3, etc. Also $Q_5 = 1$. Therefore $p_4^2 - Dq_4^2 = 24^2 - 23 \cdot 5^2 = (-1)^4 = 1$. However, Q_9 is also unity and $p_8^2 - Dq_8^2 = 1151^2 - 23 \cdot 240^2 = (-1)^8 = +1$ and similarly for $Q_{13}, Q_{17} \ldots Q_{4k+1}$. Since Q periodically takes on the value unity for every r terms, we can generalize Formula C into

$$p_{rk}^2 - Dq_{rk}^2 = (-1)^{rk}, \qquad \text{(Formula D)}$$

where k is any positive integer.

This shows that if r comes out an odd integer, solutions of

$$x^2 - Dy^2 = +1$$

or

$$x^2 - Dy^2 = -1$$

can be obtained according as k is selected even or odd. But if r comes out an even integer, no value of k can make the exponent odd and hence solutions of $x^2 - Dy^2 = -1$ are impossible in that case.

Taking $x^2 - 13y^2 = 1$ as an example, we tabulate the values for $\sqrt{13}$ and obtain the convergent $p_5/q_5 = 18/5$ corresponding to $Q_6 = 1$.

TABLE 96

CONVERSION OF $\sqrt{13}$ INTO A CONTINUED FRACTION

n	1	2	3	4	5	6	7	8	9	10	11
P_n	0	3	1	2	1	3	3	1	2	1	3
Q_n	1	4	3	3	4	1	4	3	3	4	1
a_n	3	1	1	1	1	6	1	1	1	1	6
p_n	3	4	7	11	18	119	137	256	393	649	
q_n	1	1	2	3	5	33	38	71	109	180	

Then $p_5^2 - 13q_5^2 = 18^2 - 13 \cdot 5^2 = (-1)^5 = -1$. We therefore take advantage of Formula D and let k be any even number, say 2. Then

$$p_{10}^2 - 13q_{10}^2 = (-1)^{10} = +1$$

and in fact

$$649^2 - 13 \cdot 180^2 = +1.$$

On the other hand, solutions of $x^2 - 13y^2 = -1$ are obtained when k is any odd number; the solution $18^2 - 13 \cdot 5^2 = -1$ corresponds to $k = 1$.

The reader may now wish to solve the equation $x^2 - 211y^2 = 1$ mentioned previously in this chapter, by finding the convergents to $\sqrt{211}$ but should not lose patience if $Q_{n+1} = 1$ is long in coming—it must eventually arrive.†

*   *   *

From the general relation: $p_n^2 - Dq_n^2 = (-1)^2 Q_{n+1}$, the equation $x^2 - Dy^2 = \pm c$, where c is smaller than $\sqrt{D}$, can be obtained but only if c is one of the Q's in the tabulation of a period of the convergents to $\sqrt{D}$; hence D and c cannot be arbitrarily chosen. If c is greater than $\sqrt{D}$, the method of solution becomes quite complicated and a graceful retirement before this goblin is indicated. Chrystal's *Algebra* will furnish the dauntless mathematical Siegfried the fragments to forge into a sword to attack this monster. But if one solution is known, an infinite number of others can be obtained but not quite as readily as when the right side of the equation is ± 1.

The solutions are obtained by multiplying the first solution by any one of the solutions of $x^2 - Dy^2 = \pm 1$, which is called the unit form. The terms of the product, suitably rearranged, give the required solution. If p and q satisfy $x^2 - Dy^2 = +c$ or $-c$, and r and s satisfy $x^2 - Dy^2 = +1$ or -1, we have

$$(p^2 - Dq^2)(r^2 - Ds^2) = +c \quad \text{or} \quad -c;$$

then multiplying and grouping we get:

$$(pr \pm Dqs)^2 - D(ps \pm qr)^2 = +c \quad \text{or} \quad -c.$$

Suppose we wish a number of solutions of

$$x^2 - 13y^2 = +3.$$

Table 96 shows this is possible since 3 is a Q_n, the least solution being $4^2 - 13 \cdot 1^2 = 3$. Also it was found previously that the least solution of $x^2 - 13y^2 = +1$ is $649^2 - 13 \cdot 180^2 = +1$. Then $p = 4$, $q = 1$, $r = 649$, $s = 180$, and

$$(4 \cdot 649 \pm 13 \cdot 1 \cdot 180)^2 - 13(4 \cdot 180 \pm 1 \cdot 649)^2 = 3,$$

from which either

$$4936^2 - 13 \cdot 1369^2 = 3$$

or

$$256^2 - 13 \cdot 71^2 = 3.$$

Again from $7^2 - 13 \cdot 2^2 = -3$ (Table 96 again) and $649^2 - 13 \cdot 180^2 = +1$ we obtain either

$$9223^2 - 13 \cdot 2558^2 = -3$$

or

$$137^2 - 13 \cdot 38^2 = -3.$$

By using the negative unit form, $18^2 - 13 \cdot 5^2 = -1$ with $4^2 - 13 \cdot 1^2 = +3$ we have

$$137^2 - 13 \cdot 38^2 = -3$$

or

$$7^2 - 13 \cdot 2^2 = -3.$$

And by combining the negative unit form with $7^2 - 13 \cdot 2^2 = -3$ there results:

$$256^2 - 13 \cdot 71^2 = +3$$

or

$$4^2 - 13 \cdot 1^2 = +3.$$

Finally powers of the *unit* form may be used to obtain as many other solutions as one pleases.

*   *   *

By means of the relation $Q_n = (D - P_n^2)/Q_{n-1}$ previously given in Formula 6, a series of quadratic residues of D may readily be found, this information being of considerable use in factoring the number D as described in Chapter XXI.   Clearing fractions above, we have that

$$P_n^2 - D = -Q_n Q_{n-1}, \quad \text{that is,} \quad P_n^2 \equiv -Q_n Q_{n-1} \quad \text{mod } D.$$

This means that $-Q_n Q_{n-1}$ is a quadratic residue of D.   But it will be recalled that Q_1 is *always* unity; therefore $-Q_2$ is a quadratic residue of D.   Similarly, $-Q_2 Q_3$ is a residue, but since $-Q_2$ is a residue, Q_3 must be one.   Finally we have that all Q's with odd subscripts and the negatives of those with even subscripts are quadratic residues of D.

Applying this rule to the Q's obtained from $\sqrt{13}$, Table 96, we have, $Q_1 = 1$, $Q_2 = 4$, $Q_3 = 3$, $Q_4 = 3$, $Q_5 = 4$, $Q_6 = 1$, etc., and $1, 3, 4, -4, -3, -1$ are all quadratic residues of 13.   This method does not always give *all* the quadratic residues of a modulus (for example in Table 95 there are only 3 of the 11 residues of 23), but for very large D's containing many digits, it often yields a sufficient number of small ones to materially shorten the labor of factoring D. It should not be forgotten that each Q must be prime to D in order to qualify as a genuine quadratic residue, so that any Q's obtained by this method must be tested accordingly.

Enough has been said about continued fractions to illustrate their elegance and utility in solving linear and quadratic Diophantine equations and how they may assist in factoring numbers. They are one of the all too few direct methods in number theory.

BIBLIOGRAPHY

Archibald, R. C. "Cattle Problem of Archimedes," *American Mathematical Monthly*, **25** (1918), 411.

Barlow, P. *Theory of Numbers*. London: J. Johnson & Co., 1811.

Bell, A. H. "'Cattle Problem.' By Archimedes 251 B.C.," *American Mathematical Monthly*, **2** (1895), 140.

———. "Cattle Problem of Archimedes," *Mathematical Magazine*, **1** (1882–1884), 163.

Cajori, F. *A History of Mathematics*. New York: Macmillan Co., 1919.

Carmichael, R. D. *Theory of Numbers and Diophantine Analysis*. New York: Dover Publications, Inc., 1959.

Chrystal, G. *Textbook of Algebra*. 2 vols. New York: Dover Publications, Inc., 1961.

Cunningham, A. *Quadratic Partitions*. London: F. Hodgson, 1904.

Degan, C. F. *Canon Pellianus*. Copenhagen, 1817.

Dickson, L. E. *History of the Theory of Numbers*. 3 vols. New York: Chelsea Publishing Co., 1950.

Dudeney, H. E. *Amusements in Mathematics*. New York: Dover Publications, Inc., 1958.

Evans, A. B., and Hart, D. S. "Problem: [To Find the Least Integral Solution of $x^2 - 953y^2 = \pm 1$]," *Mathematical Questions from the Educational Times*, **23** (1875), 107.

Lehmer, D. N. *Factor Stencils*. Washington, D.C.: Carnegie Institution of Washington, 1939.

Licks, H. E. *Recreations in Mathematics*. New York: D. Van Nostrand Co., 1921.

Martin, A. "Solution to Problem: Find the Least Integral Values of x and y That Will Satisfy the Equation $x^2 - 9817y^2 = 1$," *The Analyst*, **4** (1877), 154.

———. "An Error in Barlow's 'Theory of Numbers,'" *Bulletin of the Philosophical Society of Washington*, **11** (1888), 592.

———. "Solution of Problem: [$x^2 - 5658y^2 = 1$ in Integers]," *Mathematical Questions from the Educational Times*, **26** (1876), 87.

———. "Solution to Problem: Find the Least Integral Values of x and y That Will Satisfy the Equation $x^2 - 9781y^2 = 1$," *Mathematical Visitor*, **1** (1877–1881), 26.

Martin, A., and Hart, D. S. "Solution to Problems: [$241x^2 + 67x = 1$ Is a Square; $953z^2 + 87z + 1$ Is a Square; the Least Values That Will Make $x^2 - 5693y^2 = -1$]," *Mathematical Questions from the Educational Times*, **25** (1876), 97.

Merriman, M. "Cattle Problem of Archimedes," *Popular Science Monthly*, **67** (1905), 660.

Whitford, E. E.   *Pell Equation*.   New York: Columbia University Press, 1912.

Wright, H. N.   *First Course in Theory of Numbers*.   New York: J. Wiley & Sons, 1939.

Young, J. W. A.   *Monographs on Topics of Modern Mathematics*.   New York: Dover Publications, Inc., 1955.

CHAPTER XXIII

MORPHOLOGY

THE TRAVELERS in Number Land now approach the outposts of the well-nigh inaccessible Realm of Forms. Around us are nebulous shades arranging themselves into intricate and bizarre patterns. Dense, almost impenetrable vapors are forming Ternary Quadratics and Quaternary Cubics. The services of a guide are indispensable here and we overwhelm him with questions. He tells us about the leaders of this realm: Lagrange and Legendre, in the very forefront, and the venerable Karl Friedrich Gauss. We hear of the binary quadratics of Dedekind and Klein, the dexterity of Poincaré, and the discoveries of Dirichlet and Hermite, Kronecker and Cayley, Jacobi and Smith—we soon lose track of them, there are so many.

We are bewildered by the guide's vocabulary—automorphs and polymorphs, monomorphs and idoneals, proper and improper equivalence, bin-aurifeuillians. There seems to be no end to them; they sound almost like a foreign language....

*   *   *

The theory of forms is one of the most difficult branches of an inherently recondite subject. It has ramifications in almost all branches of mathematics. In our brief visit we can be introduced to only the most elementary of its elements.

Take the sum of any two squares, for instance, $1^2 + 2^2 = 5$. Multiply this number by the sum of any two squares, for example, $2^2 + 7^2 = 53$. The product 265 is also the sum of two squares—either $16^2 + 3^2$ or $12^2 + 11^2$. The product of the sum of two squares by the sum of two squares is always the sum of two squares:

$$(x^2 + y^2)(a^2 + b^2) = (ax + by)^2 + (bx - ay)^2$$
$$= (ax - by)^2 + (bx + ay)^2.$$

This is but one of numerous instances where the offspring of a mathematical union inherits the characteristics of its parents.

More remarkable still is the corresponding relation for trinomials of which the above is really a special case.   Thus

$$(x^2 + axy + by^2)(t^2 + atu + bu^2) = r^2 + ars + bs^2.$$

The numbers a and b are given constants, and this formula tells us that if two numbers M and N can be expressed as $x^2 + axy + by^2$ and $t^2 + atu + bu^2$ respectively, then it is always possible to find two integers r and s so that the product MN equals $r^2 + ars + bs^2$.   These two integers are found from the relation:

$$r = xt - byu,$$
$$s = yt + xu + ayu.$$

If $x = 4, y = 3, t = 2, u = 1$, and a and b are the numbers 7 and 5, then $M = 4^2 + 7 \cdot 4 \cdot 3 + 5 \cdot 3^2 = 145$ and $N = 2^2 + 7 \cdot 2 \cdot 1 + 5 \cdot 1^2 = 23$. Then $MN = 145 \cdot 23 = 3335$, and this number can be expressed in terms of the same a and b and numbers $r = 4 \cdot 2 - 5 \cdot 3 \cdot 1 = -7$, $s = 3 \cdot 2 + 4 \cdot 1 + 7 \cdot 3 \cdot 1 = 31$ as $(-7)^2 + 7(-7)(31) + 5 \cdot 31^2$.

Chapter XXII dealt with the Pell equation

$$x^2 - Dy^2 = 1.$$

From two solutions of this equation another can be obtained by the relation

$$(x_1^2 - Dy_1^2)(x_2^2 - Dy_2^2) = (x_1x_2 + Dy_1y_2)^2 - D(x_1y_2 + x_2y_1)^2 = 1.$$

This is another instance where the product of two expressions of a certain form yields an expression of the same form.   From the two solutions $4^2 - 15 \cdot 1^2 = 1$ and $31^2 - 15 \cdot 8^2 = 1$, there results

$$244^2 - 15 \cdot 63^2 = 1.$$

It is also true that:

$$(x_1^2 - Dy_1^2)(x_2^2 - Dy_2^2) = (x_1x_2 - Dy_1y_2)^2 - D(x_1y_2 - x_2y_1)^2.$$

Similarly,

$$(x_1^2 + Dy_1^2)(x_2^2 + Dy_2^2) = (x_1x_2 \pm Dy_1y_2)^2 + D(x_1y_2 \mp x_2y_1)^2.$$

*   *   *

A great deal of attention has been bestowed on "binary quadratic forms"—expressions like $ax^2 + bxy + cy^2$—because of certain relations by means of which a number expressed in such a form may be factored or recognized as a prime. We have already found that an odd integer which is expressible as the sum of two relatively prime squares in but one way must be a prime or one of its powers. In Chapter XXI we found how to factor a number, N, when it is expressible as the sum of two squares in two or more ways and also when it is expressible as $x^2 + Dy^2$ in two or more ways. But these methods can be greatly extended, by abstruse but engrossing considerations.

A number N which is expressible in the form $x^2 + Dy^2$ in only *one* way and where x^2 is prime to Dy^2, is a prime, a power of a prime, or the double of either of these quantities provided D does not exceed 10 and also for certain larger values of D. Stated another way, if a composite number is expressible as $x^2 + Dy^2$, where x^2 and Dy^2 are relatively prime and D does not exceed 10, then there must be at least one other way to express the composite number in this form. For $D = 7$, $x = 5$, $y = 3$, we have $N = 5^2 + 7 \cdot 3^2 = 88$, and since 88 is composite and 5^2 and $7 \cdot 3^2$ are relatively prime, there must be at least one other representation of 88 as a square plus seven times another square. This proves to be the case, because $88 = 9^2 + 7 \cdot 1^2$. Had we taken $8^2 + 7 \cdot 3^2 = 127$, and knowing that 127 is a prime, we can be assured that there is no other way of expressing this number in the form $x^2 + 7y^2$. Again, $14 = 3^2 + 5 \cdot 1^2$, but although 14 is composite, there is no other way of expressing it as $x^2 + 5y^2$ because it is twice a prime, $2 \cdot 7$.

The least value of D for which a *composite* number is expressible in the form $x^2 + Dy^2$ in only *one* way is 11, even though the number is not a prime or a power of a prime or the double of one of these and although its two terms are relatively prime. For instance, in $69 = 5^2 + 11 \cdot 2^2$, the two terms are relatively prime, 69 is not a prime or a power of a prime; nevertheless it cannot be expressed as $x^2 + 11y^2$ in any other manner.

When an integer is expressible in only one way in the form $x^2 + Dy^2$ (or $x^2 - Dy^2$), it is called monomorph; if in more than one way, polymorph. There are altogether only 65 positive values of D known for which the fact that a number is monomorph makes it definitely a prime, a power of a prime, or the double of one of these.

These 65 integers, shown in Table 97, are termed "idoneal numbers" and there are no others below the limit 100000. For other integers, D, as 11, 14, 17, 19, 20, etc., a number $x^2 + Dy^2$ may be monomorph and composite without being a power of a prime or its double.

TABLE 97

Positive Idoneal Numbers

1	16	48	120	312
2	18	57	130	330
3	21	58	133	345
4	22	60	165	357
5	24	70	168	385
6	25	72	177	408
7	28	78	190	462
8	30	85	210	520
9	33	88	232	760
10	37	93	240	840
12	40	102	253	1320
13	42	105	273	1365
15	45	112	280	1848

Idoneal numbers help in determining whether or not a number is prime. Suppose, for instance, it had been ascertained in some way that $N = 1132861 = 1043^2 + 93 \cdot 22^2$. The number 93 is an idoneal; therefore if N cannot be expressed as $x^2 + 93y^2$ in some other way it is surely a prime or a power of one. If we divide N by 93, the quotient is $12181+$, consequently y cannot be greater than the square root of 12181 or 110. It is therefore easy to verify that no other values of x and y exist satisfying the relation, and therefore N must be either a prime or an exact power of one. Were 93 not an idoneal, the fact that N is monomorph would be insufficient evidence of its character.

*   *   *

Some numbers, N, can be represented by both the form $x^2 - Dy^2$, and $Dx_1^2 - y_1^2$. Such numbers are termed "antimorphs." The values of D for which this is possible are the ones for which the Pell equation

$$x_n^2 - Dy_n^2 = -1$$

is possible. Thus since $x^2 - 13y^2 = -1$ has solutions, any number which can be expressed in the form $x^2 - 13y^2$ can also be expressed as $13x_1^2 - y_1^2$. But there is no solution for $x_n^2 - 7y_n^2 = -1$; hence $x^2 - 7y^2$ cannot be converted to $7x_1^2 - y_1^2$. The conversion when possible is accomplished by the relations:

$$
\begin{aligned}
N = x^2 - Dy^2 &= -(x^2 - Dy^2)(x_n^2 - Dy_n^2) \\
&= D(xy_n - yx_n)^2 - (xx_n - Dyy_n)^2 \\
&= D(xy_n + yx_n)^2 - (xx_n + Dyy_n)^2.
\end{aligned}
$$

As an example, $x_n = 18$, $y_n = 5$ is a solution of $x_n^2 - 13y_n^2 = -1$. Taking $N = 5^2 - 13 \cdot 1^2 = 12$ where $x = 5$, $y = 1$ we can write N in the antimorph forms:

$$13(5 \cdot 5 - 1 \cdot 18)^2 - (18 \cdot 5 - 13 \cdot 1 \cdot 5)^2 = 13 \cdot 7^2 - 25^2$$

or as

$$13(5 \cdot 5 + 1 \cdot 18)^2 - (18 \cdot 5 + 13 \cdot 1 \cdot 5)^2 = 13 \cdot 43^2 - 155^2.$$

To determine whether it is possible for a given number, N, whose composition is unknown, to be expressed as $x^2 + Dy^2$ or $x^2 - Dy^2$ where D is an assigned number, is not always an easy task.

If D is an idoneal and N is known to be a prime, the determination can be made utilizing principles depending on quadratic residues. The "linear" form of the number indicates the possibility. For values of D not exceeding 19 which are idoneals and not containing any square divisor we have Table 98.

TABLE 98

LINEAR AND QUADRATIC FORMS OF PRIMES

D	Linear Form	Quadratic Form
1	$4K + 1$	$x^2 + y^2$
2	$8K + 1, 3$	$x^2 + 2y^2$
3	$6K + 1$	$x^2 + 3y^2$
5	$20K + 1, 9$	$x^2 + 5y^2$
6	$24K + 1, 7$	$x^2 + 6y^2$
7	$14K + 1, 9, 11$	$x^2 + 7y^2$
10	$40K + 1, 9, 11, 19$	$x^2 + 10y^2$
13	$52K + 1, 9, 17, 25, 29, 49$	$x^2 + 13y^2$
15	$30K + 1, 19$	$x^2 + 15y^2$
$- 1$	$4K \pm 1$	$x^2 - y^2$
$- 2$	$8K \pm 1$	$x^2 - 2y^2$
$- 3$	$12K + 1$	$x^2 - 3y^2$
$- 5$	$10K \pm 1$	$x^2 - 5y^2$
$- 6$	$24K + 1, 19$	$x^2 - 6y^2$
$- 7$	$28K + 1, 9, 25$	$x^2 - 7y^2$
$- 10$	$40K \pm 1, 9$	$x^2 - 10y^2$
$- 11$	$44K + 1, 5, 9, 25, 37$	$x^2 - 11y^2$
$- 13$	$26K \pm 1, 3, 9$	$x^2 - 13y^2$
$- 14$	$56K + 1, 9, 11, 25, 43, 51$	$x^2 - 14y^2$
$- 15$	$60K + 1, 49$	$x^2 - 15y^2$
$- 17$	$34K \pm 1, 9, 13, 15$	$x^2 - 17y^2$
$- 19$	$76K + 1, 5, 9, 17, 25, 45, 49, 61, 73$	$x^2 - 19y^2$

If we wish to test the possibility of expressing the prime 151 in the form $x^2 + 7y^2$, we divide it by 14 and obtain a remainder of 11; therefore 151 is of the form $14K + 11$ and it must accordingly be possible to express it as $x^2 + 7y^2$ as affirmed by the table. This proves to be true, since $12^2 + 7 \cdot 1^2 = 151$. Again, for the prime 79 to be expressible as $x^2 - 5y^2$, we find that 79 is of the form $10K - 1$; hence it is possible and in fact $18^2 - 5 \cdot 7^2 = 79$ is the solution.

*   *   *

The theory of quadratic forms enables one to determine the possible forms of the divisors of a number of a given form. For example, we have already discovered that every divisor of the sum of two relatively prime squares must itself be the sum of two squares. Similarly, the divisors of $x^2 \pm 2y^2$ are of that form and also $2x^2 \pm y^2$. Every odd divisor of $x^2 + 3y^2$ and of its antimorph $3x^2 + y^2$ has the same form and this is also true of $x^2 - 5y^2$ and $5y^2 - x^2$.

The number 18000001 has the form $2(3000)^2 + 1$; therefore every prime divisor of it must have the form $2x^2 + y^2$ or $x^2 + 2y^2$, its antimorph. Table 98 shows that the linear form of primes whose quadratic form is $x^2 + 2y^2$, is $8K + 1$ or $8K + 3$. Therefore all prime numbers of the form $8K + 5$ or $8K + 7$ can be immediately excluded in testing for possible divisors of 18000001. This consideration reduces to one-half the number of primes which may be divisors of the number. The two prime divisors turn out to be $3307 = 43^2 + 2 \cdot 27^2$ and $5443 = 49^2 + 2 \cdot 39^2$. Both are of the form $8K + 3$ and $x^2 + 2y^2$.

*   *   *

Some numbers may be expressed as sums of like powers in several ways. Mention was made in Chapter XV of the forms of numbers expressible as the sum of two squares. The analysis leading to such representations for higher powers is far from easy. The smallest number representable as the sum of two cubes in really distinct ways is $1729 = 1^3 + 12^3 = 9^3 + 10^3$, and it is probable that the smallest so representable in three ways is

$$175959000 = 70^3 + 560^3 = 198^3 + 552^3 = 315^3 + 525^3.$$

There are only 10 numbers less than 100000 expressible as the sum of two cubes in two ways.   The smallest number representable doubly as the sum of two biquadrates is probably

$$635318657 = 59^4 + 158^4 = 133^4 + 134^4.$$

*   *   *

In the modern theory of quadratic forms, the coefficients a, b, and c of a form like $ax^2 + bxy + cy^2$ are detached from their variables and glide like disembodied spirits through mathematical shadow worlds far beyond the ken of ordinary mortals.   But we must hurry toward our journey's end lest profound reflections on matters morphological make our very thoughts amorphous.

BIBLIOGRAPHY

Barlow, P.   *Theory of Numbers*.   London: J. Johnson & Co., 1811.

Carmichael, R. D.   *Theory of Numbers and Diophantine Analysis*.   New York: Dover Publications, Inc., 1959.

Cunningham, A.   *Quadratic Partitions*.   London: F. Hodgson, 1904.

Dickson, L. E.   *History of the Theory of Numbers*.   3 vols.   New York: Chelsea Publishing Co., 1950.

————.   *Introduction to the Theory of Numbers*.   New York: Dover Publications, Inc., 1957.

————.   *Modern Elementary Theory of Numbers*.   Chicago: University of Chicago Press, 1939.

————.   *Studies in the Theory of Numbers*.   New York: Chelsea Publishing Co., 1962.

Mathews, G. B.   *Theory of Numbers*.   New York: Chelsea Publishing Co., 1961.

Vinogradov, I. M.   *Elements of Number Theory*.   New York: Dover Publications, Inc., 1954.

CHAPTER XXIV

THE STONE WALL

Now WE APPROACH the end of our visit to Number Land. We shall say adieu at a stone wall which has remained impenetrable to the world's most astute mathematicians. Fermat, the great Frenchman, said he had breached it but some mathematicians think he was mistaken. Against this belief we have the knowledge of his exceptional mathematical integrity; nothing which he said he had proved has ever been disproved, and in the single instance in which he stated something he believed to be true which posterity disproved, he made it clear that he could find no adequate demonstration.

Fermat owned a copy of Diophantus's work on numbers and made numerous marginal notes in it. On the margin of the page devoted to the proposition, "To divide a given square number into 2 squares," Fermat's note says, "On the other hand it is impossible to separate a cube into 2 cubes or a biquadrate into 2 biquadrates or generally any power except a square into 2 powers with the same exponent. I have discovered a truly marvelous proof of this, which however the margin is not large enough to contain." Posterity has wished many times that the margin of Bachet's *Diophantus* had been wider or Fermat less secretive.

Fermat's statement means that $x^n + y^n = z^n$ has no solution in integers or rational fractions when n is greater than 2. He was to publish a book explaining his methods of solving problems in number theory, but unfortunately death, which waits for no man, summoned him. Consequently not the least scrap of evidence is extant indicating how Fermat arrived at his conclusion, and despite the most persevering efforts of his successors, the problem is still unsolved. The equation $x^n + y^n = z^n$ is known as Fermat's "Last Theorem," not because he gasped it out and then expired nor because it was the last one he enunciated, but rather because it remains the last of his theorems which has not since been proved or refuted.

Fermat's reputation for veracity should be strong evidence for believing he had a proof. Only once has he been found incorrect

He believed that $2^{2^x}+1$ is always a prime, whereas for many values of x these "Fermat Numbers" are composite (see Chapter XVII). Finding these exceptions served merely to enhance his reputation in the light of his avowal that he could find no proof to substantiate his belief.

But reputations, even when they are as sound as Fermat's, do not establish proofs. Many real and would-be mathematicians have tried to prove or disprove his theorem. Like the quest for the Northwest Passage, the efforts of these men—and women—though vain, has resulted in the discovery of fruitful mathematical countries yielding a wealth of information that might not have been secured had the theorem been readily proved. A veritable new number continent was discovered by Kummer as a direct consequence of the attempt to solve Fermat's problem.

Wherein lies the difficulty? We have learned in Chapter XIV how to find as many solutions as we please of the equation $x^2+y^2 = z^2$. Why should there not be solutions to $x^3+y^3 = z^3$ or $x^4+y^4 = z^4$? There is no trick at all to finding two cubes whose sum is equal to that of two other cubes, for example, $12^3+1^3 = 10^3+9^3$. But there must be some subtle property of integers, which in the harmonious world of mathematics, would cause a dissonance of logic—a flaw in the pattern—were it possible to have $x^n+y^n = z^n$, or the allied equation $x^n+y^n+z^n = 0$, where n is co-prime to $x, y,$ or z.

Starting from totally dissimilar origins, investigators have proved that the equation or the allied one are impossible for all values of n smaller than 100, except perhaps 37, 59, and 67; then included these numbers among the impossibles; then extended the limit to 7000; 14000; 8332403; 253747889. It is also impossible for $n = 2^{3217} -1$, a prime. But no matter what the approach, the conclusion has always been the same—the equation is impossible in rational numbers. The theorem holds for all integral values of n except those fulfilling certain complicated conditions, yet since infinity encompasses much territory, the theorem cannot be called proven until every last exception has been thoroughly dispatched and the impossibility of the equation demonstrated for *all* values of n. W. W. R. Ball said, "But mere numerical verifications have little value; no one doubts the truth of the theorem, and its interest lies in the fact that we have not yet succeeded in obtaining a rigorous demonstration of it."

If we start with $z^n -y^n = x^n$ and factor, there results:

$$(z^{n/2}+y^{n/2})(z^{n/2}-y^{n/2}) = x^n.$$

We can take x, y, z as relatively prime, since, were there a common factor it could have been canceled out initially. Also n will be assumed co-prime to x, y, or z. Next, if the two expressions in parentheses have a common factor, so also has their sum $2z^{n/2}$. But since z and y are relatively prime, the only common factor the expressions in the two parentheses can have is 2. Then, since their product is an exact nth power, we must have either:

$$z^{n/2} + y^{n/2} = 2^{n-1}p^n \quad \text{and} \quad z^{n/2} - y^{n/2} = 2q^n$$

or

$$z^{n/2} + y^{n/2} = 2p^n \quad \text{and} \quad z^{n/2} - y^{n/2} = 2^{n-1}q^n,$$

as this will make their product $2^n p^n q^n$, which is an exact nth power as required. In either case $x = 2pq$. Solving for z and y, we have by addition and subtraction:

$$z^{n/2} = 2^{n-2}p^n + q^n, \quad y^{n/2} = 2^{n-2}p^n - q^n$$

in the first case, or

$$z^{n/2} = p^n + 2^{n-2}q^n, \quad y^{n/2} = p^n - 2^{n-2}q^n$$

in the second case. Either of the results:

$$z = (2^{n-2}p^n + q^n)^{2/n}, \quad y = (2^{n-2}p^n - q^n)^{2/n}$$

or

$$z = (p^n + 2^{n-2}q^n)^{2/n}, \quad y = (p^n - 2^{n-2}q^n)^{2/n}$$

are intractable; no solution in integers or fractions for n greater than 2 has been found nor has it been proved that solutions are impossible.

* * *

Before we try another attack on the general case, let us consider a few fundamentals and then apply them to proving that $x^4 + y^4 = z^4$ is impossible—a relatively simple demonstration and incidentally an illustration of Fermat's method of infinite descent. If two integers are relatively prime and their product is a square, a little consideration will show that each alone must be a square. For the distinguishing characteristic of a square integer, N, is that all the exponents are even when N is expressed as the product of powers of primes thus:

$$N = p_1^{2a_1} \cdot p_2^{2a_2} \cdot p_3^{2a_3} \ldots p_n^{2a_n}.$$

For instance, 1936 when expressed as the product of primes and their powers is equal to $2^4 \cdot 11^2$, and since both exponents are even, the number is a square. But $1940 = 2^2 \cdot 5 \cdot 97$, and since 5 and 97 have odd exponents (unity) the number is not a square.

If two integers are relatively prime, they cannot contain common prime factors; hence, if their product is a square, the even exponents of the primes constituting the square must have been present in each of the two factors separately, which is to say that each of the two factors was originally a square. And, of course, the same thing would hold for any number of integers which are relatively prime, each to each; if their product is an exact square, then each one of them is such a square.

Similarly, if the product of two co-prime integers is an nth power, then each number alone must be an nth power. Now consider the case $x^4 + y^4 = z^4$, where all three variables may be taken relatively prime—for if any two of them had a common factor the third would have to have it and it could be canceled out. Then $(x^2)^2 + (y^2)^2 = z^4$ will be impossible if $(x^2)^2 + (y^2)^2 = z^2$ is impossible. The latter equation requires that: $x^2 = m^2 - n^2$, $y^2 = 2mn$, $z = m^2 + n^2$ by the rules for Pythagorean triangles of Chapter XIV. Here m and n must be co-prime, otherwise x, y, z would not be; also they must be of different parity—one odd, the other even—otherwise $m^2 - n^2$ and $m^2 + n^2$ would both be even and x, y, z would have at least the common factor 2 contrary to the assumption that they are co-prime. From $x^2 = m^2 - n^2$, it follows that m cannot be even and n odd because m is obviously the hypotenuse of a primitive Pythagorean triangle and is always odd, since one of the legs is always even. Therefore, n must be even and m odd (see Formula 1 of Chapter XIV). Therefore, in $x^2 = m^2 - n^2$, we must let $n = 2pq$, $m = p^2 + q^2$, and $x = p^2 - q^2$, again by the Pythagorean triangle formulas. Then since $y^2 = 2mn$, it is also equal to $2(p^2 + q^2)(2pq) = 4pq(p^2 + q^2)$. Now p and q must also be co-prime, and since $4pq(p^2 + q^2)$ is a square, y^2, it follows that p, q and $p^2 + q^2$ are all squares. Let, therefore, $p = r^2$, $q = s^2$, $p^2 + q^2 = t^2$. Substituting the values of p and q in this last equation, we have $r^4 + s^4 = t^2$. Also, since $x = p^2 - q^2$, we have $x = r^4 - s^4$. And from $y^2 = 4pq(p^2 + q^2) = 4r^2s^2t^2$, we have $y = 2rst$. Also $z = m^2 + n^2 = (p^2 + q^2)^2 + (2pq)^2 = (r^4 + s^4)^2 + (2r^2s^2)^2 = t^4 + 4r^4s^4$. Since $z = t^4 + 4r^4s^4$, it follows that z is larger than t^4 alone or t is smaller than $z^{1/4}$.

Now comes the method of infinite descent. The equation $r^4 + s^4 = t^2$ has exactly the same form as $x^4 + y^4 = z^2$, but t is smaller than $z^{1/4}$. Therefore, if the latter equation has a solution (zeros excluded), there must be another solution in smaller integers (since t is smaller than z). Similarly, if $r^4 + s^4 = t^2$ has a solution, then there must exist still another solution with a t_1 smaller than $t^{1/4}$. This argument can be continued indefinitely. But this is absurd since if z were originally a finite positive integer, one could not indefinitely find smaller positive integers than z satisfying similar equations. Therefore, the equation $x^4 + y^4 = z^4$ must be impossible.

Some investigators have used a plausible modification of Fermat's method of infinite descent towards an attempted solution of the problem. Instead of "descending" from some starting point to a reductio ad absurdum, it has been argued that a solution is impossible if it depends on a *larger* or smaller solution. The equation forms a sort of charmed circle that cannot be penetrated. One author calls this a proof by the method of recurrence instead of by infinite descent or ascent. He says, perhaps a trifle sententiously, "When we have a complete solution of an equation (or system of equations) and this solution cannot yield solutions of a certain kind, solutions of that kind do not exist. This it cannot do when it requires us first to have such a solution before we can get such a solution, whether the required solution be smaller, equal or greater than the solution for which it is required."*

The equation $x^3 + y^3 = z^3$ is not amenable to the type of demonstration used for $x^4 + y^4 = z^4$ and the proof of its impossibility is more difficult. The Arabs knew that it was impossible 700 years before Fermat's day and even possessed a proof, albeit a faulty one.

* * *

In the general case, a proof need be given for prime exponents p only, since for any composite exponent $n = mp$ where p is a prime factor, we have $(x^m)^p + (y^m)^p = (z^m)^p$, so that if the equation is impossible for $X^p + Y^p = Z^p$ where X, Y, Z are any integers and p a prime, it will also be impossible when X, Y, Z are powers. The equation is obviously impossible when n is a multiple of 4 since we have found it impossible for $n = 4$.

Now let us review some elementary principles of factoring. The expression $x^2 + y^2$ cannot be factored, meaning thereby that it cannot be factored into "real" linear factors. If we insist on *linear* factors,

---

* C. M. Walsh, *An Attempted Proof of Fermat's Last Theorem by a New Method*, New York: G. E. Steckert & Co., 1932.

nevertheless, we must introduce the imaginary quantity $i = \sqrt{-1}$. Thus: $x^2+y^2 = (x+iy)(x-iy)$. It will be remembered that $i^2 = \sqrt{-1} \cdot \sqrt{-1} = -1$, so that $(x+iy)(x-iy)$ is equal to $x^2-i^2y^2 = x^2+y^2$. If we factor x^p+y^p, where p is an odd number, in particular an odd prime, we obtain:

$$x^p+y^p = (x+y)(x^{p-1}-x^{p-2}y+x^{p-3}y^2-x^{p-4}y^3+ \ldots -xy^{p-2}+y^{p-1}).$$

For example,

$$x^7+y^7 = (x+y)(x^6-x^5y+x^4y^2-x^3y^3+x^2y^4-xy^5+y^6).$$

The long expression is an "algebraic prime factor," that is, there is no way of factoring it into the product of two or more other expressions of lower degree. If again we force the issue and insist on linear factors, we must once more introduce the imaginary i, but this time in not quite so simple a form as it appeared when factoring x^2+y^2.

A little patience will now be required while a few somewhat difficult ideas are being expounded. Every number x has *two* square roots, $+\sqrt{x}$ and $-\sqrt{x}$. Every number has three cube roots, one real and two complex. For instance, the three cube roots of unity are $(-1+i\sqrt{3})/2$, $(-1-i\sqrt{3})/2$, and 1. Any one of these quantities cubed gives $+1$. If for convenience we represent $(-1+i\sqrt{3})/2$ by "a," then a^2 will become $(-1-i\sqrt{3})/2$, the second "complex cube root of unity," and a^3 will be simply $+1$. In a similar manner there are n nth roots of unity similarly obtainable as powers of the first one.

Our insistence on separating $x^{p-1}-x^{p-2}y+x^{p-3}y^2-x^{p-4}y^3+ \ldots -xy^{p-2}+y^{p-1})$ into linear factors injects the complex pth roots of unity into the matter. The equation $x^p+y^p = z^p$ becomes

$$(x+y)(x+ay)(x+a^2y)(x+a^3y)\ldots(x+a^{p-1}y) = z^p,$$

where each power of "a" is one of these complex pth roots of 1. These linear factors are relatively prime, and one would suppose, therefore, that each is an exact pth power since their product is z^p. This is certainly true of real numbers. Is it true of complex numbers which involve the puckish i?

Once we start questioning this, it is almost as though we begin to doubt our sanity. Our mathematical house of cards threatens to fall about our ears, and in the distance we discern the evanescent grin of Alice's Cheshire cat bearing a startling resemblance to the shade of a departed Fermat. The theory of numbers rests on the "unique factorization theorem," that is, on the fact that a number can be expressed as the product of powers of primes in one and but one way. Although true in the real number realm, it develops that this basic property of integers does not hold in every number realm.

Suppose we invent a realm comprising only integers of the form $4x+1$: 1, 5, 9, 13, 17, 21, 25, 29, 33, etc. Any other integer is beyond our ken; we shall live only in the world of $4x+1$. Would not 9 be a prime number in this realm, having only the factors unity and itself? "How about $3 \cdot 3$?" you ask. But there is no such integer as 3 in this new domain. The number 21 would also be a prime but 25 would be composite and a square to boot, since 5 and 5^2 are members of the class. The number 49 would be a prime since 7 is not in the domain.

Now we begin to arrive at some startling results. The product of 9 and 49, both "primes," is $441 = 21^2$. Both 441 and 21 belong to the new system. We have, therefore, come to the odd conclusion that the product of two primes (and prime to each other, of course) is a square! Again, the integers 9, 21, 33, and 77 are all primes in the new number system. But $693 = 9 \cdot 77 = 21 \cdot 33$, so that 693 can be expressed as the product of powers of primes (the first powers in this case) in *two* ways.

In ordinary arithmetic, an integer which divides the product of two integers without dividing either of them alone cannot be a prime. But here 693 is divisible by 21 whereas 9 and 77 are not, yet 21 *is* a prime.

The peculiar state of affairs in the realm $4x+1$ can be rectified by admitting into it the "transcendental" numbers $4x-1$. Then everything "returns to normalcy" and the birds again twitter blithely in the treetops.

The mathematician loves to reason by analogy, regardless of the bizarre conclusions he may be led to. If instead of confining ourselves to restricted realms on the "real" number planet, we take a trip to the "complex" number world characterized by such expressions as $3+2\sqrt{-1}$ or generally $a+bi$, where i again stands for the square root of minus one, and a and b are integers, what queer new mathematical inhabitants shall we find? Does the unique factorization theorem hold here?

We start with the novel idea that $\sqrt{-1}$ or i is a unit on the "complex" planet since it divides every number $a+bi$. Thus $3+2\sqrt{-1}$ or $3+2i$, when divided by i, becomes $-3i+2$. (The reader will recall from algebra that $i^2 = -1$, $i^3 = -i$, and $i^4 = 1$.) Similarly 5 is exactly divisible by the "unit," yielding the quotient $-5i$. There are four units in all in this realm, ± 1 and $\pm i$. An integer without factors of the form $a \pm bi$, where a and b are ordinary integers, is defined as a prime. When it has factors of this form, it is composite. We have for example:

$$5 = (2+i)(2-i) = 4-i^2 = 4--1 = 4+1$$
$$13 = (3+2i)(3-2i) = 9-4i^2 = 9--4 = 9+4$$
$$17 = (4+i)(4-i), \text{ etc.,}$$

all *composite* numbers. In fact since $(a+bi)(a-bi) = a^2+b^2$ and since all primes of the form $4x+1$ can be expressed as the sum of two squares, it follows that on this complex planet all ordinary primes of the form $4x+1$ are composite integers. The only real integers which are primes in this field are common primes of the form $4x-1$ such as 3, 7, 11, 19, etc. The divisors $2 \pm i$, $3 \pm 2i$, $4 \pm i$, $a \pm bi$ of the composites 5, 13, 17, etc., are also termed "primes," and lastly, the number $1-i$, which is neither real nor a divisor of a prime of the form $4x+1$, is a prime. The number 2 occupies the unique position of being a square since it is equal to $i(1-i)^2$, the product of a square and one of the units.

It so happens that every composite algebraic integer of the form $a+bi$ is the product of powers of "primes," as defined for this realm, in but a single way, just as in the case with real integers. For example, $-23+41i = (1+i)(2+i)(3+2i)(4+i)$. All these factors have no divisors of the same form;* hence they are all primes, and the product of no other prime numbers is $-23+41i$. This is also true of an algebraic integer in a realm like $a+b\sqrt{3}i$. One might hastily conclude therefore that unique factorization holds in all realms, but such is not the case.

We find that on the complex planet in the realm of $a+b\sqrt{-5}$, a number like 21 is the product of powers of "primes" in three different ways, namely, $3 \cdot 7$, or

$$(4+i\sqrt{5})(4-i\sqrt{5}) \quad \text{or} \quad (1+2i\sqrt{5})(1-2i\sqrt{5}).$$

All of these numbers are "primes," that is, they cannot be divided by integers of the realm other than the units.

---

* To demonstrate this, one assumes that a number like $3+2i$ is the product of two factors $a+bi$ and $c+di$. Their product is $(ac-bd)+i(ad+bc)$, and equating real and imaginary parts, we have $ac-bd = 3$, $ad+bc = 2$. Neither positive nor negative integers can satisfy these two equations. Hence $3+2i$ is a prime.

Again, the product of $2+i\sqrt{5}$ and $2-i\sqrt{5}$ is 9, a square, although both factors are "primes," since neither is the product of two non-unit integers of the realm.   Chaos?   Yea, verily.   When the mathematicians discovered that an "algebraic integer" could be factored in several different ways as the product of primes and their powers, they were almost beside themselves.   They must have felt like some of the modern physicists who have reduced all matter to a mathematical equation.   Of course the ploughman then, as now, plodded homeward along his weary way little recking of such disconcerting dilemmas. But he has apparently survived unscathed, so perhaps it doesn't matter very much after all.

In any case, affairs had to be put to rights in the mathematical world, and the ingenious Kummer proceeded to do it.   He reasoned as follows: If order can be restored on the real-integer planet and unique factorization effected by admitting integers of the form $4x-1$ into a restricted realm like $4x+1$, might not some numbers be discovered which, admitted into a realm on the complex planet, would also effect unique factorization?   He invented a class of numbers called "ideals" which served to restore such order to a threatened anarchy.   In the realm $a+b\sqrt{-5}$, a number T is called an ideal if T^2 equals either $c+d\sqrt{-5}$ or $c-d\sqrt{-5}$ so that $T = \sqrt{c \pm d\sqrt{-5}}$. The numbers c and d must be integers and may have a greatest common divisor which is a square or five times a square.

In this realm there are four classes into which numbers termed "primes" in our common realm fall.   Class 1 comprises common primes such as

$$29 = (3+2i\sqrt{5})(3-2i\sqrt{5})$$
$$41 = (6+ i\sqrt{5})(6- i\sqrt{5})$$
$$61 = (4+3i\sqrt{5})(4-3i\sqrt{5}),$$

each of which is representable in the form a^2+5b^2.   Such numbers are composites in the realm $a+b\sqrt{-5}$.

In the second class are 3, 7, 23, ... which cannot be expressed in the form a^2+5b^2 although their squares can:

$$3^2 = (2+i\sqrt{5})(2-i\sqrt{5})$$
$$7^2 = (2+3i\sqrt{5})(2-3i\sqrt{5})$$
$$23^2 = (22+3i\sqrt{5})(22-3i\sqrt{5}).$$

The third class contains 2, 11, 13, 17, ..., and neither they nor their squares can be expressed in the form $a^2 + 5b^2$. These numbers are primes in both the common realm and the realm $a + b\sqrt{-5}$. Last is the number 5, in a class by itself. It is a "square" number since $5 = i^2(\sqrt{-5})^2$.

The numbers of the second class are evidently the product of ideals; for instance, since $3^2 = (2 + i\sqrt{5})(2 - i\sqrt{5})$ and $\sqrt{2 + i\sqrt{5}}$ and $\sqrt{2 - i\sqrt{5}}$ are each ideals, say T_1 and T_2, we have:

$$3^2 = (\sqrt{2 + i\sqrt{5}})^2(\sqrt{2 - i\sqrt{5}})^2 = T_1^2 \cdot T_2^2 \quad \text{or} \quad 3 = T_1 \cdot T_2.$$

The ideals are a group of algebraic integers which reproduce themselves by multiplication and addition and thus form a distinct "class." We cannot here take the time to explore even a few of the implications of these numbers.

L. E. Dickson has this to say of Kummer's brain child: "The machinery is so delicate that an expert must handle it with the greatest care and [is] nowadays chiefly of historical interest in view of the simpler and more general theory of R. Dedekind." Many people, in common with the brilliant German mathematician, Leopold Kronecker, abhor such artificialities as are introduced by ideals and general "algebraic numbers." They feel with him that "*Die ganze Zahl schuf der liebe Gott, alles Übrige ist Menschenwerk.*" God created the integers; everything else is the work of man. The reader has at least learned to be wary of hasty assumptions about unique factorization, and is warned against a subtle fallacy which in the past has proved to be a Lorelei to many amateurs and professionals alike who have attempted to prove Fermat's Last Theorem.

*   *   *

But whether by erudite or elementary means, whether by simple or elaborate arguments, every proof of Fermat's Last Theorem has had a flaw in it. In 1823 and again in 1850 the Academy of Science in Paris offered a prize for a perfect proof. This opened the way for thousands of mathematical adventurers and quacks, a peculiar species of moron exhaustively and devastatingly dissected by the pungent Augustus de Morgan in his *Budget of Paradoxes*.

In 1857 the French Academy presented E. E. Kummer, the inventor of ideals, with a gold medal valued at 3000 francs in recognition of his researches in complex numbers although he was not a competitor for the prize.   Never was a mathematician more worthy of it.   It was his investigations which ruled out the possibility of the equation for all exponents smaller than 100 except 37, 59, and 67, these being subsequently dispatched by other means.   The Academy of Brussels offered a prize in 1883 and, after perusing the contributions, handed down an adverse report on all of them.

In 1908, Dr. F. P. Wolfskehl of Darmstadt, Germany, bequeathed 100000 marks for a complete proof to the Königliche Gesellschaft der Wissenschaften zu Göttingen.   "The existence of this prize money has called forth a large number of pseudo-solutions of the problem... the number of untrained workers attacking the problem seems to be increasing," deplored R. D. Carmichael.   Over 1000 false "complete" proofs were presented during the period from 1908 to 1911. Says Tobias Dantzig: "Since then, the many amateurs who had theretofore directed their energies to such problems as squaring the circle and trisecting an angle or the invention of perpetual motion machines have begun to concentrate on the Fermat Theorem.... Luckily the announcement stipulated that contributions must be printed and this may have dampened the ardor of many....   It is characteristic of all such efforts that their authors completely ignore the tremendous amount of work already accomplished; nor are they interested in learning wherein the difficulty lies."

Most of the solutions were published by the authors themselves, since no self-respecting publisher would have risked his reputation to print some of the fatuous lucubrations that were presented.   Many of the contributors would have been incapable of grasping even the beginnings of Kummer's theory of ideals.   This is not meant to imply that only through ideals can the solution to the problem be reached, but that approach seems to have struck closer to its heart than any other.

The caliber of some of the would-be rulers of Mathematica who have essayed to untie the Gordian knot may be measured by the following extracts from a pamphlet published in Boston in 1914 and modestly entitled *The Greater Fermat Theorem Proved* by G. W. Pierce.

The author starts with the brilliant observations that $1^1 + 2^1 = 3^1$ and $6^{-1} + 3^{-1} = 2^{-1}$.   He then discourses lengthily but alas not too eruditely, and triumphantly displays $12^3 + 1^3 = 10^3 + 9^3$ as though it were something unique and novel.   There are of course many such cube pairs, for example: $9^3 + 15^3 = 2^3 + 16^3$; $15^3 + 33^3 = 2^3 + 34^3$; $16^3 + 33^3 = 9^3 + 34^3$; $19^3 + 24^3 = 10^3 + 27^3$; $50^3 + 29^3 = 8^3 + 53^3$ and even three such like sums: $560^3 + 70^3 = 552^3 + 198^3 = 525^3 + 315^3$; and an infinite number of solutions can be obtained from general formulas. Apparently the author was blissfully unaware of these relations. The value of this learned treatise may best be gauged from its ending, which concludes with these strange words:

Having seen in my dream—J. B. not round—a man named "Wakefield," large dark, serious, to whom I had been directed while asleep (for profitable occupation, for the benefit, let us say, of the Belgians?) I was up by gas light writing this Sunday morning, (12/6/14) what I found, entirely New to me (except when $n = 3$, for All positive cardinal whole numbers—and negative? Today, 12/8/14—by accident years ago discovered and proved), no doubt from Fermat?—in my mind: which every test (some corrected mistakes, not God's but mine) is fixing how, at IIII, 8 P.M. just before dark, in my Belief: THE SUM OF THE nth (odd > 2) powers of many Arithmetical Progressions divided by the SUM OF THE first powers, is a whole number!? I suppose (repeated, repeated, Present, Past, Future, written and printed) a brain and spirit phaenomenon. Mother was all spirit and prophetess, "George, you'll never make a poet!" Father, body, which I inherited, and brain; to much for my (by two years) elder (first child) brother who was not *born*, a Caesar, and for (the 5th and last) a proud, sweet boy, preternaturally wise, who called me in my absence, 14 years younger, "Our George" and had dropsy upon at six, whom I somewhat Suspect of helping me on. For lasting occupation in Heaven which some people fear they may not have!! I offer Arithmetic—Algebra, my box game.

George Winslow Pierce,
A.B. Harvard College 1864
A.M.   ,,   ,,   1867
P.P. (Professor of Punctuation—
  Boston Sunday Journal (1)
  126 W. Concord St.,
  Boston, Massachusetts, U.S.A.

Author of *The Life-Romance of an Algebraist*, Boston 1891, distributed to 100 foreign libraries by my gift through The Smithsonian.
  (For sale at Old Corner Bookstore, Boston or (if ordered by mail) by the Author.
  With a Merry Christmas, Free (100 copies) to Friends Indeed.

*   *   *

Both the mercenary and the slightly irrational have become discouraged in recent years. The inflation in Germany after World War I reduced the 100000-mark prize to a fraction of a cent, which is all that these individuals will find in the crock even were they to discover the end of the rainbow. "Post mortems over the 'proofs' which fall, stillborn from the press are being held in the Sprechsaal of the Archiv der Mathematik and Physik." There are of course many careful and serious investigators ceaselessly hammering away at the problem, and it is not too rash to predict that this century may see its complete solution. A niche in the "Hall of Fame" is waiting for the man or woman who can do it.

An intrepid explorer, A. Wieferich, blazed the trail which in recent times has pushed the limit for the exponent, below which the equation is impossible, up into the millions. He discovered that if p is a prime, the equation $x^p + y^p + z^p = 0$ cannot be possible in integers unless $2^{p-1} - 1 \equiv 0 \bmod p^2$. This immediately excludes values of p below 1093 since $p = 1093$ is the least prime whose square exactly divides $2^{p-1} - 1$ (see Chapter VI). Wieferich obtained 100 marks from the interest of the Wolfskehl fund for this discovery. Quick to follow along this trail came Mirimanoff, who demonstrated that $3^{p-1} - 1$ must also be divisible by p^2, and Vandiver, who in 1914 proved that $5^{p-1} - 1$ must be so divisible. Then Frobenius arrived with 11 and 17, and it has also been shown that if p is a prime of the form $6x - 1$, then $7^{p-1} - 1$; $13^{p-1} - 1$; and $19^{p-1} - 1$ must each be divisible by p^2, if Fermat's Last Theorem is to hold. Under such restrictions, the prime exponent p was continually raised, and in 1941 it was shown that if $x^p + y^p + z^p = 0$ and no one of x, y, and z is a multiple of p, then p must be not less than 253747889. Recently it was shown that $2^{3217} - 1$, also, cannot satisfy the equation.

*   *   *

Fermat's Last Theorem was tempting bait not only to the untrained amateur but to the greatest pundits. Few could resist trying their hand at it, and some burned their fingers badly before deciding to give up the attempt. Peter Barlow, who wrote the first book on number theory in English and to whom all American admirers of the theory of numbers owe an immense debt of gratitude, was ignominiously worsted at the very outset of a fairly elaborate proof. He started with the rather plausible assumption that if you add together common fractions in lowest terms and if any denominator contains a factor not contained in all the other denominators, then the sum of the fractions cannot be an integer. But

$$\frac{1}{2} + \frac{5}{3} + \frac{5}{6} = 3,$$

even though 2 is not contained in 3, nor 6 in either. Again,

$$\frac{7}{2\cdot3}+\frac{8}{3\cdot5}+\frac{3}{2\cdot5} = 2,$$

and there is even the rather obvious

$$\frac{1}{2}+\frac{1}{3}+\frac{1}{6} = 1.$$

Lindemann, who dealt the coup de grâce to the incorrigible circle-squarers by proving π transcendental, was also snared and tarnished his escutcheon with a faulty proof. Attempts to bolster the weakness only made matters worse. Kummer began to realize the extraordinary difficulty of the task when he presented what he believed to be a complete proof based on the fact that x^p+y^p can be resolved into linear real and complex factors in but one way. The discovery that this is unfortunately not true must have proved a powerful stimulus toward his creation of the ideal number class. Later he was able to point out similar errors to other unsuspecting mathematicians. The great Gauss seems to have been wily enough to eschew a tourney with the bogey, feeling that it was but a special exercise in a much broader field.

* * *

If we take $x^n+y^n = z^n$ and divide both sides by z^n, we obtain $(x/z)^n+(y/z)^n = 1$, which for simplicity might be written $u^n+v^n = 1$. The open and closed curves of Figure 24 are graphs of this latter

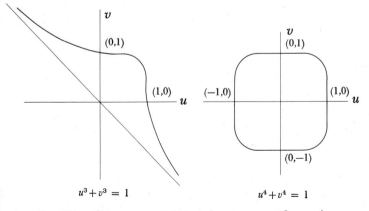

$$u^3+v^3 = 1 \qquad\qquad u^4+v^4 = 1$$

Fig. 24. Graphs of $u^n+v^n = 1$, when $n = 3$ and 4

equation when $n = 3$ and 4, respectively. Higher odd and even values of n give curves similar in character. If Fermat's Last Theorem is really true, then these curves possess the rather remarkable property that except for the intersections with the coordinate axes, there are no points on them whose coordinates are rational numbers.

* * *

Mention has already been made of like sums of two cubes such as $1^3 + 12^3 = 9^3 + 10^3$. The more general relation $x^3 + y^3 + z^3 = t^3$ also has an infinitude of solutions, the most simple of which are

$$3^3 + 4^3 + 5^3 = 6^3 \quad \text{and} \quad 1^3 + 6^3 + 8^3 = 9^3.$$

There is a fairly complicated formula for all the solutions of this equation, but the formula for all those of a certain type is simple enough to find a place here. It is the identity:

$$a^3(a^3 + b^3)^3 = b^3(a^3 + b^3)^3 + a^3(a^3 - 2b^3)^3 + b^3(2a^3 - b^3)^3.$$

When $a = 2$, $b = 1$, this gives $18^3 = 9^3 + 12^3 + 15^3$, which reduces to $6^3 = 3^3 + 4^3 + 5^3$. When $a = 3$, $b = 1$, we obtain $84^3 = 28^3 + 53^3 + 75^3$, and for $a = 3$, $b = 2$ we have $105^3 = 33^3 + 70^3 + 92^3$.

Another identity is:

$$a^3(a^3 + 2b^3)^3 = a^3(a^3 - b^3)^3 + b^3(a^3 - b^3)^3 + b^3(2a^3 + b^3)^3.$$

Here for $a = 2$, $b = 1$, we have $20^3 = 7^3 + 14^3 + 17^3$, and for $a = 3$, $b = 1$ there results $87^3 = 26^3 + 55^3 + 78^3$.

Another relation yields $11^3 + 15^3 + 27^3 = 29^3$.

Then there are more than three cubes whose sum is a cube, such as

$$1^3 + 6^3 + 8^3 = 9^3 = 1^3 + 3^3 + 4^3 + 5^3 + 8^3.$$
$$11^3 + 12^3 + 13^3 + 14^3 = 20^3.$$
$$3^3 + 4^3 + 5^3 + 8^3 + 10^3 = 12^3 = 6^3 + 8^3 + 10^3.$$
$$1^3 + 5^3 + 6^3 + 7^3 + 8^3 + 10^3 = 13^3 = 5^3 + 7^3 + 9^3 + 10^3.$$
$$2^3 + 3^3 + 5^3 + 7^3 + 8^3 + 9^3 + 10^3 = 14^3.$$

No one appears to have determined whether or not four biquadrates (fourth powers) can equal a biquadrate, but it has been proved that $x^4 + y^4 + z^4 = t^4$ is impossible. We do have, however: $4^4 + 6^4 + 8^4 + 9^4 + 14^4 = 15^4$ and $1^4 + 8^4 + 12^4 + 32^4 + 64^4 = 65^4$. Two general formulas for the sum of five such biquadrates are:

$$(8m^2 + 40mn - 24n^2)^4 + (6m^2 - 44mn - 18n^2)^4 + (14m^2 - 4mn - 42n^2)^4$$
$$+ (9m^2 + 27n^2)^4 + (4m^2 + 12n^2)^4 = (15m^2 + 45n^2)^4, \quad \text{and}$$
$$(4m^2 - 12n^2)^4 + (2m^2 - 12mn - 6n^2)^4 + (4m^2 + 12n^2)^4$$
$$+ (2m^2 + 12mn - 6n^2)^4 + (3m^2 + 9n^2)^4 = (5m^2 + 15n^2)^4.$$

Then there is a pyrotechnic burst of biquadrates:

$$1^4 + 3^4 + 4^4 + 5^4 + 9^4 + 10^4 + 11^4 + 12^4 + 14^4 + 15^4$$
$$+ 16^4 + 17^4 + 18^4 + 19^4 + 30^4 = 34^4.$$

There are also solutions of $x^4 + y^4 = u^4 + v^4$, such as

$$76^4 + 1203^4 = 653^4 + 1176^4$$
$$59^4 + 158^4 = 133^4 + 134^4$$
$$27^4 + 2379^4 = 577^4 + 729^4$$
$$7^4 + 239^4 = 157^4 + 227^4$$
$$193^4 + 292^4 = 256^4 + 257^4.$$

General formulas for some of these are: $x = a+b$, $y = c-d$, $u = a-b$, $v = c+d$, where:

$$a = n(m^2+n^2)(-m^4 + 18m^2n^2 - n^4)$$
$$b = 2m(m^6 + 10m^4n^2 + m^2n^4 + 4n^6)$$
$$c = 2n(4m^6 + m^4n^2 + 10m^2n^4 + n^6)$$
$$d = m(m^2+n^2)(-m^4 + 18m^2n^2 - n^4).$$

It is possible to continue with fifth and sixth powers:

$$4^5 + 5^5 + 6^5 + 7^5 + 9^5 + 11^5 = 12^5 \quad \text{and}$$
$$1^6 + 2^6 + 4^6 + 5^6 + 6^6 + 7^6 + 9^6 + 12^6 + 13^6 + 15^6 + 16^6 + 18^6$$
$$+ 20^6 + 21^6 + 22^6 + 23^6 = 28^6.$$

*   *   *

Fermat's Last Theorem is but one of a multitude of impossible equations with the exception, however, that the impossibility of many of these latter has been fully demonstrated. Thus $x^4 - y^4 = z^2$ is impossible, and $x^2 + y^2$ and $x^2 - y^2$ cannot simultaneously be squares. The area of a Pythagorean triangle, that is, $2mn(m^2-n^2)$, cannot be a square nor twice a square, nor can $x^2 + y^2 = ku^2$ and $x^2 - y^2 = kv^2$ exist simultaneously. The allied equations $x^2 + ky^2 = u^2$ and $x^2 - ky^2 = v^2$ are capable of solution for certain values of the "congruent" number k, but the solution is often extremely difficult (see Chapter XV). Impossible are $x^4 + 4y^4 = z^2$ and $x^4 - 4y^4 = \pm z^2$.

But none of these results helps us solve Fermat's Last Theorem. The stone wall is still insurmountable but tenacious workers are sedulously at it, chipping off a piece of granite here and another there. Some intellectual giant, rising above his fellows as did Diophantus or

Fermat or Gauss, will get through.   The only effect of that will be to create a new frontier as a stimulus to further exploration into the unknown.

*   *   *

In this land that we have so hastily explored, there have been no devastating wars nor vain mortal desires.   One can always retire to it and shut out a clamorous, all too real world.   Is this running away from life?   Perhaps.   But perhaps, too, that is better than to risk looking Medusa full in the face.   Gauss shut himself virtually all his life within the sanctuary of the Göttingen observatory, and perhaps the world might be a better place to live in were there more men as unassuming and as penetrating, as gentle and as naïve as he.

"The assimilation of some of these invigorating ideas," as E. T. Bell says in his *Men of Mathematics*, "will be found as refreshing as a drink of cold water on a hot day and as inspiring as any art."   The writer closes this book with the earnest hope that the reader has indeed found it so.

BIBLIOGRAPHY

Ball, W. W. R.   *Mathematical Recreations and Essays*.   New York: Macmillan Co., 1939.

Barlow, P.   *Theory of Numbers*.   London: J. Johnson & Co., 1811.

Bell, E. T.   *The Last Problem*.   New York: Simon and Schuster, 1961.

Cajori, F.   *A History of Mathematics*.   New York: Macmillan Co., 1919.

Carmichael, R. D.   *Theory of Numbers and Diophantine Analysis*.   New York: Dover Publications, Inc., 1959.

Cashmore, M.   *Fermat's Last Theorem*.   London: G. Bell & Sons, 1916.

Dantzig, T.   *Number: The Language of Science*.   New York: Macmillan Co., 1930.

Dickson, L. E.   *History of the Theory of Numbers*.   3 vols.   New York: Chelsea Publishing Co., 1950.

———.   *Introduction to the Theory of Numbers*.   New York: Dover Publications, Inc., 1957.

———.   "Fermat's Last Theorem and the Origin and Nature of the Theory of Algebraic Numbers," *Annals of Mathematics*, Series 2, **18** (1917), 161.

Hardy, G. H.   "An Introduction to the Theory of Numbers," *Bulletin of the American Mathematical Society*, **35** (1929), 778.

Heath, T. L.   *Diophantus of Alexandria*.   London: Cambridge University Press, 1910.

Lehmer, D. H., and Lehmer, E. "A Note on Fermat's Last Theorem," *Bulletin of the American Mathematical Society*, **38** (1932), 723.

————. "On the First Case of Fermat's Last Theorem," *Bulletin of the American Mathematical Society*, **47** (1941), 139.

Mordell, L. J. *Three Lectures on Fermat's Last Theorem*. London: Cambridge University Press, 1921.

Pierce, G. W. *Greater Fermat Theorem Proved*. Boston: G. W. Pierce, 1914.

Rosser, B. "On the First Case of Fermat's Last Theorem," *Bulletin of the American Mathematical Society*, **45** (1939), 636.

Smith, H. J. S. "Report on the Theory of Numbers," *British Association for the Advancement of Science*, **30** (1860), 120.

Uspensky, J. V., and Heaslet, M. A. *Elementary Number Theory*. New York: McGraw-Hill Book Co., 1939.

Vandiver, H. S. "Note on Some Results Concerning Fermat's Last Theorem," *Bulletin of the American Mathematical Society*, **28** (1922), 258.

————. "Fermat's Last Theorem," *American Mathematical Monthly*, **53** (1946), 555.

Vinogradov, I. M. *Elements of Number Theory*. New York: Dover Publications, Inc., 1954.

Walsh, C. M. *An Attempted Proof of Fermat's Last Theorem by a New Method*. New York: G. E. Steckert & Co., 1932.

CHAPTER XXV

TILTS AND TOURNEYS*

1. A man received a check for a certain amount of money, but on cashing it the teller mistook the number of dollars for the number of cents and conversely. Not noticing this, the man spent 68 cents and discovered to his surprise that he then had twice as much money as the check was originally drawn for. Determine the smallest amount of money for which the check could have been written.

2. Sandy McAllister promised his wife a handsome present if she could save a sufficient amount of silver dollars so that they could be arranged either in a square (such as 4 or 9 coins), a triangle (such as 3 or 6 coins), 2 triangles, or 3 triangles. What was the least number of dollars she saved? The trivial answer $1 is excluded.

He renewed his promise the following year but stipulated that she save a different amount this time. This continued for 6 years. How much was saved annually?

3. There are 3 square boards, each having an integral number of inches in its side. The second board is 5 square feet larger than the first and as much smaller than the third. What are the dimensions of the 3 boards?

4. Two church bells begin ringing at the same time. The strokes of one follow regularly at intervals of 4/3 seconds, while the intervals between two strokes of the second are 7/4 seconds. How many strokes are heard during 15 minutes if two strokes following each other in an interval of 1/2 second or less are perceived as one sound?

5. Find integers satisfying the relation $x^2 + y^2 = z^2 + 1$.

6. Divide a $12 \cdot 12$ patchwork quilt into 11 square pieces no one of which has fewer than 4 patches.

7. Find the smallest square which is the sum of more than 3 consecutive cubes but excluding the cube, unity.

* Answers or solutions to these problems begin on p. 315.

8. In Pythagorean triangles, find a formula for hypotenuses which are squares.

9. Assume that the cost of diamonds varies as the square of their weight and that of rubies as the fourth power and that a one-carat gem of these varieties costs $1000 and $2000 respectively. A jeweler traded a pair of earrings, each containing a single jewel of the same kind, in exchange for 2 stones of unequal size, the weights of all stones being an exact number of carats. Find all the possible ways in which the exchange might have been made and the smallest possible size of the stones in each case, together with their values.

10. A cattle dealer had 5 droves of animals consisting of oxen, pigs, and sheep with the same number of animals in each drove. He sold them all to 8 dealers. Each dealer bought the same number of animals, paying $17 per ox, $4 per pig, and $2 per sheep, and the dealer received $301 in all. What was the greatest number of animals the dealer could have had and how many of each kind were there?

11. Find primitive Pythagorean triangles whose perimeter is a square.

12. Each of 2 armies of unequal size consisted of a square number of men, the general being included in one of them. When they went to battle they arranged themselves into a single square but their leader remained on a hilltop 10 miles away to protect the rear. How many men were there in each of the original armies if their total number was just under 100000 men?

13. A man had 6 barrels containing 15, 16, 18, 19, 20, and 31 gallons respectively. Five barrels contained wine and one beer. He sold part of the wine to one purchaser and twice as much to another. This left him only the barrel full of beer. Which of the 6 barrels contained the beer?

14. Find the smallest and the largest number exactly divisible by 11, containing any 9 of the 10 digits.

15. A man was x years old in the year x^2. How old was he in 1960?

16. Insert the missing digits:

17. Find the largest possible divisor which will leave the same remainder when divided into the 4 numbers, 701; 1059; 1417; 2312.

18. Find all positive integers x that will make $x(x+180)$ a square.

19. A man cashed a $200 check at the bank and requested some one-dollar bills, 10 times as many twos, and the balance in fives. How did the cashier pay him?

20. Johnny said to his friend Tommy, "I have a square number of marbles. Give me some of yours and I'll have another square number of marbles." "I know just how many you need for that," said Tommy, "but if you'll give me that many instead, you'll still have a square number of marbles." What was the least number of marbles Johnny had?

21. (a) Find the dimensions of 3 square boards whose areas are in arithmetic progression with a common difference of 7 square feet, and whose sides are rational numbers.

(b) Solve this problem when the difference is 13 square feet.

(c) Solve this problem when the difference is 23 square feet.

22. Three treasure chests contained unequal numbers of gold doubloons, the difference between the number in the middle and top chest being the same as between the bottom and the middle chest. The sum of the doubloons in any 2 chests was a square number.

(a) What is the least possible number of coins in the smallest chest?

(b) What is the least possible number of total coins?

23. On a certain street the house numbers start from 1. A man noticed that the sum of the numbers up to his house but not including it equaled the sum of the numbers beyond his house. Find his house number if it exceeds 100 and is less than 1000. Solve this problem if the numbers run consecutively from 1 instead of alternately as usual.

24. Bill and Fred sent their 30 shirts to the laundry. Fred called for his laundry and explained to the laundryman that since his package contained only half the nylon and one-third the cotton shirts it should cost only $3.24. As 4 nylons cost as much as 5 cottons, Hop Along, the laundryman, lacking the traditional acumen of the Oriental, wants to know what to charge Bill for the other package.

25. A man's age at death was 1/29 of the year of his birth. How old was he in 1940?

26. Mrs. Wiggs's square cabbage patch contains 211 more cabbages than her square patch of last year. How many cabbages has she?

27. The numbers $90ABC17$; $79ABC$; $491ABC4$, where the letters stand for missing integers, have a common divisor. Find the numbers.

28. How many rails of equal length will be required to enclose a right-angled triangular field one of whose sides is 47 rails long?

29. A man had 6 barrels containing either wine or beer. They held 8, 13, 15, 17, 19, and 31 gallons respectively. A customer bought $28 worth of each beverage, paying twice as much for the wine as for the beer, and left the shopkeeper only one full barrel. What was it worth?

30. An ardent swain said to his lady love, some years ago, "Once when a week ago last Tuesday was tomorrow, you said, 'When a day just two fortnights hence will be yesterday, let us get married as it will be just this day next month.' Now sweetheart, we have waited just a fortnight so as it is now the second of the month let us figure out our wedding day."

31. Two men with equal amounts of money bet at a horse race, placing as many dollars on the poorest horse as they were offered odds of so many dollars against a single dollar. Tom bet on Sea Biscuit to win while Bill bet on him for second place. So they put up different amounts at different odds although the amount of their bets

together was equal to half their combined capital. They both won but after cashing their winnings Tom had twice as much money as Bill. What amounts were won?

32. The hot cross-bun man cried:

> Hot cross-buns, hot cross-buns,
>   One a penny, two a penny, hot cross-buns.
> If your daughters don't like them
>   Give them to your sons!
> Two a penny, three a penny, hot cross-buns.
>   I had as many daughters as I had sons,
> So I gave them seven pennies
>   To buy their hot cross-buns.

How many children were there if they were all treated alike and if there was only one way in which to purchase the buns?

33. A triangular-shaped lake is bounded by 3 square estates having areas of 74, 116, and 370 acres respectively. Find the area of the lake.

34. Find the smallest integers satisfying the equations:

(a) $x^2 - 1620\,y^2 = 1$
(b) $x^2 - 1666\,y^2 = 1.$

35. Tommy, Willie, Margaret, and Ann bought 20 pieces of candy for 40 cents. Cherries cost 8 cents apiece, caramels are 2 for a cent, and chocolate almonds 1 for a cent. How did they invest their money if each of them received an equal share of candy?

36. A roulette player had a system of playing one franc 7 times, win or lose, then 7 francs 7 times, win or lose, then 49, etc., each time 7 bets in powers of 7. How many times had he won if he finally won 777777 francs?

37. A boy piled a quantity of coconuts originally stacked in 2 pyramids with triangular bases into a single pyramid with a triangular base. What was the minimum number of coconuts he could have had?

38. A man had over 100 pennies, their number being a square. He divided them into 19 exactly equal square piles and had 81 pennies left over. What was the least number of pennies he had? Find a formula giving an infinite number of solutions.

39. A miser who had been hoarding a quantity of five, ten, and twenty-dollar gold pieces used to keep them in 5 bags, the contents of each of which were identical. While toying with his treasure he would divide it into 4 piles, each of which would be exactly alike; then to be certain that none was lost, he would take 2 of the piles and construct 3 identical heaps. How much money did this poor man have before he starved to death?

40. A tourist and a guide dashed up the steps of the pyramid of Cheops hotly pursued by a lion. The tourist could take 5 steps at a time, the guide 6, and the lion 7. At a certain instant the tourist was one step from the top, the guide 9, and the lion 19. How many steps are in the pyramid?

41. A man went into a store and spent one-half of the money that was in his pocket. When he came out he found that he had just as many cents as he had dollars when he went in, and half as many dollars as he had cents when he went in. How much money did he have when he entered the store?

42. A Chinese lady wished to purchase a puppy worth 11 dollars. Eleven Chinese coins with round holes are worth 15 dollars; 11 with square holes, 16 dollars; and 11 with triangular holes, 17 dollars. How many of each were required to purchase the puppy?

43. Express the year 1961 in the octonary system—the scale of 8.

44. An egg weighs 2 ounces and can sustain a weight of 8 pounds. How high a square pyramid may be safely piled? How high a triangular pyramid?

45. Find Pythagorean triangles whose sides are in arithmetic progression.

46. What is the least number of integral square pieces into which a 13×13 square may be cut and reassembled into 2 squares?

47. Prove that the product of 3 consecutive numbers is exactly divisible by 504 if the middle one is a cube.

48. Find all numbers N (at least 2) not exceeding 100 which have the same $\phi(N)$. $\phi(N)$ is the number of integers less than and prime to N.

49. Solve Problem 48 if N has only one prime divisor; that is, find the primes p and q and the exponents a and b such that $\phi(p^a) = \phi(q^b)$.

50. A wine merchant owned 5 large perfectly cubical vats, each measuring 9 feet on an edge. He had 15 smaller containers also perfectly cubical, only 2 of which were alike in size. He filled each of the large vats by pouring into it the entire contents of 3 small containers. What were the dimensions of the containers?

51. Find a number written in the scale of 7, with less than 40 digits, such that if the digit 3 is moved from its extreme right to its extreme left, the result (still in the scale of 7) is 4/5 of the original number.

52. An eccentric millionaire wished to distribute a million dollars in gifts of either one dollar or powers of 7 such as 7; 49; 343; 2401, etc. He had an aversion to giving more than 6 people the same sum of money but no restriction on the number of people who might taste of his bounty. How did he distribute the million dollars?

53. There are n castaways and a monkey on a desert island who have gathered a pile of coconuts which are to be divided the next day. During the night one man arises, divides the pile into n equal parts, and finds one coconut over, which he gives to the monkey. He then hides his share away from the pile. Each of the n men repeats the performance. The last man leaves a pile which is exactly divisible by n. What was the minimum number of nuts in the original pile? Solve also for the case of r monkeys.

54. Find the smallest integer consisting only of the digits 3 and 7 such that both this number and the sum of its digits are divisible by both 3 and 7.

55. Find the smallest integer consisting only of the digits 3, 5, and 7 such that both this number and the sum of its digits are divisible by these 3 digits.

56. Find the smallest integer consisting of all 10 digits *used once only*, which is divisible by all the digits from 1 to 9.

57. Find the first 100 Pythagorean triangles having consecutive legs.

58. A Sultan wished to send into battle an army that could be formed into 2 perfect squares in 12 different ways. What is the smallest number of men required to accomplish this and what are the arrangements?

59. Captain John Smith, who died in Gloucester in 1805, left the proceeds of his successful ventures in the slave trade to his 9 heirs, 5

male and 4 female, consisting of a married son, wife, and child; a married daughter, husband, and child; and a stepson, wife, and child. The will stipulated that each husband was to get as much more than his wife as she got more than her child, this difference being the same for all 3 families. The money consisted entirely of one-dollar bills and each heir received a package of sealed envelopes, each envelope containing as many one-dollar bills as there were sealed envelopes in his or her package. The heirs' names were Bill, Mary, Tom, Eliza, Hank, Susan, Ned, Sarah, and Jack. Mary and Sarah together received as much as Tom and Bill together, while Ned, Bill, and Mary together received $299 more than Hank. The needy Joneses received over one-third more than the Browns. Find the surnames of the heirs.

60. By moving the units digit D of a number N so that it becomes the first digit, a new number results which is K times the original number. Find the number and the number of its digits for $K = 2$, 3, etc., and $D = 2, 3, 4 \ldots 9$.

61. In cashing a 4-digit check, a teller paid a sum of money represented by the digits reversed. He was short by an amount represented by a square number. (a) How many such squares are possible? (b) What are they? (c) How many different amounts could the check have been written for originally?

62. Solve Problem 61 where the shortage was a cube instead of a square.

63. By adding 1 to the number, N = AAABBBCCC, it becomes a square. Find N. (A, B, and C, are unlike digits.)

64.

> "Once a bright young lady called Lillian
> Summed the numbers from one to a billion.
> But it gave her the fidgets
> To add up the *digits*;
> If you can help her, she'll thank you a million."

65. Prove $3^{2x+1} + 2^{x+2}$ is always divisible by 7 if x is a positive integer.

66. (EVE)/(DID) = .TALKTALKTALK... represents a common fraction expressed as an unending decimal. Find the digits corresponding to these letters.

67. Given a Pythagorean triangle ABC, with BF bisecting the right angle B. A perpendicular AE meets BF in E. The line GE from the midpoint, G, of the hypotenuse meets AB in D. The segment $EG = 49$. Find the sides of triangle ABC.

68. When a 3-digit number is divided by the sum of its digits, the quotient is 26. Find the smallest number meeting this condition.

69. Find the smallest integer expressible as the sum of 2 integral-squares in exactly 7 ways.

70. Find 2 numbers $aabbccddee$ so one is a perfect square and the other a perfect square increased by 7. There are 2 solutions for each case. (*Different* letters represent digits which are not necessarily different but of course *like* letters represent the same digit.)

71. Two men sold their herd of x cows at x dollars per head. With the proceeds they bought sheep at \$10 each and a single lamb costing less than \$10. Each man received the same number of animals but the one receiving the lamb had to be compensated so as to make the division equitable. How much money did he receive from the other man?

72. An army of less than 5 million men marching in a square phalanx was reinforced by 10 square companies each containing a like number of men. The entire army, now numbering more than 10 million men but less than 3 times the original army, could arrange itself into 400 equal squares or into a single square. How many men were in each of the 400 squares?

73. An old invoice showed that 72 turkeys had been purchased for \$_*_67.9_*_; the first and last digits were illegible. What were they?

74. The number $(abbbb)^2 - 1$ has 10 digits, all different. Find the number.

75. Find the smallest and largest squares in each of which all 10 digits are used once only.

76. Using all 10 digits unrepeated, find a 10-digit number which when increased by 1 million is a square. The square root of this number must be palindromic, that is, it must read the same when the order of its digits is reversed.

77. Solve Problem 76 omitting the digit zero and forming only a 9-digit number, all other conditions remaining the same.

78. Disregarding the palindromic requirement of Problems 76 and 77, find a solution for each of these problems such that the two resulting 5-digit *square roots* use all 10 digits.

79. When the census taker asked the man on the porch for the ages of the persons living at the house, the man replied, "My age is the sum of my wife's, son's, and daughter's ages, and each of our ages is a square. My father's age is the sum of my age, my wife's, and my daughter's. Although he has passed the prime of life, his age is a prime." What ages did the unstartled census taker record, and what obvious remark did he make about the wife's age?

80. Prove that $1 + [1 + (10^{10} - 1)^{99989}](10^{999890} - 1) \equiv 0$, mod 99991. $\quad 10^6 \equiv 9 \bmod m$

81. A farmer had a field shaped like a regular pentagon. Each of the 5 sides was also the side of a Pythagorean triangle. All 5 triangles were dissimilar and had their apexes outside the farmer's field. What is the least area that the 5 triangular pieces of land could have had and what was the area of the farmer's field?

82. The gross annual receipts for the sale of electronic widgits was \$3893.93, but last year business was much better since the receipts were \$8311.19. How many widgets were sold last year?

83. An old alchemist had two spherical flasks, one with a circumference of 12 inches and the other with a circumference of 24 inches. He desired to transfer their contents into two other spherical flasks of unequal size, and of a different size from the first two. What were the circumferences of the two new flasks, in rational numbers?

84. An automobile agency found that their total annual receipts for the sale of automobiles came to \$1,111,111.00, but somehow they lost the record indicating how many cars they had sold. Can you help them?

85. A merchant had 2 unequal cubical boxes whose contents totaled exactly 6 cubic feet. What were the dimensions of the boxes in rational numbers?

86. A farmer owned a 5/4-mile-square piece of land. He fenced off each of the 4 corners into right-triangular-shaped pieces, for his 4 sons. All these triangles had the same area but were dissimilar in shape, and each had an integral number of feet in each of its 3 sides. This left the farmer with a piece of land shaped like an irregular

octagon; but he still had over 96 per cent of his original square parcel left.   What was its area in square feet?

87. Find the 4 smallest primitive Pythagorean triangles that have the same perimeter.

88. Find a 9-digit square $N^2 = abcdefabc$ whose root is the product of 4 unlike primes, $a \neq 0$ and $(def) = 2(abc)$.

89. Find the smallest 3 *consecutive* integers, zero excluded, each of which is the sum of 2 squares.

90. Two digits of the 8-digit number, 273*49*5, were erased. The number is divisible by 9 and 11.   Find the missing digits.

91. The total number of heads and wings of horses and chickens in a barn is equal to the number of feet.   How many horses and how many chickens are there?

92. A student accidentally erased a long-division example.   He could recall only that the successive subtrahends starting from the top were 690; 2415; and 2070 and that the remainder was 1.   With this information he restored the problem.   Can you do likewise?

93. A 3-digit number in the scale of 7 has its digits reversed when expressed in the scale of 9.   Find the number.

94. Show that $(x^5/5) + (x^3/3) + (7x/15)$ is always an integer for integral values of x.

95. "Find me a number," said the king to his jester, "half of which is a square."   "How simple," said the jester.   "But," continued the king, "one-third of it must be a cube."   The jester looked serious for once.   "And finally," remarked the king, "one-fifth of it must be a fifth power."   The jester looked crestfallen.   "Solution by tomorrow morning," finished the king, "or you must marry my widowed mother-in-law."   The jester was crushed.   But next morning he had the answer and was thus saved from a fate worse than death.

96. Find a cube which, when diminished by a square, leaves 2,000,000.

97. Show that $61! + 1 \equiv 0$ and $63! + 1 \equiv 0$ mod 71.

98. Prove that the product of the first n consecutive integers is divisible by their sum if and only if $(n+1)$ is not a prime.

99. How many zeros are there in $(10000!)$?

100. An isosceles right triangle has each of its 2 legs equal to the hypotenuse of a primitive Pythagorean triangle. Prove that there exists another right triangle with integral legs and having a hypotenuse equal to that of the isosceles right triangle.

CHAPTER XXVI

THE QUEEN EXPLAINS:
SOLUTIONS TO PROBLEMS

Chapter I

1. $16000001 = 109 \cdot 229 \cdot 641$.

2. See Figure 4, page 111.

3. Since $5929 = 7^2 \cdot 11^2$; the number of integers less than and prime to it is $\phi(5929) = 7 \cdot 6 \cdot 11 \cdot 10 = 4620$.

4. See page 323, solutions to Chapter XXV, Problem 54.

5. If $x = p^2 - q^2 - 2pq$, $y = p^2 + q^2$, $z = p^2 - q^2 + 2pq$ where p and q are integers, then x^2, y^2, and z^2 will be in arithmetic progression. For $p = 2$, $q = 1$, the numbers are -1; 5; 7 and the squares 1; 25; 49. For $p = 3$, $q = 1$, the numbers are 2; 10; 14 and the squares, 4; 100; 196. There cannot be 4 squares in arithmetic progression.

6. See solutions to Chapter II.

7. See Chapter VII.

8. See a number-theory text such as Uspensky and Heaslet, *Elementary Theory of Numbers*, McGraw-Hill Book Company, Inc., 1939.

9. See Chapter III.

Chapter II

1. Find the least number with 100 divisors. Separate 100 into the product of 2, 3, 4 divisors as follows: $50 \cdot 2$, $25 \cdot 4$, $20 \cdot 5$, $10 \cdot 10$; $25 \cdot 2 \cdot 2$, $10 \cdot 5 \cdot 2$, $5 \cdot 5 \cdot 4$; $5 \cdot 5 \cdot 2 \cdot 2$. This gives numbers with 100 divisors of the forms $p^{49}q$, $p^{24}q^3$, $p^{19}q^4$, p^9q^9; $p^{24}qr$, p^9q^4r, $p^4q^4r^3$; p^4q^4rs. The last form gives the least solution as $2^4 \cdot 3^4 \cdot 5 \cdot 7 = 45360$.

2. Find the least number with 96 divisors. Separate 96 into the product of 2, 3, 4, 5, 6 factors. Only the factors taken 5 and 6 at a time need be examined since in the other cases the exponents are so large as to

preclude their yielding a minimum solution. This gives $6 \cdot 2 \cdot 2 \cdot 2 \cdot 2$; $4 \cdot 3 \cdot 2 \cdot 2 \cdot 2$; and $3 \cdot 2 \cdot 2 \cdot 2 \cdot 2 \cdot 2$. The number forms are then p^5qrst, p^3q^2rst, and p^2qrstu. These lead to the solutions

$$2^5 \cdot 3 \cdot 5 \cdot 7 \cdot 11, \quad 2^3 \cdot 3^2 \cdot 5 \cdot 7 \cdot 11, \quad 2^2 \cdot 3 \cdot 5 \cdot 7 \cdot 11 \cdot 13,$$

of which the second, $2^3 \cdot 3^2 \cdot 5 \cdot 7 \cdot 11 = 27720$ is the least.

Chapter V

PAGE 35

Find the magic numbers 715; 364; and 924 (or 5, 4, and -1). Let X be the unknown number and p, q, r the magic numbers to be found. Let a, b, c be the residues, modulo 7, 11, 13, respectively, of X. Then $pa + qb + rc - K \cdot 1001 = X$. Let $p = 11 \cdot 13u$; $q = 7 \cdot 13v$; $r = 7 \cdot 11w$. Then $143ua + 91vb + 77wc - X = 1001K$. Then,

$$3ua - a \equiv 0 \quad \text{mod } 7$$
$$3vb - b \equiv 0 \quad \text{mod } 11$$
$$12wc - c \equiv 0 \quad \text{mod } 13$$

and since a, b, c are prime to 7, 11, and 13, respectively, we can cancel these common factors in each congruence. This gives:

$$3u \equiv 1 \quad \text{mod } 7$$
$$3v \equiv 1 \quad \text{mod } 11$$
$$12w \equiv 1 \quad \text{mod } 13$$

whence $u \equiv 5$; $v \equiv 4$; $w \equiv 12$, modulo 7, 11, and 13, respectively. Then $p = 143u = 715$; $q = 91v = 364$; $r = 77w = 924$.

By remembering $u = 5$, $v = 4$, $w = 12$ or (-1) instead of p, q, and r, the alternate magic numbers described in Chapter V are obtained.

PAGE 38

1. $x = 37a - 1$; $y = 83 - 71a$ where a is any integer positive or negative including zero.

2. $x = 11 + 107a$; $y = 873 - 599a$ where a is any positive or negative integer including zero.

3. $1001x + 770y = 1000000 + b$. Dividing by 77, $13x + 10y = 12987 + (b+1)/77$ and $b = 76$ is the least value that will make the fraction an integer. Then $10y \equiv 1 \bmod 13$ and $y \equiv 4 \bmod 13$; whence $y = 13z + 4$. Then $13x + 130z + 40 = 12987 + 1$ or dividing by 13, $x + 10z + 3 = 999$ and $x = 996 - 10z$. There are 100 solutions corresponding to the values of z from zero to 99.

Chapter VI

We must solve

$$(2^{p-1}-1)/p = a^2$$

or

$$2^{p-1}-1 = pa^2 = (2^{(p-1)/2}+1)(2^{(p-1)/2}-1).$$

If the quantities in parentheses have a common factor, their difference, 2 has it. But these quantities are odd; hence, they cannot have a factor in common with 2 except unity. They are, therefore, co-prime and since their product is pa^2, one of them must be a square, otherwise they would not be relatively prime. Therefore, either $2^{(p-1)/2}+1 = x^2$, or $2^{(p-1)/2}-1 = x^2$. In the first case, since x is odd $= 2y+1$, we have

$$2^{(p-1)/2}+1 = 4y^2+4y+1, \quad \text{or} \quad 2^{(p-1)/2} = 4(y^2+y) = 4y(y+1).$$

Since either y or $y+1$ is odd, their product cannot be a power of 2 unless $y = 1$, in which case $p = 7$. In the second case $2^{(p-1)/2}-1 = 4y^2+4y+1$, or $2^{(p-1)/2} = 2(2y^2+2y+1)$. The quantity in parentheses is an odd number and twice an odd number is a power of 2 only when the odd number is unity, whence $y = 0$ and the corresponding value of p is 3. Hence, only for $p = 3$ and 7 does the Fermat quotient have square values; these are 1 and 9, respectively.

Chapter VIII

Which sum is greater?

```
1 2 3 4 5 6 7 8 9                           1
1 2 3 4 5 6 7 8                           2 1
1 2 3 4 5 6 7                           3 2 1
1 2 3 4 5 6                           4 3 2 1
1 2 3 4 5                           5 4 3 2 1
1 2 3 4                           6 5 4 3 2 1
1 2 3                           7 6 5 4 3 2 1
1 2                           8 7 6 5 4 3 2 1
1                           9 8 7 6 5 4 3 2 1
```

Both sums are alike.

The number

$$111222333444555666777889 = (1/81)(1/111) \cdot 10^{27}$$
$$= (1/9) \cdot (1/111) \cdot (1111111111111111111111111111)$$
$$= (1/9) \cdot (1001001001001001001001001).$$

PAGE 62

Why does the product of 15873 and multiples of 7 give a repetend of digits? The number $15873 = 3 \cdot 11 \cdot 13 \cdot 37$. Hence, $7m \cdot 15873 = m(7 \cdot 11 \cdot 13)(3 \cdot 37) = m \cdot 1001 \cdot 111 = m \cdot 111111$.

Why does $90991 \cdot 123321$ give 111111111111? Now $90991 = 9901 \cdot 7 \cdot 13$ and $123321 = 1111 \cdot 111 = 101 \cdot 11 \cdot 3 \cdot 37$. Hence,

$$90991 \cdot 123321 = (9901 \cdot 101)(7 \cdot 11 \cdot 13)(3 \cdot 37) = 1000001 \cdot 1001 \cdot 111$$
$$= 1000001 \cdot 111111 = 111111111111.$$

PAGE 65

Why do all primes, except 2 and 5, divide an infinite number of integers each a repetend of digits? By Fermat's theorem, the congruence $10^e \equiv 1 \bmod p$ always has a solution if p is a prime other than 2 or 5 (see Chapter X). Thus $10^e - 1 = 999 \ldots$ (e nines repeated) is divisible by p. (The minimum number of nines required to be divisible by p is the exponent to which 10 belongs modulo p, but any multiple of e can represent the number of nines in a number divisible by p.)

Since every prime is prime to every other prime, we can divide a repetend of nines by 9 and obtain a repetend of ones without affecting the divisibility of the repetend by another prime. Finally, we can multiply this repetend of ones by any of the remaining 7 digits without affecting the divisibility. In other words, a repetend of digits is always divisible by a prime if there is a sufficient number of digits (never more than $p-1$) in the repetend.

Chapter XII

PAGE 89

The two ways of writing 10 in the form of Formula B are: $11^0(11-1)$ and $2^0(2-1)11^0(11-1)$.

For the number 2, we have, $2^1(2-1)$, $3^0(3-1)$, and $2^0(2-1) \cdot 3^0(3-1)$.

PAGE 91

I. Give $b = \phi(N)$. Write b in the form of Formula B in every possible way.

(1) Let $b = 2^a Q$ where Q is odd. In a column headed f, list the *even* divisors f_i of b, excluding those divisors containing 2^a. However, include in the list unity and b itself. (For convenience in verifying that all the permissible divisors have been included, write each divisor as a product of powers of primes.)

(2) In a second column, headed A, list the values $(f_i + 1)$ in case they are primes and insert a dash in case they are not.

(3) Divide each f_i by the highest power B^c of its greatest prime B, and if the quotient is $B-1$, write the number B^{c+1} in a column headed B; if the quotient is not $B-1$, insert a dash.

(4) Reject all factors f_i that do not have at least one entry opposite them in either Column A or Column B.

(5) Where possible express b as a product of $1, 2, 3, \ldots (a+1)$ factors selected from the f column in all possible ways, a result arrived at by trial only. *Unity must be treated as a distinct factor.* A factor f_i may be repeated *once* only in a product and then only if there is an entry corresponding to it in *both* Columns A and B.

Reject combinations using factors where the corresponding primes listed in Columns A and B are identical. Thus in Table 99, a combination may not contain both $2 \cdot 5$ and $2 \cdot 5 \cdot 11$ because the prime 11, corresponding to these factors, is the same in both cases.

(6) To express b in the form of Formula B, write down for each f_i used in (5) the value $A_i^0(A_i - 1)$ in case there is an entry in Column A, and write down $B_i^c(B_i - 1)$ in case there is an entry in Column B. These values should be expressed as a continued product. If there is an entry in both columns, f_i furnishes two solutions.

PAGE 91

II. List the results of I in a column headed $\phi(N)$. In a column headed N, list N_i as a product of powers of primes by writing A_i for each $A_i^0(A_i - 1)$ and B_i^{c+1} for each $B_i^c(B_i - 1)$. Example:

$$b = \phi(N) = 2^3 \cdot 3 \cdot 5^2 \cdot 11.$$

See Tables 99 and 100.

TABLE 99

PRELIMINARIES FOR SOLUTION, N, GIVEN $\phi(N) = 2^3 \cdot 3 \cdot 5^2 \cdot 11$

f	A	B	f	A	B
1	2	—	$2 \cdot 3 \cdot 5^2 \cdot 11$*	—	—
2	3	2^2	$2^2 \cdot 3$	13	—
2^2	5	2^3	$2^2 \cdot 5$	—	5^2
$2 \cdot 3$	7	3^2	$2^2 \cdot 11$*	—	—
$2 \cdot 5$	11	—	$2^2 \cdot 5^2$	101	5^3
$2 \cdot 11$	23	—	$2^2 \cdot 3 \cdot 5$	61	—
$2 \cdot 5^2$*	—	—	$2^2 \cdot 3 \cdot 11$*	—	—
$2 \cdot 3 \cdot 5$	31	—	$2^2 \cdot 5 \cdot 11$*	—	—
$2 \cdot 3 \cdot 11$	67	—	$2^2 \cdot 3 \cdot 5^2$*	—	—
$2 \cdot 5 \cdot 11$	—	11^2	$2^2 \cdot 5^2 \cdot 11$*	—	—
$2 \cdot 3 \cdot 5^2$	151	—	$2^2 \cdot 3 \cdot 5 \cdot 11$	661	—
$2 \cdot 5^2 \cdot 11$*	—	—	$2^2 \cdot 3 \cdot 5^2 \cdot 11$	3301	—
$2 \cdot 3 \cdot 5 \cdot 11$	331	—	$2^3 \cdot 3 \cdot 5^2 \cdot 11$*	—	—

* These factors must be rejected, since there is no entry in either Column A or B.

TABLE 100

VALUES OF N HAVING $\phi(N) = 2^3 \cdot 3 \cdot 5^2 \cdot 11$

$\phi(N) = b$ as Product of f_i	$\phi(N) = b$ as in Formula B (Solution to I)	N (Solution to II)
$(2)(2^2 \cdot 3 \cdot 5^2 \cdot 11)$	(a) $3^0(3-1) \cdot 3301^0 \cdot (3301-1)$	$3 \cdot 3301$
	(b) $2 \cdot (2-1) \cdot 3301^0 \cdot (3301-1)$	$2^2 \cdot 3301$
$(2^2 \cdot 5)(2 \cdot 3 \cdot 5 \cdot 11)$	$5 \cdot (5-1) \cdot 331^0 \cdot (331-1)$	$5^2 \cdot 331$
$(2 \cdot 5)(2^2 \cdot 3 \cdot 5 \cdot 11)$	$11^0 \cdot (11-1) \cdot 661^0 \cdot (661-1)$	$11 \cdot 661$
$(2 \cdot 3 \cdot 11)(2^2 \cdot 5^2)$	(a) $67^0 \cdot (67-1) \cdot 5^2(5-1)$	$67 \cdot 5^3$
	(b) $67^0 \cdot (67-1) \cdot 101^0(101-1)$	$67 \cdot 101$
$(2 \cdot 5 \cdot 11)(2^2 \cdot 3 \cdot 5)$	$11 \cdot (11-1) \cdot 61^0(61-1)$	$11^2 \cdot 61$
$(1)(2)(2^2 \cdot 3 \cdot 5^2 \cdot 11)$	$2^0(2-1) \cdot 3^0(3-1) \cdot 3301^0(3301-1)$	$2 \cdot 3 \cdot 3301$
$(1)(2^2 \cdot 5)(2 \cdot 3 \cdot 5 \cdot 11)$	$2^0(2-1) \cdot 5(5-1) \cdot 331^0(331-1)$	$2 \cdot 5^2 \cdot 331$
$(1)(2 \cdot 5)(2^2 \cdot 3 \cdot 5 \cdot 11)$	$2^0(2-1) \cdot 11^0(11-1) \cdot 661^0(661-1)$	$2 \cdot 11 \cdot 661$
$(1)(2 \cdot 3 \cdot 11)(2^2 \cdot 5^2)$	(a) $2^0(2-1) \cdot 67^0(67-1) \cdot 5^2(5-1)$	$2 \cdot 67 \cdot 5^3$
	(b) $2^0(2-1) \cdot 67^0(67-1) \cdot 101^0(101-1)$	$2 \cdot 67 \cdot 101$
$(1)(2 \cdot 5 \cdot 11)(2^2 \cdot 3 \cdot 5)$	$2^0(2-1) \cdot 11(11-1) \cdot 61^0(61-1)$	$2 \cdot 11^2 \cdot 61$
$(2)(2 \cdot 5)(2 \cdot 3 \cdot 5 \cdot 11)$	(a) $3^0 \cdot (3-1) \cdot 11^0 \cdot (11-1) \cdot 331^0(331-1)$	$3 \cdot 11 \cdot 331$
	(b) $2(2-1) \cdot 11^0(11-1) \cdot 331^0(331-1)$	$2^2 \cdot 11 \cdot 331$
$(2)(2 \cdot 11)(2 \cdot 3 \cdot 5^2)$	(a) $3^0 \cdot 2 \cdot 23^0 \cdot 22 \cdot 151^0 \cdot 150$	$3 \cdot 23 \cdot 151$
	(b) $2 \cdot 1 \cdot 23^0 \cdot 22 \cdot 151^0 \cdot 150$	$2^2 \cdot 23 \cdot 151$
$(2)(2 \cdot 3 \cdot 5)(2 \cdot 5 \cdot 11)$	(a) $3^0(3-1) \cdot 31^0(31-1) \cdot 11(11-1)$	$3 \cdot 31 \cdot 11^2$
	(b) $2(2-1) \cdot 31^0(31-1) \cdot 11(11-1)$	$2^2 \cdot 31 \cdot 11^2$
$(2 \cdot 5)(2 \cdot 11)(2 \cdot 3 \cdot 5)$	$11^0(11-1) \cdot 23^0(23-1) \cdot 31^0(31-1)$	$11 \cdot 23 \cdot 31$
$(1)(2)(2 \cdot 5)(2 \cdot 3 \cdot 5 \cdot 11)$	$2^0 \cdot 1 \cdot 3^0 \cdot 2 \cdot 11^0 \cdot 10 \cdot 331^0 \cdot 330$	$2 \cdot 3 \cdot 11 \cdot 331$
$(1)(2)(2 \cdot 11)(2 \cdot 3 \cdot 5^2)$	$2^0 \cdot 1 \cdot 3^0 \cdot 2 \cdot 23^0 \cdot 22 \cdot 151^0 \cdot 150$	$2 \cdot 3 \cdot 23 \cdot 151$
$(1)(2)(2 \cdot 3 \cdot 5)(2 \cdot 5 \cdot 11)$	$2^0 \cdot 1 \cdot 3^0 \cdot 2 \cdot 31^0 \cdot 30 \cdot 11 \cdot 10$	$2 \cdot 3 \cdot 31 \cdot 11^2$
$(1)(2 \cdot 5)(2 \cdot 11)(2 \cdot 3 \cdot 5)$	$2^0 \cdot 1 \cdot 11^0 \cdot 10 \cdot 23^0 \cdot 22 \cdot 31^0 \cdot 30$	$2 \cdot 11 \cdot 23 \cdot 31$

PAGE 91

III. Impossible forms, b, for $\phi(N) = b$: For an odd number q, if $2q+1$, 2^2q+1, $2^3q+1, \ldots 2^nq+1$ are all composite and if q is not of the form $(2^{2^x} + 1)$ (where 2^x does not exceed n), then $\phi(N) = 2^nq$ cannot have solutions. Take $q = 19, n = 5$; then 39; 77; 153; 305; 609 are all composite; also 19 is not of the form $2^{2^x} + 1$; hence $2 \cdot 19 = 38$; $2^2 \cdot 19 = 76$; $2^3 \cdot 19 = 152$; $2^4 \cdot 19 = 304$; $2^5 \cdot 19 = 608$ are impossible values of $\phi(N)$.

Again, (1) if p and q are odd numbers, not both powers of 3, and (2) if $2pq+1$ is not prime, and (3) q is not equal to $2p+1$, then $\phi(N) = 2pq$ has no solutions. For $p = 3$, $q = 15$ the conditions are fulfilled and $\phi(N) = 90$ has no solutions. This also holds for $p = 5$, $q = 17$, and $\phi(N) = 170$.

PAGE 91

(a) $\phi(N) = 72$ has 17 solutions: 73; 91; 95; 111; 117; 135; 146; 148; 152; 182; 190; 216; 222; 228; 234; 252; 270.

(b) $\phi(N) = 144$ has 21 solutions: 185; 219; 273; 285; 292; 296; 304; 315; 364; 370; 380; 432; 438; 444; 456; 468; 504; 540; 546; 570; 630.

(c) $\phi(N) = 480$ has 37 solutions: 527; 533; 715; 723; 861; 915; 964; 975; 976; 992; 1054; 1066; 1144; 1148; 1155; 1220; 1232; 1240; 1300; 1400; 1430; 1446; 1464; 1476; 1488; 1540; 1584; 1716; 1722; 1800; 1830; 1848; 1860; 1950; 1980; 2100; 2310.

(d) $\phi(N) = 2^3 \cdot 3 \cdot 5^2 \cdot 11 = 6600$ has 24 solutions: $3 \cdot 3301$; $2^2 \cdot 3301$; $5^2 \cdot 331$; $11 \cdot 661$; $67 \cdot 5^3$; $67 \cdot 101$; $11^2 \cdot 61$; $2 \cdot 3 \cdot 3301$; $2 \cdot 11 \cdot 661$; $2 \cdot 5^2 \cdot 331$; $2 \cdot 67 \cdot 101$; $2 \cdot 67 \cdot 5^3$; $2 \cdot 11^2 \cdot 61$; $2^2 \cdot 11 \cdot 331$; $3 \cdot 11 \cdot 331$; $3 \cdot 23 \cdot 151$; $2^2 \cdot 23 \cdot 151$; $3 \cdot 11^2 \cdot 31$; $2^2 \cdot 11^2 \cdot 31$; $11 \cdot 23 \cdot 31$; $2 \cdot 3 \cdot 11 \cdot 331$; $2 \cdot 3 \cdot 23 \cdot 151$; $2 \cdot 3 \cdot 11^2 \cdot 31$; $2 \cdot 11 \cdot 23 \cdot 31$ (see Table 100).

(e) $\phi(N) = 1$ has the solutions $N = 1$ and 2.

TABLE 101

Solutions, N, of All Values $b = \phi(N)$ Not Exceeding 50

$\phi(N)$ = b	Solutions, N	Number of Solutions	$\phi(N)$ = b	Solutions, N	Number of Solutions
1	1; 2	2	28	29; 58	2
2	3; 4; 6	3	30	31; 62	2
4	5; 8; 10; 12	4	32	51; 64; 68; 80	7
6	7; 9; 14; 18	4		96; 102; 120	
8	15; 16; 20	5	36	37; 57; 63; 74	8
	24; 30			76; 108; 114; 126	
10	11; 22	2	40	41; 55; 75	9
12	13; 21; 26	6		82; 88; 100	
	28; 36; 42			110; 132; 150	
16	17; 32; 34	6	42	43; 49; 86; 98	4
	40; 48; 60		44	69; 92; 138	3
18	19; 27; 38; 54	4	46	47; 94	2
20	25; 33; 44	5	48	65; 104; 105; 112	11
	50; 66			130; 140; 144; 156	
22	23; 46	2		168; 180; 210	
24	35; 39; 45; 52	10			
	56; 70; 72; 78				
	84; 90				

Chapter XIV

7. Table 103, pages 328-29, gives the hypotenuse and short side of the first 100 Pythagorean triangles whose legs differ by unity.

9. The primitive Pythagorean triangle with sides 1357; 1476; 2005 has a perimeter of 4838 and an area of 1001466.

10. The primitive Pythagorean triangle each of whose sides lies between 2000 and 3000 is 2059; 2100; 2941.

PAGE 132

The six solutions of four primitive Pythagorean triangles with the same perimeter, have the following generators, m and n. The sides are $m^2 - n^2$, $2mn$, and $m^2 + n^2$; the perimeter is $2m(m+n)$.

Solution Number	Perimeter, $p = 2m(m+n)$	1		2		3		4	
		m	n	m	n	m	n	m	n
1	543660	390	307	410	253	442	173	510	23
2	554268	374	367	418	245	442	185	494	67
3	570180	390	341	430	233	442	203	510	49
4	570570	385	356	399	316	429	236	455	172
5	949620	490	479	510	421	570	263	646	89
6	986700	506	469	550	347	598	227	650	109

Chapter XV

PAGE 145

The number

$$5580731520 = 74088^2 + 9576^2 = 65016^2 + 36792^2$$
$$= 58968^2 + 45864^2 = 72072^2 + 19656^2.$$

PAGE 154

Each person must have spent a square sum of money and since each man spent $63 more than his wife, we have, $M^2 - W^2 = 63 = (M+W)(M-W) = 63 \cdot 1 = 21 \cdot 3 = 9 \cdot 7$. Solving for M and W, the men bought 32, 12, or 8 pigs; their respective wives 31, 9, or 1 pig. Therefore, Henry must have bought 32 since he bought 23 more than Catherine, the other numbers 12 and 8, purchased by the men, being smaller than 23. Then Catherine bought 9. Reasoning similarly, Ely must have bought 12 and Gertrude 1. That left 8 for Cornelius and 31 for Anna. Then Henry-Anna, Ely-Catherine, and Cornelius-Gertrude were the couples.

PAGE 154

Since each mother spent $4.05 more than her daughter, and each spent a square amount of money, $M^2 - D^2 = 405 = (M+D)(M-D) = 405 \cdot 1 = 135 \cdot 3 = 81 \cdot 5 = 45 \cdot 9 = 27 \cdot 15$. Solving for the 5 possible values of M and D and tabulating the results, together with their squares, we have:

Number of Yards Bought		Money Paid	
By Mother $= M$	By Daughter $= D$	By Mother $= M^2$	By Daughter $= D^2$
203	202	$412.09	$408.04
69	66	47.61	43.56
43	38	18.49	14.44
27	18	7.29	3.24
21	6	4.41	.36

The conditions of the problem then make it evident that the names of the daughters must be Ada Smith, Anna Brown, Emily Jones, Mary Robinson, and Bessie Evans.

PAGE 157

For three squares in A.P. with a common difference of 23, see page 317, solutions to Chapter XXV, Problem 21(c).

PAGE 159

The 9 squares whose sides are respectively 18, 15, 14, 10, 9, 8, 7, 4, 1 can be assembled into a 33 × 32 rectangle as shown in Figure 25.

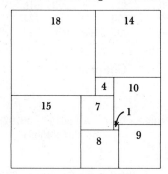

FIG. 25.   NINE SQUARES ASSEMBLED INTO A RECTANGLE

PAGE 161

A 13 × 13 square can be decomposed into squares as follows:

$$1 \cdot 7^2 + 2 \cdot 6^2 + 1 \cdot 4^2 + 2 \cdot 3^2 + 3 \cdot 2^2 + 2 \cdot 1^2 = 169$$

and the sum of the coefficients, $1 + 2 + 1 + 2 + 3 + 2 = 11$ is the *minimum* number of squares for this decomposition.   See Figure 26.

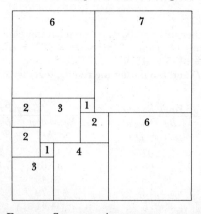

FIG. 26.   ELEVEN SQUARES ASSEMBLED INTO A SQUARE

Chapter XIX

PAGE 203

Solution of $x^2 \equiv 29 \mod 1193$
$$x \equiv \pm 534 \mod 1193.$$

Chapter XXI

PAGE 233

Factoring:

(a) $23449 = 131 \cdot 179$
(b) $394831 = 67 \cdot 71 \cdot 83$
(c) $16503593 = 3733 \cdot 4421$
(d) $18000001 = 3307 \cdot 5443$

Chapter XXII

PAGE 248

The least solution of $x^2 - 61y^2 = 1$ is

$$1766319049^2 - 61 \cdot 226153980^2 = 1.$$

Including Harold, the army must have consisted of

$$x = 3119882982860264401$$

men. Excluding the leader, the army could arrange itself into 61 squares each containing $(x^2 - 1)/61$ or 51145622669840400 men, the square of 226153980. Allowing one square foot per man, a globe three times the diameter of the earth would be required to contain the army.

PAGE 259

The least solution of $x^2 - 211y^2 = 1$ is

$$278354373650^2 - 19162705353^2 = 1.$$

Chapter XXV

PAGES 294–305

1. $10.21.

2. The following numbers are simultaneously squares, single, double, and triple triangles.

Square Number	Side of Square	Side of 1 Triangle	Side of 2 Triangles	Side of 3 Triangles
36	6	8	6; 5	5; 5; 3
1225	35	49	35; 34	33; 32; 16
41616	204	288	204; 203	192; 192; 95
1413721	1189	1681	1189; 1188	1121; 1120; 560
48024900	6930	9800	6930; 6929	6533; 6533; 3267
1631432881	40391	57121	40391; 40390	38081; 38080; 19040

The first year \$36 was saved; the sixth year it would have been necessary to save over one and one half billion dollars!

3. 31, 41, and 49 inches square.

4. 772, counting the strokes right at the beginning; otherwise, 771.

5. $x = 2ab+1$; $y = ab^2-a+b$; $z = ab^2+a+b$.

6. $12 \cdot 12 = 144 = 2 \cdot 6^2 + 3 \cdot 4^2 + 6 \cdot 2^2$.

7. In general $1^3 + 2^3 + 3^3 + \ldots + n^3 = n^2(n+1)^2/4$ so that the sum of consecutive cubes starting from unity is *always* a square. Excluding unity, $23^3 + 24^3 + 25^3 = 204^2$ is the smallest square sum of consecutive cubes, but then there are only 3 cubes whereas the problem calls for more than 3. The 5 consecutive cubes $25^3 + 26^3 + 27^3 + 28^3 + 29^3 = 315^2$ satisfy the condition but the *smallest* sum is obtained from the 12 cubes

$$14^3 + 15^3 + 16^3 + \ldots + 25^3 = 312^2.$$

8. Hypotenuse $Z = (p^2+q^2)^2$. The legs are $X = (p^2-q^2)^2 - (2pq)^2$; $Y = 4pq(p^2-q^2)$.

9. There are only 3 possible ways the exchange could have been made:

(a) A pair of diamond earrings for 2 other diamonds.
(b) A pair of diamond earrings for a diamond and a ruby.
(c) A pair of ruby earrings for 2 diamonds.

The least possible size of the gems for these cases is:

(a) A pair of 5-carat diamond earrings for a 7-carat and a 1-carat diamond.

(b) A pair of 3-carat diamond earrings for a 4-carat diamond and a 1-carat ruby.

(c) A pair of 5-carat ruby earrings for a 14-carat and a 48-carat diamond. (A second solution here is a 40- and a 30-carat diamond in exchange for the two 5-carat rubies, but the first solution involves the smallest total weights of the two stones.)

(d) The respective values of the 3 pairs of earrings were \$50000; \$18000; \$2500000; the values of the stones received in exchange were \$49000 and \$1000; \$16000 and \$2000; \$196000 and \$2304000.

Three cases are impossible:

(*a*) A pair of diamond earrings in exchange for 2 rubies.

(*b*) A pair of ruby earrings in exchange for a diamond and a ruby.

(*c*) A pair of ruby earrings in exchange for 2 rubies.

This is not a simple problem.

10. There were 3 oxen, 8 pigs, 109 sheep.

11. The sides are $b^2(4a^2-b^2)$, $4a^2(b^2-2a^2)$, $(8a^4-4a^2b^2+b^4)$, where b is odd and less than $2a$ but greater than $a\sqrt{2}$. For $a=2$, $b=3$ the sides 63; 16; 65 fulfill the conditions.

12. The largest square just under 100000 is $99856 = 316^2$, so there were 99857 men including their general, originally arranged in 2 groups of $3136 = 56^2$ and $96721 = 311^2$ men.

13. The 20-gallon barrel.

14. Smallest: 102347586. Largest: 987652413.

15. 68.

16. The only two-digit square ending having a 3 in the tens place is 36, so that must be the ending to the square. The arrangement of the work shows that the 2 left-hand digits of the square must be 10, so that the first digit of the root is 3. The arrangement also shows that the second digit of the root is 1. Barlow's table of squares gives only one four-digit number between 3100 and 3200 whose square ends in 36, namely, $3194 = 10201636$. The problem can easily be solved without resorting to a table of squares.

17. Divisor 179; remainder 164.

18. 12; 16; 60; 144; 320; 588; 1936.

19. Five ones, 50 twos, and 19 five-dollar bills.

20. 25. Had he given away 24 or received 24, he would still have had a square number. General formulas for 3 squares in arithmetic progression are given in Chapter XV.

21. (*a*) *Exactly* 11.3; 33.7; 46.3 inches square.

(*b*) 80929/1615; 106921/1615; 127729/1615 inches square.

(*c*) 1140299183/12051130; 905141617/12051130; 581618833/12051130 inches square.

The general solution of this problem, when possible, is difficult. If $(Z/Y)^2$, $(X/Y)^2$, and $(W/Y)^2$ are the 3 squares in descending order, and the common difference is A, we have: $X^2+AY^2 = Z^2$ and $X^2-AY^2 = W^2$. To solve, we first seek solutions of the auxiliary equations, $x^2+y^2 = az^2$ and $x^2-y^2 = bw^2$ where $ab = A$. Then $X = x^4+y^4$ and $Y = 2xyzw$. When $A = 23$, the auxiliary equations become $x^2+y^2 = z^2$ and $x^2-y^2 = 23w^2$. The general solution of the second of these is $x = m^2+23n^2$; $y = m^2-23n^2$; $w = 2mn$. Substituting in the first auxiliary equation, this gives $2(m^4+23^2n^4) = z^2$. If we let $n = 1$, the value $m = 17$ makes the expression a square since $2(17^4 + 23^2) = 410^2$. Then $x = 312$, $y = 266$, $w = 34$, $z = 410$. These have the common factor 2 which can be canceled, leaving $156^2 + 133^2 = 205^2$; $156^2 - 133^2 = 23 \cdot 17^2$ as the auxiliary equations. Then $X = 156^4 + 133^4 = 905141617$, $Y = 2 \cdot 156 \cdot 133 \cdot 205 \cdot 17 = 144613560$, $Z = 1140299183$, $W = 581618833$.

These solutions give the sides of the square in feet; if the answer is given in inches the sides are numerically 12 times as large. It is for this reason that the fractions given as the answers have the value of the denominator, Y, equal to 1/12 of 144613560 or 12051130.

Similar methods of attack will solve Problems 21a and 21b.

22. (a) 386; the other boxes contained 8450 and 16514 coins; total 25350.

(b) Total 10086. The boxes contained 482; 3362; and 6242 coins.

23. His number is 239 if he lives on the odd-numbered side of the street; the last number on the street is 337. If he lives on the even-numbered side, his number is 408 and the last number is 576. If the numbers run consecutively, his number is 204 and the last number is 288. The sum of the house numbers up to, but not including his house, is 14161; 41412; 20706 in the three respective cases.

24. Bill's package, containing 12 cotton and 6 nylon shirts, costs $4.68; cotton shirts cost 24 cents each for laundering, nylons cost 30 cents each.

25. He was 55 in 1940. He died in 1950 at the age of 65.

26. 11236.

27. Two solutions: ABC is 315 or 862. The common divisor is 547.

28. 2256 rails.

29. $9.50 or $19.00, depending on whether it was beer or wine.

30. Tuesday, March 17, 1936. Tuesday, March 17, 1908, is another solution but then the swain would not be very young. A lover may again say this in 1964 and a *fin de siècle* one in 1992.

31. Tom bet $15 at 15 to 1 and won $225, which with his original $25 equals $250. Bill bet $10 at 10 to 1, which with his original $25 equals $125, so that he ended up with just half as much as Tom. The solution involves a Pell equation. Other solutions are possible but the odds would be impractically large.

32. Three boys and three girls each receiving one 1/2-cent and two 1/3-cent buns. There could also have been only one boy and one girl but then the purchase could have been made in 10 ways instead of the single way as required.

33. 11 acres.

34.

$$(a) \quad 161^2 - 1620 \cdot 4^2 = 1.$$
$$(b) \quad 2449^2 - 1666 \cdot 60^2 = 1.$$

35. Four cherries and 16 caramels were purchased. Each child received 1 cherry and 4 caramels. Three cherries, 2 caramels, and 15 almonds also cost 40 cents, but these could not be equally divided.

36. The man loses 7 one-franc bets in succession, then loses 3 seven-franc bets and wins 4. He then loses 5 forty-nines and wins 2; then wins 7 on 343. He next loses 3 times on 2401 and wins 4 times, then loses 5 times on 16807 and wins twice, finally wins 7 times on 117649, winning in all 869288, losing 91511, or netting 777777. He won 26 times and lost 23 times. This problem is solved by expressing 777777 as powers of 7 with *odd* coefficients. Then the positive coefficients represent wins, the negative ones losses.

37. The original piles contained 120 and 560 nuts, having bases with 8 and 14 on a side respectively and with 36 and 105 nuts respectively in the base of the piles. The final pyramid had a total of 680 coconuts with a base having 15 on a side and containing 120 coconuts.

38. Were it not specified that he had more than 100 pennies, exactly 100 would fill the requirements since $10^2 - 19 \cdot 1^2 = 81$. The next possible value of x in $x^2 - 19y^2 = 81$ is 66, so that he had at least $66^2 = 4356$ pennies and each of the 19 smaller piles contained $15^2 = 225$ coins. The third possible solution is $105^2 = 11025$ coins and each of the 19 piles would then contain $24^2 = 576$ coins. An infinite number of solutions can be obtained from the formula:

$$x = 10 \left[\frac{(170 + 39\sqrt{19})^n + (170 - 39\sqrt{19})^n}{2} \right]$$
$$\pm 19 \left[\frac{(170 + 39\sqrt{19})^n - (170 - 39\sqrt{19})^n}{2\sqrt{19}} \right]$$
$$y = \left[\frac{(170 + 39\sqrt{19})^n + (170 - 39\sqrt{19})^n}{2} \right]$$
$$\pm 10 \left[\frac{(170 + 39\sqrt{19})^n - (170 - 39\sqrt{19})^n}{2\sqrt{19}} \right]$$

The answers are, of course, always integers; the radicals always cancel out.

Unfortunately these expressions do not yield *all* the solutions nor even the least ones given above. When $n = 1$, the two solutions obtained are: $959^2 - 19 \cdot 220^2 = 81$ and $2441^2 - 19 \cdot 560^2 = 81$.

39. He had no less than 60 coins of each denomination, making a total of $2100. Other possible solutions are multiples of 60 and of 2100.

40. The minimum number of steps is 201. The general solution is $210k + 201$ where k may be any positive integer or zero.

41. $99.98.

42. Seven with round holes and one with a square hole.

43. 3651.

44. For a triangular pyramid, 193 eggs in one line of the base, 18721 eggs in entire base, 193 layers, 1216865 eggs total.

A square pyramid with 193 eggs on one side of the base, $193^2 = 37249$ eggs in the base, and having a total of 2415009 eggs, can just be supported by its lowest layer, each of the 37249 eggs in the base being subjected to 7.979 lbs.—barely under the limit. For one additional layer, there would be 194 eggs on a side of the base, $194^2 = 37636$ in the base, and a total of 2452645 eggs. Each of the 37636 eggs in the base would be subjected to 8.0209 lbs.—just enough to crush the pile and scramble the eggs.

45. The sides are any numbers proportional to 3, 4, 5.

46. Twenty-two pieces. A 12×12 square is made up of $1 \cdot 8^2 + 4 \cdot 4^2 + 16 \cdot 1^2$, leaving a single 5×5 square. See Figures 27 and 28 for this and another solution.

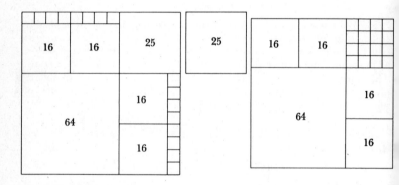

FIG. 27.   ASSEMBLING A 13×13 SQUARE INTO TWO SQUARES

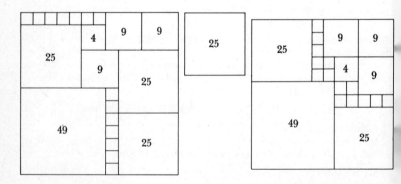

FIG. 28.   ASSEMBLING A 13×13 SQUARE INTO TWO SQUARES

47. We have $(a^3-1)a^3(a^3+1) \equiv 0 \bmod 2^3 \cdot 3^2 \cdot 7$.

By Fermat's general theorem, $a^6-1 \equiv 0 \bmod 3^2$, also by the simple theorem $a^6-1 \equiv 0 \bmod 7$. Finally either a is even, in which case a^3 is divisible by 8, or $a^3 \pm 1$ are both even, in which case one is divisible by 4 and the other by 2 so that their product is divisible by 8. Then since 2^3, 3^2, and 7 are relatively prime, $a^3(a^6-1) \equiv 0 \bmod 2^3 \cdot 3^2 \cdot 7$.

48. The solution to Problem 48 is given in Table 102.

TABLE 102

Values of N Having the Same $\phi(N)$

$\phi(N)$	N	$\phi(N)$	N
1	1, 2	24	35, 39, 45, 52, 56, 70, 72, 78, 84, 90
2	3, 4, 6	28	29, 58
4	5, 8, 10, 12	30	31, 62
6	7, 9, 14, 18	32	51, 64, 68, 80, 96
8	15, 16, 20, 24, 30	36	37, 57, 63, 74, 76
10	11, 22	40	41, 55, 75, 82, 88, 100
12	13, 21, 26, 28, 36, 42	42	43, 49, 86, 98
16	17, 32, 34, 40, 48, 60	44	69, 92
18	19, 27, 38, 54	46	47, 94
20	25, 33, 44, 50, 66	60	61, 77, 93, 99
22	23, 46	72	73, 91, 95

49. 1 and 2; 3 and 2^2; 5 and 2^3; 7 and 3^2; 17 and 2^5; 19 and 3^3; 43 and 7^2.

50. The large containers measured 108 inches on an edge. Then

$$108^3 = 104^3 + 51^3 + 13^3 = 106^3 + 38^3 + 24^3 = 96^3 + 72^3 + 12^3$$
$$= 90^3 + 72^3 + 54^3 = 89^3 + 82^3 + 15^3.$$

The smaller containers therefore measured 106, 104, 96, 90, 89, 82, 72, 72, 54, 51, 38, 24, 15, 13, and 12 inches, respectively, on an edge.

51. Let $N = 7K+3$ be the original number. If the digit 3 is placed first, a new number $3 \cdot 7^x + K$ is formed (to radix 7). Then

$$\frac{4}{5}(7K+3) = 3 \cdot 7^x + K.$$

Simplifying, $15 \cdot 7^x - 12 = 23K$ or $-8 \cdot 7^x \equiv 12 \bmod 23$. This gives $7^x \equiv 10 \bmod 23$ and $x \equiv 21 \bmod 22$. To obtain a solution of less than 40 digits, take $x = 21$. Then $K = (15 \cdot 7^{21} - 12)/23$, and

$$N = 7K+3 = [(15 \cdot 7^{22} - 84)/23] + 3 = 15(7^{22}-1)/23.$$

This answer is in the common or denary scale and written out is equal to 2549883292554122640. In the septenary scale it is equal to

4364604155323020625113.

Putting the last digit 3, first, we have that 3436460415532302062511 is 4/5 of the original number (counting in the scale of 7).

52. Writing 1000000 in the scale of 7, we have

	Dividend						Remainder
7| 1	0	0	0	0	0	0	
7| 1	4	2	8	5	7		1
7| 2	0	4	0	8			1
7| 2	9	1	5				3
7| 4	1	6					3
7| 5	9						3
7| 8							3
7| 1							1
7| 0							1

so that $1000000 = 7^7 + 7^6 + 3 \cdot 7^5 + 3 \cdot 7^4 + 3 \cdot 7^3 + 3 \cdot 7^2 + 7 + 1$. The millionaire, therefore, distributed his money as follows:

One	gift of 7^7 =	\$823543
One	„ „ 7^6 =	117649
Three	gifts „ 7^5 =	50421
Three	„ „ 7^4 =	7203
Three	„ „ 7^3 =	1029
Three	„ „ 7^2 =	147
One	gift „ 7 =	7
One	„ „ 1 =	1
		\$1000000

53. Let x equal the number of coconuts. For simplicity let:

$$(n-1)/n = A, \quad \text{then} \quad A-1 = -1/n \quad \text{and} \quad 1/(A-1) = -n.$$

The first man left $A(x-1)$ nuts.
The second man left $A[A(x-1)-1] = A^2(x-1)-A$.
The third man left $A[A^2(x-1)-A-1] = A^3(x-1)-A^2-A$, etc.
Finally,
the nth man left

$$A^n(x-1) - (A^{n-1} + A^{n-2} + \ldots + A) = A^n(x-1) - (A^n - A)/(A-1)$$
$$= A^n[x - 1 - 1/(A-1)] + A/(A-1)$$

and this is a multiple of n.
Substituting for A, we have:

$$[(n-1)/n]^n(x-1+n) - (n-1) \equiv 0 \mod n.$$
$$[(x-1+n)/n^n](-1)^n \equiv -1 \mod n.$$

Then $(x-1+n)/n^n = kn \pm 1$, the ambiguity in sign being plus when n is odd and minus when n is even. Finally,

$$x = n^n(kn \pm 1) - (n-1) = n^n[kn - (-1)^n] - (n-1).$$

k may have any integral value that will not make x negative. For the *least* value of x, $k = 0$ or 1 according as n is odd or even, resulting respectively in $n^n - (n-1)$ and $(n^n - 1)(n-1)$. When $n = 5$, $x = 5^5 - 4 = 3121$. When $n = 4$, $x = (4^4 - 1)(4-1) = 765$.

If there are n men and r monkeys, the nth man leaves

$$A^n(x-r) - r(A^{n-1} + \ldots + A) = A^n(x-r) - [r(A^n - A)]/(A-1)$$
$$= A^n[x-r-r/(A-1)] + Ar/(A-1)$$

nuts. Then $(n-1)^n[(x-r+nr)/n^n] - r(n-1) \equiv 0 \mod n$.

$$[(x-r+nr)/n^n](-1)^n \equiv -r \mod n$$
$$(x-r+nr)/n^n = kn \pm r \text{ and}$$
$$x = n^n[kn - r(-1)^n] - r(n-1).$$

The least solutions again correspond to $k = 0$ or 1, respectively, when n is odd or even, resulting in $x = rn^n - r(n-1)$ and $n^n(n-r) - r(n-1)$ for the two cases.

54. Since the sum of the digits is divisible by both 3 and 7, the digit 3 must be used a multiple of 7 times and the digit 7 a multiple of 3 times. Therefore, the required least number must have 10 digits of which 3 are sevens and 7 are threes. The number resulting from any arrangement of these digits is divisible by 3 since if the sum of the digits of a number is divisible by 3 so is the number itself. The only remaining requirement, therefore, is to permute the 10 digits to give the least number divisible by 7.

If the number consisted of 10 threes we could write it as

$$3 \cdot 10^9 + 3 \cdot 10^8 + \ldots + 3 \cdot 10^1 + 3 \cdot 10^0.$$

Finding the residues mod 7 of $3 \cdot 10^9$; $3 \cdot 10^8$; etc., we have:

Exponent, n	Residue, r, mod 7 of $3 \cdot 10^n$
0	3
1	2
2	6
3	4
4	5
5	1
6	3
7	2
8	6
9	4

Sum of residues = $36 \equiv 1 \mod 7$

Therefore 3333333333 leaves a remainder of unity when divided by 7, hence three of the terms whose residues add to 1 or 8 or 15, etc., must be removed to make the remaining sum exactly divisible by 7. Substituting three numbers of the form $7 \cdot 10^n$ will then not affect divisibility, since $7 \cdot 10^n$ is always congruent to zero modulo 7. To select three residues whose sum is 1, 8, or 15 we have only the following choices:

Exponent, n	Residue, r	Sum of Residues, $\sum r$
0, 1, 6	3, 2, 3	8
0, 2, 8	3, 6, 6	15
0, 3, 5	3, 4, 1	8
1, 3, 7	2, 4, 2	8
1, 4, 5	2, 5, 1	8
2, 3, 4	6, 4, 5	15

The greatest exponent, 4, in the last choice is less than in any of the other choices and will therefore give the smallest solution. Therefore $3 \cdot 10^2$; $3 \cdot 10^3$; and $3 \cdot 10^4$ must be removed and replaced by corresponding powers of 10 with coefficient 7. The resulting number 3333377733 is the least solution.

55. Let x be the number of times the digit 3 is used, y the digit 5, and z the digit 7. Then $3x + 5y + 7z$ must be divisible by 3, 5, and 7, that is, by 105, and the least solution will result when $x + y + z$ is a minimum in the equation $3x + 5y + 7z = 105$. Since z has the largest coefficient, 7, the sum of the three variables will be a minimum when z is large. Trying values of $z = 13, 12, 11, 10$, we find that there are three sets of possible values for x, y, and z such that their sum has the minimum value 17: $x = 3$, $y = 1$, $z = 13$; $x = 2$, $y = 3$, $z = 12$; $x = 1$, $y = 5$, $z = 11$. Therefore the required number must have at least 17 digits. Divisibility by 3 is automatically assured since the sum of the digits is divisible by 3; divisibility by 5 will occur if the number ends in 5.

Solving each of the three sets of values obtained above as an independent problem, we take first the case $x = 3, y = 1, z = 13$, where there is only one 5. This must obviously be at the extreme right in the solution. In the number 77777777777777775, three of the sevens must be replaced by threes in such positions that the resulting number is divisible by 7. Since the number above is obviously congruent to 5 mod 7, we must find three terms of $3 \cdot 10^n$ whose sum is congruent to 2 mod 7, and these should be the highest possible powers so that they may replace sevens as far to the left as possible in order to result in the smallest solution (see p. 325).

The two largest exponents correspond to residues whose sum $5 + 4$ is congruent to 2 mod 7 as required, but we need one more residue—three all told—and since no residue is zero, we cannot use the two highest. For the exponents 16 and 14, the residues are $5 + 6 \equiv 4$ mod 7 and we need another residue, 5, for the sum to be congruent to 2 mod 7. This

Exponent, n	Residue, r, mod 7 of $3 \cdot 10^n$	Exponent, n	Residue, r, mod 7 of $3 \cdot 10^n$
0	3	9	4
1	2	10	5
2	6	11	1
3	4	12	3
4	5	13	2
5	1	14	6
6	3	15	4
7	2	16	5
8	6		

is obtained from the exponent 10. Hence $7 \cdot 10^{16}$; $7 \cdot 10^{14}$; and $7 \cdot 10^{10}$ must be removed and replaced by the corresponding powers with coefficient 3, the resulting number 37377737777777775 being the smallest solution for the case of one five, 3 threes, and 13 sevens.

Solutions are obtained similarly for the other two sets of values of x, y, and z except that the problem is complicated by using more than one 5 and the fact that powers of 3 and 5 must be tabulated and the residues of the highest powers combined to give a remainder of zero mod 7. For $x = 2$, $y = 3$, $z = 12$, we obtain 33577577777777775, and for $x = 1$, $y = 5$, $z = 11$ the solution 35555777777777775. Finally, the smallest solution of the three is the second, 33577577777777775.

56. The L.C.M. of the 9 digits is 2520, so that the required number must be divisible by 2520. Obviously the number must end in zero so as to be divisible by 2 and 5. It must also be divisible by 7 and 8; then if these conditions are fulfilled it will be divisible by all of the digits since the sum of the digits in the required number is 45 and therefore it will be divisible by 3 and 9 regardless of how the digits are arranged. (The number will be divisible by 4 if divisible by 8 and divisible by 6 if it is divisible by 2 and 3.) To be divisible by 8, a number ending in zero must end in one of the following 16 triplets of *unrepeated* digits: 120; 320; 520; 720; 920; 240; 640; 840; 160; 360; 560; 760; 960; 280; 480; 680.

To obtain the least solution, assume that at least the first four digits at the left are 1, 2, 3, 4. If no solution can be obtained on this basis we can later assume that only 1, 2, 3 are at the left. Since no digits must be repeated, our assumption leaves only 560; 760; 960; and 680 for the three digits at the right end of the solution. The numbers 1234000560; 1234000760; 1234000960; and 1234000680 leave remainders of 2, 6, 3, and 3 respectively modulo 7, and therefore the unused digits in each case must be arranged to give the complementary remainders 5, 1, 4, and 4.

A table of remainders for the unused digits in the fifth, sixth, and seventh places enables us to select those permutations which have the desired residues.   The digit 7 does not appear in this table since it may be placed anywhere without affecting the divisibility.

Residues mod 7 of a·10^x

| | a = | | | |
x	5	6	8	9
3	2	1	6	5
4	6	3	4	1
5	4	2	5	3

No solution can be obtained for the first case, 1234000560; the second case gives two solutions: 1234895760 and 1234958760; the third case has one solution 1234857960, and the fourth 1234759680.   Of these the last is the least.

57. See Table 103, pages 328–29, in this chapter.

58. By Formula 1 of Chapter XV:

$$(a_1 + 1)(a_2 + 1) \ldots (a_n + 1) = 24.$$

Expressing 24 as the product of 2, 3, 4 factors, we find $24 = 12 \cdot 2$; $8 \cdot 3$; $6 \cdot 4$; $2 \cdot 2 \cdot 6$; $2 \cdot 3 \cdot 4$; $2 \cdot 2 \cdot 2 \cdot 3$.   The last of these gives the smallest values for the exponents of the number N of Chapter XV, namely, $a_1 = 2$, $a_2 = a_3 = a_4 = 1$ and the number $N = 5^2 \cdot 13 \cdot 17 \cdot 29 = 160225$ is the least possible which can be the sum of 2 squares in 12 ways.   These are: $400^2 + 15^2$; $399^2 + 32^2$; $393^2 + 76^2$; $392^2 + 81^2$; $384^2 + 113^2$; $375^2 + 140^2$; $360^2 + 175^2$; $356^2 + 183^2$; $337^2 + 216^2$; $329^2 + 228^2$; $311^2 + 252^2$; and $265^2 + 300^2$.

Formula 2 in Chapter XV would give: $(a_1 + 1)(a_2 + 1) \ldots (a_n + 1) = 25$, and factoring 25 into $25 \cdot 1$ or $5 \cdot 5$, the smallest exponents would be 4 and 4 obtained from the second resolution.   The resulting number $5^4 \cdot 13^4$, however, although expressible as the sum of 2 squares in 12 ways is much larger than $5^2 \cdot 13 \cdot 17 \cdot 29$.

59. Each heir receives a square sum of money and the amounts in one family are squares in arithmetic progression.   The 3 groups of squares all have the same common difference; call it d.   From Chapter XV we note that d must equal $4mn(m^2 - n^2)$ and there must be 3 sets of values of m and n yielding the same d.   This is satisfied by 7, 3; 7, 5; and 8, 7, giving $d = 3360$.   (It will be noted that $mn[m^2 - n^2]$ is the area of a Pythagorean triangle; to obtain 3 such triangles having equal areas, use $m_1 = m_2 = r^2 + rs + s^2$, $m_3 = r^2 + 2rs$, $n_1 = r^2 - s^2$, $n_2 = 2rs + s^2$, $n_3 = r^2 + rs + s^2$. Letting $r = 2$ and $s = 1$, we obtain the 3 sets of values, 7, 3; 7, 5; and 8, 7.)   Substituting the 3 pairs of values of m and n in the formulas for 3 squares in A.P.:

$$X = m^2 - n^2 - 2mn; \quad Y = m^2 + n^2; \quad Z = m^2 - n^2 + 2mn;$$

we obtain the 3 respective triplets:

Z^2 (Husbands)	Y^2 (Wives)	X^2 (Children)	Sum
$6724 = 82^2$	$3364 = 58^2$	$4 = 2^2$	\$10092
$8836 = 94^2$	$5476 = 74^2$	$2116 = 46^2$	16428
$16129 = 127^2$	$12769 = 113^2$	$9409 = 97^2$	38307
		Total	\$64827

The amounts in the first column belong to the husbands; the amounts in the second to the wives and those in the last column to the children. Since there are only four females there must be one daughter and two sons. From these considerations and the other conditions of the problem, we find that $5476 + 3364 = 8836 + 4 = 8840$ and $8836 + 5476 + 2116 = 16129 + 299 = 16428$. The Joneses received over a third more than the Browns so that the second and first row of numbers must be the amounts they received respectively. This completely identifies the individuals and their legacies, as follows:

Bill Jones	\$8836	Hank Smith	\$16129	Jack Brown	\$6724
Mary Jones	5476	Eliza Smith	12769	Sarah Brown	3364
Ned Jones	2116	Susan Smith	9409	Tom Brown	4
	\$16428		\$38307		\$10092

60. Let A be the number exclusive of its units digit, D. Then $10A + D = N$ is the complete number and $D \cdot 10^x + A$ is the new number where x represents the number of digits in A. Then N has $x+1$ digits, and $K(10A + D) = D \cdot 10^x + A$ or $A(10K - 1) = D(10^x - K)$. Then $A = D(10^x - K)/(10K - 1)$. Then since $N = 10A + D$, we have

$$N = D(10^e - 1)/(10K - 1)$$

where $e = x + 1$. The least value of N for a given K has e digits.

The table below shows a few values of K, and the least possible number of digits, e in N, when D is prime to $10K - 1$.

K	$10K - 1$	e
2	19	18
3	29	28
4	39	6
5	49	42
6	59	58
7	69	22
8	79	13
9	89	44
10	99	2

Thus to multiply N by 6 when its units digit is moved to first place requires a number of no less than 58 digits, but to multiply it by 4 requires

TABLE 103

Pythagorean Triangles With Consecutive Legs

Number	Short Leg	Hypotenuse
1	3	5
2	20	29
3	119	169
4	696	985
5	4059	5741
6	23660	33461
7	137903	195025
8	803760	1136689
9	4684659	6625109
10	27304196	38613965
11	159140519	225058681
12	927538920	1311738121
13	5406093003	7645370045
14	31509019100	44560482149
15	183648021599	259717522849
16	1070379110496	1513744654945
17	6238626641379	8822750406821
18	36361380737780	51422757785981
19	211929657785303	299713796309065
20	1235216565974040	1746860020068409
21	7199369738058939	10181446324101389
22	41961001862379596	59341817924539925
23	244566641436218639	345869461223138161
24	1425438846754932240	2015874949414289041
25	8308066439093374803	11749380235262596085
26	48422959787805316580	68480406462161287469
27	282229692287738524679	399133058537705128729
28	1644955193938625831496	2326317944764069484905
29	9587501471344016464299	13558774610046711780701
30	55880053634125472954300	79026329715516201199301
31	325692820333408821261503	460599203683050495415105
32	1898276868366327454614720	2684568892382786771291329
33	11063968389864555906426819	15646814150613670132332869
34	64485533470821007983946196	91196316011299234022705885
35	375849232435061491997250359	531531081917181734003902441
36	2190609861139547943999555960	3097990175491791170000708761
37	12767809934402226172000085403	18056409971033565286000350125
38	74416249745273809088000956460	105240469650709600546001391989
39	433729688537240628356005653359	613386407933224037990008001809
40	2527961881478169961048032963696	3575077977948634627394046618865
41	14734041600331779137932192128819	20837081459758583726374271711381
42	85876287720512504866545119809220	121447410780602867730851583649421
43	500523684722743250061338526726503	707847383223858622658735230185145
44	2917265820615946995501486040549800	4125636888562548868221559797461449

51	6605249862764845252797503152899061616393			9426520701020461307334377465967762860893
52	3884963735033554627306126433060073746709			5494168403412088213319314492946575538483
53	2264322280119248430855700828585363170939			3202236510704831491824492110826760228613
54	1319744043365148722403592277391441558540			1866399924998108106817753807773549480752341
55	7692031980071680830356585313791273286180303			1087817594842494384094146935430214208491185
56	4483247837064930100989915264994824827523280			6340265576556155474049670436180773577019769
57	2613026550423178998290583830586102636966995379			3695377586494494384684608709195545162004167429
58	1522983482416842468864330808606304992623296			2153823896101404153381970810068946670586980
59	8876598239458736913356694665461368083190438599			1255340561797968413560325456658820599825441401
60	5173606594335579012773490985434544921639860			7316606098177400006023755031791634132229378601
61	3015430374865547315430714792627904612107953003			4264462532526431622582204743010084193535730205
62	1757521618964992843914565538460850822234313193420			2485519009704218977246944733728487102903002629
63	1024358667603034023633308608238888738872847969319			1448661920497060706754234655502586014198100428509
64	5970399848388554211140839509857238450174448461696			8443420432013143050795983396439139805694311078509
65	3479804039568291243581706196685954331215621806659			4921186061977459802139540326078602231129590519785
66	2028178425302119325049397653000214227898163782860			2868277435971766445632533243407452060478106619164610
67	1182090471855588668230726170037868128434348992470963			1617154091327105752597320904706867125479123005225
68	6889583624813332163003736861288434348992470630839160			9743699618821859032185062018014049422747168167289
69	4015690846231433229545917407904117203543336551612930350			5670944450379838361685067121195087865231259019850
70	23405161457770261730769747657661362378036017722466919			3309896736039684426689189945253007768640094223765
71	1364152778703901070936302677188913315146177969826222719			192920360790200122723966629009085378746062694374408
72	7950865075697570752856841293736734365384174160942930			11244271191910516191710607456558219471101522240140721
73	4634103756747043378604745107015148602934461859018127900350			655361282235766188788690711839051094838649710024
74	27009364031726551371162934472554945454478435750500			38197251283235766185754495117159451117341352198002097926
75	157423112451528778701062503096132613918463085409687826329990			22262990063599368580295751731769622743474649158421395766424
76	91752931867446003669637855642332328714319087913342632749600			1297582151785925569365755531915418686112247089165170035224745
77	53477517199532561441476646305780735836714424169920			7562863018031585954955370940176191488806348422
78	3111689817889696928612163499289045208142090389654508655716438000			4407959590854777197506925775788753505185862572811137380581
79	181661353537864020150349442663175705748859449882306253045			2569147124123104601174744955175945117134135219802097925009
80	1058287830943821112768629572711384601589261058388072336140400			1497408678738383849900949541721193224181176509846185590982745009
81	617130085070911040336429671234419998909011786706873453616159143390			87275375999179994825607552664279276078458297832438763690759
82	35968972772510209080110489028825556451130981866853257512459600			50867815481219611190481419594799723844708031165842355655627524972500
83	20964256277515698508373173762344663239282994979172476812634883239			294479355552272799671946653940160950237921693327127809377646876100
84	122188639938003088968446274082083089050733118886406592931343873840000			17228003117628418941977504520717169508900830796516080383339641
85	71216758333502835300838399127624080676700101811852175477076796841803			100717057050565752708467063732809945666972957636784597194452533686285
86	415086868165013907187930214769130451756469367303024723987004376619800			587041498572269466046984734656230869007762782512066607580722069
87	241923357776945068707071718719304146723298222373493911304079			3421369193632896015978235197997184846588983731368020459391115470500
88	14100558460567240728747352261040472630440263904924540942590591371204496			11622586887852662639096563252177267614648616067640763236261182100
89	8218407740456926742087457225212176261630280665109960979545434381097359922899			677413820257080508426543915147734249403375342529877564298585985537901
90	4790039059732698975851337975515275636773903789418394682034482434007900			
91	2791839358439798614084892236947373601304260391149449852021553007450300			3948257865444863291669364766454228218086871639632186217014991729945305
92	16272032244630609270840887108648915446132966924008652445271270960944493611412000			23012128687728923973954457050725763504770654834949434439519613060000
93	94840534109496756304576378632004398504277239214886325126813858448067610219			134124515041709209010246574909362610538378547474808450884874494233025685
94	5527700924114645514531185218781929969597795202739349848166411775835471196			7817349615625263130085880518056929187734708450884074942332035891
95	32178002035945499610732639272917967170899320018746316217545852341472959			455628525433344877150506352900404595964506900683020524063593450034599
96	18778791110974526253132106234914833429579680845496156231326552922921174349896944356726499936361			26555976564438165298944449615623321563609592292114349890630693939356
97	1094445864581121201918853110177191710338528848848522223871532012142012270403			154779541323954905224972003613108748690510931182857468432566160325
98	63789209357546266589244586199797968827513668699296284684853886517475625689			9021214845049845100869842984298345884881533611602000256216894921
99	37179315593754526316272993248192429716383699446334608169199294708985345847736589			5257949253243715211078019994354590680832052145146321903025454761191215209
100	216696931486137883054797972928306716401520276689946534408169199233848549269696			30645573943232956180057997296983234588763069544508753693529117371074705467772828665

only a 6-digit number. If $K = 2$ and $D = 2$, then N is the 18-digit number 105263157894736842.

The denominator $10K - 1$ in the formula for the value of N is always prime to the digits $D = 2, 4, 5, 8$ so that for these 4 digits, the number of digits, e, in N is independent of the value of D and depends only on the value of K.   When D is not prime to $10K - 1$, the denominator is reduced and this may reduce the value of e.   The values of D and K, the resulting congruences that must be solved to obtain e, and the values of N are tabulated below:

D	$10K - 1 =$	$10^e - 1 \equiv 0 \bmod:$	N
3	$3m$	m	$(10^e - 1)/m$
6	$3m$	m	$2(10^e - 1)/m$
7	$7m$	m	$(10^e - 1)/m$
9	$9m$	m	$(10^e - 1)/m$
9	$9m \pm 3$	$3m \pm 1$	$3(10^e - 1)/(3m \pm 1)$

For $K = 5$, $10K - 1 = 49$, $e = 42$, and N has 42 digits for all values of D except 7.   For $D = 7$, N has 6 digits only, and the least solution for N is 142857.   Here the value of D had a considerable effect on N.   But dividing the modulus $10K - 1$ by 3 or 9 does not reduce e unless $10K - 1$ contains a power of 3 exceeding 9 and not necessarily even then.   Thus $K = 46$ is the *smallest* value for which the selection of the digit $D = 3, 6,$ or 9 reduces e from 48 to 16.   With any of the remaining 5 digits, $e = 48$ would be required.   For a smaller value of K making $10K - 1$ divisible by a power of 3 greater than 9, such as $K = 19$, $10K - 1 = 27 \cdot 7$, the value of e would be 6 regardless of which digit was used for D.

If K times the left-hand digit of N exceeds 9, zeros may be required in front of the significant digits in N as when $K = 10$.   If $D = 2$, then N must be taken as 02 which becomes 20 when the 2 is placed first.   Again if $K = 12$ and $D = 7$, then N has 16 digits and must be written

$$0588235294117647$$

since $12N$ equals 7058823529411764.

61. Let $1000x + 100y + 10z + u =$ face amount of check.   Then $1000u + 100z + 10y + x =$ amount paid out.   Then $999u + 90z - 90y - 999x =$ cashier's shortage $= B^2$, a square.   Then

$$111(u - x) + 10(z - y) = B^2/9 = A^2,$$

another square.   Let $u - x = L$ and $z - y = M$.   The first digit x cannot be zero, also L cannot be zero, otherwise $10(z - y)$ would have to be a square which is impossible since $(z - y) < 10$.   Hence $0 < x < 8$, and $0 < L < 9$. M may be positive or negative but not zero, since then $111L$ would have to be a square which is impossible for $(u - x) < 9$.   Then $0 < |M| \le 9$.   Then $111L + 10M = A^2$ and $M \equiv A^2 \bmod 3$, hence M is a quadratic residue of 3, namely $\pm(1, 3, 4, 7, 9)$.   Since squares terminate only in 0, 1, 4, 5, 6, 9, and $10M$ always ends in zero, it follows that $111L$ must end in one of the digits 0, 1, 4, 5, 6 (since $L < 9$). Hence $111 + 10M$, $444 + 10M$, $555 + 10M$, or $666 + 10M$ must be a square. Tabulating the possibilities we have:

Solution Type	M	L	$A = B/3$	Short-age $= B^2$	$z = y + M$	$u = x + L$	Range: x	y	Solutions $=$ Comb. of x and y
1	1	1	11	1089	$y + 1$	$x + 1$	1–8	0–8	72
2	1	6	26	6084	$y + 1$	$x + 6$	1–3	0–8	27
3	4	4	22	4356	$y + 4$	$x + 4$	1–5	0–5	30
4	7	5	25	5625	$y + 7$	$x + 5$	1–4	0–2	12
5	−3	1	9	729	$y − 3$	$x + 1$	1–8	3–9	56
6	−9	6	24	5184	0	$x + 6$	1–3	9	3
								Total	200

Thus six squares are possible, listed under B^2, and the check could have been written for 200 different amounts.

Two solutions of the 27 possible ones of Type 2 are: \$18.97 and \$30.19. Two solutions of the 56 possible ones of Type 5 are \$35.24 and \$13.02. Other solutions can be obtained by arbitrarily assigning values to x and y within their assigned limits.

62. Proceeding as in Problem 61, we have $111L + 10M = B^3/9 = 3A^3$ where $B = 3A$ and since $L < 9$ and $|M| < 10$, $3A^3 < 978$ or $A^3 < 326$. Since $7^3 > 326$, we need consider only the values $A = 1$ to 6. For these only $A = 3$ and 4 yield solution types, with $L = 1$, $M = −3$ and $L = 2$, $M = −3$ respectively. The two cube shortages are 729 and 1728. In the first case, $x = 1$ to 8, $y = 3$ to 9, $z = y − 3$, $u = x + 1$. This gives 56 solutions for the combinations of x and y. In the second case, $x = 1$ to 7, $y = 3$ to 9, $z = y − 3$, $u = x + 2$. This gives 49 solutions, making a total of 105 solutions. Examples for each solution type are \$83.09 and \$37.45.

63. (a) The number N is obviously divisible by 111.

(b) C must be 0, 5, 8, or 9 so that when N is increased by 1 a possible 3-digit ending of a square will result.

(c) C cannot be 9, otherwise the square S^2 would end in 3 zeros and squares must end in an even number of zeros. Hence S^2 must terminate only in 001, 556, or 889.

(d) $111222333 < S^2 < 999888777$ or $10546 < S < 31621$.

(e) It can easily be shown that all squares, S^2, whose last 3 digits agree with the last 3 digits of a given smallest square, T^2, are obtained from the formula $S^2 = (500K \pm T)^2$ when T is even and from $S^2 = (250K \pm T)^2$ when T is odd. Taking the even value 556, the least square T^2 having this ending is $166^2 = 27556$, and substituting in the "even" formula we have $S^2 = (500K \pm 166)^2$ represents *all* squares with this 3-digit ending. Then $(500K \pm 166)^2 - 1 \equiv 0 \bmod 111$, and $K \equiv \mp 1$, ± 3, mod 37 (a divisor of 111). Only the values $K = 34$; 36; 38; or 40 permit S

to fall within the limits set by (d) but none of the values of S meets the conditions.

Next taking the odd value 001, the least such square is 1 and substituting in the "odd" formula, $S^2 = (250K \pm 1)^2$ represents *all* squares ending in 001. Then $(250K \pm 1)^2 - 1 \equiv 0$ mod 111, and $K \equiv 0$ or ∓ 8, mod 37. Only the values $K = 45; 66; 74; 82; 103; 111; 119$ permit S to fall within the limits set by (d) and again these yield no solution.

Finally for 889, the least square $T^2 = 83^2 = 6889$. Then $S^2 = (250K + 83)^2$. Then $(250K \pm 83)^2 - 1 \equiv 0$ mod 111, for which $K \equiv \mp 3, \pm 5$, mod 37. Only the values $K = 42; 69; 71; 77; 79; 106; 108; 114; 116$ permit S to fall within the limits set by (d). The value $K = 42$ yields $S = 10583$, $S^2 = 111999889$ and the required number is 111999888. None of the other values for S gives a solution.

64. Consider the integers from 0 to $10^n - 1$; $(10^n - 1)$ consists of n nines. Pair zero with this number, pair 1 with $10^n - 2$, pair 2 with $10^n - 3$, etc. Since, including zero, there are 10^n integers, there are $10^n/2$ pairs. But each pair sums to $10^n - 1$, the sum of whose digits is $9n$. Since there are $10^n/2$ pairs, the sum of all these digits is $9n \cdot 10^n/2$, and adding 1 for the integer 10^n, we get $[9n \cdot 10^n/2] + 1 = 45n \cdot 10^{n-1} + 1$. For 1 billion, $n = 9$ and the sum is 40500000001.

65. $3^2 \equiv 2$ mod 7; $3^{2x} \equiv 2^x$ mod 7; $3^{2x+1} \equiv 3 \cdot 2^x$. Then

$$3^{2x+1} + 2^{x+2} \equiv 3 \cdot 2^x + 2^{x+2} \equiv 2^x(3 + 2^2) = 2^x \cdot 7 \equiv 0 \quad \text{mod } 7.$$

66. Let F   =   .TALKTALK...
Then 10000F = TALK.TALK...
Then 9999F = TALK.

Then $(EVE)/DID = F = (TALK)/9999$. Therefore $(TALK)/9999$ when reduced to lowest terms equals $(EVE)/DID$, hence the denominator, "DID" is a 3-digit factor of 9999, namely 101, 303, or 909.

(*a*) Assume   DID = 101.   Then $(EVE)/101 = (TALK)/9999$ or TALK = (EVE)99 = (EVE)(100 − 1) = EVE00 − EVE.   This leaves an E as the first digit which therefore cannot be T.   Therefore DID $\neq$ 101.

(*b*) Assume   DID = 909.   Then $(EVE)/909 = (TALK)/9999$ or TALK = (EVE)11 = (EVE)(10 + 1) = EVE0 + EVE and this time the units digit is E and therefore cannot be K.   Therefore DID $\neq$ 909.

(*c*) Hence if there is a solution DID = 303. Since F is a proper fraction, EVE can be only (1*1) or (2*2), leaving for trial only 121; 141; 151; 161; 171; 181; 191; also 212; 242; 252; 262; 272; 282; 292. All these except 242 repeat, in the quotient, a digit that appears in the dividend so that finally 242/303 = .79867986... is the only solution.

67. Draw BG. By hypothesis $\angle ABF = 45°$, hence $\angle BAE = 45°$, hence $AE = BE$. The midpoint G of the hypotenuse is always equidistant from the 3 vertices, hence $AG = BG$. Hence G and E determine the perpendicular bisector of AB and therefore $DG \perp AB$. Hence $AD = DB = DE$. Therefore DG which joins the midpoints of 2 sides of a $\triangle$ is equal to $1/2$ BC. Since ABC is a Pythagorean triangle, let

$BC = m^2 - n^2$, then $AB = 2mn$, then $AD = DE = mn$ and $mn + 49 = (m^2 - n^2)/2$ or $(m - n)^2 - 2n^2 = 98$. The minimum solution of this Diophantine equation is $m - n = 10$, $n = 1$, $m = 11$. Then $AB = 22$, $BC = 120$, $AC = 122$.

Had we taken instead $BC = 2mn$, then $AB = m^2 - n^2$, then $DE = (m^2 - n^2)/2$ and $(m^2 - n^2)/2 + 49 = mn$ or $(m - n)^2 + 98 = 2n^2$, another Diophantine equation whose minimum solution is $m - n = 8$, $n = 9$, $m = 17$. Then $AB = 208$, $BC = 306$, $AC = 370$.

68. Let N = number and S = sum of digits. Let $N \equiv a \bmod 9$, then $S \equiv a \bmod 9$, since when a number is divided by 9 it leaves the same remainder as does the sum of its digits. Therefore $(9K + a)/(9L + a) = 26$, whence $9(K - 26L) = 25a$. Therefore $a = 0, 9, 18$, etc.; the least value is zero. Hence $K = 26L$, and letting $L = 1$ for the smallest value, $K = 26$ and $N = 234$, $S = 9$.

69. From Formulas 1 and 2 of Chapter XV, the number of ways a number, N, can be the sum of two squares is

$$[(a_1 + 1)(a_2 + 1) \ldots (a_n + 1) - 1)]/2$$

when all the a's are even, or

$$[(a_1 + 1)(a_2 + 1) \ldots (a_n + 1)]/2$$

when at least one "a" is odd. Equating each of these to 7, we have $(a_1 + 1)(a_2 + 1) \ldots = 15$ or 14 respectively. Then $a_1 = 4$, $a_2 = 2$ or $a_1 = 6$, $a_2 = 1$. These are the exponents to be applied to primes, p, of the form $4x + 1$. This gives $N = 5^4 \cdot 13^2$ or $5^6 \cdot 13$ of which the former is least.

The finding of these seven sums of two squares is facilitated by the fact that $5^4 \cdot 13^2$ happens to be a square; hence, expressing it as the sum of two squares requires only the finding of the seven pairs of sides of Pythagorean triangles for which $5^4 \cdot 13^2$ is the square of a hypotenuse. These sides are $A = K(x^2 - y^2)$, $B = K(2xy)$ and the hypotenuse C is then $K(x^2 + y^2) = 5^2 \cdot 13 = 325$. Then $N = C^2$. Therefore factoring 325 into divisor pairs, K and $(x^2 + y^2)$, we obtain the following values:

K	$x^2 + y^2$	x	y	A	B	$C^2 = A^2 + B^2 =$ $N = 5^4 \cdot 13^2$
65	5	2	1	195	260	105625
25	13	3	2	125	300	105625
13	25	4	3	91	312	105625
5	65	8	1	315	80	105625
5	65	7	4	165	280	105625
1	325	17	6	253	204	105625
1	325	18	1	323	36	105625

The second type of solution using $N = 5^6 \cdot 13 = 203125$ is not a square and therefore the Pythagorean triangle formulas do not apply, but the seven solutions can readily be found by first factoring out the square, 5^6, 5^4, 5^2, or 5^0, expressing the quotients as the sum of two squares and then reinserting the square factor. The seven solutions are

$$5^6(2^2+3^2) = 250^2+375^2; \qquad 5^4(18^2+1^2) = 450^2+25^2;$$
$$5^4(17^2+6^2) = 425^2+150^2; \qquad 5^2(69^2+58^2) = 345^2+290^2;$$
$$5^2(86^2+27^2) = 430^2+135^2; \qquad 5^0(366^2+263^2) = 366^2+263^2;$$
$$5^0(439^2+102^2) = 439^2+102^2.$$

70. The two squares are $5500002244 = 74162^2$ and $7744000000 = 88000^2$.

The squares increased by 7 are $34641^2 + 7 = 1199998888$ and $99559^2 + 7 = 9911994488$.

71. Let x = number of cows, and L the cost of the lamb. The proceeds from the sale was x^2 dollars, and since each man received the same number of animals, lamb included, an odd number of sheep, y, were bought. Then $x^2 = 10y + L$. But if the penultimate digit of a square is odd, the last digit L must be 6. Hence the lamb cost $6.00 and the man receiving this animal should get $2.00 to equalize the transaction.

72. Let x^2 = original number, $10y^2$ the reinforcement and $400z^2$ the final number. Then $x^2 + 10y^2 = 400z^2 = (20z)^2 = w^2$. By the conditions $5,000,000 < 400z^2 < 15,000,000$ or $158 < z < 194$, hence $3160 < w < 3880$. The equation is solved by $x = K(rm^2 - sn^2); y = 2mn; w = K(rm^2 + sn^2);$ where K, m, and n can be arbitrarily chosen but rs must equal 10, the coefficient of y. Thus there are an infinite number of solutions, for example, $18^2 + 10 \cdot 4^2 = 22^2$, but to keep within the assigned limits, $K = 60$, $r = 5$, $s = 2$, $m = 3$, $n = 2$ and $x = 2220$, $y = 720$, $w = 3180$, $z = 159$. Then $2220^2 + 10 \cdot 720^2 = 4,928,400 + 5,184,000 = 10,112,400 = 3180^2 = 400 \cdot 159^2$. Thus each of the 400 squares held $159^2 = 25281$ men.

73. Since 72 is divisible by 8, the amount paid must be divisible by 8. One-thousand and higher powers of 10 are always divisible by 8, hence only 79* must be considered to make the entire cost divisible by 8. Therefore the last digit must be 2. The number of turkeys is divisible by 9; the cost must be likewise, hence the sum of the digits must be divisible by 9. Hence the first digit must be 3; the total cost was $367.92 and each turkey cost $5.11.

74.
$$85555^2 - 1 = 7319658024.$$
$$97777^2 - 1 = 9560341728.$$

75. There are altogether 87 squares using all 10 digits. The smallest is $32043 = 1026753849$. The largest is $99066^2 = 9814072356$.

76. There would be 44 solutions ranging from 35902^2 to 98182^2 were the root not palindromic. There is only *one* solution having a palindromic root: 66266. Its square diminished by 1 million is 4390182756, which is the required number.

77. There would be 26 solutions ranging from 12817^2 to 29024^2 were the root not palindromic. There is only *one* solution having a palindromic root: 18181. Its square diminished by 1 million is 329548761.

78.
$$87695^2 = 7689413025 + 10^6.$$
$$23104^2 = 532794816 + 10^6.$$

79. From the conditions, $H^2 = W^2 + S^2 + D^2$ and $F = H^2 + W^2 + D^2$ whence $2H^2 = S^2 - F$ and so the son's age is an *odd* square. With two children, even though twins 1 year old, the wife would be older than 16, hence at least 25, and the couple's ages can then be only 36/25, 49/25, 64/25, 49/36, 64/36, since any other combinations would bring the father's age over 109 and that's too old. The difference of the couple's ages is 11, 24, 39, 13, 28 respectively of which *only* 13 can be the sum of 2 squares, $S^2 + D^2$, since it has the necessary form $K^2 p$ where p is the product of primes of the form $4x + 1$. Then $S = 3^2$, $D = 2^2$, $H = 49$, $W = 36$, and $F = 49 + 36 + 4 = 89$, a prime. The wife is a "perfect 36."

80. $N = 99991 = 10^5 - 9$, a prime. Then $10^5 \equiv 9$, $10^5 + 1 \equiv 10$, $10^5 - 1 \equiv 8$ all mod N. Then $10^{10} - 1 \equiv 80$, whence $(10^{10} - 1)^{99989} \equiv 80^{99989}$. Then $1 + (10^{10} - 1)^{99989} \equiv 1 + 80^{99989}$. Also $10^{999890} = [(10^5)^2]^{99989} \equiv (9^2)^{99989} \equiv 81^{99989}$. Then $10^{999890} - 1 \equiv 81^{99989} - 1$. Then $1 + 80^{99989} = 80(1 + 80^{99989})/80 = (80 + 80^{99990})/80 \equiv (80 + 1)/80$ mod N; also $81^{99989} - 1 = 81(81^{99989} - 1)/81 = (81^{99990} - 81)/81 \equiv (1 - 81)/81 \equiv -80/81$ mod N, by Fermat's theorem. Then

$$1 + [1 + (10^{10} - 1)^{99989}](10^{999890} - 1) \equiv 1 + (81/80)(-80/81)$$
$$\equiv 1 - 1 \equiv 0 \quad \text{mod } N.$$

81. Fifteen is the smallest integer that can be the side of 5 Pythagorean triangles. Their sides are 15–20–25, 15–36–39, 8–15–17, 15–112–113, 9–12–15. The corresponding areas are 150, 270, 60, 840, and 54 respectively. Their total area is 1374 square units. The area of a regular pentagon $= (S^2/4)(25 + 10\sqrt{5})^{1/2}$. In this case $S = 15$ and the area $= (225/4)(25 + 10\sqrt{5})^{1/2}$ square units.

82. The problem requires a number which is a divisor of both numbers. To find it, obtain the greatest common divisor, G.C.D., of both numbers, as explained in an algebra or arithmetic text. The number turns out to be 887, a prime, hence each widget costs \$8.87, and 937 were sold last year.

In case a textbook is not handy, here is how to do it. Divide 389393 into 831119, giving a quotient of 2 and remainder 52333. Divide this remainder into 389393, giving a quotient of 7 and remainder 23062. Continue in this manner, dividing the remainder each time into the previous divisor. The first divisor that gives a zero remainder is the required G.C.D.

83. The volumes of similar solids are in the same ratio as the cubes of corresponding linear dimensions, hence the two spheres are in the ratio $1^3/2^3$ or 1/8. Their combined volume is therefore $9K$ cubic inches where

K is a constant by which the cube of the circumference must be multiplied to obtain the volume (here $K = 1/6\pi^2$). The problem then is to find $Kx^3 + Ky^3 = 9K$ or $x^3 + y^3 = 9$. The *smallest* values satisfying this equation are

$$x = 415280564497/348671682660,$$
$$y = 676702467503/348671682660.$$

These fractions are the respective circumferences in inches of the two required flasks.

84. The prime factors of 1111111 are 239 and 4649, hence there must have been 239 automobiles at \$4649 each.

85. The solution of $x^3 + y^3 = 6$ is $x = 17/21$, $y = 37/21$.

86. Refer to Chapter XIV. The four *smallest* Pythagorean triangles with equal area have sides of (111, 6160, 6161), (231, 2960, 2969), (1320, 518, 1418), and (280, 2442, 2458). The area of each triangle is 341880. Since a $1\frac{1}{4}$ mile square has an area of 43560000 square feet, the farmer retained all but $4(341880) = 1367520$, so he kept 42192480 square feet which is more than 96 per cent of the original.

87. See Chapter XIV. The four smallest *primitive* Pythagorean triangles having equal perimeters are

(153868, 9435, 154157),   (99660, 86099, 131701),
(43660, 133419, 140381),   (13260, 151811, 152389).

88. The number $N^2 = abcdefabc$ can be factored into $(abc)(1002001) = (abc) \cdot 7^2 \cdot 11^2 \cdot 13^2$. But $def < 1000$, therefore $abc < 500$, and must be a square. Hence its root, r, must lie between 10 and 23 and be a prime. Thus r can be only 17 or 19 since 13 has already been used. Then $r^2 = (abc) = 289$ or 361 and $N^2 = 289578289$ or 361722361. Then $N = 7 \cdot 11 \cdot 13 \cdot 17 = 17017$ or $7 \cdot 11 \cdot 13 \cdot 19 = 19019$.

89. To be the sum of two squares, an integer N must equal $N_0 m^2$ where m^2 is the largest square in N and N_0 contains no prime factor of the form $4x - 1$ (see Chapter XV). But one of every 3 consecutive numbers is divisible by 3 which is of the form $4x - 1$, hence 3 must appear to an even power in one of the numbers, and we therefore seek such a number among the multiples of 9. In 27, 54, 63, N_0 contains a prime of the form $4x - 1$; in 9 and 36 they cannot be expressed as the sum of two squares. Now 18 and 45 are so expressible but the adjacent numbers 16, 19 or 44, 46 are not. Trying 72, which is expressible as the sum of two squares, 71 will not fit but 73 and 74 are of the proper form; hence $72^2 = 6^2 + 6^2$; $73 = 3^2 + 8^2$; $74 = 5^2 + 7^2$. The smallest solution using *different* primes (instead of 6 and 6 in 72) is $232 = 6^2 + 14^2$; $233 = 8^2 + 13^2$; $234 = 3^2 + 15^2$.

90. Call the digits x and y. Adding digits, their sum is $x + y + 30$. Adding alternate digits and subtracting one set of alternates from the other, we obtain $12 + x - y$. The 8-digit number is divisible by 9 if the

sum of the digits is divisible by 9; it is divisible by 11 if $12+x-y$ is divisible by 11. Hence $x+y+3 = 0$ mod 9 and $12+x-y \equiv 0$ mod 11. Six pairs of digits satisfy the first congruence, but only the pair 7, 8 satisfy the second, hence $x = 7, y = 8$ and the number is 27374985.

91. Let h = number of horses, c = number of chickens. Then $h+c+2c = 4h+2c$, whence $c = 3h$. So there are 3 times as many chickens as horses and any numbers in the ratio 3/1 will meet the conditions.

92. Knowing the remainder and the subtrahends, we can write the corresponding minuends, 2071 and 2622, and the dividend 95221. Then the G.C.D. of the 3 subtrahends is found to be 345 and that is the divisor. The quotient then turns out to be 276.

93. In the scale of 7, the number is $a \cdot 7^2 + b \cdot 7 + c$; in the scale of 9 it is $c \cdot 9^2 + b \cdot 9 + a$. Equating these: $48a = 2b + 80c$ or $8(3a-5c) = b$. However, in the scale of 7 there is no 8, hence b must be zero and $3a = 5c$ whence $a = 5, c = 3$ and the number is 503 in the scale of 7 and 305 in the scale of 9. In the scale of 10 it is 248.

94. $(x^5/5) + (x^3/3) + (7x/15) = [(x^5-x)/5] + [(x^3-x)/3] + x$. But by Fermat's theorem $x^5 - x \equiv 0$ mod 5 and $x^3 - x \equiv 0$ mod 3, hence the entire expression is an integer.

95. A number, N, divisible by 2, 3, and 5 may have the form $N = 2^a 3^b 5^c$. Then since $N/2$ is a square, a must be odd and b and c even. Similarly a and c must be multiples of 3 and $b \equiv 1$ mod 3. Also a and b must be multiples of 5 and $c \equiv 1$ mod 5. The smallest values satisfying these conditions are $a = 15, b = 10, c = 6$ and

$$N = 2^{15} \cdot 3^{10} \cdot 5^6 = 30,233,088,000,000.$$

96. There are two solutions: $300^3 - 5000^2 = 2,000,000$; $129^3 - 383^2 = 2,000,000$. To solve $a^3 - b^2 = 2c^2$, see for example Uspensky and Heaslet's *Elementary Number Theory*, McGraw-Hill Book Company, Inc., 1939, pp. 393–395.

97. $p-i \equiv -i$ mod p, hence

$$(p-1)(p-2)\ldots(p-r) \equiv (-1)(-2)\ldots(-r) = (-1)^r r!.$$

Multiply both sides of the congruence by $(p-r-1)!$ Then

$$(p-1)! \equiv (-1)^r r!(p-r-1)!$$

Now suppose r is a number such that $(-1)^r r! \equiv 1$ mod p. Then $(p-1)! \equiv (p-r-1)!$ mod p. But by Wilson's theorem

$$(p-1)!+1 \equiv 0 \quad \text{mod } p.$$

Hence $(p-r-1)!+1 \equiv 0$ mod p.
   It is easy to verify that for $r = 7$, $(-1)^r r! \equiv 1$ mod 71, hence

$$(71-7-1)!+1 = 63!+1 \equiv 0 \quad \text{mod } 71.$$

Also since $8 \cdot 9 \equiv 1 \mod 71$, $(-1)^9 9! \equiv 1 \mod 71$, hence

$$(71-9-1)!+1 = 61!+1 \equiv 0 \mod 71.$$

98. The product of the first n consecutive integers is $n!$ and their sum is $[n(n+1)]/2$. We must prove $n!/[n(n+1)/2] = 2(n-1)!/(n+1)$ is an integer.

(a) If $(n+1)$ is composite, the largest possible prime factor in it is $(n+1)/2$ and this never exceeds $(n-1)$ (except for $n = 1, 2$ and then $n+1$ is not composite). Hence $(n-1)!$ contains $(n+1)/2$ so that $2(n-1)!/(n+1)$ is an integer.

(b) If $(n+1)$ consists of 2 equal factors (at worst 2 odd primes) so that $(n+1)$ is a square, it is necessary to show that the numerator contains 2 such factors, $(n+1)^{1/2}$. Now $(n+1)^{1/2} < (n-1)$ for $n > 3$, also $2(n+1)^{1/2} < (n-1)$ for $n > 7$. Hence $2(n-1)!$ contains the 2 factors $(n+1)^{1/2}$ and $2(n+1)^{1/2}$ and hence is again divisible by $(n+1)$. ($n = 1$, 2, 4, 5, 6 do not make $[n+1]$ a square; for $n = 3$, $2[2!]/4$ is an integer.)

(c) Finally, when $(n+1)$ is a prime, it is larger than the largest prime in $(n-1)!$, hence this is the only instance where the product of the first n consecutive integers is not divisible by their sum.

99. To find the number of zeros in 10000! it is sufficient to count the number of multiples of 5, 25, 125, . . . etc., since with each of these we can pair a power of 2 to obtain a power of 10 and there are many more such powers of 2 than required since every second factor is even. Hence

$$[10000/5]+[10000/25]+[10000/125]+[10000/625]+[10000/3125]$$
$$= 2000+400+80+16+3 = 2499 \text{ zeros.}$$

$[a/b]$ means the largest integer not exceeding a/b.

100. Each leg of the isosceles right-triangle is of the form m^2+n^2, hence the hypotenuse is $\sqrt{2}(m^2+n^2)$. It is necessary to show that a right triangle exists with integral legs x and y such that $x^2+y^2 = 2(m^2+n^2)^2$. This is satisfied by $x = |m^2-n^2+2mn|$ and $y = |m^2-n^2-2mn|$ for then $x^2+y^2 = 2m^4+4m^2n^2+2n^4 = 2(m^2+n^2)^2$. For $m = 2, n = 1$, we obtain $x = 7, y = 1$ as the legs of a right triangle whose hypotenuse is $5\sqrt{2}$. Each leg of the isosceles right-triangle is $m^2+n^2 = 5$ and the hypotenuse is also $5\sqrt{2}$. *Neither* triangle is a Pythagorean triangle, but the legs of the isosceles triangle each equal 5, which is the hypotenuse of a 3-4-5 Pythagorean triangle as required.

INDEX

CATALOG OF DOVER BOOKS

Books Explaining Science and Mathematics

WHAT IS SCIENCE?, N. Campbell. The role of experiment and measurement, the function of mathematics, the nature of scientific laws, the difference between laws and theories, the limitations of science, and many similarly provocative topics are treated clearly and without technicalities by an eminent scientist. "Still an excellent introduction to scientific philosophy," H. Margenau in PHYSICS TODAY. "A first-rate primer . . . deserves a wide audience," SCIENTIFIC AMERICAN. 192pp. 5⅜ x 8.   S43 Paperbound **$1.25**

THE NATURE OF PHYSICAL THEORY, P. W. Bridgman. A Nobel Laureate's clear, non-technical lectures on difficulties and paradoxes connected with frontier research on the physical sciences. Concerned with such central concepts as thought, logic, mathematics, relativity, probability, wave mechanics, etc. he analyzes the contributions of such men as Newton, Einstein, Bohr, Heisenberg, and many others. "Lucid and entertaining . . . recommended to anyone who wants to get some insight into current philosophies of science," THE NEW PHILOSOPHY. Index. xi + 138pp. 5⅜ x 8.   S33 Paperbound **$1.25**

EXPERIMENT AND THEORY IN PHYSICS, Max Born. A Nobel Laureate examines the nature of experiment and theory in theoretical physics and analyzes the advances made by the great physicists of our day: Heisenberg, Einstein, Bohr, Planck, Dirac, and others. The actual process of creation is detailed step-by-step by one who participated. A fine examination of the scientific method at work. 44pp. 5⅜ x 8.   S308 Paperbound **75¢**

THE PSYCHOLOGY OF INVENTION IN THE MATHEMATICAL FIELD, J. Hadamard. The reports of such men as Descartes, Pascal, Einstein, Poincaré, and others are considered in this investigation of the method of idea-creation in mathematics and other sciences and the thinking process in general. How do ideas originate? What is the role of the unconscious? What is Poincaré's forgetting hypothesis? are some of the fascinating questions treated. A penetrating analysis of Einstein's thought processes concludes the book. xiii + 145pp. 5⅜ x 8.
T107 Paperbound **$1.25**

THE NATURE OF LIGHT AND COLOUR IN THE OPEN AIR, M. Minnaert. Why are shadows sometimes blue, sometimes green, or other colors depending on the light and surroundings? What causes mirages? Why do multiple suns and moons appear in the sky? Professor Minnaert explains these unusual phenomena and hundreds of others in simple, easy-to-understand terms based on optical laws and the properties of light and color. No mathematics is required but artists, scientists, students, and everyone fascinated by these "tricks" of nature will find thousands of useful and amazing pieces of information. Hundreds of observational experiments are suggested which require no special equipment. 200 illustrations; 42 photos. xvi + 362pp. 5⅜ x 8.   T196 Paperbound **$1.95**

THE UNIVERSE OF LIGHT, W. Bragg. Sir William Bragg, Nobel Laureate and great modern physicist, is also well known for his powers of clear exposition. Here he analyzes all aspects of light for the layman: lenses, reflection, refraction, the optics of vision, x-rays, the photo-electric effect, etc. He tells you what causes the color of spectra, rainbows, and soap bubbles, how magic mirrors work, and much more. Dozens of simple experiments are described. Preface. Index. 199 line drawings and photographs, including 2 full-page color plates. x + 283pp. 5⅜ x 8.   T538 Paperbound **$1.85**

SOAP-BUBBLES: THEIR COLOURS AND THE FORCES THAT MOULD THEM, C. V. Boys. For continuing popularity and validity as scientific primer, few books can match this volume of easily-followed experiments, explanations. Lucid exposition of complexities of liquid films, surface tension and related phenomena, bubbles' reaction to heat, motion, music, magnetic fields. Experiments with capillary attraction, soap bubbles on frames, composite bubbles, liquid cylinders and jets, bubbles other than soap, etc. Wonderful introduction to scientific method; natural laws that have many ramifications in areas of modern physics. Only complete edition in print. New Introduction by S. Z. Lewin, New York University. 83 illustrations; 1 full-page color plate. xii + 190pp. 5⅜ x 8½.   T542 Paperbound **95¢**

CATALOGUE OF DOVER BOOKS

SCIENCE AND HYPOTHESIS, Henri Poincaré. Creative psychology in science. How such concepts as number, magnitude, space, force, classical mechanics were developed and how the modern scientist uses them in his thought. Hypothesis in physics, theories of modern physics. Introduction by Sir James Larmor. "Few mathematicians have had the breadth of vision of Poincaré, and none is his superior in the gift of clear exposition," E. T. Bell. Index. 272pp. 5⅜ x 8.
S221 Paperbound **$1.35**

THE VALUE OF SCIENCE, Henri Poincaré. Many of the most mature ideas of the "last scientific universalist" conveyed with charm and vigor for both the beginning student and the advanced worker. Discusses the nature of scientific truth, whether order is innate in the universe or imposed upon it by man, logical thought versus intuition (relating to mathematics through the works of Weierstrass, Lie, Klein, Riemann), time and space (relativity, psychological time, simultaneity), Hertz's concept of force, interrelationship of mathematical physics to pure math, values within disciplines of Maxwell, Carnot, Mayer, Newton, Lorentz, etc. Index. iii + 147pp. 5⅜ x 8.
S469 Paperbound **$1.35**

THE SKY AND ITS MYSTERIES, E. A. Beet. One of the most lucid books on the mysteries of the universe; covers history of astronomy from earliest observations to modern theories of expanding universe, source of stellar energy, birth of planets, origin of moon craters, possibilities of life on other planets. Discusses effects of sunspots on weather; distance, age of stars; methods and tools of astronomers; much more. Expert and fascinating. "Eminently readable book," London Times. Bibliography. Over 50 diagrams, 12 full-page plates. Fold-out star map. Introduction. Index. 238pp. 5¼ x 7½.
T627 Clothbound **$3.50**

OUT OF THE SKY: AN INTRODUCTION TO METEORITICS, H. H. Nininger. A non-technical yet comprehensive introduction to the young science of meteoritics: all aspects of the arrival of cosmic matter on our planet from outer space and the reaction and alteration of this matter in the terrestrial environment. Essential facts and major theories presented by one of the world's leading experts. Covers ancient reports of meteors; modern systematic investigations; fireball clusters; meteorite showers; tektites; planetoidal encounters; etc. 52 full-page plates with over 175 photographs. 22 figures. Bibliography and references. Index. viii + 336pp. 5⅜ x 8.
T519 Paperbound **$1.85**

THE REALM OF THE NEBULAE, E. Hubble. One of great astronomers of our day records his formulation of concept of "island universes." Covers velocity-distance relationship; classification, nature, distances, general types of nebulae; cosmological theories. A fine introduction to modern theories for layman. No math needed. New introduction by A. Sandage. 55 illustrations, photos. Index. iv + 201pp. 5⅜ x 8.
S455 Paperbound **$1.50**

AN ELEMENTARY SURVEY OF CELESTIAL MECHANICS, Y. Ryabov. Elementary exposition of gravitational theory and celestial mechanics. Historical introduction and coverage of basic principles, including: the ecliptic, the orbital plane, the 2- and 3-body problems, the discovery of Neptune, planetary rotation, the length of the day, the shapes of galaxies, satellites (detailed treatment of Sputnik I), etc. First American reprinting of successful Russian popular exposition. Follow actual methods of astrophysicists with only high school math! Appendix. 58 figures. 165pp. 5⅜ x 8.
T756 Paperbound **$1.25**

GREAT IDEAS AND THEORIES OF MODERN COSMOLOGY, Jagjit Singh. Companion volume to author's popular "Great Ideas of Modern Mathematics" (Dover, $1.55). The best non-technical survey of post-Einstein attempts to answer perhaps unanswerable questions of origin, age of Universe, possibility of life on other worlds, etc. Fundamental theories of cosmology and cosmogony recounted, explained, evaluated in light of most recent data: Einstein's concepts of relativity, space-time; Milne's a priori world-system; astrophysical theories of Jeans, Eddington; Hoyle's "continuous creation;" contributions of dozens more scientists. A faithful, comprehensive critical summary of complex material presented in an extremely well-written text intended for laymen. Original publication. Index. xii + 276pp. 5⅜ x 8½.
T925 Paperbound **$1.85**

BASIC ELECTRICITY, Bureau of Naval Personnel. Very thorough, easily followed course in basic electricity for beginner, layman, or intermediate student. Begins with simplest definitions, presents coordinated, systematic coverage of basic theory and application: conductors, insulators, static electricity, magnetism, production of voltage, Ohm's law, direct current series and parallel circuits, wiring techniques, electromagnetism, alternating current, capacitance and inductance, measuring instruments, etc.; application to electrical machines such as alternating and direct current generators, motors, transformers, magnetic magnifiers, etc. Each chapter contains problems to test progress; answers at rear. No math needed beyond algebra. Appendices on signs, formulas, etc. 345 illustrations. 448pp. 7½ x 10.
S973 Paperbound **$2.95**

ELEMENTARY METALLURGY AND METALLOGRAPHY, A. M. Shrager. An introduction to common metals and alloys; stress is upon steel and iron, but other metals and alloys also covered. All aspects of production, processing, working of metals. Designed for student who wishes to enter metallurgy, for bright high school or college beginner, layman who wants background on extremely important industry. Questions, at ends of chapters, many microphotographs, glossary. Greatly revised 1961 edition. 195 illustrations, tables. ix + 389pp. 5⅜ x 8.
S138 Paperbound **$2.00**

CATALOGUE OF DOVER BOOKS

BRIDGES AND THEIR BUILDERS, D. B. Steinman & S. R. Watson. Engineers, historians, and every person who has ever been fascinated by great spans will find this book an endless source of information and interest. Greek and Roman structures, Medieval bridges, modern classics such as the Brooklyn Bridge, and the latest developments in the science are retold by one of the world's leading authorities on bridge design and construction. BRIDGES AND THEIR BUILDERS is the only comprehensive and accurate semi-popular history of these important measures of progress in print. New, greatly revised, enlarged edition. 23 photos; 26 line-drawings. Index. xvii + 401pp. 5⅜ x 8.   T431 Paperbound **$2.00**

FAMOUS BRIDGES OF THE WORLD, D. B. Steinman. An up-to-the-minute new edition of a book that explains the fascinating drama of how the world's great bridges came to be built. The author, designer of the famed Mackinac bridge, discusses bridges from all periods and all parts of the world, explaining their various types of construction, and describing the problems their builders faced. Although primarily for youngsters, this cannot fail to interest readers of all ages. 48 illustrations in the text. 23 photographs. 99pp. 6⅛ x 9¼.   T161 Paperbound **$1.00**

HOW DO YOU USE A SLIDE RULE? by A. A. Merrill. A step-by-step explanation of the slide rule that presents the fundamental rules clearly enough for the non-mathematician to understand. Unlike most instruction manuals, this work concentrates on the two most important operations: multiplication and division. 10 easy lessons, each with a clear drawing, for the reader who has difficulty following other expositions. 1st publication. Index. 2 Appendices. 10 illustrations. 78 problems, all with answers. vi + 36 pp. 6⅛ x 9¼.   T62 Paperbound **60¢**

HOW TO CALCULATE QUICKLY, H. Sticker. A tried and true method for increasing your "number sense" — the ability to see relationships between numbers and groups of numbers. Addition, subtraction, multiplication, division, fractions, and other topics are treated through techniques not generally taught in schools: left to right multiplication, division by inspection, etc. This is not a collection of tricks that work only on special numbers, but a detailed well-planned course, consisting of over 9,000 problems that you can work in spare moments. It is excellent for anyone who is inconvenienced by slow computational skills. 5 or 10 minutes of this book daily will double or triple your calculation speed. 9,000 problems, answers. 256pp. 5⅜ x 8.   T295 Paperbound **$1.00**

MATHEMATICAL FUN, GAMES AND PUZZLES, Jack Frohlichstein. A valuable service for parents of children who have trouble with math, for teachers in need of a supplement to regular upper elementary and junior high math texts (each section is graded—easy, average, difficult —for ready adaptation to different levels of ability), and for just anyone who would like to develop basic skills in an informal and entertaining manner. The author combines ten years of experience as a junior high school math teacher with a method that uses puzzles and games to introduce the basic ideas and operations of arithmetic. Stress on everyday uses of math: banking, stock market, personal budgets, insurance, taxes. Intellectually stimulating and practical, too. 418 problems and diversions with answers. Bibliography. 120 illustrations. xix + 306pp. 5⅝ x 8½.   T789 Paperbound **$1.75**

GREAT IDEAS OF MODERN MATHEMATICS: THEIR NATURE AND USE, Jagjit Singh. Reader with only high school math will understand main mathematical ideas of modern physics, astronomy, genetics, psychology, evolution, etc. better than many who use them as tools, but comprehend little of their basic structure. Author uses his wide knowledge of non-mathematical fields in brilliant exposition of differential equations, matrices, group theory, logic, statistics, problems of mathematical foundations, imaginary numbers, vectors, etc. Original publication. 2 appendixes. 2 indexes. 65 illustr. 322pp. 5⅜ x 8.   S587 Paperbound **$1.65**

*MATHEMATICS IN ACTION, O. G. Sutton. Everyone with a command of high school algebra will find this book one of the finest possible introductions to the application of mathematics to physical theory. Ballistics, numerical analysis, waves and wavelike phenomena, Fourier series, group concepts, fluid flow and aerodynamics, statistical measures, and meteorology are discussed with unusual clarity. Some calculus and differential equations theory is developed by the author for the reader's help in the more difficult sections. 88 figures. Index. viii + 236pp. 5⅜ x 8.   T440 Clothbound **$3.50**

*INTRODUCTION TO SYMBOLIC LOGIC AND ITS APPLICATIONS, Rudolph Carnap. One of the clearest, most comprehensive, and rigorous introductions to modern symbolic logic, by perhaps its greatest living master. Not merely elementary theory, but demonstrated applications in mathematics, physics, and biology. Symbolic languages of various degrees of complexity are analyzed, and one constructed. "A creation of the rank of a masterpiece," Zentralblatt für Mathematik und Ihre Grenzgebiete. Over 300 exercises. 5 figures. Bibliography. Index. xvi + 241pp. 5⅜ x 8.   S453 Paperbound **$1.85**

*HIGHER MATHEMATICS FOR STUDENTS OF CHEMISTRY AND PHYSICS, J. W. Mellor. Not abstract, but practical, drawing its problems from familiar laboratory material, this book covers theory and application of differential calculus, analytic geometry, functions with singularities, integral calculus, infinite series, solution of numerical equations, differential equations, Fourier's theorem and extensions, probability and the theory of errors, calculus of variations, determinants, etc. "If the reader is not familiar with this book, it will repay him to examine it," CHEM. & ENGINEERING NEWS. 800 problems. 189 figures. 2 appendices; 30 tables of integrals, probability functions, etc. Bibliography. xxi + 641pp. 5⅜ x 8.
                                                                    S193 Paperbound **$2.00**

CATALOGUE OF DOVER BOOKS

THE FOURTH DIMENSION SIMPLY EXPLAINED, edited by Henry P. Manning. Originally written as entries in contest sponsored by "Scientific American," then published in book form, these 22 essays present easily understood explanations of how the fourth dimension may be studied, the relationship of non-Euclidean geometry to the fourth dimension, analogies to three-dimensional space, some fourth-dimensional absurdities and curiosities, possible measurements and forms in the fourth dimension. In general, a thorough coverage of many of the simpler properties of fourth-dimensional space. Multi-points of view on many of the most important aspects are valuable aid to comprehension. Introduction by Dr. Henry P. Manning gives proper emphasis to points in essays, more advanced account of fourth-dimensional geometry. 82 figures. 251pp. 5⅜ x 8.   **T711 Paperbound $1.35**

TRIGONOMETRY REFRESHER FOR TECHNICAL MEN, A. A. Klaf. A modern question and answer text on plane and spherical trigonometry. Part I covers plane trigonometry: angles, quadrants, trigonometrical functions, graphical representation, interpolation, equations, logarithms, solution of triangles, slide rules, etc. Part II discusses applications to navigation, surveying, elasticity, architecture, and engineering. Small angles, periodic functions, vectors, polar coordinates, De Moivre's theorem, fully covered. Part III is devoted to spherical trigonometry and the solution of spherical triangles, with applications to terrestrial and astronomical problems. Special time-savers for numerical calculation. 913 questions answered for you! 1738 problems; answers to odd numbers. 494 figures. 14 pages of functions, formulae. Index. x + 629pp. 5⅜ x 8.   **T371 Paperbound $2.00**

CALCULUS REFRESHER FOR TECHNICAL MEN. A. A. Klaf. Not an ordinary textbook but a unique refresher for engineers, technicians, and students. An examination of the most important aspects of differential and integral calculus by means of 756 key questions. Part I covers simple differential calculus: constants, variables, functions, increments, derivatives, logarithms, curvature, etc. Part II treats fundamental concepts of integration: inspection, substitution, transformation, reduction, areas and volumes, mean value, successive and partial integration, double and triple integration. Stresses practical aspects! A 50 page section gives applications to civil and nautical engineering, electricity, stress and strain, elasticity, industrial engineering, and similar fields. 756 questions answered. 556 problems; solutions to odd numbers. 36 pages of constants, formulae. Index. v + 431pp. 5⅜ x 8.   **T370 Paperbound $2.00**

PROBABILITIES AND LIFE, Emile Borel. One of the leading French mathematicians of the last 100 years makes use of certain results of mathematics of probabilities and explains a number of problems that for the most part, are related to everyday living or to illness and death: computation of life expectancy tables, chances of recovery from various diseases, probabilities of job accidents, weather predictions, games of chance, and so on. Emphasis on results not processes, though some indication is made of mathematical proofs. Simple in style, free of technical terminology, limited in scope to everyday situations, it is comprehensible to laymen, fine reading for beginning students of probability. New English translation. Index. Appendix. vi + 87pp. 5⅜ x 8½.   **T121 Paperbound $1.00**

POPULAR SCIENTIFIC LECTURES, Hermann von Helmholtz. 7 lucid expositions by a preeminent scientific mind: "The Physiological Causes of Harmony in Music," "On the Relation of Optics to Painting," "On the Conservation of Force," "On the Interaction of Natural Forces," "On Goethe's Scientific Researches" into theory of color, "On the Origin and Significance of Geometric Axioms," "On Recent Progress in the Theory of Vision." Written with simplicity of expression, stripped of technicalities, these are easy to understand and delightful reading for anyone interested in science or looking for an introduction to serious study of acoustics or optics. Introduction by Professor Morris Kline, Director, Division of Electromagnetic Research, New York University, contains astute, impartial evaluations. Selected from "Popular Lectures on Scientific Subjects," 1st and 2nd series. xii + 286pp. 5⅜ x 8½.   **T799 Paperbound $1.45**

SCIENCE AND METHOD, Henri Poincaré. Procedure of scientific discovery, methodology, experiment, idea-germination—the intellectual processes by which discoveries come into being. Most significant and most interesting aspects of development, application of ideas. Chapters cover selection of facts, chance, mathematical reasoning, mathematics, and logic; Whitehead, Russell, Cantor; the new mechanics, etc. 288pp. 5⅜ x 8.   **S222 Paperbound $1.35**

HEAT AND ITS WORKINGS, Morton Mott-Smith, Ph.D. An unusual book; to our knowledge the only middle-level survey of this important area of science. Explains clearly such important concepts as physiological sensation of heat and Weber's law, measurement of heat, evolution of thermometer, nature of heat, expansion and contraction of solids, Boyle's law, specific heat. BTU's and calories, evaporation, Andrews's isothermals, radiation, the relation of heat to light, many more topics inseparable from other aspects of physics. A wide, nonmathematical yet thorough explanation of basic ideas, theories, phenomena for laymen and beginning scientists illustrated by experiences of daily life. Bibliography. 50 illustrations. x + 165pp. 5⅜ x 8½.   **T978 Paperbound $1.00**

Classics of Science

THE DIDEROT PICTORIAL ENCYCLOPEDIA OF TRADES AND INDUSTRY, MANUFACTURING AND THE TECHNICAL ARTS IN PLATES SELECTED FROM "L'ENCYCLOPEDIE OU DICTIONNAIRE RAISONNE DES SCIENCES, DES ARTS, ET DES METIERS" OF DENIS DIDEROT, edited with text by C. Gillispie. The first modern selection of plates from the high point of 18th century French engraving, Diderot's famous Encyclopedia. Over 2000 illustrations on 485 full page plates, most of them original size, illustrating the trades and industries of one of the most fascinating periods of modern history, 18th century France. These magnificent engravings provide an invaluable glimpse into the past for the student of early technology, a lively and accurate social document to students of cultures, an outstanding find to the lover of fine engravings. The plates teem with life, with men, women, and children performing all of the thousands of operations necessary to the trades before and during the early stages of the industrial revolution. Plates are in sequence, and show general operations, closeups of difficult operations, and details of complex machinery. Such important and interesting trades and industries are illustrated as sowing, harvesting, beekeeping, cheesemaking, operating windmills, milling flour, charcoal burning, tobacco processing, indigo, fishing, arts of war, salt extraction, mining, smelting iron, casting iron, steel, extracting mercury, zinc, sulphur, copper, etc., slating, tinning, silverplating, gilding, making gunpowder, cannons, bells, shoeing horses, tanning, papermaking, printing, dying, and more than 40 other categories. 920pp. 9 x 12. Heavy library cloth.   T421 Two volume set **$18.50**

THE PRINCIPLES OF SCIENCE, A TREATISE ON LOGIC AND THE SCIENTIFIC METHOD, W. Stanley Jevons. Treating such topics as Inductive and Deductive Logic, the Theory of Number, Probability, and the Limits of Scientific Method, this milestone in the development of symbolic logic remains a stimulating contribution to the investigation of inferential validity in the natural and social sciences. It significantly advances Boole's logic, and describes a machine which is a foundation of modern electronic calculators. In his introduction, Ernest Nagel of Columbia University says, "(Jevons) . . . continues to be of interest as an attempt to articulate the logic of scientific inquiry." Index. liii + 786pp. 5⅜ x 8.   S446 Paperbound **$2.98**

*DIALOGUES CONCERNING TWO NEW SCIENCES, Galileo Galilei. A classic of experimental science which has had a profound and enduring influence on the entire history of mechanics and engineering. Galileo based this, his finest work, on 30 years of experimentation. It offers a fascinating and vivid exposition of dynamics, elasticity, sound, ballistics, strength of materials, and the scientific method. Translated by H. Crew and A. de Salvio. 126 diagrams. Index. xxi + 288pp. 5⅜ x 8.   S99 Paperbound **$1.75**

DE MAGNETE, William Gilbert. This classic work on magnetism founded a new science. Gilbert was the first to use the word "electricity," to recognize mass as distinct from weight, to discover the effect of heat on magnetic bodies; invented an electroscope, differentiated between static electricity and magnetism, conceived of the earth as a magnet. Written by the first great experimental scientist, this lively work is valuable not only as an historical landmark, but as the delightfully easy-to-follow record of a perpetually searching, ingenious mind. Translated by P. F. Mottelay. 25 page biographical memoir. 90 fix. lix + 368pp. 5⅜ x 8.   S470 Paperbound **$2.00**

*OPTICKS, Sir Isaac Newton. An enormous storehouse of insights and discoveries on light, reflection, color, refraction, theories of wave and corpuscular propagation of light, optical apparatus, and mathematical devices which have recently been reevaluated in terms of modern physics and placed in the top-most ranks of Newton's work! Foreword by Albert Einstein. Preface by I. B. Cohen of Harvard U. 7 pages of portraits, facsimile pages, letters, etc. cxvi + 412pp. 5⅜ x 8.   S205 Paperbound **$2.25**

A SURVEY OF PHYSICAL THEORY, M. Planck. Lucid essays on modern physics for the general reader by the Nobel Laureate and creator of the quantum revolution. Planck explains how the new concepts came into being; explores the clash between theories of mechanics, electrodynamics, and thermodynamics; and traces the evolution of the concept of light through Newton, Huygens, Maxwell, and his own quantum theory, providing unparalleled insights into his development of this momentous modern concept. Bibliography. Index. vii + 121pp. 5⅜ x 8.   S650 Paperbound **$1.15**

A SOURCE BOOK IN MATHEMATICS, D. E. Smith. English translations of the original papers that announced the great discoveries in mathematics from the Renaissance to the end of the 19th century: succinct selections from 125 different treatises and articles, most of them unavailable elsewhere in English—Newton, Leibniz, Pascal, Riemann, Bernoulli, etc. 24 articles trace developments in the field of number, 18 cover algebra, 36 are on geometry, and 13 on calculus. Biographical-historical introductions to each article. Two volume set. Index in each. Total of 115 illustrations. Total of xxviii + 742pp. 5⅜ x 8.   S552 Vol I Paperbound **$1.85**
    S553 Vol II Paperbound **$1.85**
    The set, boxed **$3.50**

CATALOGUE OF DOVER BOOKS

*THE THIRTEEN BOOKS OF EUCLID'S ELEMENTS, edited by T. L. Heath. This is the complete EUCLID — the definitive edition of one of the greatest classics of the western world. Complete English translation of the Heiberg text with spurious Book XIV. Detailed 150-page introduction discusses aspects of Greek and medieval mathematics: Euclid, texts, commentators, etc. Paralleling the text is an elaborate critical exposition analyzing each definition, proposition, postulate, etc., and covering textual matters, mathematical analyses, refutations, extensions, etc. Unabridged reproduction of the Cambridge 2nd edition. 3 volumes. Total of 995 figures, 1426pp. 5⅜ x 8. S88, 89, 90 — 3 vol. set, Paperbound **$6.00**

*THE GEOMETRY OF RENE DESCARTES. The great work which founded analytic geometry. The renowned Smith-Latham translation faced with the original French text containing all of Descartes' own diagrams! Contains: Problems the Construction of Which Requires Only Straight Lines and Circles; On the Nature of Curved Lines; On the Construction of Solid or Supersolid Problems. Notes. Diagrams. 258pp. S68 Paperbound **$1.50**

*A PHILOSOPHICAL ESSAY ON PROBABILITIES, P. Laplace. Without recourse to any mathematics above grammar school, Laplace develops a philosophically, mathematically and historically classical exposition of the nature of probability: its functions and limitations, operations in practical affairs, calculations in games of chance, insurance, government, astronomy, and countless other fields. New introduction by E. T. Bell. viii + 196pp. S166 Paperbound **$1.35**

DE RE METALLICA, Georgius Agricola. Written over 400 years ago, for 200 years the most authoritative first-hand account of the production of metals, translated in 1912 by former President Herbert Hoover and his wife, and today still one of the most beautiful and fascinating volumes ever produced in the history of science! 12 books, exhaustively annotated, give a wonderfully lucid and vivid picture of the history of mining, selection of sites, types of deposits, excavating pits, sinking shafts, ventilating, pumps, crushing machinery, assaying, smelting, refining metals, making salt, alum, nitre, glass, and many other topics. This definitive edition contains all 289 of the 16th century woodcuts which made the original an artistic masterpiece. It makes a superb gift for geologists, engineers, libraries, artists, historians, and everyone interested in science and early illustrative art. Biographical, historical introductions. Bibliography, survey of ancient authors. Indices. 289 illustrations. 672pp. 6¾ x 10¾. Deluxe library edition. S6 Clothbound **$10.00**

GEOGRAPHICAL ESSAYS, W. M. Davis. Modern geography and geomorphology rest on the fundamental work of this scientist. His new concepts of earth-processes revolutionized science and his broad interpretation of the scope of geography created a deeper understanding of the interrelation of the landscape and the forces that mold it. This first inexpensive unabridged edition covers theory of geography, methods of advanced geographic teaching, descriptions of geographic areas, analyses of land-shaping processes, and much besides. Not only a factual and historical classic, it is still widely read for its reflections of modern scientific thought. Introduction. 130 figures. Index. vi + 777pp. 5⅜ x 8. S383 Paperbound **$2.95**

CHARLES BABBAGE AND HIS CALCULATING ENGINES, edited by P. Morrison and E. Morrison. Friend of Darwin, Humboldt, and Laplace, Babbage was a leading pioneer in large-scale mathematical machines and a prophetic herald of modern operational research—true father of Harvard's relay computer Mark I. His Difference Engine and Analytical Engine were the first successful machines in the field. This volume contains a valuable introduction on his life and work; major excerpts from his fascinating autobiography, revealing his eccentric and unusual personality; and extensive selections from "Babbage's Calculating Engines," a compilation of hard-to-find journal articles, both by Babbage and by such eminent contributors as the Countess of Lovelace, L. F. Menabrea, and Dionysius Lardner. 11 illustrations. Appendix of miscellaneous papers. Index. Bibliography. xxxviii + 400pp. 5⅜ x 8. T12 Paperbound **$2.00**

*THE WORKS OF ARCHIMEDES WITH THE METHOD OF ARCHIMEDES, edited by T. L. Heath. All the known works of the greatest mathematician of antiquity including the recently discovered METHOD OF ARCHIMEDES. This last is the only work we have which shows exactly how early mathematicians discovered their proofs before setting them down in their final perfection. A 186 page study by the eminent scholar Heath discusses Archimedes and the history of Greek mathematics. Bibliography. 563pp. 5⅜ x 8. S9 Paperbound **$2.00**

Puzzles, Mathematical Recreations

SYMBOLIC LOGIC and THE GAME OF LOGIC, Lewis Carroll. "Symbolic Logic" is not concerned with modern symbolic logic, but is instead a collection of over 380 problems posed with charm and imagination, using the syllogism, and a fascinating diagrammatic method of drawing conclusions. In "The Game of Logic" Carroll's whimsical imagination devises a logical game played with 2 diagrams and counters (included) to manipulate hundreds of tricky syllogisms. The final section, "Hit or Miss" is a lagniappe of 101 additional puzzles in the delightful Carroll manner. Until this reprint edition, both of these books were rarities costing up to $15 each. Symbolic Logic: Index. xxxi + 199pp. The Game of Logic: 96pp. 2 vols. bound as one. 5⅜ x 8. **T492 Paperbound $1.50**

PILLOW PROBLEMS and A TANGLED TALE, Lewis Carroll. One of the rarest of all Carroll's works, "Pillow Problems" contains 72 original math puzzles, all typically ingenious. Particularly fascinating are Carroll's answers which remain exactly as he thought them out, reflecting his actual mental process. The problems in "A Tangled Tale" are in story form, originally appearing as a monthly magazine serial. Carroll not only gives the solutions, but uses answers sent in by readers to discuss wrong approaches and misleading paths, and grades them for insight. Both of these books were rarities until this edition, "Pillow Problems" costing up to $25, and "A Tangled Tale" $15. Pillow Problems: Preface and Introduction by Lewis Carroll. xx + 109pp. A Tangled Tale: 6 illustrations. 152pp. Two vols. bound as one. 5⅜ x 8. **T493 Paperbound $1.50**

AMUSEMENTS IN MATHEMATICS, Henry Ernest Dudeney. The foremost British originator of mathematical puzzles is always intriguing, witty, and paradoxical in this classic, one of the largest collections of mathematical amusements. More than 430 puzzles, problems, and paradoxes. Mazes and games, problems on number manipulation, unicursal and other route problems, puzzles on measuring, weighing, packing, age, kinship, chessboards, joiners', crossing river, plane figure dissection, and many others. Solutions. More than 450 illustrations. vii + 258pp. 5⅜ x 8. **T473 Paperbound $1.25**

THE CANTERBURY PUZZLES, Henry Dudeney. Chaucer's pilgrims set one another problems in story form. Also Adventures of the Puzzle Club, the Strange Escape of the King's Jester, the Monks of Riddlewell, the Squire's Christmas Puzzle Party, and others. All puzzles are original, based on dissecting plane figures, arithmetic, algebra, elementary calculus and other branches of mathematics, and purely logical ingenuity. "The limit of ingenuity and intricacy," The Observer. Over 110 puzzles. Full Solutions. 150 illustrations. vii + 225pp. 5⅜ x 8. **T474 Paperbound $1.25**

MATHEMATICAL EXCURSIONS, H. A. Merrill. Even if you hardly remember your high school math, you'll enjoy the 90 stimulating problems contained in this book and you will come to understand a great many mathematical principles with surprisingly little effort. Many useful shortcuts and diversions not generally known are included: division by inspection, Russian peasant multiplication, memory systems for pi, building odd and even magic squares, square roots by geometry, dyadic systems, and many more. Solutions to difficult problems. 50 illustrations. 145pp. 5⅜ x 8. **T350 Paperbound $1.00**

MAGIC SQUARES AND CUBES, W. S. Andrews. Only book-length treatment in English, a thorough non-technical description and analysis. Here are nasik, overlapping, pandiagonal, serrated squares; magic circles, cubes, spheres, rhombuses. Try your hand at 4-dimensional magical figures! Much unusual folklore and tradition included. High school algebra is sufficient. 754 diagrams and illustrations. viii + 419pp. 5⅜ x 8. **T658 Paperbound $1.85**

CALIBAN'S PROBLEM BOOK: MATHEMATICAL, INFERENTIAL AND CRYPTOGRAPHIC PUZZLES, H. Phillips (Caliban), S. T. Shovelton, G. S. Marshall. 105 ingenious problems by the greatest living creator of puzzles based on logic and inference. Rigorous, modern, piquant; reflecting their author's unusual personality, these intermediate and advanced puzzles all involve the ability to reason clearly through complex situations; some call for mathematical knowledge, ranging from algebra to number theory. Solutions. xi + 180pp. 5⅜ x 8. **T736 Paperbound $1.25**

MATHEMATICAL PUZZLES FOR BEGINNERS AND ENTHUSIASTS, G. Mott-Smith. 188 mathematical puzzles based on algebra, dissection of plane figures, permutations, and probability, that will test and improve your powers of inference and interpretation. The Odic Force, The Spider's Cousin, Ellipse Drawing, theory and strategy of card and board games like tit-tat-tce, go moku, salvo, and many others. 100 pages of detailed mathematical explanations. Appendix of primes, square roots, etc. 135 illustrations. 2nd revised edition. 248pp. 5⅜ x 8. **T198 Paperbound $1.00**

MATHEMAGIC, MAGIC PUZZLES, AND GAMES WITH NUMBERS, R. V. Heath. More than 60 new puzzles and stunts based on the properties of numbers. Easy techniques for multiplying large numbers mentally, revealing hidden numbers magically, finding the date of any day in any year, and dozens more. Over 30 pages devoted to magic squares, triangles, cubes, circles, etc. Edited by J. S. Meyer. 76 illustrations. 128pp. 5⅜ x 8. **T110 Paperbound $1.00**

CATALOGUE OF DOVER BOOKS

MATHEMATICAL RECREATIONS, M. Kraitchik. One of the most thorough compilations of unusual mathematical problems for beginners and advanced mathematicians. Historical problems from Greek, Medieval, Arabic, Hindu sources. 50 pages devoted to pastimes derived from figurate numbers, Mersenne numbers, Fermat numbers, primes and probability. 40 pages of magic, Euler, Latin, panmagic squares. 25 new positional and permutational games of permanent value: fairy chess, latruncles, reversi, jinx, ruma, lasca, tricolor, tetrachrome, etc. Complete rigorous solutions. Revised second edition. 181 illustrations. 333pp. 5⅜ x 8.
T163 Paperbound **$1.75**

MATHEMATICAL PUZZLES OF SAM LOYD, selected and edited by M. Gardner. Choice puzzles by the greatest American puzzle creator and innovator. Selected from his famous collection, "Cyclopedia of Puzzles," they retain the unique style and historical flavor of the originals. There are posers based on arithmetic, algebra, probability, game theory, route tracing, topology, counter, sliding block, operations research, geometrical dissection. Includes the famous "14-15" puzzle which was a national craze, and his "Horse of a Different Color" which sold millions of copies. 117 of his most ingenious puzzles in all, 120 line drawings and diagrams. Solutions. Selected references. xx + 167pp. 5⅜ x 8. T498 Paperbound **$1.00**

MATHEMATICAL PUZZLES OF SAM LOYD, Vol. II, selected and edited by Martin Gardner. The outstanding 2nd selection from the great American innovator's "Cyclopedia of Puzzles": speed and distance problems, clock problems, plane and solid geometry, calculus problems, etc. Analytical table of contents that groups the puzzles according to the type of mathematics necessary to solve them. 166 puzzles, 150 original line drawings and diagrams. Selected references. xiv + 177pp. 5⅜ x 8. T709 Paperbound **$1.00**

ARITHMETICAL EXCURSIONS: AN ENRICHMENT OF ELEMENTARY MATHEMATICS, H. Bowers and J. Bowers. A lively and lighthearted collection of facts and entertainments for anyone who enjoys manipulating numbers or solving arithmetical puzzles: methods of arithmetic never taught in school, little-known facts about the most simple numbers, and clear explanations of more sophisticated topics; mysteries and folklore of numbers, the "Hin-dog-abic" number system, etc. First publication. Index. 529 numbered problems and diversions, all with answers. Bibliography. 60 figures. xiv + 320pp. 5⅜ x 8. T770 Paperbound **$1.65**

CRYPTANALYSIS, H. F. Gaines. Formerly entitled ELEMENTARY CRYPTANALYSIS, this introductory-intermediate level text is the best book in print on cryptograms and their solution. It covers all major techniques of the past, and contains much that is not generally known except to experts. Full details about concealment, substitution, and transposition ciphers; periodic mixed alphabets, multafid, Kasiski and Vigenere methods, Ohaver patterns, Playfair, and scores of other topics. 6 language letter and word frequency appendix. 167 problems, now furnished with solutions. Index. 173 figures. vi + 230pp. 5⅜ x 8.
T97 Paperbound **$1.95**

CRYPTOGRAPHY, L. D. Smith. An excellent introductory work on ciphers and their solution, the history of secret writing, and actual methods and problems in such techniques as transposition and substitution. Appendices describe the enciphering of Japanese, the Baconian biliteral cipher, and contain frequency tables and a bibliography for further study. Over 150 problems with solutions. 160pp. 5⅜ x 8. T247 Paperbound **$1.00**

PUZZLE QUIZ AND STUNT FUN, J. Meyer. The solution to party doldrums. 238 challenging puzzles, stunts and tricks. Mathematical puzzles like The Clever Carpenter, Atom Bomb; mysteries and deductions like The Bridge of Sighs, The Nine Pearls, Dog Logic; observation puzzles like Cigarette Smokers, Telephone Dial; over 200 others including magic squares, tongue twisters, puns, anagrams, and many others. All problems solved fully. 250pp. 5⅜ x 8. T337 Paperbound **$1.00**

101 PUZZLES IN THOUGHT AND LOGIC, C. R. Wylie, Jr. Brand new problems you need no special knowledge to solve! Take the kinks out of your mental "muscles" and enjoy solving murder problems, the detection of lying fishermen, the logical identification of color by a blindman, and dozens more. Introduction with simplified explanation of general scientific method and puzzle solving. 128pp. 5⅜ x 8. T367 Paperbound **$1.00**

MY BEST PROBLEMS IN MATHEMATICS, Hubert Phillips ("Caliban"). Only elementary mathematics needed to solve these 100 witty, catchy problems by a master problem creator. Problems on the odds in cards and dice, problems in geometry, algebra, permutations, even problems that require no math at all—just a logical mind, clear thinking. Solutions completely worked out. If you enjoy mysteries, alerting your perceptive powers and exercising your detective's eye, you'll find these cryptic puzzles a challenging delight. Original 1961 publication. 100 puzzles, solutions. x + 107pp. 5⅝ x 8. T91 Paperbound **$1.00**

MY BEST PUZZLES IN LOGIC AND REASONING, Hubert Phillips ("Caliban"). A new collection of 100 inferential and logical puzzles chosen from the best that have appeared in England, available for first time in U.S. By the most endlessly resourceful puzzle creator now living. All data presented are both necessary and sufficient to allow a single unambiguous answer. No special knowledge is required for problems ranging from relatively simple to completely original one-of-a-kinds. Guaranteed to please beginners and experts of all ages. Original publication. 100 puzzles, full solutions. x + 107pp. 5⅜ x 8. T119 Paperbound **$1.00**

CATALOGUE OF DOVER BOOKS

THE BOOK OF MODERN PUZZLES, G. L. Kaufman. A completely new series of puzzles as fascinating as crossword and deduction puzzles but based upon different principles and techniques. Simple 2-minute teasers, word labyrinths, design and pattern puzzles, logic and observation puzzles — over 150 braincrackers. Answers to all problems. 116 illustrations. 192pp. 5⅜ x 8.
T143 Paperbound **$1.00**

NEW WORD PUZZLES, G. L. Kaufman. 100 ENTIRELY NEW puzzles based on words and their combinations that will delight crossword puzzle, Scrabble and Jotto fans. Chess words, based on the moves of the chess king; design-onyms, symmetrical designs made of synonyms; rhymed double-crostics; syllable sentences; addle letter anagrams; alphagrams; linkograms; and many others all brand new. Full solutions. Space to work problems. 196 figures. vi + 122pp. 5⅜ x 8.
T344 Paperbound **$1.00**

MAZES AND LABYRINTHS: A BOOK OF PUZZLES, W. Shepherd. Mazes, formerly associated with mystery and ritual, are still among the most intriguing of intellectual puzzles. This is a novel and different collection of 50 amusements that embody the principle of the maze: mazes in the classical tradition; 3-dimensional, ribbon, and Möbius-strip mazes; hidden messages; spatial arrangements; etc.—almost all built on amusing story situations. 84 illustrations. Essay on maze psychology. Solutions. xv + 122pp. 5⅜ x 8.
T731 Paperbound **$1.00**

MAGIC TRICKS & CARD TRICKS, W. Jonson. Two books bound as one. 52 tricks with cards, 37 tricks with coins, bills, eggs, smoke, ribbons, slates, etc. Details on presentation, misdirection, and routining will help you master such famous tricks as the Changing Card, Card in the Pocket, Four Aces, Coin Through the Hand, Bill in the Egg, Afghan Bands, and over 75 others. If you follow the lucid exposition and key diagrams carefully, you will finish these two books with an astonishing mastery of magic. 106 figures. 224pp. 5⅜ x 8. T909 Paperbound **$1.00**

PANORAMA OF MAGIC, Milbourne Christopher. A profusely illustrated history of stage magic, a unique selection of prints and engravings from the author's private collection of magic memorabilia, the largest of its kind. Apparatus, stage settings and costumes; ingenious ads distributed by the performers and satiric broadsides passed around in the streets ridiculing pompous showmen; programs; decorative souvenirs. The lively text, by one of America's foremost professional magicians, is full of anecdotes about almost legendary wizards: Dede, the Egyptian; Philadelphia, the wonder-worker; Robert-Houdin, "the father of modern magic;" Harry Houdini; scores more. Altogether a pleasure package for anyone interested in magic, stage setting and design, ethnology, psychology, or simply in unusual people. A Dover original. 295 illustrations; 8 in full color. Index. viii + 216pp. 8⅜ x 11¼.
T774 Paperbound **$2.25**

HOUDINI ON MAGIC, Harry Houdini. One of the greatest magicians of modern times explains his most prized secrets. How locks are picked, with illustrated picks and skeleton keys; how a girl is sawed into twins; how to walk through a brick wall — Houdini's explanations of 44 stage tricks with many diagrams. Also included is a fascinating discussion of great magicians of the past and the story of his fight against fraudulent mediums and spiritualists. Edited by W.B. Gibson and M.N. Young. Bibliography. 155 figures, photos. xv + 280pp. 5⅜ x 8.
T384 Paperbound **$1.25**

MATHEMATICS, MAGIC AND MYSTERY, Martin Gardner. Why do card tricks work? How do magicians perform astonishing mathematical feats? How is stage mind-reading possible? This is the first book length study explaining the application of probability, set theory, theory of numbers, topology, etc., to achieve many startling tricks. Non-technical, accurate, detailed! 115 sections discuss tricks with cards, dice, coins, knots, geometrical vanishing illusions, how a Curry square "demonstrates" that the sum of the parts may be greater than the whole, and dozens of others. No sleight of hand necessary! 135 illustrations. xii + 174pp. 5⅜ x 8.
T335 Paperbound **$1.00**

EASY-TO-DO ENTERTAINMENTS AND DIVERSIONS WITH COINS, CARDS, STRING, PAPER AND MATCHES, R. M. Abraham. Over 300 tricks, games and puzzles will provide young readers with absorbing fun. Sections on card games; paper-folding; tricks with coins, matches and pieces of string; games for the agile; toy-making from common household objects; mathematical recreations; and 50 miscellaneous pastimes. Anyone in charge of groups of youngsters, including hard-pressed parents, and in need of suggestions on how to keep children sensibly amused and quietly content will find this book indispensable. Clear, simple text, copious number of delightful line drawings and illustrative diagrams. Originally titled "Winter Nights Entertainments." Introduction by Lord Baden Powell. 329 illustrations. v + 186pp. 5⅜ x 8½.
T921 Paperbound **$1.00**

STRING FIGURES AND HOW TO MAKE THEM, Caroline Furness Jayne. 107 string figures plus variations selected from the best primitive and modern examples developed by Navajo, Apache, pygmies of Africa, Eskimo, in Europe, Australia, China, etc. The most readily understandable, easy-to-follow book in English on perennially popular recreation. Crystal-clear exposition; step-by-step diagrams. Everyone from kindergarten children to adults looking for unusual diversion will be endlessly amused. Index. Bibliography. Introduction by A. C. Haddon. 17 full-page plates. 960 illustrations. xxiii + 401pp. 5⅜ x 8½.
T152 Paperbound **$2.00**

Entertainments, Humor

ODDITIES AND CURIOSITIES OF WORDS AND LITERATURE, C. Bombaugh, edited by M. Gardner. The largest collection of idiosyncratic prose and poetry techniques in English, a legendary work in .the curious and amusing bypaths of literary recreations and the play technique in literature—so important in modern works. Contains alphabetic poetry, acrostics, palindromes, scissors verse, centos, emblematic poetry, famous literary puns, hoaxes, notorious slips of the press, hilarious mistranslations, and much more. Revised and enlarged with modern material by Martin Gardner. 368pp. 5⅜ x 8. T759 Paperbound **$1.50**

A NONSENSE ANTHOLOGY, collected by **Carolyn Wells.** 245 of the best nonsense verses ever written, including nonsense puns, absurd arguments, mock epics and sagas, nonsense ballads, odes, "sick" verses, dog-Latin verses, French nonsense verses, songs. By Edward Lear, Lewis Carroll, Gelett Burgess, W. S. Gilbert, Hilaire Belloc, Peter Newell, Oliver Herford, etc., 83 writers in all plus over four score anonymous nonsense verses. A special section of limericks, plus famous nonsense such as Carroll's "Jabberwocky" and Lear's "The Jumblies" and much excellent verse virtually impossible to locate elsewhere. For 50 years considered the best anthology available. Index of first lines specially prepared for this edition. Introduction by Carolyn Wells. 3 indexes: Title, Author, First lines. xxxiii + 279pp. T499 Paperbound **$1.25**

THE BAD CHILD'S BOOK OF BEASTS, MORE BEASTS FOR WORSE CHILDREN, and A MORAL ALPHABET, H. Belloc. Hardly an anthology of humorous verse has appeared in the last 50 years without at least a couple of these famous nonsense verses. But one must see the entire volumes—with all the delightful original illustrations by Sir Basil Blackwood—to appreciate fully Belloc's charming and witty verses that play so subacidly on the platitudes of life and morals that beset his day—and ours. A great humor classic. Three books in one. Total of 157pp. 5⅜ x 8. T749 Paperbound **$1.00**

THE DEVIL'S DICTIONARY, Ambrose Bierce. Sardonic and irreverent barbs puncturing the pomposities and absurdities of American politics, business, religion, literature, and arts, by the country's greatest satirist in the classic tradition. Epigrammatic as Shaw, piercing as Swift, American as Mark Twain, Will Rogers, and Fred Allen, Bierce will always remain the favorite of a small coterie of enthusiasts, and of writers and speakers whom he supplies with "some of the most gorgeous witticisms of the English language" (H. L. Mencken). Over 1000 entries in alphabetical order. 144pp. 5⅜ x 8. T487 Paperbound **$1.00**

THE PURPLE COW AND OTHER NONSENSE, Gelett Burgess. The best of Burgess's early nonsense, selected from the first edition of the "Burgess Nonsense Book." Contains many of his most unusual and truly awe-inspiring pieces: 36 nonsense quatrains, the Poems of Patagonia, Alphabet of Famous Goops, and the other hilarious (and rare) adult nonsense that place him in the forefront of American humorists. All pieces are accompanied by the original Burgess illustrations. 123 illustrations. xiii + 113pp. 5⅜ x 8. T772 Paperbound **$1.00**

MY PIOUS FRIENDS AND DRUNKEN COMPANIONS and MORE PIOUS FRIENDS AND DRUNKEN COMPANIONS, Frank Shay. Folksingers, amateur and professional, and everyone who loves singing: here, available for the first time in 30 years, is this valued collection of 132 ballads, blues, vaudeville numbers, drinking songs, sea chanties, comedy songs. Songs of pre-Beatnik Bohemia; songs from all over America, England, France, Australia; the great songs of the Naughty Nineties and early twentieth-century America. Over a third with music. Woodcuts by John Held, Jr. convey perfectly the brash insouciance of an era of rollicking unabashed song. 12 illustrations by John Held, Jr. Two indexes (Titles and First lines and Choruses). Introductions by the author. Two volumes bound as one. Total of xvi + 235pp. 5⅜ x 8½. T946 Paperbound **$1.00**

HOW TO TELL THE BIRDS FROM THE FLOWERS, R. W. Wood. How not to confuse a carrot with a parrot, a grape with an ape, a puffin with nuffin. Delightful drawings, clever puns, absurd little poems point out far-fetched resemblances in nature. The author was a leading physicist. Introduction by Margaret Wood White. 106 illus. 60pp. 5⅜ x 8. T523 Paperbound **75¢**

PECK'S BAD BOY AND HIS PA, George W. Peck. The complete edition, containing both volumes, of one of the most widely read American humor books. The endless ingenious pranks played by bad boy "Hennery" on his pa and the grocery man, the outraged pomposity of Pa, the perpetual ridiculing of middle class institutions, are as entertaining today as they were in 1883. No pale sophistications or subtleties, but rather humor vigorous, raw, earthy, imaginative, and, as folk humor often is, sadistic. This peculiarly fascinating book is also valuable to historians and students of American culture as a portrait of an age. 100 original illustrations by True Williams. Introduction by E. F. Bleiler. 347pp. 5⅜ x 8. T497 Paperbound **$1.35**

CATALOGUE OF DOVER BOOKS

THE HUMOROUS VERSE OF LEWIS CARROLL. Almost every poem Carroll ever wrote, the largest collection ever published, including much never published elsewhere: 150 parodies, burlesques, riddles, ballads, acrostics, etc., with 130 original illustrations by Tenniel, Carroll, and others. "Addicts will be grateful ... there is nothing for the faithful to do but sit down and fall to the banquet," N. Y. Times. Index to first lines. xiv + 446pp. 5⅜ x 8.
T654 Paperbound **$1.85**

DIVERSIONS AND DIGRESSIONS OF LEWIS CARROLL. A major new treasure for Carroll fans! Rare privately published humor, fantasy, puzzles, and games by Carroll at his whimsical best, with a new vein of frank satire. Includes many new mathematical amusements and recreations, among them the fragmentary Part III of "Curiosa Mathematica." Contains "The Rectory Umbrella," "The New Belfry," "The Vision of the Three T's," and much more. New 32-page supplement of rare photographs taken by Carroll. x + 375pp. 5⅜ x 8.
T732 Paperbound **$1.65**

THE COMPLETE NONSENSE OF EDWARD LEAR. This is the only complete edition of this master of gentle madness available at a popular price. A BOOK OF NONSENSE, NONSENSE SONGS, MORE NONSENSE SONGS AND STORIES in their entirety with all the old favorites that have delighted children and adults for years. The Dong With A Luminous Nose, The Jumblies, The Owl and the Pussycat, and hundreds of other bits of wonderful nonsense. 214 limericks, 3 sets of Nonsense Botany, 5 Nonsense Alphabets, 546 drawings by Lear himself, and much more. 320pp. 5⅜ x 8.
T167 Paperbound **$1.00**

THE MELANCHOLY LUTE, The Humorous Verse of Franklin P. Adams ("FPA"). The author's own selection of light verse, drawn from thirty years of FPA's column, "The Conning Tower," syndicated all over the English-speaking world. Witty, perceptive, literate, these ninety-six poems range from parodies of other poets, Millay, Longfellow, Edgar Guest, Kipling, Masefield, etc., and free and hilarious translations of Horace and other Latin poets, to satiric comments on fabled American institutions—the New York Subways, preposterous ads, suburbanites, sensational journalism, etc. They reveal with vigor and clarity the humor, integrity and restraint of a wise and gentle American satirist. Introduction by Robert Hutchinson. vi + 122pp. 5⅜ x 8½.
T108 Paperbound **$1.00**

SINGULAR TRAVELS, CAMPAIGNS, AND ADVENTURES OF BARON MUNCHAUSEN, R. E. Raspe, with 90 illustrations by Gustave Doré. The first edition in over 150 years to reestablish the deeds of the Prince of Liars exactly as Raspe first recorded them in 1785—the genuine Baron Munchausen, one of the most popular personalities in English literature. Included also are the best of the many sequels, written by other hands. Introduction on Raspe by J. Carswell. Bibliography of early editions. xliv + 192pp. 5⅜ x 8.
T698 Paperbound **$1.00**

THE WIT AND HUMOR OF OSCAR WILDE, ed. by Alvin Redman. Wilde at his most brilliant, in 1000 epigrams exposing weaknesses and hypocrisies of "civilized" society. Divided into 49 categories—sin, wealth, women, America, etc.—to aid writers, speakers. Includes excerpts from his trials, books, plays, criticism. Formerly "The Epigrams of Oscar Wilde." Introduction by Vyvyan Holland, Wilde's only living son. Introductory essay by editor. 260pp. 5⅜ x 8.
T602 Paperbound **$1.00**

MAX AND MORITZ, Wilhelm Busch. Busch is one of the great humorists of all time, as well as the father of the modern comic strip. This volume, translated by H. A. Klein and other hands, contains the perennial favorite "Max and Moritz" (translated by C. T. Brooks), Plisch and Plum, Das Rabennest, Eispeter, and seven other whimsical, sardonic, jovial, diabolical cartoon and verse stories. Lively English translations parallel the original German. This work has delighted millions, since it first appeared in the 19th century, and is guaranteed to please almost anyone. Edited by H. A. Klein, with an afterword. x + 205pp. 5⅝ x 8½.
T181 Paperbound **$1.00**

HYPOCRITICAL HELENA, Wilhelm Busch. A companion volume to "Max and Moritz," with the title piece (Die Fromme Helena) and 10 other highly amusing cartoon and verse stories, all newly translated by H. A. Klein and M. C. Klein: Adventure on New Year's Eve (Abenteuer in der Neujahrsnacht), Hangover on the Morning after New Year's Eve (Der Katzenjammer am Neujahrsmorgen), etc. English and German in parallel columns. Hours of pleasure, also a fine language aid. x + 205pp. 5⅝ x 8½.
T184 Paperbound **$1.00**

THE BEAR THAT WASN'T, Frank Tashlin. What does it mean? Is it simply delightful wry humor, or a charming story of a bear who wakes up in the midst of a factory, or a satire on Big Business, or an existential cartoon-story of the human condition, or a symbolization of the struggle between conformity and the individual? New York Herald Tribune said of the first edition: ". . . a fable for grownups that will be fun for children. Sit down with the book and get your own bearings." Long an underground favorite with readers of all ages and opinions. v + 51pp. Illustrated. 5⅜ x 8½.
T939 Paperbound **75¢**

RUTHLESS RHYMES FOR HEARTLESS HOMES and MORE RUTHLESS RHYMES FOR HEARTLESS HOMES, Harry Graham ("Col. D. Streamer"). Two volumes of Little Willy and 48 other poetic disasters. A bright, new reprint of oft-quoted, never forgotten, devastating humor by a precursor of today's "sick" joke school. For connoisseurs of wicked, wacky humor and all who delight in the comedy of manners. Original drawings are a perfect complement. 61 illustrations. Index. vi + 69pp. Two vols. bound as one. 5⅜ x 8½.
T930 Paperbound **75¢**

New Books

101 PATCHWORK PATTERNS, Ruby Short McKim. With no more ability than the fundamentals of ordinary sewing, you will learn to make over 100 beautiful quilts: flowers, rainbows, Irish chains, fish and bird designs, leaf designs, unusual geometric patterns, many others. Cutting designs carefully diagrammed and described, suggestions for materials, yardage estimates, step-by-step instructions, plus entertaining stories of origins of quilt names, other folklore. Revised 1962. 101 full-sized patterns. 140 illustrations. Index. 128pp. 7⅞ x 10¾.
T773 Paperbound **$1.85**

ESSENTIAL GRAMMAR SERIES
By concentrating on the essential core of material that constitutes the semantically most important forms and areas of a language and by stressing explanation (often bringing parallel English forms into the discussion) rather than rote memory, this new series of grammar books is among the handiest language aids ever devised. Designed by linguists and teachers for adults with limited learning objectives and learning time, these books omit nothing important, yet they teach more usable language material and do it more quickly and permanently than any other self-study material. Clear and rigidly economical, they concentrate upon immediately usable language material, logically organized so that related material is always presented together. Any reader of typical capability can use them to refresh his grasp of language, to supplement self-study language records or conventional grammars used in schools, or to begin language study on his own. Now available:

ESSENTIAL GERMAN GRAMMAR, Dr. Guy Stern & E. F. Bleiler. Index. Glossary of terms. 128pp. 4½ x 6⅜.
T422 Paperbound **75¢**

ESSENTIAL FRENCH GRAMMAR, Dr. Seymour Resnick. Index. Cognate list. Glossary. 159pp. 4½ x 6⅜.
T419 Paperbound **75¢**

ESSENTIAL ITALIAN GRAMMAR, Dr. Olga Ragusa. Index. Glossary. 111pp. 4½ x 6⅜.
T779 Paperbound **75¢**

ESSENTIAL SPANISH GRAMMAR, Dr. Seymour Resnick. Index. 50-page cognate list. Glossary. 138pp. 4½ x 6⅜.
T780 Paperbound **75¢**

PHILOSOPHIES OF MUSIC HISTORY: A Study of General Histories of Music, 1600-1960, Warren D. Allen. Unquestionably one of the most significant documents yet to appear in musicology, this thorough survey covers the entire field of historical research in music. An influential masterpiece of scholarship, it includes early music histories; theories on the ethos of music; lexicons, dictionaries and encyclopedias of music; musical historiography through the centuries; philosophies of music history; scores of related topics. Copiously documented. New preface brings work up to 1960. Index. 317-item bibliography. 9 illustrations; 3 full-page plates. 5⅜ x 8½. xxxiv + 382pp.
T282 Paperbound **$2.00**

MR. DOOLEY ON IVRYTHING AND IVRYBODY, Finley Peter Dunne. The largest collection in print of hilarious utterances by the irrepressible Irishman of Archey Street, one of the most vital characters in American fiction. Gathered from the half dozen books that appeared during the height of Mr. Dooley's popularity, these 102 pieces are all unaltered and uncut, and they are all remarkably fresh and pertinent even today. Selected and edited by Robert Hutchinson. 5⅜ x 8½. xii + 244p.
T626 Paperbound **$1.00**

TREATISE ON PHYSIOLOGICAL OPTICS, Hermann von Helmholtz. Despite new investigations, this important work will probably remain preeminent. Contains everything known about physiological optics up to 1925, covering scores of topics under the general headings of dioptrics of the eye, sensations of vision, and perecptions of vision. Von Helmholtz's voluminous data are all included, as are extensive supplementary matter incorporated into the third German edition, new material prepared for 1925 English edition, and copious textual annotations by J. P. C. Southall. The most exhaustive treatise ever prepared on the subject, it has behind it a list of contributors that will never again be duplicated. Translated and edited by J. P. C. Southall. Bibliography. Indexes. 312 illustrations. 3 volumes bound as 2. Total of 1749pp. 5⅜ x 8.
S15-16 Two volume set, Clothbound **$15.00**

THE ARTISTIC ANATOMY OF TREES, Rex Vicat Cole. Even the novice with but an elementary knowledge of drawing and none of the structure of trees can learn to draw, paint trees from this systematic, lucid instruction book. Copiously illustrated with the author's own sketches, diagrams, and 50 paintings from the early Renaissance to today, it covers composition; structure of twigs, boughs, buds, branch systems; outline forms of major species; how leaf is set on twig; flowers and fruit and their arrangement; etc. 500 illustrations. Bibliography. Indexes. 347pp. 5⅜ x 8.
T1016 Clothbound **$4.50**

CATALOGUE OF DOVER BOOKS

CHANCE, LUCK AND STATISTICS, H. C. Levinson. The theory of chance, or probability, and the science of statistics presented in simple, non-technical language. Covers fundamentals by analyzing games of chance, then applies those fundamentals to immigration and birth rates, operations research, stock speculation, insurance rates, advertising, and other fields. Excellent course supplement and a delightful introduction for non-mathematicians. Formerly "The Science of Chance." Index. xiv + 356pp. 5⅜ x 8.　　　　　T1007 Paperbound **$1.75**

THROUGH THE ALIMENTARY CANAL WITH GUN AND CAMERA: A Fascinating Trip to the Interior, George S. Chappell. An intrepid explorer, better known as a major American humorist, accompanied by imaginary camera-man and botanist, conducts this unforgettably hilarious journey to the human interior. Wildly imaginative, his account satirizes academic pomposity, parodies cliché-ridden travel literature, and cleverly uses facts of physiology for comic purposes. All the original line drawings by Otto Soglow are included to add to the merriment. Preface by Robert Benchley. 17 illustrations. xii + 116pp. 5⅜ x 8½.　　　　　T376 Paperbound **$1.00**

TALKS TO TEACHERS ON PSYCHOLOGY and to Students on Some of Life's Ideals, William James. America's greatest psychologist invests these lectures with immense personal charm, invaluable insights, and superb literary style. 15 Harvard lectures, 3 lectures delivered to students in New England touch upon psychology and the teaching of art, stream of consciousness, the child as a behaving organism, education and behavior, association of ideas, the gospel of relaxation, what makes life significant, and other related topics. Interesting, and still vital pedagogy. x + 146pp. 5⅜ x 8½.　　　　　T261 Paperbound **$1.00**

A WHIMSEY ANTHOLOGY, collected by Carolyn Wells. Delightful verse on the lighter side: logical whimsies, poems shaped like decanters and flagons, lipograms and acrostics, alliterative verse, enigmas and charades, anagrams, linguistic and dialectic verse, tongue twisters, limericks, travesties, and just about very other kind of whimsical poetry ever written. Works by Edward Lear, Gelett Burgess, Poe, Lewis Carroll, Henley, Robert Herrick, Christina Rossetti, scores of other poets will entertain and amuse you for hours. Index. xiv + 221pp. 5⅜ x 8½.　　　　　T1020 Paperbound **$1.25**

LANDSCAPE PAINTING, R. O. Dunlop. A distinguished modern artist is a perfect guide to the aspiring landscape painter. This practical book imparts to even the uninitiated valuable methods and techniques. Useful advice is interwoven throughout a fascinating illustrated history of landscape painting, from Ma Yüan to Picasso. 60 half-tone reproductions of works by Giotto, Giovanni Bellini, Piero della Francesca, Tintoretto, Giorgione, Raphael, Van Ruisdael, Poussin, Gainsborough, Monet, Cezanne, Seurat, Picasso, many others. Total of 71 illustrations, 4 in color. Index. 192pp. 7⅜ x 10.　　　　　T1018 Clothbound **$6.00**

PRACTICAL LANDSCAPE PAINTING, Adrian Stokes. A complete course in landscape painting that trains the senses to perceive as well as the hand to apply the principles underlying the pictorial aspect of nature. Author fully explains tools, value and nature of various colors, and instructs beginners in clear, simple terms how to apply them. Places strong emphasis on drawing and composition, foundations often neglected in painting texts. Includes pictorial-textual survey of the art from Ancient China to the present, with helpful critical comments and numerous diagrams illustrating every stage. 93 illustrations. Index. 256pp. 5⅜ x 8.　　　　　T1017 Clothbound **$3.75**

PELLUCIDAR, THREE NOVELS: AT THE EARTH'S CORE, PELLUCIDAR, TANAR OF PELLUCIDAR, Edgar Rice Burroughs. The first three novels of adventure in the thrill-filled world within the hollow interior of the earth. David Innes's mechanical mole drills through the outer crust and precipitates him into an astonishing world. Among Burroughs's most popular work. Illustrations by J. Allan St. John. 5⅜ x 8½.　　　　　T1051 Paperbound **$2.00**
　　　　　T1050 Clothbound **$3.75**

JOE MILLER'S JESTS OR, THE WITS VADE-MECUM. Facsimile of the first edition of famous 18th century collection of repartees, bons mots, puns and jokes, the father of the humor anthology. A first-hand look at the taste of fashionable London in the Age of Pope. 247 entertaining anecdotes, many involving well-known personages such as Colley Cibber, Sir Thomas More, Rabelais, rich in humor, historic interest. New introduction contains biographical information on Joe Miller, fascinating history of his enduring collection, bibliographical information on collections of comic material. Introduction by Robert Hutchinson. 96pp. 5⅜ x 8½.　　　　　Paperbound **$1.00**

THE HUMOROUS WORLD OF JEROME K. JEROME. Complete essays and extensive passages from nine out-of-print books ("Three Men on Wheels," "Novel Notes," "Told After Supper," "Sketches in Lavender, Blue and Green," "American Wives and Others," 4 more) by a highly original humorist, author of the novel "Three Men in a Boat." Human nature is JKJ's subject: the problems of husbands, of wives, of tourists, of the human animal trapped in the drawing room. His sympathetic acceptance of the shortcomings of his race and his ability to see humor in almost any situation make this a treasure for those who know his work and a pleasant surprise for those who don't. Edited and with an introduction by Robert Hutchinson. xii + 260pp. 5⅜ x 8½.　　　　　T58 Paperbound **$1.00**

CATALOGUE OF DOVER BOOKS

*GEOMETRY OF FOUR DIMENSIONS, H. P. Manning.** Unique in English as a clear, concise introduction to this fascinating subject. Treatment is primarily synthetic and Euclidean, although hyperplanes and hyperspheres at infinity are considered by non-Euclidean forms. Historical introduction and foundations of 4-dimensional geometry; perpendicularity; simple angles; angles of planes; higher order; symmetry; order, motion; hyperpyramids, hypercones, hyperspheres; figures with parallel elements; volume, hypervolume in space; regular polyhedroids. Glossary of terms. 74 illustrations. ix + 348pp. 5⅜ x 8.   S182 Paperbound **$1.95**

PAPER FOLDING FOR BEGINNERS, W. D. Murray and F. J. Rigney. A delightful introduction to the varied and entertaining Japanese art of origami (paper folding), with a full, crystal-clear text that anticipates every difficulty; over 275 clearly labeled diagrams of all important stages in creation. You get results at each stage, since complex figures are logically developed from simpler ones. 43 different pieces are explained: sailboats, frogs, roosters, etc. 6 photographic plates. 279 diagrams. 95pp. 5⅝ x 8⅜.   T713 Paperbound **$1.00**

SATELLITES AND SCIENTIFIC RESEARCH, D. King-Hele. An up-to-the-minute non-technical account of the man-made satellites and the discoveries they have yielded up to September of 1961. Brings together information hitherto published only in hard-to-get scientific journals. Includes the life history of a typical satellite, methods of tracking, new information on the shape of the earth, zones of radiation, etc. Over 60 diagrams and 6 photographs. Mathematical appendix. Bibliography of over 100 items. Index. xii + 180pp. 5⅜ x 8½.
T703 Paperbound **$2.00**

LOUIS PASTEUR, S. J. Holmes. A brief, very clear, and warmly understanding biography of the great French scientist by a former Professor of Zoology in the University of California. Traces his home life, the fortunate effects of his education, his early researches and first theses, and his constant struggle with superstition and institutionalism in his work on microorganisms, fermentation, anthrax, rabies, etc. New preface by the author. 159pp. 5⅜ x 8.
T197 Paperbound **$1.00**

THE ENJOYMENT OF CHESS PROBLEMS, K. S. Howard. A classic treatise on this minor art by an internationally recognized authority that gives a basic knowledge of terms and themes for the everyday chess player as well as the problem fan: 7 chapters on the two-mover; 7 more on 3- and 4-move problems; a chapter on selfmates; and much more. "The most important one-volume contribution originating solely in the U.S.A.," Alain White. 200 diagrams. Index. Solutions, viii + 212pp. 5⅜ x 8.   T742 Paperbound **$1.25**

SAM LOYD AND HIS CHESS PROBLEMS, Alain C. White. Loyd was (for all practical purposes) the father of the American chess problem and his protégé and successor presents here the diamonds of his production, chess problems embodying a whimsy and bizarre fancy entirely unique. More than 725 in all, ranging from two-move to extremely elaborate five-movers, including Loyd's contributions to chess oddities—problems in which pieces are arranged to form initials, figures, other by-paths of chess problem found nowhere else. Classified according to major concept, with full text analyzing problems, containing selections from Loyd's own writings. A classic to challenge your ingenuity, increase your skill. Corrected republication of 1913 edition. Over 750 diagrams and illustrations. 744 problems with solutions. 471pp. 5⅜ x 8½.   T928 Paperbound **$2.00**

FABLES IN SLANG & MORE FABLES IN SLANG, George Ade. 2 complete books of major American humorist in pungent colloquial tradition of Twain, Billings. 1st reprinting in over 30 years includes "The Two Mandolin Players and the Willing Performer," "The Base Ball Fan Who Took the Only Known Cure," "The Slim Girl Who Tried to Keep a Date that was Never Made," 42 other tales of eccentric, perverse, but always funny characters. "Touch of genius," H. L. Mencken. New introduction by E. F. Bleiler. 86 illus. 208pp. 5⅜ x 8.
T533 Paperbound **$1.00**

FARES, PLEASE! by J. A. Miller. Authoritative, comprehensive, and entertaining history of local public transit from its inception to its most recent developments: trolleys, horsecars, streetcars, buses, elevateds, subways, along with monorails, "road-railers," and a host of other extraordinary vehicles. Here are all the flamboyant personalities involved, the vehement arguments, the unusual information, and all the nostalgia. "Interesting facts brought into especially vivid life," N. Y. Times. New preface. 152 illustrations, 4 new. Bibliography. xix + 204pp. 5⅜ x 8.   T671 Paperbound **$1.50**

Dover publishes books on art, music, philosophy, literature, languages, history, social sciences, psychology, handcrafts, orientalia, puzzles and entertainments, chess, pets and gardens, books explaining science, intermediate and higher mathematics mathematical physics, engineering, biological sciences, earth sciences, classics of science, etc. Write to:

Dept. catrr.
Dover Publications, Inc.
180 Varick Street, N. Y. 14, N. Y.